Muslim Endowments, Waqf Law and Judicial Response in India

This book deals with Law of Waqf (Muslim Endowment Law) and its judicial response in India.

The volume covers several jurisprudential and historical aspects of Waqf, which include Doctrines of Waqf; Essential Requisites of Waqf; Valid Objects of Waqf; Historical Account of Waqf; Emergence of Waqf Law in India; and Constitutional Validity of Waqf in India. The chapters then go on to discuss the Waqf Act 1995 and Waqf Amendment Act 2013. The legal perspectives of each Section of Waqf Act and its amendments are elucidated with references under Reflections. The case-law has been analysed and cited under each Section of Waqf Act, wherever applicable.

This book will be of interest to scholars and researchers of law and legal studies. It will be of interest to practitioners of Waqf Jurisprudence in India, the managers of Waqf Institutions and officials involved in Waqf Administration.

P.S. Munawar Hussain works as Joint Registrar at Maulana Azad National Urdu University, India. He served as Joint Director at Civil Services Residential Coaching Academy, which was funded by the Government of India through University Grants Commission. He has been placed in various committees of the University, as Member/Convener/Secretary. He served as Law Officer of Andhra Pradesh State Waqf Board, Hyderabad. He was awarded his Ph.D. (Doctorate in Law) by Osmania University, Hyderabad, India. His research articles have been published in reputed journals. He sits on the editorial boards of several research journals and has been invited to deliver lectures at various institutions.

Muslim Endowments, Waqf Law and Judicial Response in India

P.S. Munawar Hussain

Routledge
Taylor & Francis Group
LONDON AND NEW YORK

First published 2021
by Routledge
2 Park Square, Milton Park, Abingdon, Oxon OX14 4RN

and by Routledge
52 Vanderbilt Avenue, New York, NY 10017

Routledge is an imprint of the Taylor & Francis Group, an informa business

British Library Cataloguing-in-Publication Data
A catalogue record for this book is available from the British Library

Library of Congress Cataloging-in-Publication Data
A catalog record has been requested for this book

ISBN: 978-1-138-56346-9 (hbk)
ISBN: 978-1-003-14269-0 (ebk)

Typeset in Sabon
by Deanta Global Publishing Services Chennai India

Dedicated to my parents
Rasheed P. Rasool
Zehrabi

Contents

Foreword

At the outset, I congratulate Dr. Munawar Hussain for the outstanding work on a complicated subject like the waqf. It was a research in true sense and it is in the fitness of the things that the thesis is being published in the form of a book.

Waqf is a typical phenomenon which partakes the characteristics of endowment, gift and many such sister concepts but, at the same time, stands apart. The manner in which it is made, its irrevocability and prohibition of the imposition of any conditions, are some of the typical features of the waqf. Dr. Hussain has succinctly traced the history of waqf and presented the manner in which it is understood in different parts of the world. The focus of the author was on the administration of waqf in the Indian context. Before independence, the administration of waqfs was mainly through practices and customs. After independence, the Law was codified by the Parliament in the form of the Waqf Act, 1954. Substantial amendments were made to it through the Act 69 of 1984. The amendments were indeed far-reaching and voluminous and on almost every aspect, several new provisions were added.

With a view to make the enactment comprehensive and to incorporate several new provisions that were warranted based on the experience as to the working of the 1954 Act, as amended, the Parliament enacted the Waqf Act, 1995. Detailed and comprehensive provisions touching on the aspects ranging from the manner of the institution of the waqf to the administration of the waqf properties are incorporated. The removal of encroachments upon the waqf properties is relegated to the executive wing rather than the judicial exercise. The appointment and removal of mutawallis is another complicated issue that was dealt with in detail.

It was rather a coincidence that Dr. Hussain conducted his research at the Osmania University at a time when I was Dean, Faculty of Law. As a Judge of the High Court I had to deal with the provisions of the Act on several occasions. From a glance of the work undertaken by Dr. Hussain, I can say confidently that the book would be of utmost utility for the persons connected with the administration of waqfs, for the academicians and the students. The introduction of the book would enable the reader to have a bird's-eye view of the entire work. The author has divided the subject into various chapters and each of them is detailed in its purport and presentation.

I wish the author as well as the publisher a very good response from the readers and thereby success for the publication.

Justice L. Narasimha Reddy
Chairman, Central Administrative Tribunal, New Delhi, India
Chancellor, University of Hyderabad, India

Foreword

Waqf as a concept owes its origin to Islam, as it was non-existent during the pre-Islamic Arabiya (*jahiliya*). Although the institution of waqf is not specifically mentioned in the Quran, the injunctions on charity (*Fi Sabeel Allah*) and doing good deeds in the Quran is taken to be the legal authority for establishing a waqf.

Early sayings of Prophet Muhammad (*Ahadith*) which encouraged continuous charity (*sadqat ul-jariya*) and examples of waqf at the advent of Islam undertaken by the Second Caliph Omar ibn Al-Khattaband and others validate the legality of waqf.

The underlying principle of *waqf* was philanthropy for any purpose that was considered as religious, pious or charitable. Soon waqf transformed into an important institution in the Islamic civilisation in which the religious life and socio-economic activities of Muslims were intertwined.

The evolution of the Waqf Law was a slow, gradual and complex process. Although several early Fiqh works threw significant light on the doctrine of waqf, they do not dwell much on the governance structure for *auqaf*, which was administered individually by the mutawallis, supervised by the Qadis or judges of the Sharia Courts. The differing interpretations among the four major schools of Islamic jurisprudence – Hanafi, Maliki, Hanbali and Shafi, sometimes even within the same school, added to the complexity and even inconsistency in jurisprudence relating to waqf, as different legal principles began to develop according to differing interpretations of these schools.

Consequently, the Islamic jurists had to adopt different pragmatic considerations such as public interest (*istislah*), approbation (*istihsan*), analogy (*qiyas*) and consensus (*ijma*) while adjudicating legal disputes relating to waqf. The adjudication was more a matter of individual inference and interpretation rather than reliance on codified legal statutes.

Under the Ottoman and the Safavid Empires, waqf management started getting organised and structured with the setting up of specialised institutions to look after the *auqaf*. For instance, waqf properties were under the control of an Imperial Ministry in the Ottoman Empire as early as 1826, while the Qajar dynasty of Iran set up a Ministry of Waqf in 1854 to oversee waqf affairs, thereby paving the way for the evolution and improvisation of waqf laws.

In India, the earliest reference of waqf dates back to 1185 AD in the form of Aynul Mulk Multani's book "*Insha-i-Mahru*" in which it was mentioned that a Ghorid Sultan dedicated two villages in favour of Jama Masjid in Multan. Several waqfs were reportedly created after the establishment of the Delhi Sultanate and the process continued and expanded under the Mughal rule. However, unlike the Ottomans and the Safavids, the Muslim rulers of India did not attempt to create separate departments for waqf administration.

The supervision of waqf matters was traditionally entrusted to *Qadis* or judges of the Sharia Courts who paid little or no attention to systematise waqf management or codify the laws. This practice was continued by the British until 1810, but later they decided to promulgate new statutes and regulations to govern endowments and bring about perceptible changes such as the abolition of the institution of *Qadis.*

The interpretation of waqf was now left to the English judges who rushed to apply the English legal principles to cases due to their unfamiliarity with the concept of *Sharia* or even indigenous laws and local customs and traditions, often ending up in issuing conflicting or even controversial judgements (like in *Abul Fata Mahomed Ishak* case). The problem was partly resolved with the induction of a few Indian judges as Councillors to ensure some indigenous representation at the Privy Council.

By 1900, *auqaf* became a hot topic of discussion among India's Muslim politicians and the demand for waqf reforms and promulgation of nationwide dedicated waqf laws gathered momentum. The promulgation of the Musalman Waqf Validating Act of 1913 followed by the Acts of 1923 and 1930 marked the beginning of a process of enactment of strong waqf laws in India. In the post-Independence era, the landmark Wakf Act of 1954 was enacted followed by several amendments, culminating into the Wakf Act of 1995 and its amendment in 2013.

The role of the judiciary and judicial responses to various statutes was the decisive guiding factor in dispute resolution, safeguarding waqf institutions and waqf properties and for ensuring that the desired socio-economic benefits accrue out of the waqfs.

Many such interesting historic aspects on waqf jurisprudence in India are brought out in this well-researched and informative book *Waqf Law and Judicial Response in India* by Dr. Munawar Hussain. The book deals with a range of topics such as the origin and classification of waqfs, conditions for their ownership and validity, administrative structure of waqf and the interphase between the government and waqf bodies, dextrously interpreting each of these topics in the light of judicial responses given by the Indian courts to the various waqf laws promulgated over time.

The book will prove to be invaluable to all those who are involved in waqf affairs in any capacity, as either Central or State agencies, waqf administrators, or even as waqf beneficiaries.

Dr. Ausaf Sayeed
Indian Ambassador to Kingdom of Saudi Arabia

Preface

The Waqf Law in India can be traced to the Muslim Rule. During the British Rule it has re-emerged through different enactments, beginning with the promulgation of Regulation of 1772. The British Government enacted the Wakf Validating Act in the year 1913. The first Legislation in Independent India was the Wakf Act of 1954, which has undergone several amendments with hundreds of judicial pronouncements for 40 years and culminated with the Waqf Act of 1995. After 18 years of debates and discussions, the Waqf Act 1995 has been fructified with a major overhaul of Waqf Law which resulted in Waqf Amendment Act 2013.

This book is an attempt to circumvent the Waqf Law from the Wakf Validating Act 1913, Wakf Act 1954 with its several amendments; the Waqf Act 1995 with its Amendment Act of 2013 along with the judgements rendered by the Privy Council, High Courts and Supreme Court of India.

Introduction at the beginning of the book provides the doctrines of waqf; principles governing the duties and responsibilities of Waqif and mutawalli; emergence of waqf; historical account of waqf in India, etc., for the conceptual understanding of the waqf. The legal perspectives have been incorporated under the sub-heading *reflections* under every Section of the Act in each chapter. The relevant judgements rendered by the High Courts and Supreme Court of India are quoted with observation for each Section under the heading *Judicial Response*. Citation of the cases and references of the books can be found in the footnotes. The Waqf Act 1995 has changed the sequence of Sections contained in Waqf Act 1954, hence a comparative table of Sections is provided at the beginning of the book for the convenience of the readers. The list of cases arranged in alphabetical order with their respective citations and page numbers is also incorporated. The readers can find keywords with the respective page numbers in *Index* at the end of the book. The word *waqf* is spelt as *wakf* in the Indian subcontinent at least since 1913, but by the Waqf Amendment Act 2013 it is spelt as *waqf*. So in excerpts the spelling is retained as quoted.

Every care has been taken to ensure accuracy of facts and clarity of concepts. I hope this book would be useful to the students, academics, researchers, the bar and the bench. I am grateful to my teachers, my colleagues and my friends for their guidance and encouragement to transform my research into this book. I also thank the publisher. The Readers and critics are requested to provide their valuable suggestions.

Munawar Hussain

Section-wise comparative table – I

Wakf Act 1995 with Waqf Act 1954

Wakf Act 1995	*Waqf Act 1954*	*Wakf Act 1995*	*Waqf Act 1954*	*Wakf Act 1995*	*Waqf Act 1954*	*Wakf Act 1995*	*Waqf Act 1954*
Section	*Section*	*Section*	*Section*	*Section*	*Section*	*Section*	*Section*
1	1	31	24	61	41	91	58
2	2	32	15, 15A	62	41A	92	59
3	3	33	15B	63	42	93	60
4	4	34	15C	64	43	94	61
5	5	35	15D	65	43A	95	61A
6	6	36	25	66	43B	96	62
7	6A	37	26	67	43C	97	63
8	7	38	26A	68	43E	98	63A
9	8A	39	26B	69	43F	99	64
10	8B	40	27	70	44	100	65
11	8C	41	28	71	45	101	66
12	8D	42	29	72	46	102	66A
13	9	43	30	73	46A	103	66B
14	10-11	44	31	74	46B	104	66C
15	12	45	31A	75	47	105	66D
16	13	46	32	76	47A	106	66F
17	14	47	33	77	48	107	66G
18	16	48	34	78	49	108	66H
19	17	49	35	79	50	109	67
20	18	50	36	80	51	110	68
21	19	51	36A	81	52	111	68A
22	20	52	36B	82	53	112	69
23	21	53	36C	83	55	113	70
24	21B	54	36D	84	55A		
25	21C	55	36E	85	55C		
26	21D	56	36F	86	55D		
27	22	57	37	87	55E		
28	22A	58	38	88	55F		
29	22B	59	39	89	56		
30	23	60	40	90	57		

Section-wise comparative table – II

Wakf Act 1954 with Waqf Act 1995

Wakf Act 1954	*Waqf Act 1995*	*Wakf Act 1954*	*Waqf Act 1995*	*Wakf Act 1954*	*Waqf Act 1995*	*Wakf Act 1954*	*Waqf Act 1995*
Section	*Section*	*Section*	*Section*	*Section*	*Section*	*Section*	*Section*
1	1	21B	-	37	57	55B	-
2	2	21C	25	38	58	55C	85
3	3	21D	26	39	59	55D	86
4	4	21E	-	40	60	55E	87
5	5	21F	-	41	61	55F	88
6	6	22	27	41A	62	56	89
6A	7	22A	28	41B	-	57	90
7	8	22B	29	42	63	58	91
8	-	23	30	43	64	59	92
8A	9	24	31	43A	65	60	93
8B	10	25	36	43B	66	61	94
8C	11	26	37	43C	67	61A	95
8D	12	26A	38	43D	-	62	96
9	13	26B	39	43E	68	63	97
10	14	27	40	43F	69	63A	98
11	-	28	41	44	70	63B	-
12	15	29	-	45	71	64	99
13	16	30	-	46	72	65	100
14	17	31	44	46A	73	66	101
15	32	31A	45	46B	74	66A	102
15A	-	32	46	47	75	66B	103
15B	-	33	47	47A	76	66C	104
15C	-	34	48	48	77	66D	105
15D	-	35	49	49	78	66E	-
16	18	36	50	50	79	66F	106
17	19	36A	51	51	80	66G	107
18	20/20A	36B	52/52A	52	81	66H	108
19	21	36C	53	53	82	67	109
20	22	36D	54	54	-	67A	111
21	23	36E	55/55A	55	83	68	110
21A	-	36F	56	55A	84	69	112
						70	113

Introduction

Waqf is an Islamic concept of dedication of property for the religious and welfare activities. *Waqf* means the permanent dedication of movable or immovable property for religious, educational, social and charitable purposes. When the property is dedicated as waqf, the ownership of the dedicator upon that property extinguishes. The ownership of the property is inherently transferred to God, which ensures its perpetuity.

"Waqf" is a derivative of Arabic root word "waqafa," which means to halt, detain, stop or restrain. It implies that there will be detention or restraint on the transfer of the dedicated property to another person. It means that the property in question is detained in the implied ownership of God and it is halted from alienation to a third person. Even if the purpose for which the waqf is created extinguishes, the waqf income shall be utilised for a similar purpose, but it shall not be wound up.

In North and West Africa waqf is called *Habs*, which literally means "confinement."[1] In Islamic legal terminology, it means primarily to protect the property dedicated and to prevent it from becoming the property of a third person. The renowned jurist Ameer Ali[2] says technically as Arabian jurists put it in the language of law; it signifies the dedication or consecration of property either in express terms or by implication for any charitable or religious object or to secure any benefit to human being.

Joseph Schacht, in his paper "Early Doctrines of waqf," says "the origin of the institution of waqfs cannot be traced to any single source." It is, as Heffening and Santillana[3] have seen, the result of a combination of several factors and various elements which were intimately fused during the

1 Oxford Encyclopedia of Modern Islamic World, Vol. IV – *Article: waqf*. Oxford University Press, London, 1991.

2 Ameer Ali, *Muhammadan Law*, 4th Edn. Himalayan Books, New Delhi, 1912, Rep. 1985 Vol. I, p. 194.

3 Joseph Schacht, *Early Doctrines of Waqfs*, Melanges Fuad Koprulu, (pp. 444–452) Osman Yalcin Matbaasi, Istanbul, 1953.

formative period of Muhammadan Law. Kozlowski[4] says that "the theoretical implication of creating a *waqf* suggests that the said property can never again change hands by inheritance, sale or seizure."

1. Doctrines of waqf

The word "waqf" is not found anywhere in the Quran. There are indirect references and injunctions to waqf with words like *al-birr* and *al-khair* as used in the Quran which refer to righteousness, morality and charity, respectively. The doctrines of waqf are derived from teachings of charity and morality mentioned in Chapter 2 Verses 177, 215, 262, 270, 273, 274; Chapter 4 Verse 36; Chapter 9 Verse 60; Chapter 17 Verse 26; Chapter 51 Verse 19; Chapter 57 Verses 7, 18; Chapter 63 Verse 10; Chapter 64 Verse 16 of Quran.

A study of the early doctrines relating to waqf throws light on the development of its theory. The main sources for the early doctrines are the *Mudanwana* of Sahnum, an Islamic jurist from Maliki School of Thought (d. 240H / 854 AD), in which he has collected the opinion of *Malik* the founder of Maliki School of Thought (d. 179H / 795 AD), of *Ibn al-Qasim* an early Islamic jurist (d. 191H / 806 AD) and of other early authorities of Medina; the *Kitab Ahkam-ul-waqf* by *Hilal* (d. 245H / 859 AD), which contains authentic information on the doctrines of *Abu Hanifa* (d. 150H / 767 AD), of *Abu Yusuf* (d. 182H / 798 AD) the disciple of Imam Abu Hanifa; the *kitab al-siyar-ul-kabir* of *Shaibani* (d. 189H / 804 AD). The fourth source is *Kitab-ul-Umm* of Shafii (d. 204H / 819 AD). In the words of Ameer Ali, the doctrine of wakf is thus interwoven with the entire religious life and social economy of the Mussalmans. He further says that the origin of waqf is to be seen in pursuit of the righteous and charitable deeds which are characteristic features of Islam.[5]

The doctrine of Malik, as expounded in the *Madanwana* contribution towards *habs fi-sabilillah* (dedication for the cause of Almighty) takes an important place. Hilal, in his *kitab Al-ahkam-ul-waqf*, says that *Sadaqa Mauqufa* (waqf) of animals, merchandise and garments is not valid *Sadaqa Mauqufa fi-sabil-lillah* (charities for the cause of Almighty) and that waqf of houses and land mainly is valid.[6]

Shafii describes waqf as being permanent and, according to him, its usufruct or profit is only devoted to the purpose for which the waqf has been created.

4 Gregory C. Kozlowski, *Muslim Endowments and Society in British India*, Cambridge University Press, Cambridge, 1985, p. 1.

5 Ameer Ali, *Muhammadan Law*, 4th Edn. Himalayan Books, New Delhi, 1912, Rep. 1985 Vol. I, pp. 193, 194.

6 Joseph Schacht: "*Early Doctrines on Waqf*," Mel Koprulu, 1953, pp. 443–452

> The term *mauquf* acquired its latter meaning as the consequence of a doctrinal development. On one hand, the term *mauquf* was transferred (or perhaps extended) to charities in favour of inherited groups of beneficiaries, as in the doctrines of the anonymous scholars, on the other, the doctrine gradually prevailed that such a charity should revert to the original owner not as a full property to be inherited by his heirs, but only its usufruct, to be transmitted to his next of kins.[7]

The issue of whether a waqf would take its entirety simply with the declaration of a property as waqf or the declared property has to be delivered as a possession to the procurator or administrator to completely constitute a waqf. *Durrul-Mukhtar* mentioned that a waqf is incomplete unless possession of the property dedicated is delivered to a trustee or mutawalli.[8] The two disciples of Abu Hanifa, namely Abu Yoosuf and Mohammad Shaibani, differ on this point. Mohammad maintains that handing over consecrated property of the waqf to the trustee or the mutawalli is an essential element for the waqf to be complete, whereas Abu Yoosuf says it is not an essential part of the waqf to be complete. Hedaya says:

> The two disciples therefore, hold appropriation to be absolute; and, consequently that it cannot be resumed, or disposed of by gift or sale; and that inheritance also does not obtain with respect to it. (There is indeed, one point upon which the disciples differ in opinion; for, according to Aboo Yoosuf, the appropriation is absolute from the instant of its execution; whereas Mohammad holds it to become absolute only on the delivery of it to a *mootwalee*, or procurator).[9]

The property consecrated shall be free from any kind of encumbrance and it shall be separate and identical from the cumulative property/estate.[10] The appropriation of an undefined part or portion of anything is lawful according to Abu Yoosuf. Mohammad alleges that an appropriation of this nature is unlawful; because as actual possession (by the procurator taking possession of the Article appropriated) is essential.[11]

7 *Ibid.*

8 Alauddin Haskafi*Durrul-Mukhtar, commentary of Tanvirul Absar of Md. Bin Abdullah Tarmartashi*, Tr. by B.M. Dayal Kitab Bhavan, New Delhi, 1913, Rep. 2008. p. 336.

9 Abu al-Hasan al-Marghinani, *Hedaya*, 2nd Edn. Tr. by Charles Hamilton, Kitab Bhavan, New Delhi, 1870. Rp. 1994, pp. 231–232.

10 Alauddin Haskafi *Durrul-Mukhtar, commentary of Tanvirul Absar of Md. Bin Abdullah Tarmartashi*, Tr. by B.M. Dayal Kitab Bhavan, New Delhi, 1913, Rep. 2008. pp. 336–337.

11 Abu al-Hasan al-Marghinani, *Hedaya*, 2nd Edn. Tr. by Charles Hamilton, Kitab Bhavan, New Delhi, 1870. Rp. 1994, p. 233.

Waqf of cattle is not accepted. But if a man dedicates land along with cattle it shall be valid. Durrul-Mukhtar says it is valid because the cattle remained attached to the land. This is so held by way of *Istehsan*.[12]

As soon as a waqf is consecrated the ownership of the property dedicated is transferred to Almighty God. The waqif would completely be divested himself of the ownership of the property. The waqif or the dedicator of the property will forfeit his ownership rights over the property. According to Abu Yoosuf, the disciple of Abu Hanifa, the dedication becomes absolute and the right of the person making it extinguishes by the mere fact of his declaration that he dedicates it, or has dedicated it. This rule of law laid down by *Abu Yoosuf* is in force among all the Hanafi jurists.

The great Digest prepared under the command of Aurangzeb, *Fatawa-e-Aalamgiri*, expressly declares on the compilation of the waqf that "decrees in this country (India) are given according to the doctrine of Abu Yousuf." Mohammed's views were adopted only by some of the *Bokhariot* schoolmen and have no application in any other part of the Sunni world.[13]

While fulfilling the object of waqf, attention is not paid towards repairs and maintenance of the waqf properties. *Durrul-Mukhtar* says that "the income of an endowment should first be spent over its repairs then what comes next in importance or priority."[14] *Hedaya* goes a step further in this regard and states that,

> it is incumbent that the income of an appropriation be in the first instance expended in the repairs of it, whether the appropriator may have stipulated this or not; because his design was that the income should serve as a perpetual fund and as a perpetual income cannot be drawn from the article appropriated unless it be preserved in continual repair.[15]

Once a waqf is validly constituted it takes the forms of an institution. The waqf institution is a juristic person; it can sue others and be sued. A distinguished jurist of the modern era, Sir D.F. Mulla, says "to constitute a waqf it is not necessary that the word *waqf* should be used. A grant to a *kazi* for the purpose of his performing religious duties constitutes a waqf."[16]

After perusal of these doctrines circumventing its principles, it can be concluded that waqf is an institution consecrated in perpetuity of perennial

12 Alauddin Haskafi*Durrul-Mukhtar, commentary of Tanvirul Absar of Md. Bin Abdullah Tarmartashi*, Tr. by B.M. Dayal Kitab Bhavan, New Delhi, 1913, Rep. 2008. pp. 342.

13 Abu al-Hasan al-Marghinani, *Hedaya*, 2nd Edn. Tr. by Charles Hamilton, Kitab Bhavan, New Delhi, 1870. Rp. 1994, p. 231.

14 Durrul-Mukhtar, Alauddin Haskafi's commentary of Tanvirul Absar of Md. Bin Abdullah Tarmartashi, Tr. by B.M. Dayal Kitab Bhavan, New Delhi, 1913, Rep. 2008. p. 345.

15 Abu al-Hasan al-Marghinani, *Hedaya*, 2nd Edn. Tr. by Charles Hamilton, Kitab Bhavan, New Delhi, 1870. Rp. 1994, p. 236.

16 Mulla's *Principles of Muhammadan Law*, 19th Edn. Lexis Nexis Butterworths New Delhi,1990, Rep.2007, p. 143.

or enduring properties or assets having clear title with the dedicator or the settler, whose income or usufruct is utilised for pious and/or charitable purposes, administered by an authorised committee or a person.

1.1. *Requisites of a waqf*

Various authors have described the essential requisites of a waqf differently. Some referred the property under waqf as the "subject of a waqf." Some called the "perpetuity" as "irrevocability" or "permanency." Some authors count the dedicator (waqif) as an essential requisite for a waqf. But under a "waqf by user" the dedicator or the waqif is unknown. Sometimes there need not be a dedicator, since the property assumes the character of a waqf by its utilisation over a period of time. However, the essential requisites of a valid waqf are *property*, *transfer of ownership*, *perpetuity*, *free from conditions or contingencies and valid purpose.*

1.1.1. *Property*

The dedicator (waqif) shall hold undisputed title over the property for its consecration as waqf. The property dedicated in waqf must belong to the dedicator (waqif) at the time of dedication. The property under waqf is also called the subject of waqf. The subject of the waqf must belong to the waqif, after the dedication of which its ownership is transferred to the Almighty God. The property can be movable or immovable. Lands, Buildings, Shares in Joint Stock Companies, Securities, Bonds, Promissory Notes, Units, and Currencies can be dedicated as waqf.[17] Sir D.F. Mulla says the subject of the waqf must belong to the waqif, after the dedication of which its ownership is transferred to the Almighty.[18] The appropriation of an undefined part or portion of anything is lawful according to Abu Yoosuf. Mohammad alleges that an appropriation of this nature is unlawful, because actual possession is essential[19] (by the procurator, administrator or mutawalli taking possession of the Article appropriated).

1.1.2. *Perpetuity or irrevocability*

Waqf is the detention of a property in the implied ownership of Almighty God, in such a manner that its profits may be applied for charity or for pious purposes. Once made, the dedication is absolute. The property dedicated

17 Mulla's *Principles of Muhammadan Law*, 19th Edn. Lexis Nexis Butterworths New Delhi,1990, Rep.2007, p. 144.

18 Mulla's *Principles of Muhammadan Law*, 19th Edn. Lexis Nexis Butterworths New Delhi,1990, Rep.2007, p. 144.

19 Abu al-Hasan al-Marghinani, *Hedaya*, 2nd Edn. Tr. by Charles Hamilton, Kitab Bhavan, New Delhi, 1870. Rp. 1994, p. 233.

can neither be sold nor given nor inherited. When the property (movable or immovable) is dedicated as waqf the ownership of the dedicator upon that property extinguishes. The property dedicated as waqf becomes God's property. Hence, once a waqf is always a waqf.

The objects of an appropriation must be of a perpetual nature. An appropriation is not complete, according to Hanifa and Muhammad, unless the appropriator destines its ultimate application to objects not liable to become extinct.[20] Even if the purpose for which the waqf is made extinguishes, the waqf shall be utilised for similar purposes. But it shall not be wound up.

1.1.3. Free from conditions and contingencies

The waqf should be unconditional. If the waqf is subjected to any condition or contingencies, it becomes void. Happening of uncertain events in future makes the waqf invalid. A Muslim wife can convey her property to her husband upon trust to maintain herself and her children out of the income, and hand over the property to the children on their attaining majority, and in the event of her death without leaving children, to devote the income to certain religious purposes. This dedication is subject to a contingency, i.e., the settler's death without leaving children and therefore it is not valid.[21] Hedaya gives another example that,

> if the appropriator reserves to himself a right of option with respect to his appropriation, three days by saying (for instance), "I appropriate this house to such and such purposes, with this condition, that I shall have a right of option for three days"; according to Aboo Yoosuf both the appropriation and the condition are lawful. According to Mohammad on the contrary, the appropriation is null.[22]

Dedication of the property prospectively in future makes the waqf null and void as it creates uncertainties. But if the dedicator executes a deed of waqf which contains a direction that until payment of specified debts due by him, no proceedings under the *waqfnamah* should be enforceable. The provision for the payment of debts does not entail a contingency and the waqf is valid.

"If a condition is imposed that, if the property is mis-managed it should be divided among the heirs of the waqif or that the property would be sold or utilized for the waqif's necessities, the waqf would be invalid."[23] There

20 *Ibid.*, p. 234.
21 *Ibid.*, p. 161.
22 *Ibid.*, p. 238.
23 B.R. Verma, *Islamic Law in India and Pakistan*, 6th Edn, Allahabad Law Book Co. 1986, pp. 625–626.

shall not be any uncertain conditions for the creation of waqf or for the future existence of waqf.

1.1.4. Purpose should be recognised by Islam

The purpose of the waqf should have been considered by Muslim Law as religious, pious and charitable. Even when a Non-Muslim is dedicating a property into waqf, the purpose for which the waqf is created should have been sanctioned and approved by Islam. In case the purpose for which the waqf is established no longer exists, it shall be utilised for a similar purpose.

1.2. Valid objects of waqf

S.No	*Objects/Purpose*	*Reference/Citation*
1.	Mosque and provision for Imams to conduct worship therein.	Section 104 of Waqf Act 1995. *Mahachalar* vs. *Faizur Rahman* 35 IC 880. *Syed Mohamed Labbai* vs. *Mohamed Hanifa*, AIR 1976 SC 1569.
2.	Lamps in a mosque.	*Mahazar Hussain* vs. *Abdul*, 33 All 400.
3.	*Idgah.*	Section 104 of Waqf Act 1995. *Kulsam bi* vs. *Mohamed Abdul Sattar* AIR 1948 Nag 183.
4.	*Khanquah.*	Section 104 of Waqf Act 1995.
5.	Dargah.	Section 104 of Waqf Act 1995. *Sunni Central Board of waqfs* vs. *Sirajul*, AIR 1954 All 88. *Gulam Ali* vs. *Sultan Khan,* AIR 1967 Ori 55.
6.	*Takia.*	*Advocate General* vs. *Yusufali*, 24 Bom LR 1060.
7.	*Imambara.*	Section 104 of Waqf Act 1995. *Bibi Jan* vs. *Kalb Hussain*, ILR (1909) 31 All 136; 1 IC 763.
8.	*Khaberistan* or Cemetry.	Section 104 of Waqf Act 1995. *Syed Mohammed Labbai* vs. *Mohamed Hanifa* AIR 1976 SC 1569.
9.	*Maqbara.*	Section 104 of Waqf Act 1995.
10.	*Musafirkhana* or Choultry.	Section 104 of Waqf Act 1995.
11.	Orphanage.	*Muslim Orphanage* vs. *Khatoon Bi*, AIR 1958 Mys. 28.
12.	Maintenance of tomb of a Saint.	*Advocate General* vs. *Yusufali* 24 Bom LR 1060.
13.	Performance of *Urs.*	*Aziz Unnissa* vs. *Sirdar Ali* AIR 1927 Bom 387; (1927) 29 Bom LR 434; 102 IC 129.
14.	Colleges and provision for Teachers.	*Ram Charan* vs. *Fatima* ILR (1915) 42 Cal 933; 30 IC 686.

(*Continued*)

(*Continued*)

S.No	Objects/Purpose	Reference/Citation
15.	Endowing Teacher for School.	*Hedaya,* 2nd Edn. 1870. Rp. 1994, New Delhi, p.240; *Abdul Rafey* vs. *Banni Begam,* 15 IC 36.
	Girls Education.	*Satdas* vs. *Ram Bai*, 20 IC 275.
16.	Preaching of Sermons and occasional entertainment of Holymen.	*Satdas* vs. *Ram Bai*, 20 IC 275.
17.	Starting of schools, colleges or hospitals.	*Mariam Bai* vs. *Jaffar Abdul Rahim,* AIR 1973 Mad 191.
18.	Educational Institutions.	*Mahabir Prasad* vs. *Syed Mustafa* AIR 1937 PC 174; (1937) 41 Cal WN 933; 168 IC 418.
19.	General Utilities-aqueducts, bridges, *sarais*, or tanks.	*Hedaya,* 2nd Edn. 1870. Rp. 1994, New Delhi, p.240.
20.	Celebration of the birth of Prophet Mohammed.	*Syed Ahamed* vs. *Julaiha Bibi* AIR 1947 Mad 176; (1946) 2 Mad LJ 335.
21.	Celebration of the birth of Ali Murtaza.	*Bibi Jan* vs. *Kalb Hussain* ILR (1909) 31 All 136; 1 IC 763.
22.	Observance of Moharrum Ceremonies for example making tazias, provision for camel for procession, etc.	*Ram Charan* vs. *Fatima* (1915) 42 Cal 933; 30 IC 686. *Ismail Sait* vs. *Hamidi Begam* AIR 1921 Pat 125. *Bibi Jan* vs. *Kalb Hussain* ILR (1909) 31 All 136; 1 IC 763.
23.	Observance of death anniversary of the dedicator settler and the members of his family.	*Bibi Jan* vs. *Kalb Hussain* ILR (1909) 31 All 136; 1 IC 763. *Ramanathan Chettiar* vs. *Vava Labbai* ILR (1911) 34 Mad 12.
24.	*Khadam-Shariff.*	*Phul Chand* vs. *Akbar* ILR (1896) 19 All 211.
25.	Annual Fateha of waqif and his family, prayer for their souls and alms to the poor.	*Luchimipal Singh* vs. *Amir Alam* ILR (1882) 9 Cal 176.
26.	Recitation/Reading Quran.	*Sattar Ismail* vs. *Hameed Sait* AIR 1944 Mad 504; (1944) 2 MLJ 92; *Mahazar Hussain* vs. *Abdul Hadi* ILR (1911) 33 All 400; 9 IC 753.
27.	Funeral expenses of the poor.	*Fatima Bibi* vs. *Advocate General, Bombay* ILR (1881) 6 Bom 42.
28.	Digging graves and shrouds for the dead.	*Mahachalar Rahman* vs. *Faizrur Rahman* 35 IC 880 Cal.
29.	Distribution of food or alms to the poor.	*Hashim Haroon* vs. *Gonnsali* AIR 1942 Sind 137; ILR (1942) Kant 179.
30.	Help to the poor to perform Hajj.	Abu al-Hasan al-Marghinani, *Hedaya,*Tr. Charles Hamilton, Kitab Bhavan, 2nd Edn. 1870. Rp. 1994, New Delhi, p.240.
31.	Food and Clothes to Fakirs.	*Ibrahim Khan* vs. *Ahamed Sait,* 32 All 503.

(*Continued*)

(*Continued*)

S.No	***Objects/Purpose***	***Reference/Citation***
32.	Construction of Robuth, i.e., free boarding house for pilgrims at Mecca.	*Mohamed Yusuf* vs. *Mohamed Sadiq,* AIR 1933 Lah 501; ILR (1933) 14 Lah 431; 144 IC 271.
33.	Upkeep of Hujra (Guest house).	*Yusuf Khan* vs. *Misal Khan*, 73 IC 99.
34.	Kindred of the Holy Prophet.	Tyabji's *Muslim Law*, p. 545.
35.	Family Mausoleum.	*Syed Ali* vs. *Syed Mohamed* AIR 1928 Pat 441; ILR (1928) 7 Pat 426; 116 IC 525.
36.	Feast in honour of a saint.	*Advocate General* vs. *Yusuf Ali* AIR 1921 Bom. 338; 84 IC 759; (1922) 24 Bom LR 1060.
37.	Salary and donation to servants.	*Abdul Wahab* vs. *Mst. Sughra Begam,* AIR 1932 All 248; ILR (1932) 54 All 455; 136 IC 619.
38.	The benefit of the family of the waqif.	*Syed Sibte Rasul* vs. *Sibte Nabi* AIR 1943 All 74; 1942 ALJ 722.
39.	Maintenance of poor relatives and their dependants.	*Mukarram* vs. *Anjuman-un-Nissa,* AIR 1924 All 223; ILR (1923) 45 All 152; 69 IC 836.
40.	Charity every year as atonement for sins with ultimate benefit to the poor.	*Hedaya*, Kitab Bhavan, 2nd Edn. 1870. Rp. 1994, New Delhi, p.240. *Fatima Bi* vs. *Advocate General*, ILR (1881) 6 Bom 42.
41.	Payment of debts of waqif and dedication to the poor.	*Luchmipal Singh* vs. *Ameer Alam,* ILR (1882) 9 Cal 176.
42.	Performance of Hajj every year out of the income with ultimate object to the poor in perpetuity.	*Hedaya,* Kitab Bhavan, 2nd Edn. 1870. Rp. 1994, New Delhi, p.240. *Fatima Bi* vs. *Advocate General,* ILR (1881) 6 Bom 42. *Kuttaya Routhan* vs. *Mammana Routhan,* 35 Mad 681.
43.	Performance of "Fateha."	*Ramanathan Chettiar* vs. *Vave Lebbai Marakkayar* 41 IA 21 (PC).

Waqf should not be confused with the English concept of trust or gift. There is a difference between waqf and Trust; waqf and gift; waqf and alms, which deserves to be understood to comprehend waqf.

1.3. Difference between waqf and trust

The concept of waqf gives the impression that it is similar to a trust in English Law. But a waqf is different from a trust in many ways. A trust can be wound up or revoked, but a waqf is irrevocable. A trust can be created for any lawful purpose, but a waqf should be for the discharge of pious obligation and/or for the benefit of mankind. The founder of a trust can be a beneficiary, but a waqif cannot enjoy the benefit, except to a limited extent, under Hanafi doctrines. A trustee of a trust is entrusted with enormous powers, including alienation of trust property, whereas a mutawalli is a mere curator or superintendent of waqf property. When a trust is defunct or wound up, the trust property can be reverted to its founder or its family/executors, but, in the case of waqf, the doctrine of *cy pres* is applied and income of the property is diverted towards similar purposes.

*1.4. Difference between waqf and gift (*hiba*)*

Waqf is a perennial one and it can be executed for the benefit of an unborn person and for the line of succession, but a gift (*hiba*) for an unborn person is invalid. Waqf cannot be extinguished because perpetuity is its essential character, but a gift can be extinguished.

*1.5. Difference between waqf and alms (*sadaqa*)*

Alms or *sadaqa* are charitable donations. Waqfs should not be confused with alms (*sadaqa*) or charitable donations. Alms or sadaqa can be entirely utilised, but in the case of waqf, the income derived from the property can be spent for valid purposes. A waqf requires a valid purpose for its creation, but a sadaqa does not require any such purpose. A waqf is an endowment, whereas a sadaqa is a one-time donation.

1.6. Classification of waqf

The waqf or the waqf institution can be classified on the basis of the purpose for which the waqf is created or on the basis of the circumstances under which the waqf institution has come into existence. Ameer Ali classifies waqfs as (a) public waqf, (b) quasi-public waqf, (c) private waqf/family waqf (waqf -Alal-Awlad), testamentary waqf, waqf by user, waqf for rendering services (Mashruth-ul-Khidmath) and fraudulent and fictitious waqf. He further adds that the Arabian jurists classify the waqfs or trusts under the following three heads, viz., (a) trusts in favour of the affluent and indigent alike, (b) trusts in favour of the affluent and then for the indigent, (c) trusts in favour of the indigent alone.[24] The following classification can be made to understand the types of waqfs.

24 Ameer Ali, *Muhammadan Law*, 4th Edn. Himalayan Books, New Delhi, 1912, Rep. 1985 Vol. I, p. 193.

1.6.1. *Public waqf*

A public waqf is a waqf created for the general public without mentioning the category of beneficiaries. If a library is established by a person and that person dedicates it as a waqf for the people at large without any discrimination, it is a public waqf. According to the *Bahr-ur-Raiq*, it is lawful for a Muslim to create a waqf in favour of the Non-Muslim poor and destitute. Similarly, he can endow a school for the education of Non-Muslim children and *vice versa*.[25]

1.6.2. *Quasi-public waqf*

In a quasi-public waqf, the purpose of dedication is partly for the public in general and partly for a class of people. It serves for the general people as well as for a class of individual which may be the dedicator's family.

1.6.3. *Private waqf/family waqf*

A waqf dedicated for private individuals or for the family of the settler is called a private waqf or a family waqf. In Arabic, it is called "waqf -Alal-Awlad." It is based on the notion that "charity begins at home."

1.6.4. *Testamentary waqf*

In a testamentary waqf, the waqif clearly dedicates his property towards waqf through a deed or instrument and hands it over to an administrator (mutawalli). It often carries the consent of the legal heirs of the settler or dedicator of the property, so that the legal heirs do not lay their claim over the property after his death. There are two methods of dedicating waqf under this category, viz., *waqf-bil-wasiyat* and *wasiyat-bil-waqf*. In waqf-bil-wasiyat, the property is impressed with the character of waqf on the date of the death of the testator; whereas under wasiyat-bil-waqf, a bequest is made with a direction to the executor or heirs to create a waqf as desired by the testator. One third of a person's property can be dedicated under testamentary waqf. However, for more than one third of one's property to be dedicated, the consent of one's heirs is required.

1.6.5. *Waqf by user (reputation)*

When a property is being used for decades as waqf for the purposes enshrined in Islam as pious, religious and charitable, and the dedicator is not known, it is called waqf by user. It may happen sometime that a waqf has been created

25 *Ibid.*, p. 201.

but the documents have been lost or perished. But if the property dedicated is in use as waqf, such properties are called waqf by user. It is also called waqf by reputation. In such a case, an inference or intention on the part of the owner has to be established to the effect that the owner has dedicated that property as waqf.

1.6.6. Waqf for rendering service (Mashruth-ul-Khidmath)

In waqf for rendering service (Mashruth-ul-Khidmath), a property is awarded to a person or an institution to serve towards the fulfilment of the religious or charitable purpose and is called the Mashruth-ul-Khidmath waqf. It is a grant for service of the waqf institution or carrying out the purpose of the waqf.

1.6.7. Fraudulent and fictitious waqf

Any waqf created with the intention of defeating the interest of creditors or defrauding the creditors would be a fraudulent and fictitious waqf. B.R. Verma says that

> the question whether sec. 53 of Indian Transfer of Property Act is applicable in such case is not free from doubt. Section 2 of this Act provides that nothing in Chapter II shall be deemed to affect any rule of Mohammedan law.[26]

However, Ameer Ali while admitting that a waqf created by an insolvent person is invalid, says that section 53 of the Transfer of Property Act does not affect the provision of Mohammadan Law.

1.7. Waqif

The waqif is the dedicator, settler, appropriator, consecrator or creator of the waqf. A waqif must have an undisputed title of the object or the property being dedicated. He should be in possession of the property being dedicated as waqf. He should exercise free will without coercion for the purpose of waqf. He should be major (under section 3 of Majority Act) in the Indian context. He should be competent to enter into an agreement, to sue or be sued. He should be a sane person. Even a Non-Muslim can create a waqf if the purpose of dedication is sanctioned by Muhammadan Law and the law of the religion professed by him as pious and charitable. Once a waqf is created, the waqif will not have rights over the property or object which

26 B.R. Verma, *Islamic Law in India and Pakistan*, 6th Edn, Allahabad Law Book Co. 1986, pp. 657–658.

is dedicated. The property vests with God. The waqif can function as mutawalli. He is entitled to appoint any competent person to act as mutawalli, including his family members.

Discussing the capacity of waqif, Ameer Ali says that all the schools (of Islamic jurisprudence) agreed in respect of the capacity of the waqif. "And the waqif," says the *Sharaya*, "it is required that he be of full age, sound understanding, and unrestrained in the use of disposition of his property." So the *Fatawa-i-Alamgiri*, "among the conditions (of waqf) are understanding and puberty (on the part of the waqif) as a waqf by a boy (minor) or an insane person is not valid." But the action of a mere imbecile is not absolutely invalid. "If a person who is imbecile," says the *Radd ul-Mukhtar*, "makes a waqf upon himself and after him, upon some other purpose which does not fail, it is valid according to Abu Yusuf, but the latter will take effect only upon its being sanctioned by the Judge."[27]

The waqif possesses the powers to control the affairs of the waqf which he has created as long as he is alive. His instructions and orders can supersede that of the congregation. Therefore, Ameer Ali says "he has a better title to appoint a muezzin and imam for a mosque than the congregation, unless his appointment is objectionable on the ground that the persons nominated by him are unfit."[28]

An insolvent person cannot create a waqf unless he has discharged all the dues to his creditors. Ameer Ali quotes *Durrar wal Ghurar* and *Khazanat ul-Muftiin* to say that if a person labouring death illness makes a waqf of his house, and it be found that his debts exceed his assets, then waqf is invalid.

There is some difference of opinion about the validity of a waqf created by an apostate from Islam. According to the jurist Ibn Shahna, all waqfs created by him in favour of the poor or for pious purposes of a general character remain operative. But waqfs created in favour of individuals, against the interest of heirs, are void. According to others, all waqfs created previous to apostasy are void, and such property becomes on his death part of his inheritance to which the right to Islam before his death, the waqfs come into operation again. But the waqf made by an apostate after his apostasy is void. If a woman were to make a waqf and then apostatised, her waqf would not be void.

Ameer Ali says that waqf of a person involved in debt is not void. He further says that "The rule enunciated in the *M'aruzat* of Mufti Abu S'aud and the *Fatawa –e- Ismailia* can be reconciled with the principle laid down in such high and recognized authorities as the *Fatawai Kazi Khan*, the *Fath ul-Kadir*, the *Zakhira*." In the light of the statement contained in the *Tanwir ul-Absar*, which is to this effect, "the waqf of a person whose debts

27 Ameer Ali, *Muhammadan Law*, 4th Edn. Vol. I, Himalayan Books, New Delhi, 1912, Rep. 1985, p. 195.
28 *Ibid.*, p. 441.

surround his assets should be maintained either by giving him time to pay off his debts or appointing a manager to realize the rents and profits and to pay the debts therewith." If it be wholly impossible to discharge it by that process, the judge in that case has the option of directing the sale of the property consecrated. It follows from this that the waqf of a person involved in debt is not *ipso facto* void; it is only voidable if he acts fraudulently to defeat his creditors.

The waqif can enjoy certain rights, powers and privileges. B.R. Verma says that, except in the case of a waqf for a mosque, the waqif may at the time of making the waqf reserve the following benefits for him:[29]

a. That he shall be maintained from the income of the property.
b. That he shall reserve the whole income for himself or that it may be disposed of by him in any manner during his life time.
c. That his debts shall be paid out from the income of the waqf property.
d. That he shall be entitled to a right of residence in the waqf property.
e. That he shall be entitled as the first mutawalli to a higher salary than that reserved for the succeeding mutawalli.

Thus the waqif can enjoy certain powers in respect of the administration of waqf since the waqf is consecrated by him out of his own property.

1.8. Mutawalli – the curator of waqf

Mutawalli is an administrator or manager of a waqf institution. Mutawalli is a trusted friend, sometimes referred to as curator or procurator. Mr. Gregory C. Kozlowski, in his book "*Muslim Endowment and Society in British India*," describes Mutawalli as a friend or a trusted person.[30] Ameer Ali, a well-known Islamic jurist, often refers to mutawalliship as *tawliyat*. Radd ul-Mukhtar (an authentic source of Islamic jurisprudence) gives it the expression of *wilayat* (trusteeship), referring to *mutawallisbip*.

The word "mutawalli" is a derivative of the Arabic word "wila," which literally means "trust." Similarly, "wali" means a trusted friend. Semantically mutawalli is a friend entrusted with the responsibility of the management of a waqf. Mutawalli has been referred to variously as the trustee, procurator, prosecutor, superintendent, administrator, manager, etc. Thus mutawalli is a person upon whom confidence is reposed towards the fulfilment of the purpose of (*Mansha-e-waqf*) waqf. Power to appoint a

29 B.R. Verma, *Islamic Law in India and Pakistan*, 6th Edn, Allahabad Law Book Co. 1986, pp. 644–645.
30 Gregory C. Kozlowski, *Muslim Endowments and Society in British India*, p. 1.

trustee or mutawalli rests with the founder of the waqf (waqif) and thereafter with his executors.[31]

B.R. Varma precisely describes the status of mutawalli in terms of curtailing his powers over the control of the property dedicated in waqf when he says, "The legal status and position of a mutawalli of a waqf under the Musalman Law is that of a manager or superintendent."[32]

According to the great Islamic jurists Abu Yoosuf and Hillal, the waqif may lawfully reserve the tawliath (the management of the waqf) for himself. Mohammad Shaibani, another scholar, says that the waqif cannot be a trustee of the waqf unless he has reserved trusteeship for himself at the time of consecration. But Abu Yoosuf has a different view. He says that even when the waqif does not reserve the trusteeship for himself, he will still be trustee.[33]

1.8.1. Appointment of mutawalli

Mutawalli can be appointed by the waqif, or executors of waqif. The founder of the waqf has power to appoint the first mutawalli, and to lay down a scheme for the administration of the waqf and for succession to the office of mutawalli. The waqif is primarily entitled to appoint a mutawalli for the management of the waqf. The waqif always has a right to nominate a trustee, though he has parted with the property, and his right in it has become extinguished, he still has a right to see that its proceeds are applied according to the terms of the consecration.

> He (waqif) has a better title to appoint a *muezzin* and *imam* for a mosque than the congregation, unless his appointment is objectionable on the ground that the persons nominated by him are unfit, as it is stated in the *Nawazil* and Abu-Ilaisi.[34]

The waqif is primarily entitled to appoint a mutawalli for the waqf. "If the *mutawalli* appointed by the waqif dies in his life time, the power of appointing another mutawalli rests with the waqif and not in the Kazi."[35]

A woman is also entitled to be appointed as a mutawalli, but she can't lead a prayer congregation or any other duty which is specifically earmarked by Islamic Law to be performed by a man. "But where the mutawalli has to

31 Durrul-Mukhtar, Alauddin Haskafi's commentary of Tanvirul Absar of Md. Bin Abdullah Tarmartashi, Tr. by B.M. Dayal Kitab Bhavan, New Delhi, 1913, Rep. 2008. p. 360.

32 B.R. Verma, *Islamic Law in India and Pakistan*, 6th Edn. Allahabad Law Book Co. 1986, p. 698.

33 Ameer Ali, *Muhammadan Law*, 4th Edn. Himalayan Books, New Delhi, 1912, Rep. 1985 Vol. I, p. 441.

34 Ibid.

35 *Ibid.*, p. 442.

perform religious duties or spiritual function in connection with the waqf which is regarded by men, can only be performed by a man, a women can't be appointed to the office of Mutawalli."[36]

He may nominate the successors by name, or indicate the class together with their qualifications, from whom the mutawalli may be appointed, and may invest the mutawalli with power to nominate a successor after his death or relinquishment of office. If the waqif appoints his own self as the mutawalli of a waqf and involves himself in misfeasance, he can be removed even though the waqf itself was created by him. The mutawalli will be discharged with the death of the waqif. But if the waqif appoints a mutawalli for his life, he can continue even after the death of the waqif. Mutawalli is a mere agent of the waqif for the administration of the waqf institution. The waqif can prescribe the mutawalliship to his family members or his family lineage for the future. The waqif can formulate a scheme for the appointment of mutawalli and for the administration of waqf. The waqif has the power to prescribe and formulate the scheme of administration of the waqf institution and the appointment of mutawalli. *Mulla says* " ... the founder of a waqf may appoint himself or his children and descendants or any other person even a female, or non-mohammedan to be the mutawalli of waqf property."[37] The great Digest prepared under the command of Aurangzeb *Fatawa-e-Aalamgiri* lays down the following principles in respect of the appointment of the mutawalli:

a. The mutawalli should be an adult, possess good understanding.
b. If the tawliath devolves upon a minor by virtue of a provision in the trust deed. It should be confined to make descendants of the *waqif* or the members of a particular family, the appointment of the mutawalli shall be kept in abeyance until he attains the age of majority.
c. If the tawliath is hereditary in a family and the last incumbent appoints his minor son on his death bed, to be the mutawalli the quazi (judge) shall not remove him but appoint another person to discharge the duties of the office during the minority.
d. The reason why the minor is debarred from appointment to the office of mutawalli is because of his incapacity to discharge the functions of mutawalli and to understand and comprehend the concept and functioning of the waqf. Nor a minor can appoint a deputy to discharge his duties.

"If the waqif appoints a minor as mutawalli, and no adult is associated with him, the quazi shall appoint some person to do the work until the minor

36 *Ibid*, p. 443.
37 Mulla's *Principles of Muhammadan Law*, 19th Edn. Lexis Nexis Butterworths, New Delhi, 1990, Rep. 2007 p. 173–174.

attains majority. If there is an adult associated with the minor, the quazi may appoint some person to represent the minor and act jointly with the co-mutawalli, or may empower the adult mutawalli to act for the minor."[38] Freedom and Islam are not necessary conditions.

If any person appointed as mutawalli dies, refuses to act in the trust, is removed by the court, or if the office of mutawalli otherwise becomes vacant and there is no provision in the deed of waqf regarding succession to the office, a new mutawalli may be appointed by the quazi (or the court) or by the State Waqf Board concerned.

If the waqif were to appoint two persons to be the mutawallis of a waqf after his death and one of them were to die appointing the other as his executor in the matter of the waqf, the survivor would be entitled to act as the sole mutawalli.[39] Abu Yoosuf holds that if a waqif were to appoint a mutawalli during his lifetime, without mentioning that such appointment should continue in force after his death, the mutawalli would vacate his office on the death of the waqif. The rule of law, however, is that when an appointment is made without mentioning its duration, it does not cease on the death of the appointer (waqif).

If a person makes a waqf during his lifetime and does not appoint a mutawalli even when death comes upon him, but instead appoints an executor, such an executor will be the executor as well as the mutawalli of the waqf, according to Abu Yoosuf. If, however, the waqif appointed a mutawalli for the waqf during his lifetime, his executor will not be the mutawalli of the waqf.[40]

If the waqif has appointed no mutawalli, and the quazi has appointed one, the waqif has no power to remove the person appointed by the quazi. When the waqif dies without appointing a mutawalli or leaving an executor, in that case, the quazi will have the power of appointing the superintendent of the waqf.[41] If the mutawalli wants to resign from the post, he shall inform that quazi to relinquish him from the post.

1.8.2. Office of mutawalli under the Waqf Law in India

Waqf Act 1995 defines mutawalli as "mutawalli" means any person appointed, either verbally or under any deed or instrument by which a waqf has been created, or by a competent authority, to be the mutawalli of a waqf and includes any person who is a mutawalli of a waqf, *sajjadanashin*, *Amin* or other person appointed by a mutawalli to perform the duties of a

38 Ameer Ali, *Muhammadan Law*, 4th Edn. Vol. I, Himalayan Books, New Delhi, 1912, Rep. 1985, p. 446.
39 *Ibid.*, p. 448.
40 *Ibid.*, p. 449.
41 *Ibid.*, p. 450.

mutawalli and save as otherwise provided in this Act, any person, committee or corporation for the time being managing or administering any waqf or waqf property:[42]

With the enactment of the Waqf Act 1995, the power of appointment of mutawalli vests with the Waqf Boards of the respective states. The Waqf Boards are empowered to regulate the functioning of the waqfs. In such a case, the Waqf Board or the State Government concerned can constitute a managing committee to look after the affairs of the waqf institutions, or it may take the waqf institutions under its direct management and control vide section 65 of the Act. But the Waqf Board can't proceed arbitrarily against any mutawalli without giving him sufficient time to present his point of view and explanation, constitute a committee to discharge the duties of mutawalli and to manage the affairs of waqf. When there is a vacancy in the office of the mutawalli of a waqf, and there is no one to be appointed under the terms of the deed of the waqf, or where the right of any person to act as mutawalli is disputed, the State Waqf Board may appoint any person to act as mutawalli for such period and no such conditions as it may think fit. The state Waqf Board, instead of appointing a person as mutawalli, can take the waqf institution under its direct control.

The office of mutawalli is neither transferable nor heritable, unless otherwise specifically provided in the deed of waqf (*waqfnamah*). The office of mutawalli is not hereditary in the case of a public waqf. However, in the case of *waqf al-Aulad*, the office of the mutawalliship can be a hereditary one. "The office of Mutawalli is an office of personal trust, and a person who cannot discharge the duties of the trust personally, nor be responsible for their due discharge, cannot appoint a deputy." "The office of mutawalli can't be attached in execution of a personal decree against the mutawalli" as decided in the case of *Sarkum* vs. *Rehman Baksh*.[43]

1.8.3. Remuneration of mutawalli

The founder may provide for the remuneration of the mutawalli. Such remuneration may be a fixed sum or it may be a residue of the income of the waqf. If no provision is made by the founder for the remuneration of the mutawalli, the court may fix a sum not exceeding one-tenth of the income of the waqf property. If the amount fixed by the founder is too small, the court may increase the allowance, but it must not exceed the limit of one-tenth.[44]

The Mutawalli can't expend any income of the waqf institutions for his personal gains. However, he can take up to ten per cent of the total income

42 Waqf Act (Act 43 of 1995) 1995.
43 1896–1824, Cal. 83, p. 91.
44 Ameer Ali, *Muhammadan Law*, 4th Edn. Vol. I, Himalayan Books, New Delhi, 1912, Rep. 1985, p. 469.

towards his personal expenditure in respect of the administration of the waqf. The mutawalli can manage and administer the waqf properties. He can lease the waqf properties for not more than 12 months.

The mutawalli of a waqf plays a pivotal role in the administration of waqf. The appointment, removal, duties and responsibilities of a mutawalli have been contentious issues before the courts of law. In the early 20th century, the status of a mutawalli was compared with that of a trustee in English law. Though there are some similarities, there is a lot of difference between these two. Section 50 of the Waqf Act 1995 discusses the duties of mutawalli. As per section 15 of the Indian Trust Act, a trustee is bound to deal with the trust property as if it were his own, whereas the Waqf Act 1995 imposes many restrictions on mutawalli in the administration of the waqf institutions.

1.8.4. Removal of mutawalli

As regards the power of the waqif to remove a *mutawalli* whom he has appointed, there is a difference of opinion between Abu Yoosuf and Mohammad. Abu Yoosuf holds that the waqif is absolutely entitled to remove the mutawalli appointed by himself, whether he has reserved the power or not. Mohammad differs, holding that it is only when the waqif has reserved the power that he can remove the mutawalli without any misfeasance, and the *Fatwa* is according to Mohammad's view.[45] As far as the waqf jurisprudence is concerned, a waqif can remove the mutawalli if he has reserved for himself the right to remove a mutawalli or appoint a new mutawalli.

The *Radd-ul-Mukhtar* states the principle thus: "When a mutawalli is appointed by the *waqif*, he will become discharged on the death of the *waqif*." This is according to Abu Yoosuf's rule on which is the *Fatwa*, for such a mutawalli is merely an agent on behalf of the waqif. But when the waqif appoints a mutawalli "for his life and after his death," such a mutawalli will not become discharged in consequence of the waqif's death.

> If the waqif appoints as mutawalli a person who is absent, the Kazi has the power of nominating in his place another for the time – being, and when the mutawalli appointed by the waqif arrives the trust will revert to him.[46]

A mutawalli can be removed by the waqif, by the court, by the Waqf Board or by the government, if he involves himself in misconduct or misfeasance,

45 *Radd-ul-Mukhtar*, Vol. III, p. 638, as quoted by Ameer Ali, *Mohammadan Law*, cited, p. 458.

46 *Ibid.*, p. 447.

or if his continuation is detrimental to the interest of the waqf. The details of circumstances and reasons under which a mutawalli can be removed have been enumerated under section 64 of Waqf Act 1995. Honesty and integrity shall be indispensable qualities of a mutawalli, without which the purpose for which the waqf is dedicated would be jeopardised.

2. Historical account of waqf

It has been observed by some authors that there was no system of waqf prior to the advent of Islam. However, some scholars consider *Ka'aba* (the most revered place of worship for Muslims in Makkah) as the first structure dedicated as waqf for worship. Quran mentions *Ka'aba* as the first house of worship.[47] However, after the advent of Islam, "the first mosque to be built was the mosque of *Quba* in Medina (in the first year Hijri) in 622 AD."[48]

When the Second Caliph acquired a piece of land in the canton of Khaibar and approached the Prophet to seek his advice, the Prophet suggested dedicating the land and devoting its income for the benefit of mankind and that the property should not be sold, gifted or inherited. He followed the Prophet's advice and created a waqf out of this property. It is said that he appointed Hufsa to be the mutawalli of this waqf after his death.

Prophet Mohammed himself dedicated a piece of land he had acquired in the canton of Khaibar for the support of travellers.[49] The Fourth Caliph Ali established a waqf in Yenbo (Valley of *Q'ara*) for the beggars, the indigent and the worshipers. There have been instances of creation of waqfs by Ayesha (wife of Prophet Muhammad), Asma (the daughter of First Caliph Hazrat Abu Bakar) Safia, Um-e-Habiba (wife of Prophet Muhammad, Sa'ad bin Abi Waqas, Khalid bin Walid, Jaber bin Abdullah, Abdullah bin Zubair and Zaid bin Thabit (the companions of the Prophet).[50]

The earliest recorded instance of waqf is considered to be dedicated by Fa'iq-al Hadin ibn Abd-Allali-al Siquilli in 912 AD in the Ramallah City in Palestine. This waqf was established with a Caaravan Sarai (Rest House) for merchants and travellers.

The practice of dedication of waqf began to develop in the first century AH and assumed rigid legal form in the second century AH. Heffening says that some foreign influence might have also worked on the development of the institution. Henry Cattan does not agree with this view and says that

47 Holy Quran Chapter 3 verse 96.

48 *The Oxford Encyclopedia of the Modern Islamic World*. Vol. IV, *Art. Waqf*, Oxford University Press, London 1991.

49 Ameer Ali, *Muhammadan Law*, 4th Edn. Himalayan Books, New Delhi, 1912, Rep. 1985 Vol. I, p. 193.

50 *Ibid.*

> the institution of waqf has developed with Islam and there is no evidence that such a complex system of appropriating usufruct as a life interest to varying and successive classes of beneficiaries existed prior to Islam. Although the separation of ownership from the usufruct was not a new legal concept, the settlement of usufruct of property on successive generations in perpetuity for an immediate or ultimate charitable purpose, is an institution developed by the jurists during the first three centuries of Islam.[51]

In the administration of waqf institutions, quazis played an important role during the *Ummaid* and *Abbassid* period in the Arab countries. But the mutawallis were basically entrusted with the responsibility of day-to-day administration of the waqfs. The quazis had the supervisory role. Von Kremer, a German orientalist, suggests that the quazis exercised supervisory control over the waqf institutions.[52] Philip K. Hitti also subscribes to the views expressed by Von Kremer, when he says that sometimes the quazis directly administered the pious foundations and estates of orphans and imbeciles.[53]

3. Waqf in India

Waqf in India is as old as Islam and Muslim rule in India. The rulers, the nobles and the philanthropists have constructed mosques and other shrines. They have also dedicated their properties as waqf for the cause of mankind. Athar Hussain and Khalid Rashid, in their book titled "Waqf Law and Administration," give a detailed account of the history of waqf in India. They say that the earliest descriptions of waqf in India are found in a rare book, *Insha-i-Mahru*, written by Aynul Mulk Multani, who is described by Barni as one of the officers of Jalal Uddin Firoz Khilji (1290–1296 AD). The author of the book *Insha-i-Mahru* says that Sultan Muizuddin Sam Ghaor (who reached his zenith of power during 1185–1195 AD), dedicated two villages in favour of Jama Masjid of Multan, and handed its administration to the Shaikh-ul-Islam (highest Ecclesiastical Officer of the empire). The book also refers to the creation of a waqf by *Salatin-e-Maziyyah* (kings of the past), *Danishmandan-i-Mashaikh* (men of wisdom) and *Umara* (nobles). After the establishment of Delhi Sultanate in 1206 AD, many more waqfs were created. A description by Ibn Batuta provides interesting evidence as to the mode of administration by, and discretionary powers of, the mutawallis

51 Henry Cattan, *Law in the Middle East*, Vol. I, Middle East Institute, Washington, 1955, p. 205.

52 Von Kremer, *The Orient under the Caliphs*, Tr. by S. Khuda Buksh, University of Calcutta, 1920, p. 285.

53 Philip K. Hitti, Tlie *History of Arabs*, 2nd Edn. Macmillan, London, 1940, p. 225.

during the Sultanate period. Ibn Batuta himself was appointed the mutawalli of the waqfs in favour of the tomb of Sultan Qutub-ud-Din.[54]

When in 1526 AD the Mughals ousted the Delhi Sultans, they continued to follow the traditions laid down by their predecessors, and there exists abundant evidence to establish that a very large number of waqfs were created during this period.[55] Some people believe that the beautiful monument that is the Taj Mahal, constructed by the Mughal Emperor Shah Jahan in the year 1631 at Agra, which is considered to be the eighth wonder of the world, along with a mosque and *Ibadat Khana* (prayer hall), having 30 villages and a parganah yielding a total income of Rs. 100,000 a year in those days, is also a waqf as it has a place of worship and graves of the Emperor and his Queen.

During the Muslim rule in India, the quazis played an important role in the administration of waqfs, as was the practice during the *Ummaid* and *Abbassid* period in the Arab countries. *Aina-e-Akbri*[56] and Insha-i-Mehru[57] throw light on the administration of waqf institutions during this period. *Quasbah Quazis* and *Parganah Quazis* were appointed to solemnise the Muslim marriages during the Akbar Rule. These quazis were also entrusted with the responsibility of supervision of waqf institutions. They were also responsible for the arrangement for waqf administration and appointment of mutawallis. The *Sudre Subah*, the Chief of the Province, was the controlling authority of waqf. The ultimate controlling authority rested with *Sadrus-Sudur*.

During the Muslim rule in India, a large number of properties were dedicated for the maintenance of mosques and schools, and to provide for the salaries (*Suyurghal or Madad-e-ma'ash*) of those who were in the service of the waqf institutions. But these institutions and their properties were systematically destroyed. W.W. Hunter, the famous British historian, says in his book *Indian Mussalmans*[58] that around 1765, about one fourth of the land holdings in Bengal consisted of *Suyurghal* lands. The British (East India Company) confiscated the nature of these lands in Bengal and took control of them. The income derived from these lands, which was supposed to be the waqf income, was diverted towards English education and the propagation of Christianity. Hunter states that:

> The English Government devoted an estate left expressly for the pious uses of Islam to founding an institution subversive in its very nature of

54 Athar Hussain, *waqf Law and Administration in India*, 2nd Edn. Eastern Book Company, Lucknow, p.14.

55 *Ibid*., p.15.

56 *Aina-e-Akbri*, Translated by Bloachmann, Vol. I, 2nd Edn. Asiatic Society of Bengal, Calcutta, 1927, p. 281.

57 *Insha-e-Mehru*, Manuscript in Asiatic Society of Bengal, Calcutta. pp. 32, 33.

58 W.W.Hunter, *Indian Mussalman*; Trubner and Company, London 1876 p. 156.

> the principles of Islam and from which the Muhammadans were practically excluded. At this moment i.e. 1871 the head of the (Calcutta) College is an English gentleman ignorant of a single word of Persian or Arabic, who draws 1,500 British Pounds a year from a Mohammadan Religious Endowment for teaching things hateful to every Mussalman. It is not, of course his fault, but the fault of the government which placed him there, and which for 35 years has been deliberately misappropriating this great educational fund. In vain it attempted to cloak so gross a breach of trust by attaching a small Mohammadan School to the English College. Besides the misappropriation of accumulated funds in building the college, it annually diverted 5,000 British Pounds to its maintenance. This is to say, out of an income of 5,260 British Pounds it devoted only 350 Pounds to the little Mohammadan School which alone remained to bear the original character of the trust (waqf). It is painful to dwell on this charge of misappropriation because it is impossible to rebut it out of 300 hundred boys in the English College not one percent were Mussalmans.

The waqf properties were in the control of the East India Company, as is evident from the proceedings of the home department.[59] The description and illustration of the misuse of waqf properties in the above paragraphs shows that mismanagement of waqf properties is not a new phenomenon. This was further strengthened by the reportage of newspapers like *Watan*[60] of Lahore, *Curzon Gazette*[61] of Delhi and *Ahsan-ul-Akhbar*[62] of Calcutta, which reiterated the demand for a fair and just administration of waqf institutions, recovery of the alienated waqf properties and action against those who indulged in the swindling of income derived from waqf properties.

4. Emergence of Waqf Law in India

The idea of charity and welfare of mankind is as old as the human race.

> Virtually all societies have set aside a certain lots of land and buildings as places of worship. For ages, temples, churches and other forms of construction have been built and devoted to religious practices. Moreover, the pharaohs of Egypt assigned land for the benefit of monks, and Ancient Greek and Romans dedicated properties exclusively for libraries and education.[63]

59 Proceedings of the home department (Legislative), No. 884, dated 20 September 1845.
60 *Watan* dated 22 August 1902 p. 3 col. 1.
61 *Curzon Gazette* dated 1 September 1902 p. 2 col. 1.
62 *Ahsan-ul-Akhbar* dated 24 October 1902 p. 7.
63 Oxford Encyclopedia of Modern Islamic World, Vol. IV – *Article: waqf*. Oxford University Press, London 1991

In Islam the companions of the Prophet, the nobles and the philanthropists have dedicated their properties for religious, charitable purposes and for the benefit of mankind. The principles or the doctrines enunciated by the Islamic jurists have evolved into waqf jurisprudence.

Historically, the origin of waqf is traced to the prescriptions and sayings (hadith) of the Prophet Muhammad as direct references to waqf are not found in the Islamic Holy Book, the Quran. The practice of waqf has been handed down in succession by the followers of the Prophet. "The validity of waqfs," says the author of *Ghait–ul–Bayan* "is founded on the rule laid down by the Prophet himself ... and handed down succession by Ibn Auf, Nafe and Ibn Omar as stated in the Jami' -Tirmizi."[64]

When the East India Company appeared on the scene and was entrusted with Diwany of the Province (*Subah*) of Bengal as a result of the battle of Buxer in 1765 by a Royal *Firman*, issued by Shah Alam, it decided to leave the personal laws of Hindus and Muslims untouched. It was with this object in view that the famous Regulation of 1772 was passed, section 27 of which provided that

> in all suits regarding inheritance, succession, marriage, castes and other religious usages or institutions, the laws of the Quran with respect to Mohammedans and those of the *Shastras* with respect to *Gentoos* (Hindus) shall be invariably adhered to.

Hindu and Mohammadan Law Officers were appointed under Regulation XII of 1793, for the administration of justice in religious matters pertaining to Hindus and Muslims.

Warren Hastings was not inclined to impose English ideas on people who were not accustomed to them. In his dispatch to the Court of Directors, dated as the 3 November 1772, he wrote that "We have endeavored to adopt our Regulations to the manners and understanding of the people and the exigencies of the country adhering, as closely as we are able, to their ancient usages and institutions."

The East India Company did not interfere in the administration of waqfs or trusts until 1810. The administration of waqfs and trusts continued as it was under the *Moghals*. The promulgation of Regulation XIX of 1810 of the Bengal Code has given a new direction in the administration of justice in waqf matters. Its preamble says that

> Whereas considerable endowments have been granted in land by the preceding Governments of this country, and by individuals, for the support of mosques, Hindu temples, colleges and other pious and beneficial

64 Ameer Ali, *Muhammadan Law*, 4th Edn. Himalayan Books, New Delhi,1912, Rep. 1985 Vol. I, p. 192.

> purposes, and whereas there are grounds to suppose that the produce of such land is used in many instances contrary to the intentions of the donors ... and whereas it is an important duty of every Government to provide that all such endowments be applied to the real interest and will of the granter ... the following rules have been framed.

As a result of this Regulation (XIX) of the Bengal Code 1810 and Regulation (VII), of the Madras Code 1817, the general superintendence of waqfs was vested with the Board of Revenue. The Commissioners in the several districts used to supervise the administration of religious endowments, including waqf institutions, subject to the overall control of the Board of Revenue. In the case of lands granted for the support of mosques, temples, colleges and other purposes, the Board of Revenue and the local agents were put in possession of lands and other properties. These Regulations tried to ensure that the income derived from the endowed properties was duly appropriated for the purposes for which the endowments were created.

During the year 1839 there was an agitation from the Christian Missionaries that it was not the function of a Christian Government to administer Hindu and Muslim endowments and provide for their maintenance as stated by S.A. Kader.[65] The government in Bengal and Madras Provinces gradually withdrew its control over the Hindu and Muslim's endowment, which is evident in the letter dated 10 August 1840 addressed by the Governor-General-in-Counsel to the Government of Madras, which states as under:

> The administration of the affairs and funds of the native religious institutions should be vested in individuals professing the faith to which the institutions belong and who may be best qualified to conduct such administrations with fidelity and regularity, being responsible, together with their subordinate officers, to the courts of justice for any breach of the duties assumed by them which can be made the grounds of a civil action.

S.A. Kader further reveals that between 1840 and 1863 no supervision of any kind was exercised by the Government over the administration of Hindu and Muslim institutions, though Regulation XIX of 1810 of the Bengal Code and Regulation VII of 1817 of the Madras Code continued to remain in the statute book. The inevitable result was mismanagement and embezzlement of temple and mosque funds, there being no proper control under the general law in the absence of any supervising authority. The evil came to an alarming head in or about 1860.[66] But in the year 1863, both these

65 S.A.Kader, T*he Law of Waqfs*, 2nd Edn. Eastern Law House, Kolkata, 1999 p. 7.
66 *Ibid.*, p. 7.

regulations were repealed with the enactment of Religious Endowments Act 1863 (Act 20 of 1863).

In 1860 Societies Registration Act was passed which allowed the functioning of a society as an entity. This Act also provided for the registration of religious and charitable institutions. This Act paved the way for better administration of waqf institutions as well.

Prior to 1864, both Hindu and Mohammadan laws were administered by the Pandits and quazis in their own courts. The quazis used to be the *de facto* guardians of the waqf institutions. All the disputes pertaining to waqf were dealt and resolved by the quazis. In 1864, the Kazis Act (II of 1864) was passed abolishing Hindu and Mohammadan Law Officer appointed under Regulations XII of 1793.[67] With this the quazis were absolved of the responsibility of waqf administration. The disputes pertaining to the waqfs were referred to the courts.

The need for an effective law for the control and supervision of religious endowments was felt in all quarters of society. The British Government enacted Religious Endowments Act 1863 which repealed Regulation XIX of 1810 and Madras Regulation VII of 1817. It provided for the control and management of endowments by manager or managing committees under the supervision of Board of Revenue. This Act was ineffective to deal with misappropriation and mismanagement of the funds and income of endowment properties. Mac Callum Scott, a British Member of Parliament admitted that "owing the defects in the drafting, the Religious Endowments Act 1863 has failed to secure the efficient management of endowments."[68] The managers and the members of the committee held office for life and their services could not be terminated. The power and functions of the committees were not clearly defined, which led to mischief and malpractices.

In the year 1890 legislation was enacted known as the Charitable Endowments Act 1890 (Act VI of 1890), which provided for better administration of the properties held in trusts for charitable purposes. This Act also provided for the appointment of a Treasurer of Charitable Endowments by the Central/Provisional Governments. It also provided for the framing of schemes for the better administration of properties vested in the charitable trusts. It covered charitable endowments relating to relief of the poor, education, medical relief and advancement of any other object of general public utility but excluding a purpose which related exclusively to religious teaching or worship.

The British Government in India accepted in a Dispatch of 1876[69] to the Madras Government that the Religious Endowments Act 1863 failed

67 Athar Hussain, *waqf Law and Administration in India*, 2nd Edn. Eastern Book Co., Lucknow p. 21.

68 Proceedings of the Home Department (Judicial) Government of India, January 1913, No. 672, Part-B.

69 Proceedings of the Home Department (Public) Government of India, March 1876, p. 381.

to prevent mismanagement of religious endowments and protection of the endowed properties. It invited efficacious draft regulation for the protection of endowed properties. The waqf administration was being reduced to dismal. The judgements rendered by the English Judges were not in consonance with Islamic Laws, because of which the Muslim minds were agitated. The Calcutta Mohammadan Union had submitted two memorials in 1902 to the Viceroy demanding Government intervention to take corrective measures for efficient waqf administration. These memorials were rejected and the Secretary to the Government of India recorded a rather sarcastic observation in these words. "The memorialists want us to substitute executive for the judicial procedure, the odium of which would be upon our shoulders." The Viceroy concurred with the observation of the Secretary and accordingly a reply was sent to Calcutta Muhammadan Union.[70]

Representations were also submitted around the same time to the Viceroy by the Society for the Preservation of Waqfs, Support of Widows in India and Anjuman-i-Himyat-i-lslam, Lahore, but to no avail.[71] For the next ten years, several representations were submitted to the British Crown for conducting an inquiry into the mismanagement of the waqf properties and for efficacious law for the administration of waqf institutions.

A conference of officials and non-officials representing Hindu, Muslim, Sikh and Buddhist religions was held in March 1914. The deliberations of the conference made in a representation to the British Crown. This resulted in the passing of the Charitable and Religious Trusts Act 1920. This Act provided for the initiation of legal action by any person interested in endowment against a person involved in misappropriation of funds pertaining to an endowment. The district judges were authorised to try such cases.

During the second half of the 19th century and the early 20th century, the British Government took control of the justice delivery system and appointed judges trained in English Law. These judges were ignorant of the local laws, more particularly Hindu and Muslim laws. The institutions of quazis and pandiths were discontinued. The Judgement rendered by these English trained judges were not in conformity of the local laws, thus resulting in miscarriage of justice. Mohammad Yusoof Khan Bahadur says "it is very seldom that we come across a decision on a disputed question of Mohammadan Law, which is consistent with the instincts of Mohammadan Law."[72] One such case was witnessed in the case of Russomoy, Dur Chowduri vs. Abul Fata Muhammad,[73] wherein the judges Tottenham and Travelion of the Calcutta High Court declared waqf allal Aulad as invalid. When the

70 Proceedings of the Home Department (Public) 1903, No.121 Part-A.

71 *Ibid.*, Nos. 115, 116, Part-A.

72 Mohammad Yusoof Khan Bahadur, *Review of Mohammadan Law of waqf*, Calcutta, 1906, p. 113.

73 ILR(1891) 18 Cal 399.

matter went to appeal in 1894, the Privy Council in Abul Fata Muhammad vs. Russomoy, Dur Chowduri[74] declared waqf-alal-Aulad (family waqf) to be an invalid waqf.

This decision in *Abul Fata Muhammad* vs. *Russomoy, Dur Chowduri* rendered by the Privy Council stirred up the Muslim society and caused resentment against the British administration. A number of representations and memoranda were submitted by leading Muslim intellectuals and leading men of India to the Viceroy and to Her Majesty's Government. It ultimately resulted in the enactment of the Waqf Validating Act, (VI of 1913) 1913, which restored the validity of the waqf. This is the first piece of legislation on waqf in India. This Act declared the right of Mussalmans to make settlements of property by way of waqf in favour of their families, children and descendants, and for the benefit of the poor or for religious, pious or charitable purpose. It seeks to remove doubts regarding the validity of waqfs. But this Act did not have any provision for waqfs created before its enforcement. Therefore, the British Government enacted another Act in 1930, i.e., The Mussalman Waqf Validating Act, (XXXII) of 1930. This Act, while giving retrospective effect to the 1913 Act, says that whereas the Mussalman Validating Act 1913 (VI of 1913) does not apply to the waqfs created before its enactment, it is expedient to validate such waqfs without infringing any rights contrary thereto as it may have already accrued or been required.

Justice Hamilton of Kenya has an interesting observation with regard to *waqf-alal-Auladad*, when he says

> A study of the question shows that while the (Islamic) Law uninfluenced from outside sources permitted perpetuities and the erection of Auqaf for the family (benefit), solely the influence of English Judges and of the Privy Council have gradually encroached on this position.[75]

The Civil Procedure Code (Act V) of 1908, provides for taking action against the breach of trust and for the issue of direction by the court for proper administration of religious or charitable trusts, including waqfs, under sections 92 and 93. Under these sections, any two or more persons interested in a trust, waqf or endowment could bring a suit against the management of the trust or a mutawalli of a waqf with the prior approval of the Advocate General. However the provision in section 69 of the Waqf Act 1954 made the section 92 of Civil Procedure Code ineffective as far as waqfs are concerned.

74 22 IA 76.

75 Talibu Bin Mwijaka V. Executors of Siwa Haji as quoted in East African Law Review (1967) p. 33.

Another Act which is directly or indirectly related to the administration of waqf under the British Rule was the Official Trustees Act 1913. Under section 4 of this Act, some specified persons can be appointed as trustees by any person intending to create a waqf for secular purposes or for purposes that are other than religious.

The British Government has enforced several laws for the administration of waqfs, such as Mussalman Waqf Validating Act VI of 1913, Charitable and Religious Trusts Act XIV of 1920 and Mussalman Waqf Act XLII of 1923.

4.1. Mussalman Wakf Validating Act VI of 1913

Mussalman Waqf Validating Act VI of 1913 was the first enactment directly concerned with the subject of waqf. The Preamble of the Mussalman Waqf Validating Act 1913 was as under:

> An Act to declare the rights of Mussalmans to make settlements of property by way of 'waqf' in favour of their families, children and descendants.
>
> WHEREAS doubts have arisen regarding the validity of waqfs created by persons professing the Mussalman faith in favour of themselves, their families, children and descendants and ultimately for the benefit of the poor or for other religious, pious or charitable purposes; and whereas it is expedient to remove such doubts.

4.2. The Mussalman Wakf Act, 1923 (No. 42 of 1923)

The Mussalman Wakf Act, 1923 (No. 42 of 1923), was enacted for the whole of India. This Act merely provided for the submission of audited accounts by the mutawallis to the District Judges concerned.

4.3. Mussalman Wakf Validating Act of 1930 (Act No. 32 of 1930)

The Judicial Committee of the Privy Council, while dealing a case in *Khajah Soleman* vs. *Nawab Sir Salimullah*,[76] came across an argument that the Mussalman Wakf Validating Act 1913 did not have retrospective effect, hence could not apply to the waqfs created prior to its enactment. Several representations were made to the British Crown. Therefore, the Mussalman Wakf Validating Act of 1930 (Act No. 32 of 1930) was enacted. Its Preamble reads as under:

76 AIR 1922 PC 107; ILR 49 Cal 820.

> WHEREAS the Mussalman Wakf Validating Act, 1913, does not apply to waqfs created before its enactment;
>
> AND WHEREAS it is expedient to validate such wakfs without infringing any rights contrary thereto which may have already accrued or been acquired;

Ultimately, the Mussalman Wakf Validating Act 1913 was accorded retrospective effect.

4.4. The Provincial and Local Laws

The princely State of Hyderabad had promulgated Endowments Regulation Act in the year 1939 (1349 Fasli). In the erstwhile Hyderabad State, there was a separate department called *Umoor-e-Mazhabi* (Ecclesiastical Department) to look after the religious affairs. This department was headed by a Commissioner and assisted by two Deputy Commissioners. The waqf matters were also looked after by this department. The Hyderabad Endowments Regulation provides for registration of waqf properties, maintenance of waqf register and lays emphasis on the duties of the mutawalli.

Likewise, in other provinces of the country, different Acts and Regulations were in vogue before independence. Prominent among them are Bihar and Orissa Mussalman Waqf Act 1926, Bengal Wakf Act 1934, Bombay Mussalman Wakf Act 1935, Uttar Pradesh United Provinces Muslim Wakfs Act 1936, Delhi Muslim Wakf Act 1943, Bombay Mussalman Wakfs (Amendment) Act, 1945, etc.

4.5. Wakf Act 1954 (XXIX) of 1954

Indian Wakf Act (XXIX) of 1954 was legislated as the first piece of legislation on waqf in independent India. It received the assent of the president of India on 21 May 1954 and published in the Gazette of India.[77] The Act aimed for better administration and supervision of waqfs. Its statement of objects and reasons states that:

> The management of waqfs though it vests immediately in a mutawalli is a subject which requires the supervision of the State. The need for supervision has been felt, and in addition to various enactments dealing with the subject of the charitable endowments, the Mussalman waqf Act, 1923 (No. 42 of 1923), was enacted for the whole of India. This Act merely provides for the submission of audited accounts by the Mutawallis, to the District Judges. This Act did not prove of much practical value. The Mussalman waqf (Bombay Amendment) Act, 1935

77 Gazette of India (Extraordinary) Part II Section1 p. 871, dated 24 May 1954.

> (XVIII of 1935) amended the Mussalman waqf Act, 1923 (42 of 1923). The Bengal waqf Act, 1934 (XIII of 1934) was enacted to create a machinery for the supervision of waqfs in Bengal. The U. P. followed suit and the United Provinces Muslim waqfs Act. 1936 (XIII of 1936) was passed creating a Central waqf Board. Similarly Bihar also passed a legislation almost on the same lines. The working of these Acts has brought out the necessity of some amendments. Further many of the States have got no Act for the purpose. It. is therefore, necessary that one uniform and consolidated legislation may be passed by the Centre, which may be adopted as a model Act by the various States. It is with this view that the present Bill is introduced.[78]

The Wakf Act 1954 (Act XXIX of 1954) provided for the incorporation of Waqf Boards in every state. It also provided for the investigation, survey and registration of waqf properties. With the passage of this legislation, many of the State Acts were repealed, except the Bengal Wakf Act 1934 and the Uttar Pradesh United Provinces Muslim Wakf Act 1936. In Maharashtra, this Act was applicable in the Marathwada Region; in Gujarat, this Act was applicable only in the Kutch Region. In rest of the areas of Maharashtra and Gujarat States, the Bombay Public Trust Act 1950 was applicable. This means that two systems of waqf administration were prevalent in the same state and the waqf institutions were governed by different laws in the country.

4.6. *Amendment to Wakf Act 1954 for Removal of Anomalies*

The Wakf Act of 1954 could not meet the emerging challenges. Hence it underwent several amendments with the passage of time, such as Wakf Act Amendment 1956, Public waqf (Extensions of Limitations) Act 1959 (Act XXIX of 1959), Wakf Amendment Act of (XXXIV) of 1964, Wakf Amendment Act (XXXVIII) of 1969 and Wakf Amendment Act (XXXXXXIX) of 1984.

4.7. *Wakf Amendment Act 1956*

After the enactment of the Wakf Act 1954, the country witnessed the reorganisation of federal states on linguistic basis. Due to state reorganisation, some of the newly formed states left without the statutory body of Waqf Boards, which were the custodians of the waqf properties in the respective states. It had complicated the waqf administration. This necessitated empowering the Union Government to make arrangements to surmount

78 Gazette of India 1952, Part II, Section 2, p. 285.

such incongruity. Therefore the Wakf Amendment Act 1956 was enacted mainly to empower the State and Union Governments to constitute Inter-State or Intra-State Waqf Boards.

4.8. Public Wakfs Extension of Limitation Act 1959

It was observed that the waqf properties were in adverse possession more particularly in the western federal states largely due to partition after independence. The waqf institutions were abandoned and its properties were encroached up by unscrupulous elements. The waqf properties were found to be in an adverse position. The situation in the rest of the country was no better. Though the Wakf Act was legislated in 1954 it could not help because of the adverse position of the property and statutory limitation. The provision of statutory limitation under Article 142 and 144 of the Indian Limitation Act (Act IX of 1908) 1908 (now this Act is called the Limitations Act 1963) was a major hurdle. Hence a legislation called Public Wakf (Extension of Limitation) Act 1959[79] was passed by the Parliament. It extended the statutory limitation for filing suits for recovery of waqf properties dispossessed after 14 August, 1947 and before 7 May 1954, up to 15 August, 1967. It enabled the waqf management and the Waqf Boards to file suits for recovery and possession of alienated waqf properties. It received the assent of the President of India on 1 September 1959. This period of limitation was extended by the Amendment Act 1969 (Act IX) of 1969 from 15 August 1967 to 31 December 1970.

4.9. Wakf Amendment Act 1964

After ten years of the enactment of the Wakf Act 1954, it was felt in 1964 that the functioning of the Waqf Boards was not satisfactory. The mutawallis were alienating the waqf properties without the knowledge of the Waqf Board. The Waqf Boards required sufficient powers to take disciplinary action against the erring Mutawallis and even to remove them to safeguard the waqf properties.

The Wakf Amendment Act of 1964 added new Chapter II (A) comprising sections 8A, 8B, 8C and 8D providing for the establishment, functioning, account and powers of the Central Waqf Council. Finally, the Central Waqf Council was constituted in the year 1965. This Amendment Act also provided for the constitution of a separate Waqf Board for Shia Waqfs if the Shia Waqf properties constitute 15 per cent of the total waqf properties in the state or the waqf income in any state is more than 15 per cent of the total waqf income. This Amendment Act paved the way for the establishment of the Central Waqf Council.

79 Gazette of India (Extraordinary) Part II, Section I p. 220, dated 2 September 1959.

4.10. The Wakf Amendment Act (Act IX of 1969) 1969

Many of the administrators of the waqf institutions could not take advantage of the extension of limitation as envisaged in Public Wakf Extension of Limitation Act 1959 for recovery and possession of the alienated waqf properties. The limitation period lapsed on 15 August 1967. The stakeholders of the waqfs stared at the Indian Parliament for a further extension of limitation, since many of the waqf properties could not be recovered due to adverse possession. Hence the Wakf Amendment Act 1969 was enacted, which extended the period of limitation to 31 December 1970.

4.11. Wakf Amendment Act 1984

The Waqf Act was again subjected to amendment by the Wakf (Amendment) Act 1984 (Act XXXXXXIX of 1984), largely based on the recommendations of the Waqf Inquiry Committee set up in December 1970. Waqf Inquiry Committee was constituted in response to a demand made in Parliament by the members during a discussion on the Waqf (Amendment) Bill 1969. This Committee held discussion with stakeholders and inquired into the administration of waqfs at all levels. It submitted its report in 1976. The statement of objects and reasons for this Wakf Amendment Act (XXXXXXIX) of 1984 reads as under:[80]

> The Waqf Act 1954 (29 of 1954) provides for the better administration and supervision of waqfs. The working of the waqf Boards established under the Waqf Act is however not satisfactory and in most cases these boards have failed to achieve the very purpose for which they have been established. Further the financial position of most of these boards is also not happy. The question of toning up of the administration of the waqfs so as to protect and properly manage waqf properties by taking necessary measures, including legislation, has been engaging the attention of the Central Government. A committee known as the waqf Inquiry Committee was accordingly constituted by the Central Government for the purpose of verifying the working of the Waqf Act and for making enquiry into the administration of waqfs at all levels in respect of States to which the provisions of the Waqf Act are applicable. The waqf Enquiry Committee made a large number of recommendations which envisage a thorough restructuring of waqf administration designed to improve the financial positions of the waqf institutions and to plug the loopholes noticed in the working of the waqf Act. The report of the waqf Enquiry Committee was examined by the Central Government in consultation with the State Governments, the Central waqf Council,

80 Gazette of India Dated 22 April 1964, Part II, Section 2, Ext., p. 317.

> Chairman of the waqf Boards, Muslim members of Parliament and Minorities Commissions. Various views and different shades of opinion on the subject were expressed at different forums. The Bill, which is mainly based on the recommendations of the waqf Enquiry Committee, takes into consideration the various views expressed in this behalf.

Only two provisions of Wakf (Amendment) Act 1984 could, however, be enforced because of strong opposition to its various provisions from some quarters of the Muslim Community. The two provisions are related to:

i. Increasing the period of limitation for filing suits in respect of waqf properties in adverse possession from 12 years to 30 years; and
ii. Application of the provisions of Waqf Act 1954, to the Evacuee properties.

The main criticism related to provisions concerned the powers of the Waqf Commissioner. It was stated that the Waqf Commissioner had been given overriding powers and the Waqf Board had been made subordinate to him. The other criticisms were that the Amendment Act 1984 was a gross interference by the State and the Central Government in the day-to-day management and administration of the waqfs by the trustees and mutawallis of waqfs.

4.12. Exclusive enactments for Waqf institutions

Apart from the laws governing the administration of waqfs in India, the British Government brought in specific Acts for the administration of specific waqf institutions of importance. In the year 1878, Hussainabad Endowment Act (Act 15 of 1878) was enacted to deal with the administration of Hussainabad Imambara in Lucknow. This waqf institution is venerable to the Shia Community because of spiritual importance.

Similarly, in 1936, an Act (Act 22 of 1936) was passed to regulate the affairs of the famous Shrine of Sufi Saint Hazrat Khwaja Moinuddin Chishti in Ajmer, popularly known as Dargah Khwaja Saheb, which is one of the most revered spiritual shrines of the Muslim Community in India. This waqf institution was governed under the ambit of Religious Endowments Act 1863 (Act 20 of 1863) until 1936. In the year 1936, Dargah Khwaja Saheb Act (Act 22 of 1936) was passed to regulate the administration of this Dargah. It provided for the Nazims to receive Nazars. With the enactment of Dargah Khwaja Saheb Act 1955 (Act 36 of 1955)[81] the 1936 Act (Act 22 of 1936) was repealed. The Dargah Khwaja Saheb Act 1955 was notified vide Notification No. S.R.O. 482 (E) dated 24 February 1956, published in the Gazette of India.

81 Gazette of India (Extraordinary) Part II Section 3 (I), dated 1 March 1956.

4.13. Dargah Khwaja Saheb Act 1955 (Act 36 of 1955)

The Government of India had constituted an inquiry committee in 1949, under the chairmanship of Justice Gulam Hassan, the then judge of Allahabad High Court, to inquire into the administration affairs of Dargah Khwaja Saheb of Ajmer and to submit recommendations for its efficient administration. The committee in its report took account of the appointment of the Sajjadahnashin (the spiritual head) and the appointment of Mutawalli Administrator (the temporal office). The committee observed that the Office of the Mutawalli and Sajjadahnashin were wisely kept separately. The Sajjadahnashin took care of the spiritual matters while the mutawalli took care of the temporal matters. The merger of these two offices could have resulted in the abuse of power and misuse of waqf income.[82]

This inquiry report paved the way for the enactment of Dargah Khwaja Saheb Act 1955 (Act 36 of 1955). Its statement of objects and reasons states that

> In 1949 the Government of India appointed a committee under the chairmanship of Justice Gulam Hassan, the then judge of Allahabad High Court, to report on the affairs of the Durgah Khwaja Saheb, Ajmer, and to make recommendations for its efficient management in the interest of the devotees. The present Bill seeks to implement the decisions of Government on the recommendations of the Committee.

The Principal provisions are as follows:

(i) The administration, control and management of the Durgah are to vest in a high power committee consisting representative Muslims to be appointed by the Central Government.
(ii) A paid Nazim is to be appointed a Member-Secretary of the Committee and to administer the Durgah.
(iii) An Advisory Committee is to be set up to advise the Nazim in the discharge of his functions.
(iv) The remuneration of the Sajjadanashin and the manner of determining succession to that office are laid down.
(v) The soliciting or receiving of offerings on behalf of the Durgah is to be prohibited except through the Nazim or a person authorised by him.
(vi) A Board of Arbitration is to be set up to settle disputes not relating to any religious usage or custom or to the performance of any religious office.

82 Report of Dargah Khwaja Saheb (Ajmer) Committee of Inquiry, New Delhi, 1949.

This Act declares in its preamble that this is an Act to make provisions for the proper administration of the Dargah and the endowment of Dargah of Khwaja Moinuddin Chishti, generally known as Dargah Khwaja Saheb Ajmer. With the enactment of this Act, Dargah Khwaja Saheb (Emergency Provisions) Act 1950 has been repealed. This Act has an overriding effect notwithstanding anything contained in the Religious Endowments Act, 1863 (Act 20 of 1863). The Managing Committee of Durgah Khwaja Saheb, exercising the powers conferred by section 20 of the Durgah Khwaja Saheb Act 1955, formulated the Bye-Laws for the administration of the Durgah affairs which were published in the Gazette of India.[83] These Bye-Laws describe the procedural matters for the day-to-day administration of the Durgah.

Dargah Khwaja Saheb Act 1955 could not efficiently control the mismanagement and maladministration of affairs of Durgah. It was felt necessary to provide for penal action against the erring persons. Therefore, this Act was amended by the Amendment Act (Act 20 of 1964).[84] The statement of objects and reasons of this Act reads as under:

1. The Durgah Khwaja Act 1955 was enacted to provide inter alia for proper control and efficient management of the Durgah Endowments as defined in the Act.
2. A large number of pilgrims who come to offer prayers at the Durgah Khwaja Saheb make offering of *Nazars* in the forms of cash or in kind, which are meant for the Durgah Khwaja Saheb and form part of the Durgah Endowment. The Act expressly provides in Section 2(d) (v) and 14 that only the *Nazim* or a person authorised by him is entitled to receive on behalf of the Durgah, *Nazars* and offering given by the pilgrims. In contravention of these express provisions of the Act some individuals have been collecting the *Nazars* and offerings made at the shrine and have been misappropriating them. In the absence of a specific penal clause in the Act it has not been found possible to take action against them, in order to prevent them from doing so. The acceptance of the offerings and *Nazars* which are a source of substantial income to the Durgah by unauthorised persons affects the interest of the shrine. It is, therefore, considered necessary to make a specific provision for penalising persons who solicit or receive *Nazars* and offerings meant for the Durgah in an unauthorised manner. The present Bill seeks to amend the Durgah Khwaja Saheb Act 1955, by providing for such a penal clause for this purpose.

83 Gazette of India (Extraordinary) Part II Section 3 (I), dated 25 October, 1958.
84 Gazette of India (Extraordinary) Part II Section 3 (I), dated 1 June 1964.

4.14. Central Waqf Council

The Government of India had organised an Inter-State Conference on waqf in 1960. The idea of a Central Waqf Council, to supervise the functioning of the Waqf Boards and to advise the Central Government on matters of waqf emerged in the conference, though the Kazmi Bill of 1952 had proposed the establishment of such a central agency. Accordingly, the Ministry of Irrigation and Power (there was no Ministry of Minority Affairs in those days) passed a resolution on 20 September 1961 in this regard. It necessitated an amendment to the Waqf Act in 1954. Therefore, the Waqf Amendment Act 1964 (Act XXXIV of 1964) was enacted to make a provision for the establishment of the Central Waqf Council. Finally, the Central Waqf Council was constituted in 1965. Presently it functions under the Ministry of Minority Affairs and the Chairman of this council is the Minister in charge of Minority Affairs.

4.15. Waqf Inquiry Committee Recommendations

In December 1970 the Government of India constituted the Waqf Inquiry Committee to inquire into waqf administration in the country and to examine the working of the Central Waqf Council. The committee advocated sufficient powers to Central Waqf Council for its efficient functioning. The Final Report[85] of the Waqf Inquiry Committee further says that:

> Following a detailed review of the actual working of the Council and the reports of the various sub-Committee (constituted by the council) we are convinced that in the absence of specific well defined functions and clear cut role the council has been wasting its efforts in all directions ... It is distressing to note that out of one percent contribution collected from the awquaf almost all the amount is spent on the travelling allowance and daily allowance of the members of the council attending the annual or bi-annual meetings of the council held in New Delhi just for a day. The balance goes to the traveling allowance and daily allowance of the members of various committees and the permanent staff of the council.

It recommended that the administrative expenses towards the functioning of the Central Waqf Council shall be incurred from the annual grants of the Central Government instead of generating income from the one per cent waqf fund contribution from the State Waqf Boards.

85 Final Report of the Waqf Inquiry Committee Government of India, Ministry of Law and Justice, Government of India Press, Simla, 1976, pp. 3–4.

4.16. Waqf Act 1995 (Act 43 of 1995)

The waqf administration continued to slip into decadence. The waqf properties were falling prey to the nefarious designs of land sharks, politicians and the accommodating Mutawallis. The matter was discussed several times in the Parliament and in the State Legislatures. Joint Parliamentary Committees were constituted to submit recommendations for the effective protection and efficient administration of the waqfs. A Committee was constituted under the Chairmanship Mrs. Bajpai, the then-Minister for Social Welfare in 1986.

After a careful consideration of the objections to the various provisions of the 1984 (Amendment) Act, and after holding wide-ranging discussions with the leaders of the Muslim Community, it has been decided to bring in a new comprehensive Bill on waqf matters incorporating the features of 1954 Act and such provisions of the 1984 Act in respect of which there was a near consensus.

After a long deliberation in different fora, the Waqf Act 1995 (Act 43 of 1995) was enacted. It provided bright hopes for better administration of waqf and matters connected therewith. The statement of objects and reasons of the Waqf Act 1995 states that

> The actual working of Waqf Act 1954 had brought out many deficiencies in it as also in the set up of the waqf Boards, especially their powers of superintendence and control over the management of individual waqfs. To clarify some of these matters – the Act had to be amended three times – in 1959, in 1964 and in 1969 – within a period of 15 years.

The Waqf Act 1995 (Act 43 of 1995) received the assent of the President of India on 22 November 1995. It was published in the Gazette of India.[86] This Act came into force on 1 January 1996 and nullified all the previous Acts except the Dargah Khwaja Saheb Act 1955 (Act 36 of 1955) and its Amendment Act (Act 20 of 1964).

Now the new Law (Waqf Act 1995) will have *inter alia* the following features:

a. Waqf Boards for the States and for the Union Territory of Delhi shall have not less than 7 and not more than 13 members of which the majority will comprise such persons as are elected from amongst Muslim Members of Parliament, Muslim Member of State Legislatures, Muslim Members of the Bar Council in a State and Mutawallis of waqfs having an annual income of Rs. 1 lakh or more. The nominated members will be from Muslim organizations of the State eminence, recognized scholars

86 Gazette of India (Extraordinary) Part II Section I pp. 1–55, dated 22 November 1995

in Muslim theology and a representative of the State Government not below the rank of Deputy Secretary. In a State where there are shia waqfs but no separate shia waqf Board, at least one of the Members shall be a Shia Muslim. A smaller Waqf Board is envisaged for Union Territories other than Delhi.

b. The other important feature is about distribution of powers between the Waqf Board and the waqf Commissioner which would now be redesignated as the Chief Executive Officer and would be subordinate to the waqf Board.
c. Provisions are also being made for appointment of the Executive Officer in respect of waqfs whose performance is not satisfactory and whose annual income is Rs. 5 lakhs or more.
d. To strengthen the finances of the waqf Board, one of the measures being contemplated is to raise the rate of the contribution by a waqf to the Waqf Board from 6 per cent of its annual income to 7 per cent.
e. It is also intended to put certain restrictions on the powers of Mutawallis in the interest of better management of waqf properties.
f. An important provision in the proposed Bill relates to setting up waqf Tribunals to consider questions and disputes pertaining to waqfs.
g. There are instances of misuse of waqf properties either with or without the connivance of the Mutawallis. It is now proposed to incorporate in the bill a provision so that the alienation of waqf properties will not be easy.
h. At present, the Waqf Act 1954 is not applicable to Uttar Pradesh, West Bengal, parts of Gujarat, parts of Maharashtra and some of the North – Eastern states. With the enforcement of this legislation there will be uniformity in respect of waqf administration throughout the country except in Jammu and Kashmir State.

In spite of the efforts by the Government and lawmakers of the country to have the efficient law through several amendments for the waqf administration, there have been many issues that were left unattended, such as a survey of the waqf institutions and their properties, the infirmities in the definitions of waqf and encroacher, powers and functions of the Waqf Board, the Waqf Tribunal and Central Waqf Council, effective measures for the protection of the waqf properties. Hence the Waqf Act 1995 was amended in 2013.

4.17. Waqf Amendment Act 2013 (Act 27 of 2013)

In order to remove infirmities and deficiencies in the existing Waqf Act 1995, a bill Called Waqf Amendment Bill 2010 was introduced in the Lower House of Parliament on 27 April 2010. After discussions and deliberations, it was referred to the Select Committee of the Upper House of Parliament, which submitted its report on 16 December 2011 to the Parliament. Ultimately, it was passed by the Parliament in 2013. It received the assent of the President of India on the 20 September 2013, and was published in the Gazette[87] of India Extraordinary Part II Section I No. 37 New Delhi, dated 23 September 2013. The salient features of this Amendment Act is as follows:

a. It has been made obligatory on the part of the state governments to appoint survey commissioners to conduct survey and publish the survey reports in the official gazette. The cost of the publication is to be borne by the State Government.
b. Some of the definitions in the 1995 Act have reframed. It provides that waqf can be created by any persons irrespective of his religious faith. The scope of the word encroacher has be broadened to include public and private institutions and persons whose tenancy / licence has expired, to empower the State waqf Boards and the waqf Tribunals to protect the waqf properties from encroachments.
c. The waqf Tribunal can now assess the damages due to unauthorised occupation and pass orders for recovery through the Districts/ Magistrates.
d. The Central waqf Council has been entrusted with the powers to issue directions to the state waqf boards for the survey of and maintenance of waqf records. A provision has been made for the adjudication of disputes between Central Waqf Council and State waqf Boards to a Board of Adjudication presided over by a retired Supreme Court/High Court Judge.
e. The Waqf Act 1995 had a provision for the representation of a Muslim Member of the State Bar Council. However due to non availability of such Muslim Member, in the respective State the vacancy could not be filled up. Now the Amendment Act of 2013 provides that if a Muslim Member in the respective State Bar Council is not available the State Government can nominate any senior Muslim Advocate from that State to the State Waqf Board.
f. The period of tenancy has been enhanced from 3 years to 30 years for commercial, educational or residential purposes.
g. The Amendment Act 2013 ensures that the District Magistrate or the Additional District Magistrate and the Sub-Divisional Magistrate shall implement the decisions of the State Waqf Board.
h. If waqf land is required under the Land Acquisition Act, no order shall be passed without consultation of the State Waqf Board.
i. New penal provision is introduced as 52(A) which imposes rigorous imprisonment up to 2 years for alienation or purchase or permanently acquiring waqf property without prior sanction of the State waqf Board. Such offence is made a cognisable and non-bailable one.

87 Gazette of India (Extraordinary) Part II Section I No. 37, dated 23 September 2013.

j. The Chief Executive Officer may make an application to the Waqf Tribunal for the eviction orders of unauthorised occupants under the provisions of Section 54 of the Amendment Act of 2013.
k. The Waqf Tribunal no longer be a single member Tribunal. It will not have a District /Sessions Judge or Class I Civil Judge as Chairperson and other Member who is an expert of Muslim Law and Jurisprudence.
l. The words *wakf* and *wakif* have been spelt as *waqf* and *waqif* in the entire Amendment Act of 2013.

After 18 years of debate and discussion in different fora, the Waqf Act 1995 has been fructified with major overhaul when the Waqf Amendment Act 2013 (Act 27 of 2013) was enacted by the Parliament of India. This Amendment Act changed the contents under many of the sections of the Principal Act, i.e., the Wakf Act 1995.

5. Constitutional validity of Waqf Law in India

The Constitution of India ensures freedom of religion and expression, freedom of conscience, freedom to manage religious affairs under Articles 25 and 26, which are mentioned below.

Article 25:

1. *Subject to public order, morality and health and to the other provision of this Part, all persons are equally entitled to freedom of conscience and the right freely to profess, practice and propagate religion.*
2. *Nothing in this Article shall effect the operation of any existing law or prevent the State from making any law-*
   (a) *Regulating or restricting any economic, financial, political or other secular activity which may be associated with religious practice;*
   (b) *Providing for social welfare and reform or the throwing open of Hindu religious institutions of a public character to all classes and sections of Hindus.*

Article 26 of the Constitution further gives freedom to the citizens to manage their religious affairs and it reads as under:

Subject to public order, morality and health, every religious denomination or any section thereof shall have the right.

(a) *To establish and maintain institutions for religious and charitable purposes;*
(b) *To manage its own affairs in matters of religion;*
(c) *To own and acquire movable and immovable property; and*
(d) *To administer such property in accordance with law.*

The above constitutional provisions have been interpreted in the following judgements of the Supreme Court and High Courts and upheld the constitutional validity of waqf laws and the Waqf Boards constituted under these laws.

- The judgment in Commissioner, Hindu Religious and Charitable Endowments, Madras vs. Sri Lakshmindra Thirtha Swamiar of Shirur Mutt[88] rendered by seven-judge Bench of the Supreme Court while dealing with the constitutional validity of the Madras Hindu Religious and Charitable Endowments Act 1951.
- Five-judge Bench of the Supreme Court in Ratilal Panashanit Gandhi vs. State of Bombay.[89]
- Supreme Court judgment delivered by seven-judge Bench while dealing with the validity of the Nathdwara Temple Act 1959 in Tilkayat Shri Govindlalji Maharaj vs. State of Rajasthan.[90]
- High Court of Allahabad in *Hafiz Mohamed Zafar Ahamed* vs. *Uttar Pradesh Sunni Central Board of waqfs*.[91]
- High Court of Calcutta, in *Basheer Ahamed* vs. *State of West Bengal*.[92]

Thus the Parliament enactment pertaining to administration of waqf institutions, waqf properties and regulating the activities of stakeholders in waqf is constitutionally valid.

6. Recent developments

The definition of waqf in the Waqf Laws in India, which prescribes that it is the dedication of waqf property by *a person professing Islam*, is disturbing. The Islamic Law, as said in the preceding paragraph, does not prohibit a Non-Muslim to create a waqf or to dedicate property in waqf. According to *Hanafi* and *Maliki* schools of thought, the object must be valid, according to the Islamic Law as well as the Personal Law of the dedicator. However, the *Shaifai* and *Hambli* schools of thought require that the object of waqf shall be in consonance with the Islamic Law only, the belief or the religion of the dedicator does not matter. Khadar Ali Khan Enquiry Commission appointed by State Government of Andhra Pradesh, also suggested deletion of these words.[93] This issue has been put to rest by the Waqf Amendment of 2013.

It becomes necessary that the Survey Commissioner of waqf shall have the powers vested in a civil judge as per the provisions of the Civil Procedure Code to call for any record in possession of any person, government servant

88 AIR 1954 SC 282.
89 AIR 1954 SC 388.
90 AIR 1963 SC 1638.
91 AIR 1965, All 33.
92 AIR 1976 Cal 142.
93 Khadar Ali Khan Inquiry Commission Report, Government of Andhra Pradesh, Hyderabad, 1984, p. 150.

or authority, and to institute an inquiry with regard to the waqfs. He shall also be entitled to get the waqf registered with the Waqf Board.

The Honourable Prime Minister of India appointed a high power committee on 9 March 2005 to conduct a survey of Social, Economic and Educational Status of the Muslim Community in India headed by Justice Rajindar Sachar. This Committee submitted its report on 17 November 2006. The report of this committee was placed before the Parliament of India on 30 November 2006.

Justice Sachar Committee report states that there are more than 4.9 lakhs of registered waqfs spread over different states and union territories of India. A large concentration of waqf properties is found in West Bengal. The total area under waqf properties all over India is estimated at about 6 lakh acres and the book value at about Rs. 6,000 Crores. The market value of these properties is considered to be a higher manifold. For instance, a recent estimate of the current value of waqf properties in Delhi alone is in excess of Rs. 6,000 Crores. The current annual income from these properties is only about Rs. 163 Crores, which amounts to a meagre rate of return of 2.7 per cent. Justice Sachar says that, as the book values of waqf properties are about half a century old, the current value can safely be estimated to be several times more and the market value of the waqf properties can be put at Rs. 1.2 lakh Crores (Rs. 1,200 billion). If these properties are put to efficient and marketable use they can generate at least a minimum return of 10 per cent, which is about 12,000 Crores per annum.[94] These estimated values of the waqf properties is 13 years old. Now the market price of real estate in India over the years has increased by more than tenfold. Hence it can be fairly estimated the value of waqf properties in India to be Rs. 12, Lakh Crores or Rs. 12,000 billion. In terms of US Dollars it would be more than 171 billion.

Some of the major recommendations of Justice Sachar pertaining to waqf are as follows:

a. A large number of states have not framed the waqf Rules; this is one of the main reasons for non-implementation of the provisions of the Waqf Act and perpetuation of corruption and lack of accountability.
b. The Public Premises (Eviction of Unauthorized Occupants) Act, 1971 should be applied to remove encroachment from waqf properties and arrears of rent, at market rates, should be recovered as arrears of land revenue. It also recommends that Rent Control Act, Land Reforms Act, Agricultural Land Ceilings Act, Urban Land Ceiling Act, Registration of Properties Act, Tenancy Act, Stamp Duty Act, Court Fee Act, Income-tax Act, Private Forest Vesting and Assignments Act may be amended without hurting their general public objective which

94 Justice Sachar Committee Report 2005, Government of India p. 219.

would strengthen the functioning of the waqfs. This recommendation could go a long way to bring such statutes in harmony with the Waqf Act 1995.

c. The application of the RCA (Rent Control Act) to waqfs is damaging the noble interests of waqfs and hurting the entitlements of the beneficiaries. Therefore, an amendment exempting the waqf properties from the purview of the RCA within the waqf is urgently needed. This can be done by introducing an over-riding provision in the waqf Act. Section 85of the Waqf Act though bars the jurisdiction of Civil Courts, but it cannot have retrospective effect.
d. The period of limitation should be extended till 2035 with retrospective effect.
e. The Central waqf Council is authorized to issue general instructions and directives to the State Waqf Boards. Therefore it is more appropriate that it should frame standard rules and regulations for the smooth functioning and administration of waqf institutions as well as the Waqf Boards in the country.

The Indian Parliament constituted a Joint Parliamentary Committee to examine and submit recommendations for the improvement of the waqf administration in the country. The Joint Parliamentary Committee in its 9th Report[95] presented to the Parliament on 23 October 2008 recommended the computerisation of the waqf records in all the states. Accordingly, a budgetary allocation of Rs. 25 Crores was made for this purpose and all the State Waqf Boards were asked to digitise their records.

Consequent to the Sachar Committee Recommendations 2005 the Ministry of Minority Affairs, Government of India amended the Waqf Act 1995 in the year 2013. A Public Sector Undertaking, namely National Waqf Development Corporation (NAWADCO), has been incorporated with an authorised share capital of Rs. 500 Crores and paid up capital of Rs. 100 Crores to finance the development of waqf properties for public purposes throughout the country. Model Waqf Regulations have been drafted. Again in 2016 the Ministry of Minority Affairs prepared a 92-page document containing Model Waqf Rules to be adopted by the State Waqf Boards with suitable modifications if any.

The dismal performance of waqf institutions in India cannot be attributed to a single reason. It can be the dishonesty of the mutawallis or committees, apathy of the officials, absence of consistent persuasion of the Waqf Boards, ulterior motives of the politicians and/or misinterpretation of law in the courts. The Waqf Law and its various amendments could not be successful to protect the waqf administration from slipping into shambles.

95 Joint Parliamentary Committee on Waqf 9th Report, Government of India, New Delhi, 2008.

It took a hundred years from the first piece of legislation, i.e., Mussalman Waqf Validating Act VI of 1913 to the present Waqf Amendment Act of 2013. But the law of waqf has come a long way in a journey of about two and half centuries from the promulgation of Regulation of 1772 to the modern legislative history of India. The success and efficacy of this Amendment Act 2013 will depend on the judicious actions of all the stakeholders.

I PRELIMINARY

Synopsis

The journey of the Waqf Law in Independent India since the legislation of Waqf Act 1954 and its amendment in 1956, 1959, 1964 and 1984, and the subsequent enactment of Waqf Act 1995 with its amendment in 2013 coupled with judicial response therein, have led to the emergence of a strong waqf jurisprudence. But the Waqf Law as in vogue up to 1995 could not prove to be efficacious enough for the protection of waqf institutions and their properties. The Waqf Act 1995 incorporated significant changes such as democratised composition of Waqf Boards, Establishment of Waqf Tribunals in every state, providing statutory status to the Central Waqf Council, removal of the restrictions of statutory limitation under the Limitation Act 1963 (Act 36) of 1963. The Waqf Act 1995 (Act 43 of 1995) received the assent of the President of India on 22 November 1995. It was published in the Gazette of India.[1] This Act came into force on 1 January 1996 and nullifies all the previous Acts except the Dargah Khwaja Saheb Act 1955 (Act 36 of 1955) and its Amendment Act (Act 20 of 1964).

This Act has been amended vide Waqf Amendment Act 2013 (Act 27 of 2013). It received the assent of the President of India on 20 September 2013 and gazette notified in the Gazette of India.[2] The salient features of the Amendment Act are that it rephrases the definitions, extends the tenancy period from 3 years to 30 years, allows even a Non-Muslim to create a waqf, rigorous imprisonment for unauthorised alienation of waqf properties, provides for the implementation of the decisions of the State Boards by the District Magistrate/Additional District Magistrates, Strengthening of Waqf Tribunal with additional Members, etc.

The prefatory statement of the Act (43 of 1995) says that it is "an Act to provide for the better administration of Waqfs and for matters connected therewith or incidental thereto."

1 Gazette of India Extraordinary, Part II Section I pp. 1–55, dated 7 November 1995.
2 Gazette of India Extraordinary, Part II Section I No. 37, dated 23 September 2013.

Keywords: Waqf, Beneficiary, Encroacher, Purpose, Person interested, Waqif

****

Section 1

Short title, extent and commencement:-

(1) ***This Act may be called the Waqf Act, 1995.***
(2) ***It extends to the whole of India except the State of Jammu and Kashmir.***
(3) ***It shall come into force in a State on such date as the Central government may, by notification in the Official Gazette, appoint; and different dates may be appointed for different areas within a State and for different provisions of this Act, and any reference in any provision to the commencement of this Act, shall, in relation to any State or area therein, be construed as reference to the commencement of that provision in such state or area.***

Reflections

Analogous section under Wakf Act 1954 is S.1

The Waqf Act 1995 has changed the composition of the Waqf Board. It has democratised the process of the constitution of the Waqf Board. This Act provides for the establishment of Waqf Tribunal by the State government. The Amendment Act 2013 has put to rest the confusion about the jurisdiction of the Waqf Tribunal which had attracted incoherent judgements by various High Courts across the country. The constitutional validity of the Act was challenged in the court of law. The following judgements upheld the constitutional validity of the Act.

Judicial response

The Constitutional validity of Waqf Law can be traced in the seven-judge Bench of the Supreme Court, in Commissioner, Hindu Religious and Charitable Endowments, Madras vs. Sri Lakshmindra Thirtha Swamiar of Shirur Mutt[3] while dealing with the constitutional validity of the Madras Hindu Religious and Charitable Endowments Act 1951 observed that:

3 AIR 1954 SC 282.

> It will be seen that besides the right to manage its own affairs in matters of religion, which is given by clause (b), the next two clauses of Article 26 guaranteed to a religious denomination the right to acquire and own property and to administer such properties in accordance with law. The administration of its property by a religious denomination has thus been placed on a different footing from the right to manage its own affairs in matters of religion. The latter is a fundamental right which no legislature can take away, whereas, the former can be regulated by laws which the legislature can validly impose. It is clear; therefore, that questions merely relating to administration of properties belonging to a religious group or institution are not matters of religion to which clause (b) of the Article applies. A law which takes away the right of administration from the hands of a religious denomination altogether and vests it in any other authority would amount to a violation of the right guaranteed under clause (d) of Article 26.

The validity of the Wakf Act 1954 and its several provisions was considered by the Indore Bench of the High Court of Madhya Pradesh in Nawab Usman Ali Khan vs. Choudary Faezulla[4] wherein the provisions of sections 11, 18, 52, 62, 63, 64, 67(a), (b), (c), (d), (h), (i), (k) and (n) of the Act were challenged as unconstitutional and violative of Article 25 and 26 of the Constitution. The learned single judge after referring to the decisions of the Supreme Court in Commissioner, Hindu Religious and Charitable Endowments, Madras vs. Sri Laksmindra Thirtha Swamiar of shrur Mutt[5] and Ratilal Penashant Gandhi vs. State of Bombay[6] held that:

> In view of these pronouncements of the Supreme Court and the purpose and general scheme of the Act as is discernible by the general survey of the principal provisions of the Act made above, it is futile to contend that the question regarding wakf, in so far as it relates to the properties comprised therein and the right of Mutawalli or any person to manage the same properly falls under Article 26(b) of the Constitution. It falls under Article 26(d) of the Constitution and as such is subject to the law made by the parliament. The legislative competence of the Parliament therefore to make aforesaid Act cannot be questioned.

In Hafiz Mohamed Zafar Ahamed vs. Uttar Pardesh Sunni Central Board of wakfs,[7] the validity of the Uttar Pradesh Muslim Wakfs Act 1960 came up for consideration. The High Court of Allahabad observed:

4 AIR 1959 MP 377.
5 AIR 1954 SCC 282.
6 Air 1954 SC 388.
7 AIR 1965 All 33.

> A Mutawalli's right is purely a right of management of the property and is not a proprietary right. The duties of a Mutawalli are purely of a secular character. His duties are not of a religious character. He has no beneficial interest of any kind in the property which he administers ... The right to manage the property of a wakf is a secular right and is not hit by Article 26 of the Constitution. Under section 19 of the Act only general superintendence of all wakfs vests in the Board. The Act does not deprive religious institutions of their right to manage their own affairs either in religious matter or in the administration of the property in accordance with law.

In Amir Alam Khan vs. State of Uttar Pradesh,[8] the Division Bench of Allahabad High Court pointed out that sections 19 and 20 of the Act place the "member" and the "Chair-Person" on the same footing or at the same place. The definition clause does not begin with the words "Not withstanding anything contained in any section of this Act." From this it is evident that if the Parliament, while enacting section 3(h) intended to attach a different meaning to the words "Member" and "Chair-Person," it would have been mentioned in section 3(h) of the Wakf Act. Their Lordships therefore held that the definition of "Member" is exhaustive and not restrictive, and that the "Member" of the Board includes "Chair-Person." As the term of the "Member," which is coterminous with the term of the Board, the term of the Chair-Person, in accordance with the aforesaid section, will be five years.

In Ratilal Panashanit Gandhi vs. State of Bombay[9] a five-judge Bench of the Supreme Court observed that:

> The language of the two clauses (b) and (d) of Article 26 would at once bring out the difference between the two. In regard to affairs in matters of religion, the right of management given to a religious body is a guaranteed fundamental right which no legislation can take away. On the other hand, as regards administration of property which a religious denomination is entitled to own and acquire, it has undoubtedly the right to administer such property but only in accordance with law. This means that the State can regulate the administration of trust properties by means of laws validly enacted; but here again it should be remembered that under Article 26 (d) it is the religious denomination itself which has been given the right to administer its property in accordance with any law which the statute may validly impose. A law, which takes away the right of administration altogether from the religious denomination and vests it in any other or secular authority, would amount

8 AIR 2002 All 215.
9 AIR 1954 SC 388.

> to violation of the right which is guaranteed by Article 26 (d) of the Constitution.

Another seven-judge Bench of the Supreme Court, while dealing with the validity of the Nathdwara Temple Act 1959 in Tilkayat Shri Govindlalji Maharaj vs. State of Rajasthan,[10] observed that:

> If the practice in question is purely secular or the affair which is controlled by the statute is essentially and absolutely secular in character, it cannot be urged that Article 25 (1) or Article 26 (b) has been contravened. Though the task of disengaging the secular from the religious may not be easy, it must nevertheless be admitted in dealing with the claims for protection under Articles 25 (1) and 26 (b). The right to manage the properties of the temple is a purely secular matter and it cannot, in our opinion, be regarded as a religious practice so as to fall under Article 25 (1) or as amounting to affairs in matters of religion.

A case pertaining to the validity of the Bengal Wakf Act 1934 as amended by the Bengal Wakf (Amendment) Act 14 of 1973 came up for consideration by Justice Sabyasachi Mukharji, of the High Court of Calcutta, in Basheer Ahamed vs. State of West Bengal.[11] The learned judge held that:

> Law regulating the management is permissible under clause (d) of Article 26 of the Constitution. I am therefore unable to accept that there has been violation of any provisions of Article 25 or Article 26 of the Constitutions by the provisions of the Bengal Wakf Act 1934 as amended by the Amendment Act of 1973. The provisions of the Act to which I have referred to herein before are essentially provisions for the preservation protection and improvement of the Wakf properties.

Thus the provisions under article 26 (b) and 26 (d) strengthen the concept of waqf and the establishment of waqf institutions and the right of citizens to manage them.

****

10 AIR 1963 SC 1638.
11 AIR 1976 Cal 142.

Section 2

Application of the Act:-

Save as otherwise expressly provided under this Act, this Act shall apply to all auqaf whether created before or after the commencement of this Act:

Provided that nothing in this Act shall apply to Durgah Khawaja Saheb, Ajmer to which the Durgah Khawaja Saheb Act, 1955 (36 of 1955.) applies.

Reflections

Analogous section under Wakf Act 1954 is S.2

This Act also does not apply to Durgah Khaja Saheb, Ajmir whose affairs are regulated by Durgah Khwaja Saheb Act, 1955 (Act 36 of 1955).

Judicial response

Judicial response pertaining to this section is not found.

****

Section 3

Definitions:-

In this Act, unless the context otherwise requires-

(a) ***"beneficiary" means a person or object for whose benefit a waqf is created and includes religious, pious and charitable objects and any other objects of public utility sanctioned by the Muslim law;***

(b) ***"benefit" does not include any benefit which a mutawalli is entitled to claim solely by reason of his being such mutawalli;***

(c) ***"Board" means a Board of Waqf established under sub-section (1), or as the case may be, under sub-section (2) of section 13 and shall include a common Waqf Board established under section 106;***

(d) ***"Chief Executive Officer" means the chief Executive Officer appointed under sub-section (1) of Section 23;***

(e) ***"Council" means the Central Waqf Council established under section 9;***

(ee) "encroacher" means any person or institution, public or private, occupying waqf property, in whole or part, without the authority of law and includes a person whose tenancy, lease or licence has expired or has been terminated by mutawalli or the Board;[12]

(f) *"Executive Officer" means the Executive Officer appointed by the Board under sub-section (1) of Section 38;*

(g) *"list of auqaf" means the list of auqaf published under sub-section (2) of Section 5 or contained in the register of auqaf maintained under Section 37;*[13]

(h) *"member" means a member of the Board and includes the Chairperson;*

(i) *"mutawalli" means any person appointed, either verbally or under any deed or instrument by which a waqf has been created, or by a competent authority, to be the mutawalli of a waqf and includes any person who is a mutawalli of a waqf by virtue of any custom or who is a naib-mutawalli, khadim, mujawar, sajjadanshin, amin or other person appointed by a mutawalli to perform the duties of a mutawalli and save as otherwise provided in this Act, any person, committee or corporation for the time being managing or administering any waqf or waqf property:*

Provided that no member of a committee or corporation shall be deemed to be a mutawalli unless such member is an office bearer of such committee or corporation;

Provided further that the mutawalli shall be a citizen of India and shall fulfil such other qualifications as may be prescribed:

Provided also that in case a waqf has specified any qualifications, such qualifications may be provided in the rules as may be made by the State Government;

(j) *"net annual income", in relation to a waqf, means net annual income determined in accordance with the provisions of the Explanations to sub-section (1) of section 72;*

(k) *"person interested in a waqf" means any person who is entitled to receive any pecuniary or other benefits from the waqf and includes-*

(i) *any person who has a right to offer prayer*[14] *or to perform any religious rite in a mosque idgah, imambara, Dargah, khanqah,*

12 Inserted by Act 27 of 2013, S. 5 (i).

13 Substituted by Act 27 of 2073, S. 5 (ii), for Cl. (g). Prior to its substitution, Cl. (S) read as under:- "(g) 'list of wakfs' means the list of wakfs, published under sub-section (2) of section 5;"

14 Substituted by Act 27 of 2013, s. 5 (iv) for "workship" and "khangah," respectively.

peerkhana and karbala, maqbara, graveyard or any other religious institution connected with the waqf or to participate in any religious or charitable institution under the waqf;

(ii) *the wakif and any descendant of the wakif and the mutawalli;*

(l) *"prescribed," except in Chapter III, means prescribed by rules made by the State Government;*

(m) *"regulations" means the regulations made by the Board under this Act;*

(n) *"Shia waqf" means a waqf governed by Shia law;*

(o) *"Sunni waqf" means a waqf governed by Sunni law;*

(p) *"Survey Commissioner" means the Survey Commissioner of Waqf appointed under sub-section (1) of section 4 and includes any Additional or Assistant Survey Commissioners of auqaf under sub-section (2) of Section 4;*

(q) *"Tribunal", in relation to any area, means the Tribunal constituted under sub-section (1) of section 83, having jurisdiction in relation to that area;*

(r) *"waqf" means the permanent dedication by any person, of any movable or immovable property for any purpose recognised by the Muslim law as pious, religious or charitable and includes-*[15]

(i) *A waqf by user but such waqf shall not cease to be a waqf by reason only of the user having ceased irrespective of the period of such cesser;*

(ii) *a Shamlat Patti, Shamlat Deh, Jumla Malkkan or by any other name entered in a revenue record.*

(iii) *"grants" including mashrut-ul-khidmat for any purpose recognised by the Muslim law as pious religious or charitable; and*

(iv) *a waqf-alal-aulad to the extent to which the property is dedicated for any purpose recognised by Muslim law as pious, religious or charitable, provided when the line of succession fails, the income of the waqf shall be spent for education, development, welfare and such other purposes as recognised by Muslim Law, and "waqif" means any person making such dedication,*

(s) *"waqf deed" means any deed or instrument by which a waqf has been created and includes any valid subsequent deed or instrument by which any of the term of the original dedication have been varied;*

(t) *"Waqf Fund" means a waqf fund formed under sub-section (1) of section 77.*

----

15 Substituted by Act 27 of 2013, s. 5 (v) for Cl. (r). Prior to substitution, Cl. (r) read as under:- (r) "wakf" means the permanent dedication by a person professing Islam, of any movable or immovable property for any purpose recognised by Muslim law as pious religious or charitable and includes-

Reflections

Analogous section under Wakf Act 1954 is S.3.

"Waqf" is a derivative of the Arabic root word "Waqafa," which means to halt, detain, stop, or restrain. It implies the detention of an object or property in dedication against the transfer of the same to another person as the property dedicated becomes the property of God (Allah), thus making the waqf perpetual. In North and West Africa Waqf is called *Habs*, which literally means "confinement."[16]

The Islamic jurists consider that the waqf dedicated even by a Non-Muslim is valid as long as the purpose of dedication is as per the tenets of Islam. But the words, "a person professing Islam" in Section 3(r) in the Principal Act of 1995 (Act 43 of 1995) leads to believe that the waqf properties dedicated by Non-Muslims rulers and nobles are not valid wakf. Whereas there have been grants of lands and buildings, etc., by the non-Muslims rulers and nobles for mosques, dargahs, etc. The words "a person professing Islam" appeared to be superfluous and unnecessary. This expression created an impression that the waqfs dedicated by Non-Muslims are not valid, though Sec. 104 attempts to remove this confusion. The words a person professing Islam also appears in the Wakf Act 1954. Khadar Ali Khan Inquiry Commission appointed by Government of A.P., suggested the deletion of these words.[17] However, some academics feel that there is no problem in retaining these words in the definition of the waqf. However, the Waqf Amendment Act 2013 (Act 27 of 2013) settled this issue by removing these words.

The definition of mutawalli includes naib-mutawalli, khadim, mujawar, sajjadanashin, amin or any other person appointed by a mutawalli to perform the duties of a mutawalli.

Naib-mutawalli is a deputy of the mutawalli.

A Khadim means a servant in a waqf, either for remuneration or on a voluntary basis.

Mujawar is a person designated to discharge sundry religious duties in a waqf institution more particularly in durgahs, ashorkhanas, takias, etc.

Sajjadanashin is a spiritual head of an Islamic religious sect and a person who leads a khanquah or a sect or institutions of mashaique, darvesh, peers, faquirs, etc. Such institutions are similar and analogous to Christian Monasteries or a Hindu Mutt. The term Sajjadanashin literally means a man who sits on a sajja or prayer mat.

Amin. "Amin" literally means an honest and trusted person. In other words, a person who has been entrusted with the responsibility of financial and administrative matters of a waqf.

16 Oxford Encyclopedia of Modern Islamic World, Vol. IV – Article: Wakf.
17 Khadar Ali Khan Enquiry Commission Report, 1984, p. 150.

The naib-mutawalli, khadim, mujawar, amin and any other person appointed by a mutawalli to perform the duties of a mutawalli are included in the definition for the sake of convenience and for the proper implementation of the provisions of the Waqf Act.

Committee or Corporation means a group of persons joined together for a common cause and to be known by a name agreed by them.

The term "mutawalli" includes naib-mutawalli, khadim, mujawar, amin, any person appointed by a mutawalli, or a committee or corporation, managing or administering any waqf or waqf property have been included in the definition of a mutawalli since different waqf institutions have adopted different nomenclatures for the administration of the waqf institutions.

Judicial response

The strength, weakness and character of waqf have been under the consideration before various courts. Dealing with such an issue, the Supreme Court of India in Chhedilal Misra vs. Civil Judge, Lucknow,[18] held that:

> It was only thereafter in 1958, that is, after 32 years that the Wakif filed a collusive suit which was decreed on compromise. The Wakif did not, however, question the registration of the waqf under the provisions of the 1936 Act, nor did he challenge the Gazette notification published in January 1954.

The Supreme Court of India in U.P. Sunni Central Board of Wakfs vs. Mazhar Hassan,[19] observed that:

> If a property is set apart for a definite purpose, such property would become "dedicated" for a purpose ... It is out of the moneys given by the general public a property is purchased for public purpose which is religious or charitable in character, we do not think, such property will lose the character of a "Wakf" as defined under the Act.

Muslim Law provides for a creation of waqf for the benefit of the family and descendants of the wakif (settler). The Waqf Act 1995, while giving the definition of waqf under section 3 (r) (iii), includes Waqf-alal-aulad as well. The High Court of Patna, in Syed Hassan Francis Imam vs. Muzaffarpur Properties Pvt. Ltd,[20] has observed that even though the Waqf-alal-aulad was created in the year 1931 when the Mussalman Wakf Validating Act 1930 was in force, the title suit or any appeal or revision arising out of it will

18 2007(4) SCC 632.
19 AIR 2001 SC 3359.
20 AIR 2008 (NOC) 2675 (PAT).

have to be governed by the provisions of the Wakf Act 1954, but will not be affected by the Wakf Act 1995, which had no retrospective effect.

The Supreme Court in Mohammed vs. Mohammed,[21] dealing with the validity of the waqf, has observed that:

> There was no dedication and public was not allowed to have any prayers on the property as mosque; nor the public had access to it. During the lifetime of the father himself, the appellant had cancelled the deed. Under these circumstances the necessary tests laid down by this court have not been satisfied to conclude that a Wakf has been created in respect of the above properties.

Justice Mahmud of Allahabad High Court in Jawahara vs. Akbar Hussain,[22] observed that:

> The rule of Mohammaden Law on the subject is that when anyone has resolved to devote his property to religious purposes, as soon as his mind is made up and his intention declared by some specific act, such as delivery, etc., an endowment is immediately constituted. This act deprives him of all ownership in the property and to use the technical language of Mohammadan Lawyers vests it in God, in such a manner as subjects it to the rules of divine property whence the appropriator's right in it is extinguished, and it becomes a property of God by the advantage of it result into His Creatures.

The Islamic Law says that once a waqf is created it is irrevocable, and the notion that once a waqf is always a waqf has been reaffirmed by various courts. The Judicial Committee of the Privy Council in Vidya Varuthi Thirtha Swamigal vs. Balusamy Iyer[23] rendered an excellent judgement way back in 1921 describing the creation of waqf. Mr. Ameer Ali speaking for the Board observed:

> Neither under the Hindu Law nor in the Mohammadan system is any property conveyed to a shebait or a mutawalli in the case of a dedication nor is any property vested in him; whatever property he holds for the idol or the institution, he holds as manager with certain beneficial interest regulated by custom or usage. Under the Mohammadan Law, the moment a wakf is created all rights of property passed out of the wakif and vest in God Almighty.

21 (1996) 10 SCC 705.
22 ILR 7 All 178 (FB).
23 AIR 1922 PC 123; (1921) 48 IA 302; ILR 44 Mad 831; 65 IC 161.

A waqf can be private one, or for a limited category of a person or a group, for which Ameer Ali terms them as "private wakfs" as discussed under concepts of waqf under introduction. Such waqfs are valid. In a case pertaining to an alleged family waqf for consideration before a Division Bench of High Court of Allahabad in Khalil Ahamad vs. Sheik Mohammed,[24] the Bench observed that:

> Like a private chapel in England or private Hindu temple in India, there could also be a private mosque for offering prayers by the owner and the members of his family. Such private mosques were not unknown in India. We have two glaring examples of such mosques in the Red Fort at Delhi and Agra Fort, where the members of the Moghul Royal family used to offer prayers in the mosques situated within the four walls of their forts. Obviously, it could not have been suggested that simply because those buildings were shaped and doomed like mosque and the members of the Royal family regularly offered prayers therein, the same had become Wakf property so as to entitle the general public to get into such private mosque and offer prayers in congregation as of right.

In the above case, the Allahabad High Court accepted the existence of private waqfs. The Supreme Court, while dealing in detail the validity of dedication for a public mosque, has made significant observation in the case of Syed Mohamed Salie Labbai vs. Md. Hanifa.[25] In this, the Supreme Court enumerated the conditionalities for the creation of a public waqf. It also said that there was no need for a form of declaration.

> It is not necessary for the dedication of a public mosque that a mutawalli or Pesh Imam should be appointed, which could be done later by the members of the Muslim community. All that is necessary is that there should be a declaration of the intention to dedicate either expressly or impliedly and a divestment of his interest in the property by the owner followed by delivery of possession. Here also the delivery of possession does not involve any ritual formality or any technical rule. For instance, in the case of a mosque if the Mohammadans of the village, town or the area are permitted to offer their prayers either on the vacant land or in a mosque built for the said purpose that amounts to delivery of possession and divestment and after the prayers have been offered the dedication becomes complete.
>
> No particular form of declaration is necessary. The declaration may be presumed from the conduct of the founder either express or implied.

24 AIR 1965 All 320.
25 AIR1976 SC 1569.

> Even if there is no actual delivery of possession the mere fact that the members of the Mohammadan public are permitted to offer prayers with azan or ikamat, the Wakf is complete and irrevocable.

The Judicial Committee of the Privy Council in Baqar Ali Khan vs Anjuman Ara Begam[26] has observed that a person from a Shia community can create a waqf by will. He can ask somebody through a will to dedicate his properties to consecrate a waqf. In this judgement, the Judicial Committee of the Privy Council states that:

> A Shia may create a wakf. He can make a gift of the kind known as a wakf. He can make a will and can, speaking generally, give a gift by will. It would seem to follow as a logical inference that he can make a gift by a will, as can a Sunni. And in substance and effect it is admitted that he can indirectly do so. It is admitted that he can give a gift of property by will and require the donee to apply it as wakf; the contention is that the testator, though he can do this, cannot himself directly create the wakf by his will.

Further, in another case, the Judicial Council of the Privy Council in Mt. Ali Begam vs. Badr-ul-Islam Ali Khan[27] observed that:

> If the will can be read as intending that on the death of the testator these two properties should become Wakf, it would be in no way unlawful that a life interest in the usufruct should be reserved for the beneficiaries above named. On the other hand a direction that the property should become Wakf after the death of a person surviving the testator is contrary to the principles applied by the Shia law to dedications, inter vivos.

A Bench of the High Court of Calcutta in Commissioner of Wakfs, West Bengal vs. Kazi Razshid Ali,[28] has ruled that:

> It is almost beyond controversy that the rule of contingency which hits a Wakf under the Mohammadan Law would affect the present disposition. That would be the position under the general law of Wakfs under the Mohammadan system of jurisprudence and the position in that respect is not altered by anything in the Wakf Validating Act. That Act, undoubtedly, authorises or sanctions a postponement of the ultimate gift to charity which would not have been valid under the general law. It does not however abrogate the rule of contingency.

26 ILR (1902) 25 All 236; 30 IA 111.
27 AIR 1938 PC 184; (1938) 65 IA 198.
28 AIR 1958 Cal 413.

A five-judge Bench of the Supreme Court in Nawab Zain Yar Jung vs. Director of Endowments[29] summarised the possibility of creating public religious, charitable waqf in a non-religious sense. It observed that:

> Having noticed this broad distinction between the wakf and the secular trust of a public and religious character, it is necessary to add that under Muslim Law there is no prohibition against the creation of a trust of the latter kind. Usually followers of Islam would naturally prefer to dedicate their property to the Almighty and create a wakf in the conventional Mohammadan sense. But that is not to say that the follower of Islam is precluded from creating a public religious or a charitable trust which does not conform to the conventional notion of a wakf and which purports to create a public religious charity in a non-religious secular sense. This position is not in dispute.

While relying on the above judgment of the Supreme Court in Nawab Zain Yar Jung vs. Director of Endowments,[30] the High Court of Madras in Kassimiah Charities Rajagiri vs. Madras State Wakf Board,[31] observed as follows:

> The essential characteristic of a Wakf under the Muslim law is that if it were to be religious it should be only for the benefit of the members of the Muslim community and if it were to be secular the charity should be to the poor alone. A public utility like a school, college or hospital, bridge, etc. cannot obviously be restricted to the poor alone or to the Muslims alone. Under the common law therefore Muslim lawyers recognised that public utilities could be wakfs notwithstanding the fact that non-Muslims were intended to participate in the benefits. But the Wakf Act is perhaps enacted for designedly with a view to exclude those that confer benefits on non-Muslims.

A Non-Muslim can also dedicate property in waqf which has been confirmed in the judgment of the Lahore High Court in Arur Singh and others vs. Badar Din and others[32] in the following terms:

> "Secondly, there seems to be no clear authority to show that dedication of land by a Hindu for the purpose of a Muslim graveyard would be invalid either according to Hindu or Muslim law ..."

If a property is in use for the purposes enshrined in Islam as religious, pious and charitable, even if that property is not formally dedicated or registered

29 AIR 1963 SC 985.
30 *Ibid.*
31 AIR 1964 Mad 18.
32 [AIR 1940 Lahore 119],

as waqf, the Muslim law provides that such property shall be a Wakf by User or Waqf by Reputation. The Supreme Court in Syed Mohamed Salie Labbai vs. Mohamed Hanifa,[33] held that:

> "It is also well settled that where a mosque has been in existence for a long time and prayers have been offered therein, the Court will infer that it is not by leave and license but that the dedication is complete and the property no longer belongs to the owner."

Even before this judgment of Supreme Court the High Court of Allahabad in Miru vs. Ramgopal,[34] observed in the year 1935 that:

> Where there is a mosque or a temple, which has been in existence for a longtime, and the terms of the original grant of the land cannot now be ascertained, there would be a fair presumption that the sites on which mosques or temples stand are dedicated property.

The Bench of the High Court of Andhra Pradesh in Andhra Pradesh Wakf Board vs. Dowlat Bibi,[35] has interpreted the definition of wakf in clear words. It observed that:

> All that is required is that the grant should be for a purpose recognised by Muslim law a pious, religious or charitable. The contention is that the two requirements or ingredients, as they may be called, in the main limb of the definition, equally apply to grants contemplated by cl. (ii). But, if it were so, there was no reason for the Parliament to repeat the words "for any purpose recognised by Muslim law as pious, religious or charitable," in cl. (ii) because those words are already found in the main limb of the definition. Repeating of these words while omitting the words "by a person professing Islam" in cl. (ii) would indicate that the requirement that the dedication should be by a person professing Islam does not apply in the case of grants contemplated by cl. (ii). This would be more evident if we look at cl. (i) in the second half of the definition. Wakf by User means a Wakf which is being used as Wakf since time immemorial and where the identity of the grantor is not known nor is the time of grant verifiable. If the appellant's contention is correct, even in the case of a Wakf by User, it should be established that grant was made by a person professing Islam, which is impossibility. We are, therefore, of the opinion that in the case of grants burdened with the condition of service contemplated by cl. (ii) in the second half of the

33 AIR 1976 SC 1569.
34 AIR 1935 All 891; 1935 All LJ 1269;
35 AIR 1983 AP 57.

> definition, it is not necessary to prove that the grant was made by a person professing Islam.

The purpose of waqf is one of the essential elements of a valid wakf. The purpose to be valid should have been recognised in Islam as religious and/or charitable. The High Court of Rajasthan in the case of Gora Devi & Ors. vs. Rajasthan Board of Muslim Waqf,[36] has held that:

> Thus, where evidence led on the side of plaintiff, was found to be sufficient to prove the property to be wakf property, and there being no evidence in rebuttal, on the side of the defendant, the property would be termed as wakf property.

Muslim Law provides for a creation of waqf for the benefit of the family and descendants of the wakif (settler). The Waqf Law in India also recognises the concept of Waqf-alal-aulad. In Rasamaya Dur Chowduri vs. Abul Fata Mohamed,[37] a Bench of the Calcutta High Court, consisting of Tottenham and Travelion, observed that:

> We cannot believe that the authors of Mohammedan Law intended that under the cover of a pretended dedication to Almighty God, the owners of property should be enabled to secure it for their own use, protect it forever from their own and their descendants' creditors and repeated alienation in respect of which they have received full consideration. In our opinion, then, the deed before us cannot be sustained as a valid Wakfnama.

In 1894 this matter went in appeal before the Privy Council. After careful consideration, and with reference to Bikanimia vs. Shukhlal,[38] the Privy Council observed that:

> If a man was to deliver a Crore of rupees and provides ten for the poor that would be at once recognised as illusory. It is equally illusory to make a provision for the poor under which they are not entitled to receive a rupee till after the total extinction of a family; possibly not for hundreds of years; possibly not until the property had vanished away, under the wasting agencies of litigation or malfeasance or misfortune; certainly not as long as there exists on the earth one of those objects whom the donors really cared to maintain in a high position. Their Lordships agree that the poor have been put into this settlement merely

36 AIR, 2009 (NOC) 1393, Raj.
37 ILR (1891) 18 Cal 399.
38 ILR (1893) 20 Cal 116 (FB).

> to give it a colour of piety and so to legalise arrangements meant to serve for the aggrandizement of the family.

In Bikanimia vs. Shukhlal,[39] a similar matter of waqf-alal-Aulad came up before a five-judge Bench at the High Court of Calcutta, Ameer Ali, which, while delivering the dissenting judgement, observed that:

> It must be remembered that in Mohammedan Law and Mohammedan law books, there is a distinction between a waqf for a man's family and a waqf for any other purpose. They all stand on the same footing. The Mutawalli whether Wakif himself or anybody else has no interest in the waqf beyond that which is expressly provided at the time of dedication. He has no power to sell, mortgage or lease without the sanction of the Judge, and is just in the same position as a Manager of a minor's property. To hold that a Wakf, the benefaction of which is bestowed wholly or in part on the Wakif's family and his descendants, is invalid, would have the effect, in my opinion, of sweeping away an important branch of Muslim Law, with which are associated and intermixed the dearest religious interests of the people.

Again the High Court of Calcutta in Ali Bakhtiyar vs. Khondkar Altaf Hossain,[40] Justice Mitter, speaking for the Bench observed that:

> We are of the opinion that section 3 of the Mussalman Wakf Validating Act applies to waqfs which are in the nature of family settlement pure and simple where the ultimate benefit is expressly or impliedly reserved for the poor or for any other purpose recognised by the Mussalman law as a religious, pious or charitable purpose of a permanent character.

Justice Venkataraman, of Madras High Court in the amatter of Mohamed Mahin vs. Madras State Board,[41] has observed that a settlement both for the benefit of the persons mentioned therein and charitable acts mentioned therein will plainly be a wakf-alal-aulad within the meaning of Section 3 (1) (iii) of Act XXIX of 1964, and that it will be a waqf for the purpose of the control of the Wakf Board to the extent to which the properties have been dedicated for the religious and charitable acts. This is the case-law on the subject. The High Court of Madras in Kadir Murthuza vs. Mohamed Murthuza,[42] observed that:

39 *Ibid.*
40 AIR 1933 Cal 581; ILR (1933)60 Cal 790; 145 IC 638.
41 (1967) 1 M.L.J. 65 at 74.
42 AIR 1943 Mad 234; (1942) 2 Mad LJ 672.

> On the other hand, it seems to me that the words "wholly or partially" have application only to the income of the properties settled under the wakf. In another words, "wholly" will refer to a type of wakf where the entire income for the time being is devoted to the maintenance and support of the family, children or descendants of the settler and the word "partially" will apply to a kind of wakf where only a part of the income for the time being is so devoted, the other part being divided simultaneously for religious or charitable purposes.

The matter pertaining to the creation of wakf-alal-aulad had also come up before the Bombay High Court in Abdul Karim Adenwalla vs. Rahima Bai[43] for its consideration. Justice Chadla made the following observations:

> It is open to a settler when he belongs to Hanafi sect, to reserve for his maintenance and support during his life time the income of trust property. In this case, what the settler has done is that he has reserved for himself during his life for his absolute use the whole income of the trust property ... Now a reservation of a life interest of income of a trust property is a very different thing from securing to himself for his own maintenance and support the income of the trust property. The difference in law between these two provisions is clear and of considerable importance.

The matter of family wakf or waqf-alal-Aulad has been under consideration of many a number of courts. One such matter came up before a Bench of the Allahabad High Court also in Rashid Unnisha vs. Ata Rasool,[44] the Bench observed that:

> The Plaintiff No. 1 may have been included in the category of ayal during the lifetime of Amanet Razool as at that time she being his wife was entitled to be maintained by him. But on the death of Amanet Razool when she became a widow, she could no longer claim to be a person who was entitled to be maintained by Amanet Razool or his estate. She therefore ceases to belong to the category of ayal. If she is remarried as alleged by the defendants, she has become a wife of another person and has ceased to be a member of the family of Amanet Razool altogether. The fact that the wakif did not provide that his widow would forfeit her right as a result of remarriage, appears to be immaterial because as a widow she would not have been a beneficiary of the wakf at all, and there was therefore no necessity for making any provision for her forfeiture of such a right as a result of any future event like remarriage.

43 AIR 1946 Bom 342; (1946) 48 Bom LT 67.
44 AIR 1958 All 67.

Another case of Wakf-alal-Aulad came up before a division Bench of Patna High Court in Asma Jafar Imam vs. State of Bihar,[45] and the Bench observed that:

> If it is held that all Wakfs-alal-aulad and every part of them are included in the definition of "Wakf", then the words "to the extent to which the property is dedicated for any purpose recognised by Muslim Law as pious, religious or charitable", will become surplusage and redundant. It is settled canon of interpretation that a statute is not supposed to use words without a meaning and it is better to adopt the construction which would give some effect to the words, rather than that which will give none.

Again in the year 1979 a Bench of the Madras High Court dealt with the intricacies of Wakf-alal-aulad in Tamil Nadu Wakf Board vs. M. Ibrahim Musuee.[46] Speaking for the Bench Justice Ismail interpreted the concept of wakf in the following words:

> The ultimate provision for poor is for the purpose of importing an element of permanency to the wakf, so that it will not fail under any circumstance as there will always be poor people – so it was thought – and the provision for the poor is not the only basis for sustaining the validity of the wakf as having been created for a pious, religious or charitable purpose ... Therefore, the provision in the wakf for the maintenance of the family and relations of the wakif was itself considered to be a pious and charitable object under the Muslim Law.

A division of the High Court of Kerala in A.P. Moidu V.P.V. Narayanan[47] ruled that dedication, subject and object are the necessary elements of waqf. Mere stipulation that income will have to be utilised for religious purposes does not constitute a waqf and an absence of dedication to the Almighty does not constitute a waqf.

The Judicial Committee of the Privy Council in Masjid Shahid Ganj vs. Shiromani Gurdwara Parbandhak Committee,[48] gave the following observations:

> Their Lordships, with all respect to the High Court of Lahore, must not be taken as deciding that a juristic personality may be extended for any purpose to Muslim institutions generally or to mosques in particular. On this general question they reserve their opinion; but they think it

45 AIR 1965 Pat 48.
46 AIR 1979 Mad 231.
47 AIR 2017 (NOC) 287 KER.
48 AIR 1940 PC 116.

> right to decide the specific question which arises in the present case and hold that suits cannot competently be brought by or against such institutions as artificial persons in British India courts.

The Judicial Committee of the Privy Council discussed the matter about appointment of mutawalli in Mohamed Islam vs. Ahamed Moola.[49] The observation in this case also throws light on the role of Quazi in the justice delivery system in those days. It thus observed that:

> The Mussalman Law, like the English Law, draws a wide distinction between public and private trusts. Generally speaking in the case of a waqf or a trust created for specific individuals or a determinate body of individuals, the kazi, whose place in the British Indian system is taken by the civil court, has in carrying the trust into execution, to give effect, so far as possible, to the express wishes of the founder. With respect, however to public religious or charitable trust, of which a public mosque is a common and well-known example, the Kazi's discretion is very wide. He may not depart from the intentions of the founder or from any rule fixed by him as to the objects of the benefaction: but as regards management which must be governed by circumstances, he has complete discretion. He may defer to the wishes of the founder so far as they are conformable to changed conditions and circumstances, but his primary duty is to consider the interest of the general body of the public for whose benefit the trust is created. He may in his judicial discretion vary any rule of management which he may find either not practicable or not in the best interest of the institution.

The High Court of Rajasthan, in the case of Gora Devi & Ors. vs. Rajasthan Board of Muslim Wakf,[50] has held that:

> Thus, where evidence led on the side of plaintiff, was found to be sufficient to prove the property to be waqf property, and there being no evidence in rebuttal, on the side of the defendant, the property would be termed as waqf property.

As observed by Mohammad Noor, J. In Syed Shah Mohammad Kazim vs. Syed abi Saghir:[51]

> Khangahs cannot exist and continue without a sajjadanshin. In other systems the personal expenditure of the head of such an institution has

49 43 IA 127.
50 AIR, 2009 (NOC) 1393, Raj.
51 AIR 1932 PC 123; 48 IA 302; ILR 44 Mad 831; 65 IC 161.

> been curtailed to almost nothing by enjoining celibacy, as for instance in the case of Christian monasteries or Hindu Mutts. But Islam prohibits celibacy and a saint with a family is the rule rather than an exception. In these circumstances devotees and adherence of khangahs have always made provision for maintenance of the sajjadanashin and his family so that he may devote all his time to imparting religious and spiritual instructions to his disciples and be free from secular cares. A sajjadanshin is an integral part of the institution and the central figure so as to speak therein. Its existence depends on his personality. In him is supposed to continue the spiritual line. Therefore provision for his maintenance and that of his descendants is a provision for him as the head of the institution. It is a trust and not a personal grant.

The full Bench of Allahabad High Court, in the matter of Moattar Raza vs. Joint Director of Consolidation U.P.,[52] has ruled that:

> The legal status and position of a Mutawalli under a Wakf under the Mussalman law is that of a manager or superintendent.

Justice Ameer Ali in the case of Vidya Varuthi Thirtha Swamigal vs. Balusamy Iyer,[53] speaking for the judicial committee of the Privy Council observed that:

> The manager of the wakf is mutawalli, the governor superintendent or curator. In Jeevandas Shah's case the Judicial Committee called him "procurator" which related to a Khankha, a Mohammadan institution analogous in many respects to a Mutt where Hindu religious instruction is dispensed. The head of these Khankhas which exist in large numbers in India is called Sajjadanashin. He is the teacher of religious doctrines and rules of life and the manager of the institution and the administrator of its charities and has in most cases a larger interest in the usufruct than an ordinary mutawalli. But neither the sajjadanashin nor the mutawalli has any right in the property belonging to the Wakf; the properties are not vested in him and he is not a trustee in the technical sense.

The above observation of Justice Ameer Ali differentiates between a mutawalli and a sajjadahnashin. The Waqf Act 1995 includes sajjadahnashin in the definition of a mutawalli.

The waqf Act 1995 as amended vide Amendment Act 2013 defines a person interested in waqf as any person who is entitled to receive any pecuniary or other benefits from the waqf, and includes any person who has a right to

52 AIR 1933 All 407.
53 AIR 1922 PC 123; 48 IA 302; ILR 44 Mad 831; 65 IC 161.

offer prayer or to perform any religious rite in a mosque, idgah, imambara, Dargah, khanqah, peerkhana and karbala, maqbara, graveyard or any other religious institution connected with the waqf, or to participate in any religious or charitable institution under the waqf, a person interested in waqf also includes the wakif and any descendant of the wakif and the mutawalli;

The High Court of Madras in Tamil Nadu Wakf Board vs. S.J. Syed Basha[54] described a person interested in waqf as "a person interested" in the Trust, which means the Mutawalli or any person connected with the Trust and a stranger who has nothing to do with the waqf cannot be said to be "a person interested in the waqf" and consequently any failure on the part of the stranger to institute a suit under section 6 of the Waqf Act will not affect his rights.

A Division Bench of the High Court of Rajasthan in Radhakrishnan vs. State of Rajasthan[55] had the occasion to make observations on a person interested in waqf:

> In our opinion the words "any person interested therein" appearing in sub-section (1) of section 6 mean no more than a person interested in a wakf as defined in clause (h) of section 3 of the Act ... It could never have been the intention of the Legislature to cast a cloud on the right, title or interest of persons who are not Muslims. That is, if a person who is a non-muslim whether he be a Christian, a Hindu, a Sikh, a Parsee or of any other religious denomination and if he is in possession of certain property, his right, title and interest cannot be put in jeopardy simply because their property is included in the list published under sub-section (2) of section 5. The Legislature could not have meant that he should be driven to file a suit in a civil court for declaration of his title simply because the property in his possession is included in the list. Similarly, the Legislature could not have meant to curtail the period of limitation available to him under the Limitation Act and to provide that he must file a suit within a year or the list would be final and conclusive against him. In our opinion sub-section (4) makes the list final and conclusive only between the Wakf Board, the Mutawalli and the person interested in the Wakf.

This view of the Division Bench of the High Court of Rajasthan has been affirmed by the Supreme Court in the Board of Muslim Wakfs, Rajasthan vs. Radhakrishnan.[56]

54 (2000) 2 LW 510.
55 AIR 1967 Raj 1.
56 AIR 1979 SC 289.

Dealing with the concept of a person interested in waqf a Division Bench of High Court of Madras in Jainulabudeen vs. Jainulabudeen,[57] has observed that:

> It has to be seen that the former part of the definition, apart from stating that a person interested in a Wakf means any person who is entitled to receive any pecuniary benefits, also states that it means any person who is entitled to other benefits from the Wakf. The expression "person who is entitled to receive other benefits from the Wakf" is of the widest connotation, and there is neither reason nor principle to restrict the scope of that expression only to certain types of benefits analogous to pecuniary benefits. Ramanujam, J. would appear to have taken the view that only persons who have been given pecuniary or other benefits under the Wakf deed which they could claim as a right, would come within the scope of the expression "persons interested in a Wakf". We are of the opinion that whenever a benefit is reserved for the public in general without restricting the persons who will be entitled to participate therein either with references to the religious or with reference to the age, or with reference to the social status, any person who will fall within the particular category of the persons for whom the benefit is reserved will be a person entitled to receive that benefit as of right and such a person will certainly the entitled to invoke the jurisdiction of a body like the Wakf Board under section 44.

The Himachal Pradesh High Court in Jeet Mohammaed vs. Jatinder Kaur & another[58] says that any person who professes Islam is a person interested in the management of waqf and observed that:

> A bare reading of this provision shows that any person who receives any benefits from the wakf whether pecuniary or otherwise is a person interested in the Wakf. The definition is inclusive in nature and includes any person who has a right to worship in a mosque, idgah, imambara, dargah, khanqah, maqbara, graveyard etc. the petitioner who professes muslim religion definitely has the right to worship in a mosque and other institutions mentioned in this section. Therefore, he is a person interested in a Wakf.

The Andhra Pradesh High Court, while dealing with this subject of a person interested in a waqf matter in Madrasa Ahle Sunnath Bahrul Uloom, Visakhapatnam vs. State of A.P. and others,[59] has observed that:

57 (1981) 1 MLJ 332 (DB).
58 AIR 2009 HP, 44.
59 2004 (2) ALD 365.

> It is obvious that "person" in the above definition is natural person and not a juristic person. Hence, a company, or an incorporated body with perpetual succession cannot be treated as "person interested" in Wakf. Admittedly the petitioner is a society interested in educational and economic welfare of Muslims. It does not claim to be a person interested as per sub-clause (i) of clause (k) of Section 3 of the Act nor does it claim as wakif, descendant of wakif or mutawalli. Therefore, in the considered opinion of this Court, petitioner cannot be treated as "person interested" in the Wakf. It is well settled principle of judicial review that the power can be exercised only at the instance of aggrieved party. Every person, be it natural person or juristic person remotely connected with the case cannot be conferred with locus standi to invoke this Court's power of judicial review. The Writ Petition is liable to be dismissed on that ground alone.

The High Court of Karnataka in C.K. Mohammed Khasim & Ors, vs. Karnataka State Board of Waqfs Rep. by Chief Executive Officer, Bangalore & Ors,[60] has ruled that a person who is not an ordinary resident for a period of the preceding 12 months in a town where the waqf is situated cannot be considered as a person interested in waqf. Whereas the Himachal Pradesh High Court in Jeet Mohammaed vs. Jatinder Kaur & Another[61] has held that any Muslim is a person interested in waqf and can approach the Waqf Tribunal to file a petition in respect of a waqf matter. It observed that:

> When these aspects are kept in mind, it is obvious that any person who professes Islam is a person interested in the management of the Wakf Board. He can raise dispute(s) before the Wakf Tribunal that such property is being frittered away or are being sold against the intention of the creator of the Wakf.

The expression "person interested therein" came up for consideration before a Division Bench of the High Court of Rajasthan in Radhakrishnan vs. State of Rajasthan.[62] The Bench observed:

> In our opinion the words "any person interested therein" appearing is sub-section (1) of section 6 mean no more than a person interested in a Wakf as defined in clause (h) of section 3 of the Act ... It could never have been the intention of the Legislature to cast a cloud on the right, a person who is non-Muslim whether he be a Christian, a Hindu, a Sikh,

60 AIR, 2009 (NOC) 1706 (Kar).
61 AIR 2009 HP, 44.
62 AIR 1967 Raj 1.

> a Parsee or of any other religious denomination and if he is in possession of a certain property, his right, title and interest cannot be put in jeopardy simply because their property is included in the list published under sub-section (2) of section 5. The Legislature could not have meant that he should be driven to file a suit in a civil court for the declaration of his title simply because the Legislature could not have meant to curtail the period of limitation available to him under the Limitation Act and to provide that he must file a suit within a year or the list would be final and conclusive against him. In our opinion sub-section (4) makes the list final and conclusive only between the Wakf Board, the Mutawalli and the person interested in the wakf.

The Supreme Court of India in Hindu Public vs. Rajdhani Puja Samithee,[63] (Civil Appeal Nos. 2546 of 1992) their Lordships Justice Jagannadha Rao and Justice B.M. Shah after referring with approval to the decision of the Allahabad High Court and the Madras High Court, referred to above, stated the law as follows:

> "According to the learned counsel for the Society, the words `charitable purposes' used in the Preamble and sections 1 and 20 of Act 21/1860 do not include `religious purposes."
>
> In our opinion, this contention is not well founded. More than ninety years ago, such a contention raised under Act 21 of 1860 was negatived by the Allahabad High Court in Anjuman Islamia of Muttra vs. Nasiruddin [(1906) ILR 28 All. 384]. It was contended in that case that the registration of a society called "Anjuman Islamia" under Act 21 of 1860 was not permissible as the society was formed for "religious purposes only" and not for charitable purposes. The Allahabad High Court rejected the said contention and held that a society for religious purposes would ordinarily be a society for charitable purposes. A similar question arose before the Madras High Court in Khaji Muhammed Hussain Sahib vs. Masjiday Mehmood Jamait Managing committee, Puddupet [AIR 1940 Madras 167]. A Division Bench consisting of Wadsworth and Venkataramana Rao, JJ. held that the Act 21/1860 was passed in 1860 when, according to English law, a gift for the advancement of religion or promotion of religious worship was treated as a charitable purpose and, therefore, a society formed for such a purpose would be a charitable society under Act 21/1860. The only condition was that it should be for the benefit of the public. No doubt, in some statutes enacted subsequent to Act 21 of 1860, the legislature used the words "charitable" and "religious" but the definition of these words

63 1999 (2) SCC 583.

> was expressly stated to be for the purposes of those Acts. The subsequent legislation, the Madras High Court held, would not be helpful in interpreting the words "charitable" in Act 21 of 1860. The real question was: "What did the term mean in 1860"? We are in agreement with the view of the Allahabad and Madras High Courts. In fact, Lord McNaughten in his celebrated judgment in Commissioner of Income Tax vs. Pemsel [1891 AC 531 (581)] said that charitable purposes which came within the language and spirit of the statute of Elizabeth (43 Eliz ch 4) could be grouped into four heads (i) relief of poverty, (ii) education, (iii) advancement of religion and (iv) other purposes beneficial to the community not coming under any of the preceding heads. The words in Act 21/1860 are, therefore, to be understood as including religious purposes also. Point No.1 is held against the society.

The above judgement leads to an understanding that a society registered under the Societies Registration Act can also administer a waqf institution.

A member of the Waqf Board includes its Chair-Person. The period of appointment/nomination of a Member is coterminous with that of the period of the Wakf Board.

In Amir Alam Khan vs. State of Uttar Pradesh[64] the Division Bench of Allahabad High Court pointed out that sections 19 and 20 of the Act place the "Member" and the "Chair-Person" on the same footing or at the same place. There is no provision in the Act, from where a contrary intention of the Legislature can be inferred. The definition clause does not begin with the words "Not withstanding anything contained in any section of this Act." From this it is evident that if the Parliament, while enacting section 3(h) intended to attach a different meaning to the words "Member" and "Chair-Person," it would have been mentioned in section 3 (h) of the Waqf Act. Their Lordships therefore held that the definition of "Member" is exhaustive and not restrictive and the "Member" of the Board includes "Chair-Person." As the term of the "Member" which is coterminous with the term of the Board, the term of the Chair-Person, in accordance with the aforesaid section, will be five years.

The Hon Supreme Court in Sattar alias Sattar Khan V, High School Boarding Committee[65] upheld the order of High Court of Madhya Pradesh order directing the Madhya Pradesh authorities to consider handing over of 2.49 acres of land to the Madhya Pradesh Waqf Board, for the burial ground which is already in use as a Muslim Burial Ground.

64 AIR 2002 All 215.
65 (2018) 4 SCC 613.

II SURVEY OF AUQAF

Synopsis

Chapter II of the Waqf Act 1995 under sections 4 to 8 deals with the provisions regarding survey of waqf properties, appointment of survey commissioner and determination of the issues such as whether a particular property is a waqf or not; if it is a waqf, whether it is Shia Waqf or a Sunni Waqf; publication of the list of Waqf in official gazette, etc. As per the Amendment Act of 2013 it is mandatory on the part of the State Government to appoint a Survey Commissioner of Waqf to conduct the survey of the waqf properties and publish the same in the official gazette. The expenditure to be incurred towards the publication of the waqf institutions and their properties shall be borne by the State Government.

Keywords: Auqaf, Survey, Aggrieved, Gazette, Shia, Sunni

****

Section 4

Preliminary survey of Auqaf:-

(1) ***The State Government may, by notification in the Official Gazette, appoint for the State a Survey Commissioner of Auqaf and as many Additional or Assistant Survey Commissioners of Auqaf as may be necessary for the purpose of making a survey of auqaf in the State.***[1]

(1A) Every State Government shall maintain a list of auqaf referred to in sub-section (1) and the survey of auqaf shall be completed within a period of one year from the date of commencement of the

1 Substituted by Act 27 of 2013, S. 6 (a), for "wakfs existing in the state at the date of the commencement of this Act."

Waqf (Amendment) Act, 2013, in case such survey was not done before the commencement of the Waqf (Amendment) Act, 2013:[2]

Provided that where no Survey Commissioner of Waqf has been appointed, a Survey Commissioner for auqaf shall be appointed within three months from the date of such commencement";

(2) *All Additional and Assistant Survey Commissioners of Auqaf shall perform their functions under this Act under the general supervision and control of the Survey Commissioner of Auqaf.*

(3) *The Survey Commissioner shall, after making such inquiry as he may consider necessary, submit his report, in respect of auqaf existing at the date of the commencement of this Act in the State or any part thereof, to the State Government containing the following particulars, namely:-*
  - (a) *the number of auqaf in the State showing the Shia auqaf and Sunni auqaf separately;*
  - (b) *the nature and objects of each waqf;*
  - (c) *the gross income of the property comprised in each waqf;*
  - (d) *the amount of land revenue, cesses, rates and taxes payable in respect of each waqf;*
  - (e) *the expenses incurred in the realisation of the income and the pay or other remuneration of the mutawalli of each waqf; and*
  - (f) *such other particulars relating to each waqf as may be prescribed.*

(4) *The Survey Commissioner shall, while making any inquiry, have the same powers as are vested in a Civil Court under the Code of Civil Procedure, 1908 (5 of 1908) in respect of the following matters, namely:-*
  - (a) *summoning and examining any witness;*
  - (b) *requiring the discovery and production of any document;*
  - (c) *requisitioning any public record from any court or office;*
  - (d) *issuing commissions for the examination of any witness or accounts;*
  - (e) *making any local inspection or local investigation;*
  - (f) *such other matters as may be prescribed.*

(5) *If, during any such inquiry, any dispute arises as to whether a particular waqf is a Shia waqf or Sunni waqf and there are clear indications in the deed of waqf as to its nature, the dispute shall be decided on the basis of such deed.*

(6) *The State Government may, by notification in the Official Gazette, direct the Survey Commissioner to make a second or subsequent*

2 Inserted by Act 27 of 2013.

> *survey of waqf properties in the State and the provisions of sub-sections (2), (3), (4) and (5) shall apply to such survey as they apply to a survey directed under sub-section (1):*
>
> *Provided that no such second or subsequent survey shall be made until the expiry of a period of ten years[3] from the date on which the report in relation to the immediately previous survey was submitted under sub-section (3):*
>
> *Provided further that the waqf properties already notified shall not be reviewed again in subsequent survey except where the status of such property has been changed in accordance with the provisions of any law.[4]*

Reflections

Analogous section under Wakf Act 1954 remains S.4 with certain amendments.

This section provides for the appointment of a Survey Commissioner of Waqf and as many Additional Survey Commissioners and Assistant Commissioners as may be necessary by the State Government. It enumerates the duties and responsibilities of such Commissioners. The Survey Commissioner of Waqf shall hold an enquiry while conducting survey of waqf to conclude whether a particular property is a waqf property or not; if it is a waqf property whether it is a shia waqf or a sunni waqf. Sub-section (3) under this section discusses the particulars to be incorporated in the survey reports to be submitted to the State Government. The second and subsequent survey shall be conducted after the expiry of ten years. The survey Commissioner is vested with the powers of a Civil Court under the Code of Civil Procedure 1908 (6 of 1908). The cost of such a publication shall be borne by the State Government.

Judicial response

The matter pertaining to the survey of waqf properties and its notification in the Official Gazette came up for consideration before the High Court of Karnataka in Karnataka Waqf Board vs. Government of India and Others.[5] The Court observed that:

3 Substituted by Act 27 of 2013, S. 6 (c) (i), for "twenty years."
4 Inserted by Act 27 of 2013, S. 6 (c) (ii),
5 1995 AIHC 6666.

> What is contemplated under Section 4(3) is a full fledged enquiry to enable the Commissioner to determine whether a particular property is existing wakf and make a request to the Wakf Board to enable it to publish a list of such Wakfs. If no such enquiry is conducted by the Commissioner then the publication of the list of wakf under Section 5 will be illegal.

A Division Bench of the Andhra Pradesh High Court, while deciding a batch of Writ Petitions in D. Venkata Krishna Rao and Others vs. Government of A.P., Rep. by Principal Secretary, Revenue Department and Others,[6] observed that:

> Under Section 4(6) of the Wakf Act, the Government can direct the Survey Commissioner to make second or subsequent survey of the wakf properties in accordance with Section 4. While conducting enquiry, as per the explanation to sub-section (1) of Section 6, the Survey Commissioner is under obligation to give reasonable opportunity to every "person interested." The said phrase means "any person who is entitled to receive any pecuniary or other benefits of the wakfs and includes any person who has a right to worship or to perform any religious rite in a mosque, idgah, imambara, dargah or khangah."

The High Court further added that:

> An analysis of the above provision would show that the Wakf Board can itself collect information regarding any wakf property which it has reason to believe to be wakf property. This power of the Wakf Board to collect information on its own is not subordinate to the power of the State Government under Section 4(1) to appoint Survey Commissioners.

A bench of the High Court of Rajasthan has held in Radhakrishnan vs. State of Rajasthan:[7]

> The law does not require the Commissioner to make a survey of wakf properties which have already become extinct as such. If he mentions in his report that certain properties were once wakf properties and can still be recovered as such, then the proper course, in our opinion, for the Board is to file a suit, get them declared as wakf properties and to recover their possession. If a dispute about the existence of a wakf is raised by a person who is stranger to the wakf, then it is neither fair nor proper for the Board to include such properties in the list published in the official gazette ... Again, if a dispute whether a particular

6 2012 (4) ALD 144; 2012 (6) ALT 379 (DB).
7 AIR 1967 Raj 1.

> property is a wakf property or not is raised by a non-muslim and a stranger to the wakf, the Board of Wakfs has no jurisdiction to decide the matter in its own favour under Section 27 and enter it in the register. The Board's decision under Section 27 would not be binding against such persons for the same reason, the Board would not be able to recover possession of the property from such persons under Section 36B of the Act.

But this decision of the High Court of Rajasthan has been reversed by the Supreme Court in the Board of Muslim Wakfs, Rajasthan vs. Radhakrishnan.[8] The Supreme Court of India in this case has articulated the powers and functions of the Survey Commissioner of Waqf. The learned Judges of the Supreme Court held that:

> The Commissioner of wakfs acted within his jurisdiction in holding the disputed property to be wakf property. The whole purpose of the survey of the wakfs by the Commissioner under s. 4(1) is to inform the Board of Wakfs as to existence of the wakfs in the State in order that all such wakfs should be brought under the supervision and control of the Board.

"The words "for the purpose of making a survey" are the key to the construction of the section. If the Commissioner has the power to make a survey it is but implicit that in the exercise of such power he should enquire whether or not a wakf exists. The making of such an enquiry is a necessary concomitant of the power to survey. The High Court was, therefore, wrong in holding to the contrary.

> It would be illogical to hold that while making a survey of wakf properties existing in the State the Commissioner of wakfs should have no power to enquire whether a particular property was wakf property or not. After making the survey the Commissioner is required to submit a report to the State Government in regard to the several matters referred to in clauses (a) to (f) thereof ... While making such an enquiry, the Commissioner is invested with the powers vested in a Civil Court under the code of Civil Procedure, 1908. In view of the comprehensive provisions contained in the Act the enquiry which the commissioner makes is not purely of an administrative nature but partakes of a quasi-judicial character in respect of persons falling within the scope of s. 6(1).

Justice N.R.L. Nageshwar Rao, of Andhra Pradesh High Court in the case of All India Federation of Minorities Welfare Association, Hyderabad and

8 AIR 1979 SC 289.

Others vs. Syed Shah Akbar Nizamuddin Hussaini and Others,[9] took the view that when the Government that allotted pattas for housing disowns the land and subsequently the Survey Commissioner and the revenue authorities find it to be wakf land, the allottees lose interest over the land. The court held that:

> The right of the petitioners is only through the Government which they want to agitate and when the Government itself disowns its interest in the property, the petitioners cannot be said to be interested parties to dispute the order of the Wakf Tribunal and the judgment in OS No. 39 of 2008 passed by the Wakf Tribunal ... Therefore, in view of the report of the Collector which was implemented by virtue of the decree, the petitioners cannot agitate and seek to challenge the above said decree.

The High Court of Uttarakhand, in Mohd. Idris alias Idris Baba vs. Uttaranchal Wakf Board through its Chief Executive Officer[10] made the following observation in respect of the Powers of the Survey Commissioner of Waqfs vis-à-vis the appointment of a mutawalli, observed that "Work of Assistant Survey Commissioner has been defined in sub-section (2) of section 4 of the Act, wherein there is no mention that he has a power even to appoint ad hoc Administrator to perform the act of mutawalli under the Act."

****

Section 5

Publication of list of Auqaf:-

(1) ***On receipt of a report under sub-section (3) of section 4, the State Government shall forward a copy of the same to the Board.***

(2) ***The Board shall examine the report forwarded to it under sub-section (1) and forward it back to the Government within a period of six months for publication in the Official Gazette*[11] *a list of Sunni auqaf or Shia auqaf in the State, whether in existence at the commencement of this Act or coming into existence thereafter, to which the report relates, and containing such other particulars as may be prescribed.***

(3) ***The revenue authorities shall-*[12]**

   (i) ***Include the list of auqaf referred to in sub-section (2), while updating the land records, and***

   (ii) ***Take into consideration the list of auqaf referred to in sub-section (2), while deciding mutation in the land records.***

9 2011 (6) ALD 722.

10 AIR 2013 Uttarakhand 72.

11 Inserted by Act 27 of 2013, S:7-(b).

12 Inserted by Act 27 of 2013, S:7-(b).

(4) ***The State Government shall maintain a record of the lists published under sub-section (2) from time to time.***[13]

Reflections

Analogous section under Wakf Act 1954 is S.5 with certain amendments.

After completion of the survey as prescribed in the foregoing section the State Government shall forward the report to the Waqf Board. The Board after examining the report within six months shall return it back to the State Government for publication in the official gazette. Sub-section (3) imposes a responsibility upon the revenue authorities to refer the list of waqfs while updating the land records and while deciding mutation in the land records.

Judicial response

The Karnataka High Court in Gulisthan Shadi Mahal Trust, Bangalore, vs. Karnataka Board of Wakfs, Bangalore,[14] while dealing with the question of whether the list of waqfs published under section 5 (2) of the Wakf Act can be challenged under Article 226 of the Constitution by invoking writ jurisdiction of the High Court. The High Court of Karnataka held that:

> The purpose of Section 6 of the Act is to confine the dispute between the Board, the mutawalli and persons interested in the wakf. Unless a suit is filed in a Civil Court of competent jurisdiction within one year of the date of publication of the list of wakfs for decision of the question whether a particular property is a wakf property or not or whether a wakf is a Shia Wakf or Sunni Wakf, the list so published would be final and conclusive between the Board, the mutawalli and the person interested in the wakf ... At this stage, it may be mentioned that the challenge to list of wakf properties under Section 5(2) of the Act, in these proceedings filed under Article 226 of the Constitution of India, in my opinion, the same is impermissible, in view of the fact that a civil suit is maintainable to challenge the list published under Section 5(2) of the Act. At this stage, I must also add that much before Trust could be registered, the property in question had been notified as a wakf property in the list that was published on 27-7-1965 and therefore, neither the decision to register nor the registration of wakf as a Trust in the year 1972 cannot bind the Wakf Board.

13 Inserted by Act 27 of 2013, S:7-(b).
14 2002 AIHC 999 Karn. H.C.

If, any property has been omitted by inadvertence or otherwise then it is for the Wakf Board to take action as provided under Section 27 of the Act. In Tamil Nadu Wakf Board vs. Hadhija (dead) by LRs,[15] the Supreme Court in its judgement rendered by Justice Rajender Babu observed that:

> The High Court is justified in holding that the Wakf Board had no right to institute suit for declaration that any property is a wakf property as the scheme of the Act clearly indicates. The High Court further found that as far as the appellant is concerned with regard to title of any property, it must comply with the requirements of Sections 4, 5, and 6 or 27 of the Act, which means that if any property is not published as wakf property as required under Section 5(2) of the Act or the Board has not invoked the special power under Section 27, the Wakf Board cannot file a suit for declaration and possession and on that basis upheld the order made by the Trial Court as affirmed by the First Appellate Court.

In another case, M.P. Wakf Board vs. Subhan Shah,[16] the Supreme Court held that:

> The power vested under Section 27 in the Wakf Board to declare the property as wakf and its decision is final and the Wakf Tribunal under 1995 Act being an adjudicatory body cannot usurp the power and it should be left to the Board which is statutorily empowered there for.

It was also held that: "When the Wakf Board issues notification attaching any property to the wakf it can only be invalidated by the Wakf Tribunal and it cannot frame a scheme for managing the affairs of the Dargah."

A Division Bench of the High Court of Andhra Pradesh in M. Bikshapathi vs. Government of Andhra Pradesh,[17] held that:

> We are of the considered view that reading both the sections together and permitting them to operate in their totality, it is within the jurisdiction of the Tribunal to determine whether the wakf property has been rightly leased or wrongly leased or any questions relating to wakf property.

The High Court of Andhra Pradesh in Dr. T.S.A. Guptha vs. Joint Collector-II and Ors[18] observed that:

> Once the lands have been notified as wakf property under Section 5(2) of the Wakf Act, 1995, the aggrieved persons are entitled to raise a dispute under Section 6(1) of the Wakf Act by instituting a suit before the

15 AIR 2002 SC 402; (2002)1 LW 384 (SC).
16 (2006) 10 SCC 696.
17 1999 (6) ALD 270 (DB).
18 2008 (2) ALD 184.

> Wakf Tribunal and unless the notification is modified under Section 6(4) of the Wakf Act, the said notification shall be deemed to have become final and conclusive.

When the A.P State Wakf Board went in appeal for declaration of the suit property as wakf against the order of the lower court, a Bench of the High Court of Andhra Pradesh in Andhra Pradesh State Wakf Board ... vs. Mavuru Sundaramma W/O Sundararao[19] observed that:

> Therefore the expression "any person interested in a waqf" must mean "any person interested in what is held to be a waqf." It is only persons who are interested in a transaction which is held to be a waqf who would sue for a declaration that the decision of the Commissioner of the Waqfs in that behalf is wrong, and that the transaction in fact is not a waqf under the Act.

In the case of Smt. Kamla Mohini vs. H.P. Waqf Board Shimla and another[20] it was claimed that "the property in question was purchased from the President of India by the predecessor in title, and in Revenue Records it is shown as owner in possession. The Hon High Court of Himachal Pradesh upheld the finding of the Wakf Tribunal that defendant No. 1 and her predecessor in title in collusion with officials of the Revenue Department had themselves got recorded as owner in possession. The property in dispute was never sold by his Excellency, the President of India, in 1958, wherein the area and the boundaries were not mentioned. The High Court of Himachal Pradesh stated that it was more than settled that property can either be sold by boundaries or by area, especially when the same is clearly discernible from the document of title. It further observed that:

> The findings recorded by the learned Tribunal are pure findings of fact, based upon the correct appreciation of the pleadings and the evidence on record, therefore, in absence of any perversity I am not inclined to interfere with the judgment passed by the learned Wakf Tribunal.

****

Section 6

Disputes regarding Auqaf:-

(1) ***if any question arises whether a particular property specified as waqf property in the list of auqaf is waqf property or not or whether a waqf specified in such list is a Shia waqf or Sunni waqf, the Board or the***

19 2007 (5) ALD 267, 2007 (6) ALT 365.
20 AIR 2019 HIMACHAL PRADESH 1.

mutawalli of the waqf or any person aggrieved[21] *may institute a suit in a Tribunal for the decision of the question and the decision of the Tribunal in respect of such matter shall be final:*

Provided that no such suit shall be entertained by the Tribunal after the expiry of one year from the date of the publication of the list of auqaf:

Provided further that no suit shall be instituted before the Tribunal in respect of such properties notified in a second or subsequent survey pursuant to the provisions contained in sub-section (6) of section 4.

[22]*[***]*

(2) *Notwithstanding anything contained in sub-section (1), no proceeding under this Act in respect of any waqf shall be stayed by reason only of the pendency of any such suit or of any appeal or other proceeding arising out of such suit.*
(3) *The Survey Commissioner shall not be made a party to any suit under sub-section (1) and no suit, prosecution or other legal proceeding shall lie against him in respect of anything which is in good faith done or intended to be done in pursuance of this Act or any rules made there under.*
(4) *The list of auqaf shall, unless it is modified in pursuance of a decision of the Tribunal under sub-section (1), be final and conclusive.*
(5) *On and from the commencement of this Act in a State, no suit or other legal proceeding shall be instituted or commenced in a court in that State in relation to any question referred to in sub-section (1).*

Reflections

Analogous section under Wakf Act 1954 is S.6 with certain amendments.

This section provides for a resolution of the disputes regarding waqf properties. The question of whether a particular property is waqf or not, and, if it is a waqf, whether it is a Sunni waqf or a Shia Waqf, shall be determined by the Waqf Tribunal. Sub-section 1 has been suitably amended by the Amendment Act 2013 by substituting the words "by any person aggrieved" for the words "any person interested therein." This has removed the confusion regarding the scope of the meaning of person interested.

21 Substituted by Act 27 of 2013, S. 8 (a), for "any person interested therein."
22 Explanation omitted by Act 27 of 2013, S. 8 (c).

The explanation under sub-section (1) has been omitted by the Waqf Act 2013 (Act 27 of 2013). The explanation runs as under:

> Explanation for the purpose of this section and section 7, the expression 'any person interested therein' shall in relation to any property specified as wakf property in the list of wakfs published after the commencement of this Act, shall include also every person who, though not interested in the wakf concerned, is interested in such property and to whom a reasonable opportunity had been afforded to represent his case by notice served on him in that behalf during the course of the relevant inquiry under section 4.

The Waqf Board cannot register the waqf institutions and their properties without proper enquiry and without providing reasonable opportunity to the persons connected therewith. It should give a notice to the persons/parties concerned about its intended action to register a particular property as waqf. Such kind of notice may be by way of publishing in at least two newspapers having circulation in the area where the property is situated. Notice can also be pasted at a conspicuous place at the waqf institution and at a reasonable place where the property is situated. It should also hear the version of the aggrieved person.

The list of auqaf, unless modified by the Tribunal, shall be final. The survey Commissioner of Waqf shall not be made a party to the suits.

Judicial response

The Supreme Court in Karnataka Waqf Board vs. State of Karnataka,[23] while upholding the decision of a Bench of the Karnataka High Court, held that the petitioners were strangers and not interested in waqf and hence the suit filed by them prior to insertion of explanation to section 6 (1) by the amendment Act 69 (84) was not applicable to them. Hence the suit is not barred by the law of limitation. While passing the orders, the Supreme Court held that:

> According to the appellant's counsel, these suits, having been filed after a period of one year were not maintainable and they were barred by time. This plea was not accepted by the High Court, in our view, rightly, as the plaintiff in both these suits cannot be construed as "persons interested in the Wakf." It is pertinent to note that the Explanation to Section 6(1) was added by Act 69 of 1984.
>
> At the time when these plaintiffs filed the suits, they were strangers and they were not interested in the Wakf as such. The Explanation

23 AIR 2003 SC 2467.

> added to Section 6(1) can operate against these plaintiffs only after the insertion of the same in Section 6 of the Act. Therefore, the inhibition provided under Proviso to Section 6 regarding the period of limitation was not applicable to the plaintiffs at the time when they filed the suits.

In the case of rival claims by Shia and Sunni communities on a waqf property in Gulam Abbas vs. State of Uttar Pradesh,[24] the Supreme Court held that:

> In the result we hold that the petitioners and through them the Shia community of Mohalla Doshipura, Varanasi have established their existing customary rights to perform their religious rites, practices, observances, ceremonies and functions minus the recitation and utterance of Tabarra (detailed in the writ petition) over the Plots and structures in question and respondents 5 and 6 and the Sunni community of Mohalla Doshipura are permanently restrained by an injunction from interfering with the exercise of said rights in any manner by the petitioners or members of Shia community and respondents 1 to 4, particularly the executive magistracy of Varanasi is directed, if action under s. 144 Cr. P.C. is required to be taken …

The All India Shia Conference filed a case for declaration of all the Panjas, Alams, Ashur Khanas, Asthanas and Imambadas as Shia Wakfs. The matter went up to the Supreme Court in A.P. State Wakf Board, Hyd. v All India Shia Conference.[25] The Hon'ble Supreme Court observed that:

> But we are of the view that, on the basis of the above proposition. It cannot be straightaway declared that every institutions known as "Ashtanas, Imambadas, Ashurkhanas or Alams" is a Shia Wakf and that it cannot be a Sunni Wakf. Whether any particular institution even if it is known by the above names, is prima facie a Shia Wakf or not is a matter upon which it will be necessary to lead evidence in relation to each one of the institutions.

The Supreme Court, while discussing the construction of sub-section (1) of section (6) in the case of Punjab Wakf Board vs. Gram Panchayat & Gram Sabha,[26] observed as under:

> In order to understand the meaning of the Word "therein" in our view, it is necessary to refer to the preceding words `the Board or the

24 AIR 1981 SC 2198.
25 AIR 2000 SC 1751; 2000 (2) SCR 78.
26 AIR 2000 SC 3488.

mutawalli of the wakf. The word "therein" must necessarily refer to the wakf which immediately precedes it. It cannot refer to the "wakf property"; Sub-section (1) of Section 6 enumerates the persons who can file suits and also the questions in respect of which such suits can be filed. In enumerating the persons who are empowered to file suits under this provision, only the Board, the mutawalli of the Wakf, and "any person interested therein," thereby necessarily meaning any person interested in the Wakf, are listed, it should be borne in mind that the Act deals with Wakfs, its institutions and its properties. It would, therefore, be logical and reasonable to infer that its provisions empower only those who are interested in the Wakf, to institute suits.

Obviously, the intention of Parliament was to say that if a suit was not filed within one year, the Notification would be binding not only on those interested in the trust but even strangers, claiming interest in the property in question, provided they were given notice in the inquiry under Section 4 preceding the Notification under Section 5(2).

In the case of Sayyed Ali and Ors vs. Andhra Pradesh Wakf Board,[27] the Supreme Court observed that:

> Consequently, the finding of the Tahsildar that the property is not a wakf property would not constitute res judicata in the subsequent suit filed by the Wakf Board. It is well settled that if a decision of a court or a tribunal is without, jurisdiction, such a decision or finding cannot operate as res judicata in any subsequent proceedings. The plea of res judicata presupposes that there is in existence a decree or judgment which is legal, but when the judgment is non est in law, no plea of res judicata can be founded on such a judgment.

The Supreme Court further observed that:

> It may be stated that a wakf is a permanent dedication of property for purposes recognized by Muslim law as pious religious or charitable and the property having been found as Wakf would always retain its character as a Wakf. In other words, once a Wakf always a Wakf and the grant of patta in favour of Mokhasadar under the Inams Act does not, in any manner, nullify the earlier dedication made of the property constituting the same as Wakf. After a Wakf had been created, it continues to be so for all time to come and further continues to be governed by the provisions of the Wakf Act and a grant of patta in favour of Mokhasadar does not affect the original character of the wakf property.

27 (1998) 2 SCC 642; [1998] 1 SCR 398.

While considering a similar matter in the case of Abdul Rais and Ors vs. Madhya Pradesh Wakf Board and Ors,[28] the Supreme Court remanded the case since the principles laid down in Punjab Wakf Board V. Gram Panchayat,[29] Sayyed Ali. vs. A.P. Wakf Board,[30] Board of Muslim Wakfs vs. Radha Kisan,[31] were not considered. A Bench of the High Court of Andhra Pradesh, while dealing the case of Andhra Pradesh State Wakf Board vs. Mavuru Sundaramma,[32] referred to the above said judgements and observed as under:

> Having regard to the aforesaid principles laid down by the Supreme Court in the above said decisions, it quite clear that the proviso to aforesaid Section 6 of the Wakf Act, and the bar created there under, much less, the period of limitation, as prescribed there under, would in any way apply to the third parties who are in no way concerned with the Wakf.

A Division Bench of the Andhra Pradesh High Court, while deciding a batch of Writ Petitions in D. Venkata Krishna Rao and Others vs. Government of A.P., Rep. by Principal Secretary, Revenue Department and Others,[33] observed that:

> The appointment of Survey Commissioner is not one time exercise of power. Under Section 4(6) of the Wakf Act, the Government can direct the Survey Commissioner to make second or subsequent survey of the wakf properties in accordance with Section 4. While conducting enquiry, as per the explanation to sub-section (1) of Section 6, the Survey Commissioner is under obligation to give reasonable opportunity to every "person interested." The said phrase means "any person who is entitled to receive any pecuniary or other benefits of the wakfs and includes any person who has a right to worship or to perform any religious rite in a mosque, idgah, imambara, dargah or khangah."
>
> In view of the clear provisions as briefly pointed out hereinabove, it is not possible to accept the submission of the State and its supporting parties that the impugned errata notification is ultra vires. For issuing the impugned errata notification, in our opinion, it may not be necessary for the Government to appoint a second Survey Commissioner nor

28 (2005) 1 SCC 741; 2005 (2) ALD3 (SC).
29 AIR 2000 SC 3488.
30 (1998) 2 SCC 642; [1998] 1 SCR 398.
31 AIR 1979 SC 289.
32 2007 (5) ALD 267; 2007 (6) ALT 365.
33 2012 (4) ALD 144; 2012 (6) ALT 379 (DB).

> for him to submit a report. Section 40 is wide enough to confer such powers on the Wakf Board.

The High Court of Andhra Pradesh in B. Gowra Reddy vs. Government of Andhra Pradesh[34] observed as under:

> The report as such has to conform to the requirements of Section 4 of the Act as has been held by the Supreme Court in the catena of decisions referred to above ... Further the requirements under Section 25 of the Wakf Act 1954 have to be complied with. There is not even an iota of proof of dedication by Abbas Ali Khan nor is there any Wakf deed.

The Supreme Court while dealing with the jurisdiction of the High Court under Article 226 in deciding the matters pertaining to survey of waqfs and the reports of the survey commissioner, in the case of Board of Muslim Wakfs vs. Smt. Hadi Begum[35] held that:

> The order dated July 9, 1962 passed by the Wakfs Commissioner and the list of wakf properties dated December 2, 1965 as amended by notification dated June 29, 1967, published under Sub-section (2) of Section 5 of the Act were not open to challenge before the High Court under Article 226 of the Constitution on the ground that the finding recorded by the Wakfs Commissioner was not supported by the evidence on record.

****

Section 7

Power of Tribunal to determine disputes regarding auqaf:-

(1) ***If, after the commencement of this act, any question or dispute arises,[36] whether a particular property specified as waqf property in a list of auqaf is waqf property or not, or whether a waqf specified in such list is a Shia waqf or a Sunni waqf, the Board or the mutawalli of the waqf, or any person aggrieved by the publication of the list of auqaf under section 5[37] therein, may apply to the Tribunal having jurisdiction in relation to such property, for the decision of the question and the decision of the Tribunal thereon shall be final:***

34 AIR 2002 AP 313, 2002 (3) ALT 439.
35 AIR 1992 SC 1083, 1993 Supp (1) SCC 192.
36 Substituted by Act 27 of 2013, S. 9 (a) (i), for "any question."
37 Substituted by Act 27 of 2013, S. 9 (a) (ii), for "or any person interested."

Provided that-

(a) *in the case of the list of auqaf relating to any part of the State and published after the commencement of this Act no such application shall be entertained after the expiry of one year from the date of publication of the list of auqaf; and*

(b) *in the case of the list of auqaf relating to any part of the State and published at any time within a period of one year immediately preceding the commencement of this Act, such an application may be entertained by Tribunal within the period of one year from such commencement:*

Provided further that where any such question has been heard and finally decided by a civil court in a suit instituted before such commencement, the Tribunal shall not re-open such question.

(2) *Except where the Tribunal has no jurisdiction by reason of the provisions of sub-section (5), no proceeding under this section in respect of any waqf shall be stayed by any court, tribunal or other authority by reason only of the pendency of any suit, application or appeal or other proceeding arising out of any such suit, application, appeal or other proceeding.*

(3) *The Chief Executive Officer shall not be made a party to any application under sub-section (1).*

(4) *The list of auqaf and where any such list is modified in pursuance of a decision of the Tribunal under sub-section (1), the list as so modified, shall be final.*

(5) *The Tribunal shall not have jurisdiction to determine any matter which is the subject-matter of any suit or proceeding instituted or commenced in a civil court under sub-section (1) of section 6, before the commencement of this Act or which is the subject-matter of any appeal from the decree passed before such commencement in any such suit or proceeding or of any application for revision or review arising out of such suit, proceeding or appeal, as the case may be.*

(6) *The Tribunal shall have the powers of assessment of damages by unauthorised occupation of waqf property and to penalise such unauthorised occupants for their illegal occupation of the waqf property and to recover the damages as arrears of land revenue through the collector:*[38]

38 Inserted by Act 27 of 2013.

> ***Provided that whosoever, being a public servant, fails in his lawful duty to prevent or remove an encroachment, shall on conviction be punishable with fine which may extend to fifteen thousand rupees for each such offence.***[39]

Reflections

Analogous section under Wakf Act 1954 is S.6A introduced with the amendment act of 1984 (act 69 of 1984) with certain amendments.

This section delegates the powers to the Waqf Tribunal to determine any dispute regarding waqf matters. The question regarding whether a particular property is a waqf property or not, and, if it is, whether it is a Sunni Waqf or a Shia Waqf shall be determined by the Waqf Tribunal. No suit or application shall be entertained by the Tribunal after the expiry of one year from the date of publication of the list of the auqaf in the Official Gazette.

Under sub-section (6) the Tribunal is authorised to assess the damages caused due to unauthorised occupation, pass orders for the recovery of the damages as arrears of land revenue. It is also authorised to penalise the illegal occupants which may extend up to 15,000 rupees for each such offence. The decision of the Tribunal shall be final. The Chief Executive Officer of the Waqf Board shall not be made a party to any application under subsection (1).

Judicial response

The Waqf Act 1995 for the first time provides for the constitution of the Waqf Tribunal or Tribunals in every State to try and adjudicate the cases pertaining to matters of waqf. But there was confusion whether all the pending cases in the matters of waqf in different Civil Courts shall be transferred to the Tribunal irrespective of their date of initiation. In some states, the registry of High Courts have issued notifications that all those matters pertaining to waqf filed on or after 1 January 1996 shall be transferred to the waqf Tribunal. The Supreme Court has put this confusion to rest in Sardar Khan vs. Syed Najmul Hasan[40] by ruling that:

> On a conjoint reading of sub-section (5) of Section 7 and Section 85, the result would be that the Act will not be applicable to the pending suits or proceedings or appeals or revisions which have commenced

39 Inserted by Act 27 of 2013.
40 (2007) 3 MLJ 366 (SC).

prior to 1.1.1996, i.e., coming into force of the Wakf Act, 1995 ... Consequently, the impugned order passed by the learned Single Judge is set aside and the matter is remitted back to the High Court for deciding the appeal in accordance with law, expeditiously.

A Bench of Kerala High Court in Badagara Jumayath Palli Dharas Committee vs. Peedikayalakath Ummar Kutty Haji and Others,[41] held that:

> Further, we find that Section 7 (5) of the Act merely says that the tribunal shall not have jurisdiction to determine any matter which is the subject-matter of any suit or proceedings instituted or commenced in a civil court under sub-section (1) of Section 6, before the commencement of this Act or which is the subject-matter of any appeal from the decree passed before such commencement. Section 7(5) of the Act clearly exempts appeal from the bar of jurisdiction. Hence, we are of the view that this court is perfectly competent to decide the question regarding Wakf in this appeal.

The High Court of Andhra Pradesh in T. Shivalingam vs. A.P. Wakf Tribunal,[42] while dealing with the jurisdiction of the Wakf Tribunal, observed that:

> So it is Section 83 which grants jurisdiction to the Tribunals to entertain any dispute with regard to Wakf property. Section 7 of the Act is not a bar for entertaining of such suits but it only lays down that disputes regarding nature of property as to whether it is Wakf property or not can be decided only by the Tribunal. This Writ Petition is misconceived and deserves dismissal and is accordingly dismissed.

The order of the Wakf Tribunal restraining the Sub-Registrar not to register the Sale Deed, without impleading him in the case or even without serving him notice cannot be not sustainable as held by High Court of Hyderabad in Kagitala Venkata Chalapati Rao vs. Smt. Sabarunnisa Begum[43]

****

<u>*Section 8*</u>

<u>*State Government to bear Cost of Survey:-*</u>

41 AIR 2002 Ker. 56.
42 1999 (3) ALD 646.
43 AIR 2018 (NOC) 137, HYD.

The total cost of making a survey including the cost of publication of the list or lists of auqaf under this Chapter shall be borne by the State Government.[44]

Reflections

Analogous section under Wakf Act 1954 is S.7.

This Act has been suitably amended by making a provision through the Amendment Act of 2013 that the cost of the survey and the publication of the list of the auqafs shall be borne by the State Government. Whereas hitherto the mutawallis were required to bear the cost of survey and cost of publication of lists. Prior to this Amendment under the Amendment Act 2013, this section read as under:

8. Recovery of costs of survey.-

(1) The total cost of making a survey including the cost of publication of the list or lists of wakfs under this chapter shall be borne by all the mutawalli of the wakfs the net annual income whereof exceeds five hundred rupees, in proportion to the net annual income accruing in the state to such wakfs, such proportion being assessed by the Survey Commissioner.

(2) Notwithstanding anything contained in the deed or instrument by which the wakfs was created, any mutawalli may pay from the income of the wakf any sum due from him under sub-section (1).

(3) Any sum due from a mutawalli under sub-section (1) may, on a certificate issued by the State Government, be recovered from the property comprised in the wakf in the same manner as an arrear of land revenue.

Judicial response

Judicial response pertaining to this section is not found.

44 Substituted by Act 27 of 2013, S. 10.

III CENTRAL WAQF COUNCIL

Synopsis

This chapter from section 9 to 12 of the Act, (analogous to Sections 8A, 8B, 8C and 8D of Chapter IIA of Wakf Act 1954), pertains to the establishment, composition and functions of the Central Waqf Council. The Central Waqf Council is a statutory body established in the year 1964 by the Government of India under section 8A of the Wakf Act 1954 (present sub-section 1 of section 9 of Wakf Act 1995). The provision for the establishment of the Council was made vide Wakf Amendment Act (Amendment Act 34 of 1964). This amendment was incorporated in the Wakf Act 1954 by inserting Sections 8A, 8B, 8C and 8D. The Kazmi Bill of 1952 had also made a provision for the establishment of Central Wakf Council.

The Council consists of 20 members assorted from different segments as mentioned in section 9 (2) of this Act. The Union Minister in charge of the Waqf shall be Chair-Person of the Council.

The main function of the Central Waqf Council is to advise the Central and the State Governments and the State Waqf Boards on matters pertaining to the administration of waqfs. It formulates schemes for the development of urban waqf properties. It identifies potential waqf lands for development by National Waqf Development Corporation Limited. It also establishes Industrial/Vocational Training Centres.

The provision for the constitution of the Central Wakf Council was marred by criticism. The Council was considered unnecessary and superfluous. Some considered it as fifth wheel of a coach. But a body at the central level to advise the Central and the State Government and the State Wakf Boards would be helpful to act as a nodal agency between and among the stakeholder at the Central and State levels.

Keywords: Council, Composition, Statutory, Adjudications, Parliament, Fifth wheel

****

Section 9

Establishment and Constitution of Central Waqf Council:-

(1) *The Central Government may, by notification in the Official Gazette, establish a Council to be called the Central Waqf Council, for the purpose of advising the Central Government, the State Government and the Boards on matters concerning the working of Boards and the due administration of auqaf.*[1]

(1A) The Council referred to in sub-section (1) shall issue directives to the Boards, on such issues and in such manner, as provided under sub-section (4) and (5).[2]

(2) *The Council shall consist of-*
   (a) *the Union Minister in charge of auqaf - ex officio Chairperson;*
   (b) *the following members to be appointed by the Central Government from amongst Muslims, namely:-*
      (i) *three persons to represent Muslim organisations having all India character and national importance;*
      (ii) *four persons of national eminence, one each from the fields of administration or management, financial management, engineering or architecture and medicine,*[3]
      (iii) *three Members of Parliament of whom two shall be from the House of the People and one from the Council of States;*
      (iv) *chairpersons of three Boards by rotation;*
      (v) *two persons who have been Judges of the Supreme Court or a High Court;*
      (vi) *one advocate of national eminence;*
      (vii) *one person to represent the Mutawallis of the waqf having a gross annual income of rupees five lakh and above;*
      (viii) *three persons who are eminent scholars in Muslim Law:*

Provided that at least two of the members appointed under sub-clauses (i) to (viii) shall be women.[4]

1 Substituted by Act 27 of 2013, S. 11 (a), for sub-s. (1). Prior to its substitution, sub-s. (1) read as under:- "(1) for the purpose of advising it, on matters concerning the working of Boards and the due administration of waqfs, the central Government may by notification in the official gazette, establish a council to be called the central waqf council."

2 *Ibid.*

3 Substituted by Act 27 of 2013, S. 11 (b) (i) for sub-CI. (ii) prior to its substitution, sub-CI (ii) read as under:- "(ii) four persons of national eminence of whom two shall be from amongst persons having administration and financial expertise;"

4 Inserted by Act 27 of 2013, S. 11 (b) (ii).

(3) ***The term of office of, the procedure to be followed in the discharge of their functions by, and the manner of filling casual vacancies among, members of the Council shall be such as may be prescribed by rules made by the Central Government.***

(4) ***The State Government or, as the case may be, the Board, shall furnish information to the council on the performance of Waqf Boards in the State, particularly on their financial performance, survey, maintenance of waqf deeds, revenue records, encroachment of waqf properties, annual reports and audit reports in the manner and time as may be specified by the Council and it may suo motu call for information on specific issues from the Board, if it is satisfied that there was prima facie evidence of irregularity or violation of the provisions of this Act and if the council is satisfied that such irregularity or violation of the Act is established, it may issue such directive, as considered appropriate, which shall be complied with by the concerned Board under intimation to the concerned State Government.***[5]

(5) ***Any dispute arising out of a directive issued by the Council under sub-section (4) shall be referred to a Board of Adjudication to be constituted by the Central Government, to be presided over by a retired judge of the Supreme Court or a retired Chief Justice of a High Court and the fees and travelling and other allowances payable to the Presiding Officer shall be such as may be specified by that Government.***

Reflections

Analogous section under Wakf Act 1954 is S.8A. The role of the Central Waqf Council has so far been advisory. Now with the amendment act of 2013 it can issue directions to the State Waqf Boards, apart from advising the State and Central Government on matters of waqf. This section describes the composition of the council. It comprises the Union Minister in charge of waqfs as the Chair-Person, three persons to represent Muslim organisations having national importance, four persons of national eminence representing the fields of Administration, Management Engineering, Medicine, etc., three Members of Parliament – two from Lower House and one from Upper House, Chair-Persons of three Boards by rotation; two persons who have been Judges of the Supreme Court or a High Court; one advocate of national eminence, one person to represent the mutawallis of the waqf having a gross annual income of rupees five lakh and above; three persons who are eminent scholars in Muslim Law. However, at least two members shall be women.

5 Inserted by Act 27 of 2013, S. 11 (c).

This section provides that the state governments shall furnish annual reports to the Council. If the Council is not satisfied with any aspect of the report it can issue a directive to the State Waqf Board. Any dispute arising out of such matters shall be referred to a Board of Adjudication presided over by a retired Judge of the Supreme Court, or a retired Chief Justice of a High Court.

Judicial response

Judicial response pertaining to this section is not found.

****

Section 10

Finance of Council:-

(1) ***Every Board shall pay from its Waqf Fund annually to the Council such contribution as is equivalent to one per cent, of the aggregate of the net annual income of the auqaf in respect of which contribution is payable under sub-section (1) of section 72:***

Provided that where the Board, in the case of any particular waqf has remitted under sub-section (2) of section 72 the whole of the contribution payable to it under sub-section (1) of that section, then for calculating the contribution payable to the Council under this section the net annual income of the waqf in respect of which such remission has been granted shall not be taken into account.

(2) ***All monies received by the Council under sub-section (1) and all other monies received by it as donations, benefactions and grants shall form a fund to be called the Central Waqf Fund.***

(3) ***Subject to any rules that may be made by the Central Government in this behalf, the Central Waqf Fund shall be under the control of the Council and may be applied for such purposes as the Council may deem fit.***

Reflections

The analogous section under Wakf Act 1954 is S.8B.

This section compels the State Waqf Boards to contribute one per cent of its net annual income to the Central Waqf Council. There are Waqf Boards which are unable to protect the waqf properties or provide basic amenities at the waqf institutions due to a paucity of funds. Hence this provision could have been avoided. The Central Government shall allocate the necessary budget to cater to its financial requirement under the Ministry of Minority Affairs. This section entitles the Council to receive donations grants and benefactions which should form the Central Waqf Fund. The Council can use this fund for such purposes as it deems fit.

Judicial response

The Hon Supreme Court in the year 2011 in the case of Praful Goradia vs. Union of India[6] held that the subsidy offered by the Government of India in the airfare of Haj pilgrims was not unconstitutional. While observing that the parliament has the legislative competence to enact the Haj Committee Act in view of entry 20 to list 1 of the seventh schedule to the constitution which states "pilgrimage to places outside India," the Supreme Court held that:

> It is nowhere mentioned in the writ petition as to what percentage of any particular tax has been utilized for the purpose of the Haj pilgrimage. If only a relatively small part of any tax collected is utilized for providing some conveniences or facilities or concessions to any religious denomination that would not be violative of Article 27 of the Constitution. Thus, there is no violation of Article 27 as also Articles 14 and 15 of the Constitution.

The expenditure towards the Central Waqf Council shall not be deemed to be an expenditure incurred for a religious denomination. Proper administration of endowments and redeeming the endowed properties from maladministration of the waqf institutions are the responsibilities of the Government of the day.

****

Section 11

Accounts and Audit:-

(1) ***The Council shall cause to be maintained such books of account and other books in relation to its accounts in such form and in such manner as may be prescribed by rules made by the Central Government.***
(2) ***The accounts of the Council shall be audited and examined annually by such auditor as may be appointed by the Central Government.***

6 [2011] 1 S.C.R. 579.

(3) ***The costs of the audit shall be paid from the Central Waqf Fund.***

Reflections

Analogous section under Wakf Act 1954 is S.8C.

This section provides for maintenance of books of accounts, audit of the accounts of Central Wakf Council. The audit shall be conducted by the auditor as may be appointed by the Central Government and the cost of such an audit shall be paid from the Central Wakf Fund. When the Council is the Statutory Body headed by the Union Minister concerned, the audit could have been conducted by the office of the Comptroller and Auditor General (C.A.G.) of India. If the audit is conducted by the C.A.G.'s, i.e., the Government's auditors, the question of the cost of audit or the payment of fee to auditors would not have arisen.

Judicial response

Judicial response pertaining to this section is not found.

****

Section 12

Power of Central Government to make rules:-

(1) ***The Central Government may, by notification in the Official Gazette, make rules to carry out the purposes of this Chapter.***

(2) ***In particular, and without prejudice to the generality of the foregoing power, such rules may provide for all or any of the following matters, namely:-***

   (a) ***the term of office of, the procedure to be followed in the discharge of their functions by, and the manner of filling casual vacancies among, the members of the Council;***

   (b) ***control over and application of the Central Waqf Fund;***

   (c) ***the form and manner in which accounts of the Council may be maintained;***

(3) ***Every rule made by the Central Government under this Chapter shall be laid, as soon as may be after it is made, before each House of Parliament, while it is in session for a total period of thirty days, which may be comprised in one session or in two or more successive sessions, and if, before the expiry of the session immediately following, the session or the successive sessions aforesaid, both Houses agree in making any modification in the rule or both House agree that the***

rule should not be made, the rule shall thereafter have effect only in such modified form or be of no effect, as the case may be; so, however, that any such modification or annulment shall be without prejudice to the validity of anything previously done under that rule.

Reflections

Analogous section under Wakf Act 1954 is S.8D.

This section confers powers to the Central Government to frame rules for the purpose of carrying out of the purposes and functions of the Central Waqf Council. Sub-section (3) under the section renders that the rules formulated by the Central Government shall be placed before both the Houses of Parliament when they are in session at least for 30 days. According to sub-section (1) of section 9 of this Act, the function of the Central Waqf Council is to advise the Central Government, the State Government and the Boards on matters concerning the working of Boards and the due administration of auqaf. The Central Waqf Council may prepare model guidelines/ regulations on different aspects of the administration of waqf to be adopted by the State Waqf Boards with or without modifications to have uniformity and cohesion in the waqf administration.

Judicial response

Judicial response pertaining to this section is not found.

IV ESTABLISHMENT OF BOARDS AND THEIR FUNCTIONS

Synopsis

The Wakf Act 1995 in chapter IV provides for the establishment of Wakf Boards in every state. It deals with incorporation, composition, powers and functions of the Waqf Boards under sections 13 to 35. It makes a provision for a separate Shia Waqf Board if the number of Shia Waqfs are more than 15 per cent of all the auqaf in the State or if the income of the properties of the Shia auqaf in the State constitutes more than 15 per cent of the total income of the properties of all the auqaf in the State. In Section 13, Sub Section 2A has been inserted in this regard. It also makes a provision for the nomination of Senior Advocate of State concerned, if the Muslim Member of the State Bar Council is not available. The Waqf Board can conduct an inquiry against the mutawalli or waqf institution and its properties to ascertain the factual position and to initiate suitable action as per law.

Keywords: Succession, Composition, Election, Removal, Resignation, Disqualification

****

Section 13

Incorporation:-

(1) ***With effect from such date as the State Government may, by notification in the Official Gazette, appoint in this behalf, there shall be established a Board of Auquaf under such name as may be specified in the notification:***

Provided that in case where a Board of Waqf has not been established, as required under this sub-section, a Board of Waqf shall, without prejudice to the provisions of this Act or any other Law for the time

being in force, be established within six months from the date of commencement of the Waqf (Amendment) Act, 2013.[1]

(2) *Notwithstanding anything contained in sub-section (1), if the Shia auqaf in any State constitute in number more than fifteen per cent of all the auqaf in the State or if the income of the properties of the Shia auqaf in the State constitutes more than fifteen per cent of the total income of properties of all the auqaf in the State, the State Government may, by notification in the Official Gazette, establish a Board of Auqaf each for Sunni auqaf and for Shia auqaf under such names as may be specified in the notification.*

(2A) Where a Board of Waqf is established under sub-section (2) of section 13, in the case of shia waqf, the members shall belong to the Shia Muslim and in the case of sunni waqf, the members shall belong to the Sunni Muslim.[2]

(3) *The Board shall be a body corporate having perpetual succession and a common seal with power to acquire and hold property and to transfer any such property subject to such conditions and restrictions as may be prescribed and shall by the said name sue and be sued.*

Reflections

Analogous section under Wakf Act 1954 is section 9, as Amended vide Act 34 of 1964 and Act 69 of 1984.

This section provides for Incorporation of Waqf Board in every State. The board shall be established by the State Government by notification in the official gazette. A proviso under sub-section (1) has been inserted by the Waqf Amendment Act 2013 (Act 27 of 2013) which contemplates that if the Waqf Board in any state is not constituted it shall be constituted within six months of the date of commencement of the Waqf Amendment Act 2013.

Separate Shia Waqf Board may also be constituted if the Shia Waqfs in any state comprise more than fifteen per cent of the total waqfs in that state or if the income from Shia Waqfs is more than fifteen per cent of the total income from waqfs in that state.

Section (2A) has been inserted by Waqf Amendment Act 2013 which clarifies that in case of establishment of separate boards for Sunni Waqfs

1 Inserted by Act 27 of 2013, S. 12 (a).
2 Inserted by Act 27 of 2013, S. 12 (b).

and Shia Waqfs, the Members of such boards shall belong to Sunni and Shia Muslims communities respectively.

Sub-section of the Act says that the Waqf Board is a body corporate. A body corporate is an artificial person created to have a perpetual succession and a common seal of its own. Ramanatha Iyer's Law Lexicon gives a comprehensive meaning of a corporation.[3] It says:

> A corporation is an artificial being, invisible, intangible and existing only in contemplating of law. Being the mere creator of law it possesses only those properties which the charter of the creating confers upon it, either expressly or as incidental to its very existence. These are such as are supposed best calculated to effect the object for which it was created. Among the most important ones immortality and if the expression may be allowed, individuality; properties by which a perpetual succession of many persons are considered as the same and may act as a single individual. They enable a corporation to manage its own affairs and to hold property without the perplexing intricacies, the hazardous and endless necessity, of perpetual conveyances for the purposes of transmitting it from hand to hand. It is chiefly for the purpose of clothing bodies of men, in succession with these qualities and capacities, that corporations were invented and are in use. By these means a perpetual succession of individuals are capable of acting for the promotion of the particular object like one immortal being.

Judicial response

The validity of the constitution of Waqf Boards and their powers was questioned in Usman Ali Khan vs. Faezullah[4] in the High Court of Madhya Pradesh. It was argued that the powers of the Waqf Board are violative of the right as guaranteed under Article 26 of the Constitution of India. But the High Court of Madhya Pradesh, while referring to the judgements of the Supreme Court in The Commissioner, Hindu … vs. Sri Lakshmindra Thirtha Swamiar[5] and in Ratilal vs. State of Bombay,[6] rejected these averments and held that:

> The legislative competence of the Parliament therefore to make the aforesaid Act cannot be questioned. There is nothing in the impugned Sections which deprives the religious denomination namely Muslims of their right of administration or administering properties owned and

3 Ramanatha Iyer, Law Lexicon, 1940, p. 247.
4 AIR 1959 MP 377.
5 AIR 1954 SC 282 at p. 289.
6 AIR 1954 SC 388.

> acquired by it altogether with a view to vest it in any other or secular authority.

The legal entity of the Waqf Board has not been disputed in any court of law. But whether the Waqf Board is a religious denomination, has been the bone of contention in some of the cases. Syed Fazal Pookoya Thangal the then-chairperson of Kerala State Waqf Board challenged the constitutional validity of section 4 (2) of Muslim women (protection of right on divorce) Act and the order passed by the judicial magistrate as violating Article 26 (b) and (d) of the Constitution of India. The High Court of Kerala in Syed Fazal Pookoya Thangal vs. Union of India,[7] after referring to the definition of religious denomination by the Supreme Court in Commissioner, Hindu Religious and Charitable Endowments vs. Sri Lakshmindra Thirtha Swamiar of Shirur Mutt,[8] observed in this case that:

> The Wakf Board is not a conglomeration of individuals. It is not even akin to a company where a number of individuals join together to constitute it. It is a statutory body, pure and simple. It is not a representative body of the Muslim community. It has no soul and no faith, except the faith of dutiful performance of its functions and duties under the Act. It is well known that management of Wakf properties has since long been controlled by the State. Various laws have been enacted from time to time in various parts of the country by either the Central Legislature or the State Legislatures for achieving this purpose. ....It is the power so exercised by the State that now stands vested in the Wakf Boards in each State, specially established for the purpose. What the Wakf Board does is to carry out functions which were hitherto being undertaken by the State. It is exercising a part of the State's functions and is an instrumentality of the State. The Wakf Board is a creature of the Wakf Act. It has no existence otherwise. It stands or falls with the Wakf Act. It has to exercise those functions and powers which are vested in it under the provisions of the Wakf Act. It is not a collection of individuals, or a sect or body with a common faith which alone will make it a denomination for the purpose of Article 26. If it is not a denomination, it has no rights under Article 26, liable to be violated by Section 4(2) of the Act or the order Ext. P1 by casting the liability to make payment of maintenance to a destitute divorced woman. Article 26 is therefore out of operation so far as the Wakf Board is concerned.

The composition of the Waqf Board under various clauses Waqf Act 1995 has been a matter of debate and discussion whenever the election to

7 AIR 1993 KER 308.
8 AIR 1954 SC 282.

the board is declared. A writ petition was filed by the Association of A.P. Sajjadanashins, Mutawallis and Khidmat Guzaran of Wakfs, Hyderabad challenging the inclusion of mutawallis of waqf institutions having an income of more than one lakh and exclusion of other mutawallis for the composition of an electoral college representing mutawallis as unconstitutional. The Bench of the High Court of Andhra Pradesh, in the case of Association of A.P. Sajjada Nasheens, Mutawallis and Khidmat Guzaran of Wakfs, Hyderabad vs. Union of India and others,[9] has observed that:

> Keeping in view, all these aspects, therefore, I am of the view that the provisions of Section 14(b) (iv) of the Act are clearly discriminatory as they discriminate Mutawallis by treating them in two different classes. The said differentiation among the Mutawallis as a class is unsupported by any intelligent criteria and the said differentiation has absolutely no nexus with the object of giving representation to the Mutawallis over the Board. The composition of the Board giving representation to the eminent Muslims from different sections of the society apart from the Mutawallis conveys the object behind the composition of the Board to give wide representation to various categories. The said object, therefore, is defeated if large number of Mutawallis are to be excluded from consideration on the ground that the income of the wakfs under their management is less than Rs. 1,00,000/-. The said classification, therefore, has no apparent justification and it is clear and apparent that all Mutawallis, who are equals, are being treated unequally and thereby Article 14 of the Constitution of India is violated.
>
> In the result, the writ petitions are allowed declaring the Section 14(b) (iv) of the Wakf Act, 1995 is discriminatory, violative of Article 14 of the Constitution of India and is arbitrary and accordingly struck down. There shall be a direction to the respondents 1 and 2 to forthwith ensure completion of survey of wakf institutions in the State, within a period of six (6) months from today, containing all particulars thereof as required under the Wakf Act and the respondents shall file a compliance report relating to the above direction before the Registry of this Court on or before 31.5.2010.

The High Court of Bombay, in Shaikh Yusuf Bhai Chawala vs. State Of Maharashtra,[10] disposing of a batch of Writ Petitions respect of constitution of separate Shia Board and registration of Trusts as Waqfs, made the following observations:

9 2010 (4) ALD 136 (DB).
10 AIR 2012 (NOC) 112 (Bom).

> In our opinion, the provisions of sub-section 2 of Section 13 have to be read with the provisions of sub-section 3 of section 4 of the Act. Sub-section 3 of Section 4 of the Act casts a duty on the Survey Commissioner to collect information as to the number of Shia wakfs and Sunni Wakfs separately. He is also required to collect information on the income, expenditure and properties of Shia Wakfs and Sunni Wakf separately. A duty on the Survey Commissioner is cast by sub-section (3) of Section 4 to collect information in that regard obviously to enable the State Government to take a decision, which is contemplated by sub-section (2) of Section 13 of the Act.

This matter went in appeal before Honourable Supreme Court in Maharashtra State Board of Wakfs vs. Shaikh Yusuf Bhai Chawla and Ors[11] the Supreme Court in an interim order gave the following observation:

> Accordingly, at this stage, we direct that in relation to wakf properties, as distinct from Trusts created by Muslims, all concerned, including the Charity Commissioner, Mumbai, shall not permit any of the persons in management of such wakf properties to either encumber or alienate any of the properties under their management, till a decision is rendered in the pending Special Leave Petitions.

****

Section 14

Composition of Board:-

(1) ***The Board for a State and the <u>National Capital Territory of Delhi</u> shall consist of-***
   (a) ***a Chairperson;***
   (b) ***one and not more than two members, as the State government may think fit, to be elected from each of the electoral colleges consisting of-***
      (i) ***Muslim Members of Parliament from the State or, as the case may be, <u>the National Capital Territory of Delhi,</u>***
      (ii) ***Muslim Members of the State Legislature,***
      (iii) ***<u>Muslim Members of the Bar Council of the concerned State or Union Territory:</u>***[12]

11 2012 (5) SCR 1014.

12 Substituted by Act 27 of 2013; S. 13 (1) (ii) (a), for sub-CI. (iii) Prior to its substitution, sub-CI. (III READ AS UNDER:-"(iii) Muslim Members of the Bar council of the states, and ..."

Provided that in case there is no Muslim member of the Bar Council of a State or a Union territory, the State Government or the Union Territory administration, as the case may be, may nominate any senior Muslim advocate from that state or the Union Territory and;

(iv) *Mutawallis of the auqafs having an annual income of rupees one lakh and above.*

Explanation I. For the removal of doubts, it is hereby declared that the members from categories mentioned in sub-clauses (i) to (iv), shall be elected from the electoral college constituted for each category.[13]

Explanation II. For the removal of doubts it is hereby declared that in case a Muslim member ceases to be a Member of Parliament from the State or National Capital Territory of Delhi as referred to in sub-clause (i) of clause (b) or ceases to be a Member of the State Legislative Assembly as required under sub-clause (ii) of clause (b), such member shall be deemed to have vacated the office of the member of the Board for the State or National Capital Territory of Delhi, as the case may be, from the date from which such member ceased to be a Member of Parliament from the State or National Capital Territory of Delhi, or a Member of the State Legislative Assembly, as the case may be;

(c) *one person from amongst Muslim, who has professional experience in town planning or business management, social work, finance or revenue, agriculture and development activities, to be nominated by the State Government;*[14]

(d) *one person each from amongst Muslim, to be nominated by the State Government from recognised scholars in shia and sunni Islamic Theology.*

(e) *an person amongst muslims, to be nominated by the State Government from amongst the officers of the State Government not below the rank of Joint Secretary to the State Government;*

(1A) No Minister of the Central Government or, as the case may be, a State Government, shall be elected or nominated as a member of the Board:[15]

Provided that in case of a Union Territory, the Board shall consist of not less than five and not more than seven members to be appointed by

13 Inserted by Act 27 of 2013, S.4 for "wakfs."

14 Substituted by Act 27 of 2013, S. 13 (I) (iii), for cls. (c) to (e).

15 Inserted by Act 27 of 2013, S. 13 (II).

the Central Government from categories specified under sub-clauses (i) to (iv) of clause (b) or clauses (c) to (e) in sub-section (1):

Provided further that at least two members appointed on the Board shall be women:

Provided also that in every case where the system of mutawalli exists, there shall be one mutawalli as the member of the Board.

(2) *Election of the members specified in clause (b) of sub-section (1) shall be held in accordance with the system of proportional representation by means of a single transferable vote, in such manner as may be prescribed:*

Provided that where the number of Muslim Member of Parliament, the State Legislature or the State Bar council, as the case may be, is only one, such Muslim Member shall be declared to have been elected on the Board:

Provided further that where there are no Muslim Members in any of the categories mentioned in sub-clauses (i) to (iii) of clause (b) of sub-section (1), the ex-Muslim Members of Parliament, the State Legislature or ex-member of the State Bar Council, as the case may be, shall constitute the electoral college.

(3) *Notwithstanding anything contained in this section, where the State Government is satisfied, for reasons to be recorded in writing, that it is not reasonably practicable to constitute an electoral college for any of the categories mentioned in sub-clause (i) to (iii) of clause (b) of sub-section (1), the State Government may nominate such persons as the members of the Board as it deems fit.*

(4) *The number of elected members of the Board shall, at all times, be more than the nominated members of the Board except as provided under sub-section (3).*

(5) *[***] Sub Section 5 omitted*[16]

(6) *In determining the number of Shia member or Sunni members of the Board, the State Government shall have regard to the number and value of Shia auqaf and Sunni auqafs to be administered by the Board and appointment of the members shall be made, so far as may be, in accordance with such determination.*

(7) *[***] Sub Section 7 omitted*[17]

16 Sub-section (5) omitted by Act 27 of 2013, S. 13 (III).
17 Sub-section (7) omitted by Act 27 of 2013, S. 13 (IV).

(8) ***Whenever the Board is constituted or re-constituted, the members of the Board present at a meeting convened for the purpose shall elect one from amongst themselves as the Chairperson of the Board.***

(9) ***The members of the Board shall be appointed by the State Government by notification in of Official Gazette.***

Reflections

Analogous sections under Wakf Act 1954 are S.10 and S.11.

This section enumerates various categories of members to be elected or nominated for the constitution of Waqf Board. The Waqf Act 1995 has democratised the process of constitution of Waqf Board by making provision for election of Members from different electoral colleges/segments. At all times the number of elected Members shall be more than nominated Members.

Sub-clause (iii) of clause (b) under sub-section (1) has been substituted by Waqf Amendment Act 2013 (Act 27 of 2013). Before substitution this clause read as under:

"(iii) Muslim Members of the Bar council of the states, and"

Clauses (c) and (e) have been substituted by Waqf Amendment Act 2013 (Act 27 of 2013). Prior to their substitution these clauses read as under:

> (c) one and not more than two members to be nominated by the state government representing eminent Muslim organisations; (d) one and not more than two members to be nominated by the State Government, each from recognised scholar in Islamic theology (e) an officer of the state government not below the rank of 'Deputy Secretary.'

Sub-sections (5) and (7) have been omitted by Waqf Amendment Act 2013 (Act 27 of 2013). Prior to their omission Sub-Sections (5) and (7) read as under:

> (5) where there are shia wakfs but no separate wakfs boards exists, at least one of the members from the categories listed in sub-section (1) shall be Shia Muslim.
>
> (7) in the case of Union territory other than Delhi, the Board shall consist of not less than three and not more than five members to be appointed by the central government from amongst the categories of persons specified in sub-section (1):
>
> Provided that there shall be one mutawalli as the Member of the Board.

After completion of the process of election and nomination of the Members the State Government shall issue a notification in the official gazette to this effect. Then the meeting of the Members shall be convened for the election of the chairperson from amongst these Members.

This Act came in to force on 1 January 1996. The validity of the Waqf Boards constituted before the commencement of this Act and which continue on or after 1 January 1996 was challenged before the courts.

Section 24 of General Clauses Act makes it clear that the actions taken under the previous Act, which is repealed or re-enacted with or without modifications, shall be valid unless otherwise expressly provided in the newly enacted or Amended Act. The section 24 of General Clauses Act states that:

> Where any Central Act or Regulation is, after the commencement of the Act, repealed and re-enacted with or without modification, then, unless it is otherwise expressly provided, any appointment, notification, order, scheme, rule, form or bye-law, made or issued under the repealed Act or Regulation shall, so far as it is not inconsistent with the provision re-enacted, continue in force and be deemed to have been made or issued under the provisions so re-enacted, unless and until it is superseded by any appointment, notification, order, scheme, rule, form or bye-law, made or issued under the provisions so re-enacted.

Hence the waqf administration flows in continuity even after the enforcement of the Waqf Act 1995 which nullifies the previous waqf legislations.

Judicial response

The validity of Waqf Board constituted under the provisions of previous Act, i.e., Wakf Act 1954, was questioned in Muslim Minority Front vs. Andhra Pradesh[18] before the High Court of Andhra Pradesh, which held that:

> All members of the Board appointed under Section 11 of the Wakf Act, 1954 shall vacate their office the moment notification Under Section 14(9) of the Wakf Act, 1995 is issued. They can hold the office, thus, pursuant to the judgment in W.A. 401/95 and batch until the composition of the Board under the Wakf Act, 1954 (sic. 1995) is completed, but not a day more. The new Board shall assume office on the appointment of the members thereof and the members appointed Under Section 11 of the Wakf Act, 1954 shall have no claim whatsoever for any office in the Board.

The term of the Rajasthan Waqf Board expired on 2 January 1995. When the government of Rajasthan appointed an administrator for the Waqf Board on the expiry of the term of the board constituted under the Waqf Act 1954. The petitioner challenged the decision of the government of Rajasthan in

18 (1996) 2 ALT 30.

appointing an administrator to the Waqf Board. The Rajasthan High Court, while dealing this case in Shoukat Ali Ansari vs. State of Rajasthan,[19] held that:

> There is no question of colourable exercise of powers in this type of cases. In fact, it appears that because of certain reasons, the past Govt. continued their term even though their initial term of five years came to an end way back in 1995 itself. The constitution of the Board is to be first made under Section 14 of the new Act by the State Govt. and then the members have to elect their Chairperson. In my opinion, the petitioner has no such right to continue till the new Wakf Board is constituted.

The matter pertaining to inclusion of managing committees of the waqf institutions in the electoral college for the election of the mutawallis as Members of the Waqf Board came up for consideration before Andhra Pradesh High Court in Abdul Khadeer Beig vs. Government of Andhra Pradesh,[20] and the court held that:

> However to avoid any uncertainties, we make it clear that the committees that are existing as on the date of notification issued in terms of Section 14 of the Act, and on the date of actual polling, should be held to be entitled to be part of the electoral colleges.

The Delhi High Court in W.P. (C) No.9980/2017, Rana Parween Siddiqui vs. Union of India and Others[21] ruled that under Section 14 (1)(b) (iii) a senior Muslim Advocate can be nominated to the Waqf Board only if a there is no existing Muslim Member of the State Bar Council or Ex-Member (Muslim) of the State Bar Council.

****

Section 15

Term of Office:-

> ***The members of the Board shall hold office for a term of five years <u>from the date of notification referred to in sub-section (9) of section 14</u>.***[22]

----

19 AIR 1999 Raj. 175.
20 2008 (2) ALD 33.
21 AIR 2018 Delhi 90.
22 Inserted by Act 27 of 2013, S. 14.

Reflections

Analogous section under Wakf Act 1954 is S.12.

Section 15 prescribes a term of five years for the board under sub-section (9) of section (14). The Chair-Person can be removed through a no-confidence motion with the prior permission of the State Government concerned after a lapse of 12 months from the date of election of such a Chair-Person.

Judicial response

A Bench of High Court of Punjab and Haryana in Haji Anwar Ahamed khan vs. Punjab Waqf Board[23] while dealing in the case no-confidence motion against the Chair-Person of the Waqf Board has held that:

> It is in the fitness of things keeping in view the larger public policy as well that a meeting, which has to consider the motion of No Confidence against the Chairman should be convened by the Government and if the motion of No Confidence is carried, the members in the same meeting may be able to elect a new Chairman in accordance with Rule 6 ...

A division bench of Kerala High Court, in T.A. Ahammed Kabeer vs. State of Kerala and others,[24] held that membership of the Waqf Board in the category of Muslim Members of Parliament and State Legislature is co-terminus with dissolution or expiry of their Membership of Parliament or State Legislature. The Members in this category are deemed to have vacated office of Member of Waqf Board from the date he ceases to be Member of State Legislature or Parliament.

****

Section 16

Disqualification for being appointed or for continuing as, a member of the Board:-

A person shall be disqualified for being appointed, or for continuing as, a member of the Board if-

(a) ***he is not a Muslim and is less than twenty-one years of age;***
(b) ***he is found to be a person of unsound mind;***
(c) ***he is an undischarged insolvent;***

23 AIR 1980 P&H 306.
24 AIR 2017 (NOC) 72 KER.

(d) ***he has been convicted of an offence involving moral turpitude and such conviction has not been reversed or he has not been granted full pardon in respect of such offence;***

(da) he has been held guilty of encroachment on any waqf property;[25]

(e) ***he has been on a previous occasion-***
   (i) ***removed from his office as a member or as a mutawalli, or***
   (ii) ***removed by an order of a competent court or tribunal from any position of trust either for mismanagement or for corruption.***

Reflections

Analogous section under Wakf Act 1954 is S.13.

This section describes the disqualification for a Member and prescribes encroachment on waqf property as one of the disqualifications under newly inserted clause (da). This section attempts to eliminate corrupt persons from being the Member of the Waqf Board.

Judicial response

Continuous absence for three consecutive meetings is not a valid ground for disqualification of a Member. In the case of P.K.M. Kutty Haji vs. State of Kerala & Ors,[26] the Kerala High Court has held that mere absence of a Member of the Board for three consecutive meetings is not a reasonable ground to attract section 20 (1) (b) to issue show cause notice (for disqualification).

****

Section 17

Meetings of the Board:-

(1) ***The Board shall meet for the transaction of business at such time and places as may be provided by regulations.***
(2) ***The Chairperson, or in his absence, any member chosen by the members from amongst themselves shall preside at a meeting of the Board.***

25 Inserted by Act 27 of 2013, S. 15.
26 AIR 2009 (NOC) 596 (Ker).

(3) ***Subject to the provisions of this Act, all questions which come before any meeting of the Board shall be decided by a majority of votes of the members present, and in the case of equality of votes, the Chairperson or, in his absence, any other person presiding shall have a second or casting vote.***

Reflections

Analogous section under Wakf Act 1954 is S.14.

The meetings shall be presided over by the Chair-Person. In the absence of the Chair-Person for any reason, a Member chosen by the Members present shall preside over the meetings. All the decisions in the meeting shall be presided and resolved by a majority of votes of the Members present and, in the case of a tie, the chair can exercise a casting vote.

Judicial response

Judicial response pertaining to this section is not found.

****

Section 18

Committees of the Board:-

(1) ***The Board may, whenever it considers necessary, establish either generally or for a particular purpose or for any specified area or areas committees for the supervision of auqaf.***
(2) ***The constitution, functions and duties and the term of office of such committees shall be determined from time to time by the Board: Provided that it shall not be necessary for the members of such committees to be members of the board.***

Reflections

Analogous section under Wakf Act 1954 is S.16.

This section empowers the Waqf Board to constitute committees for specified area or areas for the supervision of auqaf. The duties and functions of such committees shall be determined by the board from time to time. The committee as has been mentioned under this section shall not be construed as a managing committee of a waqf. This section authorises the Waqf Board to constitute as many numbers of committees and as many types of committees for an area or for areas to be specified for the supervision of a waqf. A managing committee can be appointed in place of a mutawalli under section 63 of the Act as the definition of the mutawalli includes a committee or a corporation.

Judicial response

The High court of Karnataka in the case of Abdul Khaleel vs. Karnataka Wakf Board[27] held that the board is entitled to constitute any number of committees and more than one type of committees for the supervision of waqfs.

A Division Bench of the Andhra Pradesh High Court in Andhra Pradesh Wakf Board vs. Mohammad Hidayatulla[28] has held that:

> We have already seen that it is only in a case where the mutawalli has been removed by a proper order or a mutawalli cannot be appointed in certain circumstances that the Board can either under Section 43 (5) or under Section 43-A direct the records to be handed over. As long as the mutawalli is effectively working in office and as long as there are no other proceedings pending against him, we do not think the Board has any power to direct the mutawalli to hand over the record to the committee or to the Board.
>
> The Wakf Board, without assuming direct management of the wakf or removing the mutawalli, cannot keep back in its custody or possession the records relating to the wakf. It has to hand over the entire property belonging to the wakf to the mutawalli. It is true that the Board has special powers of supervision directly or indirectly through the committee constituted under Section 16 of the Act. But that does not mean that the Board can direct the mutawalli to hand over the entire property to the managing committee or to the Board without having any recourse to Section 43 or S, 43-A.

The Karnataka High Court in Janab Shastry Khaja Hussain vs. Karnataka Board of Wakf,[29] observed that:

> Suffice it to say that since the terms subject to which the Committee was appointed themselves authorised the Board to wind up the Committee at its pleasure, it is difficult to see how any such order of dissolution could be said to be bad particularly when the Members of the Committee so

27 1988 (1) CLJ 251.
28 AIR 1974 AP 287.
29 1997 AIHC 4146.

> appointed had accepted the said appointment on those terms without any reservation. In the totality of the above circumstances therefore I see no reason to interfere.

In Md. Saleem ur Rahman vs. A.P. State Wakf Board,[30] the Bench of High Court of Andhra Pradesh lead by L. Narasimha Reddy, held that:

> The administration of a Wakf predominantly vests with the Mutawalli, appointed through succession or otherwise. The appointment of a Committee arises only when the Wakf does not have a Muthawalli. Conversely, no Committee can be appointed as long as the Mutawalli functions for a Wakf.

The above judgements have underlined the difference between supervision of the waqfs and management of the waqf institutions. A supervisory committee is distinct from a mutawalli or a managing committee. Thus, a supervisory committee cannot enter in to the shoes of a mutawalli.

****

Section 19

Resignation of Chairperson and members:-

> ***The Chairperson or any other member may resign his office by writing under his hand addressed to the State Government:***
>
> ***Provided that the Chairperson or the member shall continue in office until the appointment of his successor is notified in the Official Gazette.***

Reflections

Analogous section under Wakf Act 1954 is S.17.

The Chair-Person or any Member of the Waqf Board may resign from his office by addressing a resignation letter to the State Government concerned and he/she shall relinquish his/her office after appointment of the successor is notified in the official gazette.

30 2007 (4) ALT 834.

Judicial response

Judicial response pertaining to this section is not found.

****

Section 20

Removal of Chairperson and member:-

(1) ***The State Government may, by notification in the Official Gazette, remove the Chairperson of the Board or any member thereof if he-***
   (a) ***is or becomes subject to any disqualifications specified in section 16; or***
   (b) ***refuses to act or is incapable of acting or acts in a manner which the State Government, after hearing any explanation that he may offer, considers to be prejudicial to the interests of the auqaf; or***
   (c) ***fails in the opinion of the Board, to attend three consecutive meetings of the Board, without sufficient excuse.***

(2) ***Where the Chairperson of the Board is removed under sub-section (1), he shall also cease to be a member of the Board.***

Reflections

Analogous section under Wakf Act 1954 is S.18.

This section specifies the disqualifications for the Chair-Person and any Member and for their removal.

Judicial response

Mere misbehaviour of a Member of the Wakf Board with the Chair-Person of the Wakf Board does disqualify him from the membership to initiate action against him under Section 18(1) (b) of Wakf Act 1954 (now refer under section 20 of Waqf Act 1995) as held by the Andhra Pradesh High Court in Akthar Ahmad vs. State of Andhra Pradesh.[31] The Court while referring to a decision of the Court of Appeal in Picture Houses vs. Wednesbury Corpn,[32] observed that:

> Merely because a Statute gives power to an administrative authority to arrive at a subjective determination, it does not at all mean that any order,

31 AIR 1964 AP 244.
32 (1947) 2 KB 680 p. 682.

however patently unreasonable and arbitrary it be, can be passed by it under cover of mat statute it passes such an order, it arrogates to itself a power and a jurisdiction which the statute did not Intend to confer on it.

Continuous absence for three consecutive meetings is not a valid ground for disqualification of a Member. In the case of P.K.M. Kutty Haji vs. State of Kerala & Ors,[33] the Kerala High Court has held that mere absence of a Member of the Board for three consecutive meetings is not a reasonable ground to attract section 20 (1) (b) to issue show cause notice (for disqualification).

****

Section 20A

Removal of chairperson by vote of no confidence:- [34]

Without prejudice to the provisions of section 20, the chairperson of a Board may be removed by vote of no confidence in the following manner, namely:-

(a) *No resolution expressing a vote of confidence or no confidence in any person elected as chairperson of a Board shall be moved except in the manner prescribed and twelve months have not elapsed after the date of his election as a Chairperson and be removed except with prior permission of the State Government,*
(b) *Notice for no confidence shall be addressed to the State Government stating clearly the grounds on which such motion is proposed to be moved and shall be signed by at least half the total members of the Board;*
(c) *At least three members of the Board signing the notice of no confidence shall personally present to the State Government, the notice together with an affidavit signed by them to the effect that the signatures on no confidence motion are genuine and have been made by the signatories after hearing or reading the contents of the notice;*
(d) *On receipt of the notice of no confidence, as provided hereinabove, the State Government shall fix such time, date and place as may be considered suitable for holding a meeting for the purpose of the proposed no confidence motion:*

Provided that at least fifteen days notice shall be given for such a meeting;

(e) *Notice for the meeting under clause (d) shall also provide that in the event of no confidence motion being duly carried on or, election of the*

33 AIR 2009 (NOC) 596 (Ker).
34 Inserted by Act 27 of 2013, S. 16.

new Chairperson, as the case may be, shall also be held in the same meeting.

(f) *The State Government shall also nominate a Gazetted Officer (other than an officer of the department which is concerned with supervision and administration of the Board) to act as presiding officer of the meeting in which the resolution for no confidence shall be considered;*

(g) *The quorum for such a meeting of the Board shall be one-half of the total number of members of the Board;*

(h) *The resolution for no confidence shall be deemed to be carried out, if passed by a simple majority of the members present;*

(i) *If a resolution for no confidence is carried out, the Chairperson shall cease to hold office forthwith and shall be succeeded by his successor who shall be elected by another resolution in the same meeting;*

(j) *Election of the new Chairperson shall be conducted under clause (i) in the meeting under the chairmanship of the said presiding officer referred to in clause (f), in the following manner, namely:*

  (A) *Chairperson shall be elected from amongst the elected members of the Board;*

  (B) *Nomination of candidates shall be proposed and seconded in the meeting itself and election after withdrawal, if any, shall be held by method of secret ballot;*

  (C) *Election shall be held by simple majority of the members present in the meeting and in case of equality of votes, the matter shall be decided by drawing of lots; and*

  (D) *Proceedings of the meeting shall be signed by the presiding officer;*

(k) *New chairperson elected under clause (h) shall hold the office only up to the remainder of the term of the Chairperson removed by the resolution of no confidence; and*

(l) *if the motion for passing the resolution of no confidence fails for want of quorum or lack of requisite majority at the meeting, no subsequent meeting for considering the motion of no confidence shall be held within six months of the date of the previous meeting."*

Reflections

This is a new Section inserted under the Section 16 of Amendment Act of 2013. Hence there is no analogous section under Wakf Act 1954.

This is a new section inserted vide Waqf Amendment Act 2013 (Act 27 of 2013) providing for removal of a Chair-Person through a motion of no confidence. But a no-confidence motion can be moved only with the prior permission of the State Government concerned after a lapse of 12 months from the date of the election of such a chairperson.

Judicial response

A Bench of the High Court of Punjab and Haryana in Haji Anwar Ahamed khan vs. Punjab Waqf Board[35] has observed that:

> It is accepted principle of common law relating to the removal of the holder of an office that the body which has authority to elect its Chairman has the inherent and implied power to remove the Chairman. If the Chairman holds his office at pleasure, then he can be removed at will, but if he holds his office otherwise than at pleasure, he can be removed only for cause after notice and hearing. In view of the principles of common law stated above, until and unless there is a provision in the statute barring the removal of the Chairman by a vote of no confidence it has to be held that the members who had the power to elect the Chairman have the power to remove the Chairman by a majority of votes. This principle is also enshrined in the provisions of S. 21 of the General Clauses Act, 1897.

This issue of admissibility of no-confidence motion against the chairperson of the Waqf Board has been put to rest by the insertion of Section 20 A.

****

Section 21

Filling of a vacancy:-

> ***When the seat of member becomes vacant by his removal, resignation, death or otherwise, a new member shall be appointed in his place and such member shall hold office so long as the member whose place he fills would have been entitled to hold office, if such vacancy had not occurred.***

Reflections

Analogous section under Wakf Act 1954 is S.19.

This section specifies that, in the case of a vacancy, the newly appointed Member shall hold office for the remaining period of the relinquished Member in whose place the new Member is elected or nominated.

35 AIR 1980 P&H 306.

Judicial response

Judicial response pertaining to this section is not found.

****

Section 22

Vacancies etc., not to invalidate proceedings of the Board:-

> ***No act or proceeding of the Board shall be invalid by reason only of the existence of any vacancy amongst its members or any defect in the constitution thereof.***

Reflections

Analogous section under Wakf Act 1954 is S.20.

This section validates the proceedings of the board in spite of any vacancy of a Member or any shortcomings in the constitution of the board.

Judicial response

Judicial response pertaining to this section is not found.

****

Section 23

Appointment of Chief Executive Officer and his term of office and other conditions of service:-

(1) *There shall be a full-time Chief Executive Officer of the Board who shall be a Muslim and shall be appointed by the State Government, by notification in the Official Gazette, from a panel of two names suggested by the Board and who shall not be below the rank of Deputy Secretary to the State Government, and in case of non-availability of a Muslim officer of that rank, a Muslim officer of equivalent rank may be appointed on deputation.*[36]

(2) ***The term of office and other conditions of service of the chief Executive Officer shall be such as may be prescribed.***

36 Substituted by Act 27 of 2013, S. 17.

(3) ***The Chief Executive Officer shall be ex officio Secretary of the Board and shall be under the administrative control of the Board.***

Reflections

Analogous section under Wakf Act 1954 is S.21.

The sub-section 1 under this section (23) has been redrafted and inserted vide Waqf Amendment Act (Act 27 of 2013). Before substitution, this section read as under:

> "(1) there shall be a Chief Executive Officer of the Board who shall be a Muslim and shall be appointed by the State Government, in consultation with the board, by notification in the Official Gazette."

Previously, the State Government concerned used to appoint the Chief Executive Officer in consultation with the board concerned. Now, under the present provision, the State Government shall appoint the Chief Executive Officer from among the panel of two names forwarded by the board.

The term of office and conditions of service may be such as prescribed. The Chief Executive Officer shall be the Ex-officio Secretary of the Board.

Judicial response

Judicial response pertaining to this section is not found.

****

Section 24

Officers and other employees of the Board:-

(1) ***The Board shall have the assistance of such number of officers and other employees as may be necessary for the efficient performance of its functions under this Act, details thereof shall be determined by the Board in consultation with the State Government.***
(2) ***The appointment of officers and other employees, their term of office and conditions of service shall be such as may be provided by regulations.***

Reflections

Analogous section under Wakf Act 1954 is S.21 B inserted by Amendment Act of 69 of 1984.

Under this section, the Waqf Board shall recruit such a number of employees as may be necessary for the efficient functioning of the board. The service conditions of the employees shall be regulated as per the regulations framed for this purpose. It is always better if the service conditions of the employees are at par with the employees of the State Government. It is advisable if the State Government provides annual administrative grants to the board under a non-plan budget to meet the administrative expenses, including the salaries of the employees.

Judicial response

Judicial response pertaining to this section is not found.

****

Section 25

Duties and powers of Chief Executive Officer:-

(1) ***Subject to the provisions of this Act and of the rules made there under and the directions of the Board, functions of the chief Executive Officer shall include-***
   (a) ***investigating the nature and extent of auqaf and waqf properties and calling whenever necessary, an inventory of waqf properties and calling, from time to time for accounts, returns and information from mutawallis;***
   (b) ***inspecting or causing inspection of waqf properties and account, records, deeds or documents relating thereto;***
   (c) ***doing generally of such acts as may be necessary for the control, maintenance and superintendence of auqaf.***

(2) ***In exercising the powers of giving directions under sub-section (1) in respect of any waqf, the Board shall act in conformity with the directions by the wakif in the deed of the waqf, the purpose of waqf and such usage and customs of the waqf as are sanctioned by the school of Muslim law to which the waqf belongs.***

(3) ***Save as otherwise expressly provided in this Act, the Chief Executive Officer shall exercise such powers and perform such duties as may be assigned to him or delegated to him under this Act.***

Reflections

Analogous section under Wakf Act 1954 is S.21 C inserted by Amendment Act of 69 of 1984.

The Chief Executive Officer is the administrative and executive head and Ex-officio Secretary of the State Waqf Board. He can call for the inventory of the waqf properties and assets of the waqf institutions. He has powers to inspect the records, deeds, documents and accounts of the waqf institutions and their properties. He can also inspect or cause to inspect the waqf properties and their extent.

He has every power for the superintendence and control of waqfs. His powers are quasi-judicial in nature. But at the same time the Chief Executive Officer shall have due regard for the instructions of the wakif, customs and traditions followed by a waqf institution. He shall discharge his duties under the administrative control of the Waqf Board.

Judicial response

The powers of the Waqf Board and the powers of the Chief Executive Officer are not analogous and the same. The Andhra Pradesh High Court, in Gajjala Venkateshwarlu and Another vs. A.P. State Wakf Tribunal, Hyderabad,[37] observed that the powers of the Wakf Board are different and distinct from those of the Chief Executive Officer.

The High Court of Bombay in Mansoor Kasim Mulla vs. Guddu Saheb Ibrahim Mugale & Anr,[38] has held that the orders passed by the Chief Executive Officer can be recalled by the Chief Executive Officer himself.

The Andhra Pradesh High Court in Agrapu Venkatamma vs. Revenue Divisional Officer, Srikakulam and others,[39] held that the powers of the Chief Executive Officer are quasi-judicial in nature and observed that:

> Throughout its length, Section 54 of the Act empowers the Chief Executive Officer alone, and it does not enable him to delegate his powers to any other authority. Admittedly, in the instant case, the notice referable to Sub-section (1) was issued by the third respondent. Therefore, it is per se without jurisdiction. Further, the said notice did not entail in passing of any final orders.
>
> "Another aspect of the matter is that, after the exercise contemplated under Section 54 becomes final, and the removal of encroachment does not materialize, the second respondent is empowered under Section 55, to request or approach the revenue authority to cause removal of encroachments. Here again, there is a serious lapse. The first respondent

37 2003 (3), ALD 269.
38 AIR 2010, (NOC) Bom, 835.
39 2007 (2), ALT 595.

did not refer to any request made by the second respondent. Viewed from any angle, the impugned action cannot be sustained.

The High Court of Bombay, in Farid Abdul Latif Noorani vs. Sayed Sadiq Ali Qadri & Others[40] also held that the powers of the Chief Executive Officer were quasi-judicial in nature.

****

Section 26

Powers of Chief Executive Officer in respect of orders or resolutions of Board:-

Where the Chief Executive Officer considers that an order or resolution passed by the Board-

(a) ***has not been passed in accordance with the law; or***
(b) ***is in excess of or is an abuse of the powers conferred on the Board by or under this Act or by any other law; or***
(c) ***if implemented, is likely to-***
    (i) ***cause financial loss to the Board or to the concerned waqf or to the auqaf generally; or***
    (ii) ***lead to a riot or breach of peace; or***
    (iii) ***cause danger to human life, health or safety; or***
(d) ***is not beneficial to the Board or to any waqf or to auqaf generally,***

he may, before implementing such order or resolution place the matter before the Board for its reconsideration and, if such order or resolution is not confirmed by a majority of vote of the members present and voting after such reconsideration, refer the matter to the State Government along with his objections to the order or resolution, and the decision of the State Government thereon shall be final.

Reflections

Analogous section under Wakf Act 1954 is S.21 D inserted by Amendment Act of 69 of 1984.

The Waqf Act provides an exclusive power to the Chief Executive Officer empowering him to submit the resolution of the board for its reconsideration if he is of the opinion that the resolution or order passed

40 AIR 2009, (NOC) 1935 (Bom).

by the board is improper or it is not in the interest of waqf or the board. While submitting any resolution for the reconsideration of the board, he shall also give the objections, suggestions and reasons in writing in support of his contention. This is an important power and function bestowed on the Chief Executive Officer of the Waqf Board. But if such a resolution or order fails to be confirmed by the majority of votes of the Members present, then such resolution shall be referred to the State Government for its decision.

Judicial response

The Andhra Pradesh High Court in M.A. Azeem Baig vs. Chief Executive Officer, A.P.[41] observed that:

> This Court has perused the note file as well as the draft proceedings and other relevant documents in the file, which would clinchingly show that the decision to place the petitioner under suspension pending enquiry was in fact taken by the Special Officer of Waqf Board on the ground that the CEO is not competent to pass orders, therefore, the impugned proceedings cannot be invalidated.

****

Section 27

Delegation of powers by the Board:-[42]

> *The Board may, by a general or special order in writing, delegate to the Chairperson, any other member, the Chief Executive Officer or any other officer or servant of the Board or any area committee, subject to such conditions and limitations as may be specified in the said order, such of its powers and duties under this Act, as it may deem necessary, except the powers and functions of the Board mentioned under clauses (c), (d), (g) and (j) of sub-section (2) of section 32 and section 110.*

----

41 2005 (6) ALD 858; AIR.
42 Substituted by Act 27 of 2013, S. 18, for S. 27.

Reflections

Analogous section under Wakf Act 1954 is S.22.

The board is empowered to pass orders to delegate powers to its chairperson, its Member, Secretary/Chief Executive Officer, any area committee or any other officer or employee of the board by specifying the extent of such powers and duties.

This section has been substituted by the Waqf Amendment Act 2013 (Act 27 of 2013). Prior to its substitution, S. 27 read as under:

> 27. Delegation of powers by the Board: The Board may, by a general or special order in writing, delegate to the chairperson, any other member, the secretary or any other officer or servant of the Board or any area committee, subject to such condition and limitation as may be specified in the said order, such of its powers and duties under this Act, as it may deem necessary.

While delegating the powers, limitations and restrictions may be imposed. But, in any case, the powers and functions of the board mentioned under clauses (c), (d), (g) and (j) of sub-section (2) of section 32 and section 110 should not be delegated.

Judicial response

Section 27 of the Waqf Act 1995 provides for delegation of powers by the Waqf Board to the Chair-Person, a Member, Secretary or any other officer of the board or any area committee. The Andhra Pradesh High Court in M.A. Aziz vs. A.P. State Wakf Board and another[43] held that the Wakf Board cannot make blanket delegation of all its powers to any person indiscriminately and observed that:

> It is fundamental to note that whenever any stigma is cast on any individual or Committee or group of persons, before passing any order by the statutory authority, some opportunity is bound to be given as otherwise it would offend the principles of natural justice... Therefore, with all anxiety this Court is dealing with the matters to set the things right and to remind the Wakf Board and the authorities under the Act to act in accordance with the principles of natural justice.

****

43 AIR 1998 AP 61.

Section 28

Power of District Magistrate, Additional District Magistrate or Sub-Divisional Magistrate to implement the directions of the Board.—[44]

> *Subject to the provisions of this Act and the rules made there under, the District Magistrate or in his absence an Additional District Magistrate or Sub-Divisional Magistrate of a District in the State shall be responsible for implementation of the decisions of the Board which may be conveyed through the Chief Executive Officer and the Board may, wherever considers necessary, seek directions from the Tribunal for the implementation of its decisions.*

Reflections

Analogous section under Wakf Act 1954 is S.22 A, inserted by Amendment Act 69 of 1984.

This section has been completely overhauled and substituted by the Waqf Amendment Act 2013 (Act 27 of 2013). Previously, the Chief Executive Officer was entitled to exercise his powers with the approval of the Waqf Board through the District Collector/Magistrate or any other officer authorised on his behalf. The previous section runs as under:

> 28 (1) Subject to the provisions of this Act and of the rules made there under, the Chief Executive Officer may exercise all or any of the powers conferred on him by or under this Act with the previous approval of the Board through the Commissioner of the division or the Collector of the district in which the concerned Waqf property is situated or through any other Gazetted Officer whom he may appoint for such purpose and may, from time to time, delegate any of his powers to any such Commissioner of the division or Collector or any other Gazetted Officer and may, at any time revoke the delegations so made by him.
>
> 28 (2) Where any delegation of powers is made by the Chief Executive Officer under sub-section (1), the person to whom such delegation is made may exercise those powers in the same manner and to the same extent as if they have been conferred on him directly by this Act and not by way of delegation.

But under the present section, the District Magistrate, or, in his absence, an Additional District Magistrate or Sub-Divisional Magistrate of a District

44 Substituted by Act 27 of 2013, S. 19, for S. 28.

in the State, shall be responsible for the implementation of the decisions of the board, which may be conveyed through the Chief Executive Officer and the board may, wherever it considers necessary, seek directions from the Tribunal for the implementation of its decisions.

Judicial response

Judicial response pertaining to this section is not found.

****

Section 29

Powers of Chief Executive Officer to inspect records, registers, etc.:-

(1) *The Chief Executive Officer or any officer of the Board duly authorised by him in this behalf shall, subject to such conditions as may be prescribed*[45] *be entitled to all reasonable time to inspect in any public office, any records, registers or other documents relating to a waqf or movable or immovable properties which are waqf properties or are claimed to be waqf properties*[46].

(2) *The mutawalli or any other person having the custody of any document related to waqf properties shall produce the same, within the prescribed period, before the Chief Executive Officer on being called upon to do so in writing.*[47]

(3) *Subject to such conditions as may be prescribed, an agency of the Government or any other organisation shall supply, within ten working days, copies of the records, registers of properties or other documents relating to waqf properties or claimed to be waqf properties, to the Chief Executive Officer on a written request to this effect from him:*

Provided that before taking any course of action as mentioned in subsections (2) and (3), the Chief Executive Officer shall obtain approval of the Board."

----

45 Substituted by Act 27 of 2013, S.20 (A).

46 S. 29 renumbered as sub-S.(1) thereof by Act 27 of 2013, S. 20.

47 Inserted by Act 27 of 2013, S. 20 (b).

Reflections

Analogous section under Wakf Act 1954 is S.22 B, inserted by Amendment Act 69 of 1984.

This section has been substantially modified; two new sub-sections have been inserted by Waqf Amendment Act 2013 (Act 27 of 2013).

The words "subject to such conditions as may be prescribed" have been substituted by the Waqf Amendment Act 2013 (Act 27 of 2013) for the words "subject to such conditions and restrictions as may be prescribed and subject to the payment of such fees as may be leviable under any law for the time being in force."

Under the unamended section, the board could authorise the Chief Executive Officer or any other officer to inspect the records at any reasonable time. The previous section states as under:

> The Chief Executive Officer or any officer of the Board duly authorised by him in this behalf shall, subject to such conditions and restrictions as may be prescribed and subject to the payment of such fees as may be leviable under any law for the time being in force, be entitled at all reasonable time to inspect, in any public office, any records, registers or other documents relating to a waqf or movable or immovable properties which are Waqf properties or are claimed to be Waqf properties.

Now the Amendment Act of 2013 has made it mandatory on the part of the Government Departments and Agencies to provide copies of the document within ten days from the date of such requisition.

Judicial response

Judicial response pertaining to this section is not found.

****

Section 30

Inspection of records:-

(1) ***The Board may allow inspection of its proceedings or other records in its custody and issue copies of the same on payment of such fees and subject to such conditions as may be prescribed.***
(2) ***All copies issued under this section shall be certified by the Chief Executive Officer of the Board in the manner provided in section 76 of the Indian Evidence Act, 1872(1 of 1872)***
(3) ***The powers conferred on the Chief Executive Officer by sub-section (2) may be exercised by such other officer or officers of the Board as***

may either generally or specially be authorised in this behalf by the Board.

Reflections

Analogous section under Wakf Act 1954 is S.23.

While section 29 provides for obtaining the documents by the Waqf Board or its Chief Executive Officer, this section makes it obligatory on the part of the Waqf Board to provide certified copies of the documents under its custody by levying the appropriate fee as may be prescribed. The copies of the documents issued under this section shall be certified by the Chief Executive Officer or any other officer authorised on his behalf, in the manner provided in section (76) of the Indian Evidence Act 1872 (Act 1 of 1872).

> The Indian Evidence Act under section 76 prescribes that any certified copy must be issued under signature and seal of the authorised officer and show the date of issue in order to verify that it is a true copy of the document.

The Right to Information Act 2005 (Act 22 of 2005) also makes it mandatory for every Government establishment to provide certified copies of documents to the applicants. This section endeavours to keep the documents or the information in public domain.

Judicial response

Judicial response pertaining to this section is not found.

****

Section 31

Prevention of disqualification for membership of Parliament:-

> ***It is hereby declared that the office of the Chairperson or members of a Board shall not be disqualified and shall be deemed never to have been disqualified for being chosen as, or being, a Member of Parliament or a Member of Union Territory Legislature or a Member of a State Legislature if so declared under a law made by the appropriate State Legislature.***[48]

----

48 Inserted by Act 27 of 2013, S. 21.

Reflections

Analogous section under Wakf Act 1954 is S.24.

This section declares that the office of the Chair-Person or the membership of the board shall not be a disqualification for being a Member of Parliament or the Member of Legislature of the State or Union Territory. The immunity from such disqualifications was made available to the Members of Parliament/Legislature. The words "or a Member of Union Territory Legislature or a Member of a State Legislature if so declared under a law made by the appropriate State Legislature" are inserted by the Waqf Amendment Act 2013 (Act 27 of 2013).

Judicial response

Judicial response pertaining to this section is not found.

****

Section 32

Powers and function of the Board:-

(1) *Subject to any rules that may be made under this Act, the general superintendence of all auqaf in a State shall vest in the Board established or the State; and it shall be the duty of the Board so to exercise its powers under this Act as to ensure that the auqaf under its superintendence are properly maintained, controlled and administered and the income thereof is duly applied to the objects and for the purposes for which such auqaf were created or intended:*

Provided that in exercising its powers under this Act in respect of any waqf, the Board shall act in conformity with the directions of the waqf, the purposes of the waqf and any usage or custom of the waqf sanctioned by the school of Muslim law to which the waqf belongs.

Explanation.-For the removal of doubts, it is hereby declared that in this sub-section, "waqf" includes a waqf in relation to which any scheme has been made by any court of law, whether before or after the commencement of this Act.

(2) *Without prejudice to the generality of the foregoing power, the functions of the Board shall be-*

(a) *to maintain a record containing information relating to the origin, income, object and beneficiaries of every waqf;*

(b) *to ensure that the income and other property of auqaf are applied to the objects and for the purposes for which such auqaf were intended or created;*

(c) *to give directions for the administration of auqaf;*

(d) *to settle schemes of management for a waqf;*
Provided that no such settlement shall be made without giving the parties affected an opportunity of being heard;

(e) *to direct-*
   (i) *the utilisation of the surplus income of a waqf consistent with the objects of a waqf;*
   (ii) *in what manner the income of a waqf, the objects of which are not evidence from any written instrument, shall be utilized,*
   (iii) *in any case where any object of waqf has ceased to exist or has become incapable of achievement, that so much of the income of the waqf as was previously applied to that object shall be applied to any other object, which shall be similar, or nearly similar or to the original object or for the benefit of the poor or for the purpose of promotion of knowledge and learning in the Muslim community:*

Provided that no direction shall be given under this clause without giving the parties affected an opportunity of being heard.

Explanation.-For the purpose of this clause, the powers of the Board shall be exercised-

(i) *in the case of a Sunni waqf, by the Sunni members of the Board only; and*
(ii) *in the case of a Shia waqf, by the Shia members of the Board only:*

Provided that where having regard to the number of the Sunni or Shia members in the Board and other circumstances, it appears to the Board that the power should not be exercised by such members only, it may co-opt such other Muslims being Sunnis or Shias, as the case may be, as it thinks fit, to be temporary members of the Board for exercising its powers under this clause;

(f) *to scrutinise and approve the budget submitted by mutawallis and to arrange for the auditing of account of auqaf;*
(g) *to appoint and approve and remove mutawallis in accordance with the provisions of this Act;*
(h) *to take measures for the recovery of lost properties of any waqf;*
(i) *to institute and defend suits and proceedings relating to auqaf;*
(j) *to sanction lease of any immovable property of a waqf in accordance with the provisions of this Act and the rules made there under;*[49]

49 Substituted by Act 27 of 2013, S. 22(I) (a), for CL. (j).

Provided that no such sanction shall be given unless a majority of not less than two-thirds of the members of the Board present cast their vote in favour of such transaction:

Provided further that where no such sanction is given by the Board, the reasons for doing so shall be recorded in writing.

(k) *to administer the Waqf Fund;*

(l) *to call for such returns, statistics, accounts and other information from the mutawallis with respect to the waqf property as the Board may, from time to time, require;*

(m) *to inspect, or cause inspection of, waqf properties, accounts, records or deeds and documents relating thereto;*

(n) *to investigate and determine the nature and extent of waqf and waqf property, and to cause, whenever necessary, a survey of such waqf property;*

(na) to determine or cause to be determined, in such manner as may be specified by the Board, market rent of the waqf land or building;

(o) *generally do all such acts as may be necessary for the control, maintenance and administration of auqaf.*

(3) *Where the Board has settled any scheme of management under clause (d) or given any direction under clause (e) of sub-section (2), any person interested in the waqf or affected by such settlement or direction may institute a suit in a Tribunal for setting aside such settlement or directions and the decision of the Tribunal thereon shall be final.*

(4) *Where the Board is satisfied that any waqf land, which is a waqf property, has the potential for development as an educational institution, shopping centre, market, housing or residential flats and the like,*[50] *market, housing flats and the like, it may serve upon the mutawalli of the concerned waqf a notice requiring him within such time, but not less than sixty days, as may be specified in the notice, to convey its decision whether he is willing to execute the development works specified in the notice.*

(5) *On consideration of the reply, if any, received to the notice issued under sub-section (4), the Board, if it is satisfied that the mutawalli is not willing or is not capable of executing the works required to be executed in terms of the notice, it may, [******]*[51] *take over the property, clear it of any building or structure thereon, which, in the opinion of the Board is necessary for execution of the works and execute such works*

50 Substituted by Act 27 of 2013, S. 22(II), for "offers a feasible potential for development as a shopping center."

51 The words "with the prior approval of the Government, "omitted by Act 27 of 2013, S. 22 (III).

from Waqf funds or from the finances which may be raised on the security of the properties of the waqf concerned, and control and manage the properties till such time as all expenses incurred by the Board under this section, together with interest thereon, the expenditure on maintenance of such works and other legitimate changes incurred on the property are recovered from the income derived from the property:

Provided that the Board shall compensate annually the mutawalli of the concerned waqf to the extent of the average annual net income derived from the property during the three years immediately preceding the taking over of the property by the Board.

(6) *After all the expenses as enumerated in sub-section (5) have been recouped from the income of the developed properties, the developed properties shall be handed over to mutawalli of the concerned waqf.*

Reflections

Analogous section under Wakf Act 1954 is S.15; sub-sections (4), (5) and (6) are comparable to section 15A of the Wakf Act 1954, as inserted by the Wakf Amendment Act 1984 (Act 69 of 1984).

This section comprehensively discusses the powers and functions of the Waqf Board. As a custodian of the waqf properties in the State concerned, it is the duty and responsibility of the Waqf Board to take care of the administration of the waqf, preparation of scheme of administration, leasing of the waqf property, recovery of the lost properties, etc., as per law. Clause (j) has been substituted by the Waqf Amendment Act 2013 (Act 27 of 2013). Before substitution, this clause read as under:

> (j) to sanction any transfer of immovable property of a wakf by way of sale, gift, mortgage, exchange or lease, in accordance with the provisions of this Act: Provided that no such sanction shall be given unless at least two-thirds of the members of the Board vote in favour of such transaction:

This section provides extensive powers to the Waqf Board. However, the intentions of the wakif and traditional customs and usages shall be respected.

Judicial response

The validity of the powers of the Waqf Board in controlling the functions and duties of the mutawalli was challenged as unconstitutional and violative of Article 26 (b) of the Constitution before the High Court of Madhya

Pradesh in the case of Usman Ali Khan vs. Faezulla.[52] But the court, while rejecting this contention, upheld the Constitutional validity of such powers of the Waqf Board stating that "it is not without significance that Section 42 under which the Board acted in appointing a Committee has not been assailed as unconstitutional."

The Waqf Board has to ensure the proper safeguarding of the waqf properties and the proper management of waqf institutions. It can prepare the scheme of administration of the waqf institution. But, in some cases, courts have prepared schemes for the administration of waqf institutions. A Bench of the High Court of Madras, in Narayanamoorthi vs. Achayya Sastrulu,[53] observed that:

> It is far from desirable that courts should assume to themselves the continued supervision of institutions, for the management of which they are called upon to frame schemes. In fact, under such schemes the courts of law constitute themselves in some manner as temple committees and the whole burden of such functions for all time is thrown upon the courts. It is very undesirable that the courts should be burdened with such tasks. Even in the interests of the institutions themselves it is doubtful if such provisions are calculated to promote their improvements or efficiency.

In State of Madras vs. Sri Mahalingaswami Devasthanam (1957) 1 M.L.J. 350 : I.L.R. (1957) Mad. 752, dealing with the provisions of the Madras Hindu Religious and Charitable Endowments Act, a Division Bench of this Court has observed that the power to call for a budget, though vested in the Court under the scheme, vests in the Commissioner after the commencement of the Act and the Civil Court has no jurisdiction to call for or approve a budget, and that after the coming into force of the Act, the trustee should submit the budget only to the Commissioner and not to the Court. In Mayadhar vs. Orissa Board of Waqfs, dealing with an application by the mutawalli for the sanction of a lease, the Court observed that, after the passing of the Wakf Act, 1954, the board had been given specific powers for grant of lease for a term exceeding three years, that such a provision barred the jurisdiction of the civil Courts to take cognisance of an application asking for sanction of such leases and that it was open to the parties to make such an application to the Board itself which alone was competent to accord sanction.

The Waqf Board is the custodian of the waqf properties in the State concerned. The general superintendence and control over the administration of waqf institutions is the duty of the Waqf Board. In C.S. Peeran Sahib vs.

52 AIR 1959 MP 377.
53 AIR 1925 Mad 411; (1924) 47 M.L.J. 714 and 718.

State Wakf Board, Madras,[54] the High Court of Madras, while referring to the above judgements, held that the Wakf Act 29 of 1954 vested the powers of superintendence and control of all waqfs on the board and further observed that:

> It is the duty of the Mutawalli to obey the directions of the Board in the matter of getting the suit properties registered under the Act and submitting accounts etc., to it, notwithstanding the fact that there is a scheme framed by the Civil Court in force.

While discussing the powers of the Wakf Board vis-à-vis the powers of the State and Central Governments in regulating the activities of wakf institutions, the High Court of Madras, in Raichand J. Shah vs. State of Tamil Nadu & Secretary, Tamil Nadu Wakf Board,[55] extensively analysed the powers of the Waqf Board in relation to the powers of the Central and State Governments and observed that:

> The power vested in the Wakf Boards so constituted under the Wakf Act is a power which itself is in the nature of a trust and even in the exercise of that power, the Board does not enjoy unlimited authority.
>
> Resolutions made by the Board, which in the opinion of the State Government are detrimental to the interest of the wakfs, are certainly capable of being interfered with and in respect of which directions are capable of being given by the State Government for which express provision is made in section 63 of the Wakf Act 1954" [section 97 of the Wakf Act 1995].

The High Court of Andhra Pradesh in Yousuf Begum vs. Wakf Board, Hyderabad and Another,[56] has held that:

> If it is a service inam the question of the petitioner getting the absolute title would not arise in view of the proviso to Section 4(1) of the Andhra Pradesh (Telangana Area) Abolition of Inams Act, 1955. Therefore, even if the property was initially brought into the custody of the Wakf Board pending the dispute, the Wakf Board cannot be compelled to abdicate their duties to protect the property of the institution in view of Sections 27, 32 and 40 of the Wakf Act.

54 AIR 1969 Mad 350; (1968) 2 MLJ 365.
55 (2002) 4 LW 213.
56 2010 (6) ALD 273.

The High Court of Karnataka, in Syed Shah Muhammad-Al-Hussaini vs. Union of India and Others,[57] held that:

> The scheme of the Act does not in any way show the interference of the State in the matters of religion thus allegedly violating the guarantee as provided under Article 25 and 26 of the Constitution. The Writ petition appears to have been filed upon unfounded apprehensions and concocted grounds. The allegation made in the petition is based upon hypothesis, which has nothing to do with the reality.

The section 32 of the Waqf Act 1995 discusses the powers and functions of the Waqf Board to ensure the proper safeguarding the waqf properties and proper management of waqf institutions. The Waqf Law authorises the courts and the boards to formulate schemes for the administration of any waqf institution. Several courts have upheld the authority of the board and the courts in formulating the scheme for the administration of waqf institutions.

The High Court of Andhra Pradesh, in Manjula Varsheney and Another vs. A.P. State Wakf Board and Others,[58] while discussing the powers of the Waqf Board, observed that:

> In the given situation, the Wakf Board can certainly act for and on behalf of Mutawalli, so as to ensure that the wakf is properly maintained and administered and for the protection of its properties ... Section 32(2) (i) of 1995 Act, confers power upon the Wakf Board to institute and defend suits and the proceedings relating to Wakfs. In the instant case, the property in question was granted on lease by the then Mutawalli under the express permission of the Wakf Board. Under those circumstances, it cannot be said that the Wakf Board has no jurisdiction or authority to issue the impugned notice terminating the lease and determining the same.

In the case of Ali Makin Naqvi, etc., vs. U.P. Shiya Central Board of Wakf & Others,[59] the High Court of Allahabad ruled that, when the Waqf Board, as a quasi-judicial authority has passed an order (for registration of waqf) on merit after hearing both the parties, it cannot review its order in the absence of powers to review.

The High Court of Madras, in Mahboob Basha vs. Tamil Nadu Wakf Board,[60] dealt with the powers of the Waqf Board in framing the scheme

57 AIR 1999 Kant 112.
58 2000 (1) ALD 452, 1999 (6) ALT 725.
59 AIR 2009 (NOC) 593.
60 C.R.P. NPD. Nos. 1816 and 2164 of 2012.

for the administration of the waqf. The learned judge, while interpreting the legal maxims and principles of interpretation of statues such as "verba generalia generaliter sunt intelligenda," observed as under:

> The cumulative reading of those maxims and the above general interpretation of statutes would amply and unequivocally, ... highlight the point that once the statutory authority, namely Wakf Board, has been vested with the power to deal with the wakfs of all kinds, including the ones already covered by any court judgement or scheme decree, then such statutory authority, namely, the Wakf Board is not enjoined to go before the court and seek permission to take over the control from the court to that of itself. But this basic principle has not been considered by the lower court.

The lower court, in the above judgement cited supra, simply assumed and presumed as though, despite the passing of the Wakf Act, 1995, it had jurisdiction and could give directions as contained in the impugned order. Such a course would be totally antithetical to the object of the Wakf Act and no more elaboration in this regard is required.

As such, I would like to set aside the order passed by the lower court, giving liberty to the Board to act as per Section 32 of the Wakf Act, 1995, adhering to the principle of "audi alteram partem."

The High Court of Uttarakhand, in Mohd. Idris alias Idris Baba vs. Uttaranchal Wakf Board, through its Chief Executive Officer,[61] made the following observation in respect of the Powers of the Survey Commissioner of Waqfs vis-à-vis appointment of a mutawalli:

> It is to be seen whether the revisionist was appointed by a competent person. In the case at hand, revisionist was appointed by Assistant Survey Commissioner. Work of Assistant Survey Commissioner has been defined in sub-section (2) of section 4 of the Act, wherein there is no mention that he has a power even to appoint adhoc Administrator to perform the act of mutawalli under the Act.

****

Section 33

Powers of inspection by Chief Executive Officer or persons authorised by him:-

(1) ***With a view to examining whether, by reason of any failure or negligence on the part of a mutawalli in the performance of his executive***

61 AIR 2013 Uttarakhand 72.

or administrative duties, any loss or damage has been caused to any waqf or waqf property, the Chief Executive Officer or any other person authorised by him in writing[62] *with the prior approval of the Board, [****]*[63] *may inspect all movable and immovable properties, which are waqf properties, and all records, correspondences, plans, accounts and other documents relating thereto.*

(2) *Whenever any such inspection as referred to in sub-section (1) is made, the concerned mutawalli and all officers, and other employees working under him and every person connected with the administration of the waqf shall extend to the person making such inspection, all such assistance and facilities as may be necessary and reasonably required by him to carry out such inspection, and shall also produce for inspection any movable property or documents relating to the waqf as may be called for by the person making the inspection and furnish to him such information relating to the waqf as may be required by him.*

(3) *Where, after any such inspection, it appears that the concerned mutawalli or any officer or other employee who is or was working under him has mis-appropriated, misapplied or fraudulently retained, any money or other waqf property, or had incurred irregular, unauthorised or improper expenditure from the funds of the waqf, the chief Executive Officer may, after giving the mutawalli or the person concerned a reasonable opportunity of showing cause why an order for the recovery of the amount or property, should not be passed against him and after considering such explanation, if any, as such person may furnish, determine the amount or the property, which has been mis-appropriated, misapplied or fraudulently retained, or the amount of the irregular, unauthorised or improper expenditure incurred by such person, and make an order directing such person to make payment of the amount so determined and to restore the said property to the waqf, within such time as maybe specified in the order.*

(4) *A mutawalli or other person aggrieved by such order may, within thirty days of the receipt by him of the order, appeal to the Tribunal:*

Provided that no such appeal shall be entertained by the Tribunal unless the appellant first deposits with the Chief Executive Officer the amount which has been determined under sub-section (3) as being payable by the appellant and the Tribunal shall have no power to make any order staying pending the disposal of the appeal, the operation of the order made by the Chief Executive Officer under sub-section (3).

62 Inserted by Act 27 of 2013, S. 23 (a).

63 The word "either himself or any other person authorised by him in writing in this behalf" omitted by Act 27 of 2013, S. 23 (b).

(5) ***The Tribunal may, after taking such evidence as it may think fit, confirm, reverse or modify the order made by the Chief Executive Officer under sub-section (3) or may remit, either in whole or in part, the amount specified in such order and may make such orders as to costs as it may think appropriate in the circumstances of the case.***

(6) ***The order made by the Tribunal under sub-section (5) shall be final.***

Reflections

Analogous section under Wakf Act 1954 is S.15B, inserted by the Amendment Act 69 of 1984.

This section authorises the Chief Executive Officer, or an officer authorised by him with the prior approval of the board, to conduct inspection of the waqf properties and to ascertain such properties are being utilised for the purposes for which they have been dedicated. The mutawalli, managing committee or the persons working under them shall produce the records, documents and the properties before the officer conducting the enquiry. The Chief Executive Officer can pass appropriate orders to restore such properties if he has reason to believe that such properties are being misused. The Chief Executive officer can also penalise the responsible persons and the tribunal shall not interfere in such matters unless and until the amount of penalty and the orders of the Chief Executive Officers are complied with. The appeal against the order of the Chief Executive Officer shall be made within 30 days to the Tribunal. The order of the Tribunal is final; however, it is subject to revision by the High Court under Section 83(9).

Judicial response

Judicial response pertaining to this section is not found.

****

Section 34

Recovery of the amount determined under section 33:-

Where any mutawalli or other person who has been ordered, whether under sub-section (3) or sub-section (5) of section 33, to make any payment or to restore the possession of any property, omits or fails to make such payment or restoration within the time specified in such order, the Chief Executive officer, with the prior approval of the Board shall, take such steps as he may think fit for the recovery of possession of the property aforesaid and shall also send a certificate to the Collector of the district in which the property of such mutawalli or other person is situate, stating therein the amount that has been determined by him or by the Tribunal, as the case may be, under section 33, as being payable by such mutawalli or other person, and, thereupon, the Collector shall recover the amount specified in such certificate as if it were an arrear of land revenue and on the recovery of such amount, pay the same to the Chief Executive Officer, who shall, on receipt thereof, credit the amount to the funds of the concerned waqf.

Reflections

Analogous section under Wakf Act 1954 is S.15C inserted by the Amendment Act 69 of 1984.

This section is the continuation of section 33 and provides for the compliance of the orders passed by the Chief Executive Officer as confirmed or otherwise by the Tribunal under section 33 and for the recovery of waqf property and the penalty (if any). The Chief Executive Officer, with the prior approval of the board, shall send a Certificate to the District Magistrate/Collector concerned to recover the said amount as an arrear of land revenue and remit it to the Chief Executive Officer who shall credit the same to the account of the waqf concerned.

As far as the possession of the waqf property is concerned, requisition may be issued to the District Magistrate/Collector concerned under section (52) of the Waqf Act 1995 or the Waqf Tribunal may be approached by way of suit.

Judicial response

Judicial response pertaining to this section is not found.

****

Section 35

Conditional attachment by Tribunal:-

(1) *Where the Chief Executive Officer is satisfied that the mutawalli or any other person who has been ordered under sub-section (3) or sub-section (5) of section 33 to make any payment, with intent to defeat or delay the execution of the said order,-*

(a) *is about to dispose of the whole or any part of his property; or*

(b) ***is about to remove the whole or any part of his property from the jurisdiction of this Chief Executive Officer, he may, with the prior approval of the Board, apply to the Tribunal for the conditional attachment of the said property or such part thereof, as he may think necessary.***

(2) ***The Chief Executive Officer shall, unless the Tribunal otherwise directs, specify in the application the property required to be attached and the estimated value thereof.***

(3) ***The Tribunal may direct the mutawalli or the person concerned, as the case may be, within a time to be fixed by it, either to furnish security, in such sum as may be specified in the order, to produce and place at the disposal of the Tribunal when required, the said property or the value of the same or such portion thereof as may be sufficient to satisfy the amount specified in the certificate referred to in section, 34, or to appear and show cause why he should not furnish such security.***

(4) ***The Tribunal may also in the order direct the conditional attachment of the whole or any portion of the property so specified.***

(5) ***Every attachment made under this section shall be made in accordance with the provisions of the code of Civil Procedure, 1908, (5 of 1908) as if it were an order for attachment made under the provisions of the said Code.***

Reflections

Analogous section under Wakf Act 1954 is S. 15 D inserted by the Amendment Act 69 of 1984.

The subject matter of this section is again the continuation of the previous two sections. This section provides for the application to be made by the Chief Executive Officer with the prior approval of the board, before the Wakf Tribunal for the conditional attachment of the property if he apprehends that the mutawalli or the person concerned is trying to dispose of such property to avoid compliance of such orders or payment of penalty. The provisions of the Code of Civil Procedure, 1908 (5 of 1908) shall be followed for every attachment made under this section.

Judicial response

Judicial response pertaining to this section is not found.

V REGISTRATION OF AUQAF

Synopsis

In this chapter, sections 36 to 43 (corresponding to sections 25 to 30 of the Waqf Act 1954) deal with the registration of waqf properties, maintenance of Register of Auqaf, etc. The Act under section 36 provides for registration of every waqf institution by the mutawalli, waqif and descendants of waqif or by a beneficiary with the Waqf Board. The Waqf Board may prescribe a proforma and call for any further information and make such inquiries as it may think fit in respect of the genuineness and validity of the application and correctness of the particulars therein, before registration of a waqf institution. The application for registration of waqf shall provide all relevant information pertaining to the waqf institution, such as (a) a brief introduction to and purpose of the waqf; (b) a description of the waqf properties sufficient for the identification thereof; (c) the gross annual income from such properties; (d) the amount of land revenue cess, rates and taxes annually payable in respect of the waqf properties; (e) an estimate of the expenses annually incurred in the realisation of the income of the waqf properties; (f) the amount set apart to achieve the purpose of waqf; (g) the salary of the mutawalli and salaries and allowances of the individuals, if any; (h) purely religious purposes; and (i) any other information.

The Waqf Board is also required to maintain a register of auqaf under section 37 of the Act which shall provide the details as to the class of the waqf, the name of the mutawalli, the rule of succession to the office of mutawalli under the Waqf Deed or by custom or by usage, particulars of all waqf properties and all title deeds and documents relating thereto, particulars of the scheme of administration and the scheme of expenditure at the time of registration, such other particulars as may be provided by regulations. The Act also provides under section 43 that the waqfs registered before the commencement of this Act shall be deemed to have been registered.

If any question arises whether a particular property is a waqf property or not, and, if it is a waqf property, whether it belongs to a Sunni Waqf or Shia

Waqf, the matter shall be decided by the Waqf Tribunal whose decisions shall be final as per section 40.

Keywords: Registration, Register, Waqif, Substitute, Revenue, Descendant

****

Section 36

Registration:-

(1) *Every waqf, whether created before or after the commencement of this Act, shall be registered at the office of the Board.*

(2) *Application for registration shall be made by the mutawalli:*

Provided that such applications may be made by the waqif[1] *or his descendants or a beneficiary of the waqf or any Muslim belonging to the sect to which the waqf belongs.*

(3) *An application for registration shall be made in such form and manner and at such place as the Board may by regulation provide and shall contain following particulars:-*

- (a) *a description of the waqf properties sufficient for the identification thereof:*
- (b) *the gross annual income from such properties;*
- (c) *the amount of land revenue, cesses, rates and taxes annually payable in respect of the waqf properties;*
- (d) *an estimate of the expense annually incurred in the realisation of the income of the waqf properties;*
- (e) *the amount set apart under the waqf for -*
  - (i) *the salary of the mutawalli and allowances to the individuals;*
  - (ii) *purely religious purposes;*
  - (iii) *charitable purposes; and*
  - (iv) *any other purposes*
- (f) *any other particulars provided by the Board by regulations.*

(4) *Every such application shall be accompanied by a copy of the waqf deed or if no such deed has been executed or a copy there of cannot be obtained, shall contain full particulars, as far as they are known to the applicant, of the origin, nature and objects of the waqf.*

(5) *Every application made under sub-section (2) shall be signed and verified by the applicant in the manner provided in the Code of Civil Procedure, 1908 (5 of 1908) for the signing and verification of pleading.*

1 Substituted by Act 27 of 2013, S. 24 for "made by the wakf."

(6) *The Board may require the applicant to supply any further particulars or information that it may consider necessary.*
(7) *On receipt of an application for registration, the Board may, before the registration of the waqf make such inquiries as it thinks fit in respect of the genuineness and validity of the application and correctness of any particulars therein and when the application is made by any person other than the person administering the waqf property, the Board shall, before registering the waqf, give notice of the application to the person administering the waqf property and shall hear him if he desires to be heard.*
(8) *In the case of auqaf created before the commencement of this Act, every application for registration shall be made, within three months from such commencement and in the case of auqaf created after such commencement, within three months from the date of the creation of the waqf;*

Provided that where there is no board at the time of creation of a waqf, such application will be made within three months from the date of establishment of Board.

Reflections

Analogous section under Waqf Act 1954 is S.25. The expression "Waqf Commissioner" is substituted for "Board." Proviso to sub-section (8) is inserted. Sub-sections (9) and (10) are deleted.

The Waqf Act 1995 makes it mandatory for all concerned for the registration of waqf institutions along with their properties with the State Waqf Board. It also provides detailed information about the waqf institution to be incorporated in the Register of Auqaf. This section ensures that the particulars regarding the waqf institutions and waqf properties are incorporated in the Register of Auqaf.

The Waqf Board shall prepare an application form for the registration of the waqf institutions. The application form shall contain information as sought under sections (36) and (37). An undertaking shall be obtained that information provided is true and correct. Personal details of the individual or individuals who make such applications shall also be sought for verification to avoid fictitious and frivolous registrations.

Judicial response

The waqf institution and its properties have to be registered by the Waqf Board on the basis of the inquiry and findings of the Survey Commissioner of Waqf. The High Court of Jharkhand in Managing Committee of Ekra

Mosque vs. State of Bihar[2] set aside the orders of the minister in the State Government, which cancelled the registration of the mosque as a waqf under section 25 of the Waqf Act 1954 (section 36 of Waqf Act 1995). The Honourable High Court held that the order of cancellation of registration by the Honourable Minister was without jurisdiction and was liable to be set aside. The court held that:

> Thus, the Waqf Act is a special legislation and consequently, ousts the applicability of the general law. It is therefore held that the Societies Registration Act has no role to play in matters relating to the administration, supervision and management of wakfs ... The Societies Registration Act therefore cannot be invoked for purposes of management of a mosque / religious places as this falls within the exclusive domain of the Waqf Board. Thus the Order of the minister (Annexure-1 of C.W.J.C. No. 4323 of 1998) authorizes the Society which was registered under the provisions of the Societies Registration Act, 1860 under the presidentship of the Respondent No. 8 to manage the Eqra Mosque and properties appertaining thereto, is wholly without jurisdiction.

The Supreme Court in Karnataka Board of Wakfs vs. Government of India[3] held that civil suits cannot be decided on the basis of historical facts without proper records and documents. While rejecting the claim of the Waqf Board on the lands acquired by the Government of India under the Ancient Monuments Preservation Act 1904, the court observed that borderline historical facts would lead to erroneous conclusions. The Honourable Supreme Court referred to the case-law in S.M. Karim vs. Bibi Sakinal,[4] Parsinni vs. Sukhi[5] and D.N. Venkatarayappa vs. State of Karnataka[6] and observed that:

> Adverse possession is a hostile possession by clearly asserting hostile title in denial of the title of true owner. It is a well settled principle that a party claiming adverse possession must prove that his possession is "nec vi, nec clam, nec precario," that is, peaceful, open and continuous. The possession must be adequate in continuity, in publicity and in extent to show that their possession is adverse to the true owner. It must start with a wrongful disposition of the rightful owner and be actual, visible, exclusive, hostile and continued over the statutory period.

The Appeal of the Karnataka Board of Wakfs was dismissed.

2 AIR 2004 Jhar 3, 2003 (4) JCR 122 Jhar.
3 (2004) 10 SCC 779.
4 AIR 1964 SC 1254.
5 (1993) 4 SCC 375.
6 (1997) 7 SCC 567).

In the case of Ali Makin Naqvi vs. U.P. Shiya Central Board of Wakf and Ors,[7] the High Court of Allahabad has ruled that when the Waqf Board, as a quasi-judicial authority, has passed an order (for registration of Waqf) on merit after hearing both the parties, it cannot review its order in the absence of powers of review conferred under the statute.

The High Court of Andhra Pradesh in Md. Ahmed Ali and Ors vs. Arastu Talimi Trust and Anr[8] held that:

> A wakf once registered and entered in the Register of Wakfs need not be entered again under the provisions of the subsequent enactments. Ex.A-63-Gazette Notification and Ex.A-110-letter of the first plaintiff amply established that the wakf was registered and entered in the Register of Wakfs.

****

Section 37

Register of Auqaf[9]

(1) ***The Board shall maintain a register of auqaf which shall contain in respect of each waqf copies of the waqf deeds, when available and the following particulars, namely:-***
   (a) ***the class of the waqf;***
   (b) ***the name of the mutawalli;***
   (c) ***the rule of succession to the office of mutawalli under the waqf deed or by custom or by usage;***
   (d) ***particulars of all waqf properties and all title deeds and documents relating thereto;***
   (e) ***particulars of the scheme of administration and the scheme of expenditure at the time of registration;***
   (f) ***such other particulars as may be provided by regulations.***

(2) ***The Board shall forward the details of the properties entered in the register of auqaf to the concerned land record office having jurisdiction of the waqf property.***[10]

(3) ***On receipt of the details as mentioned in sub-section (2), the land record office shall, according to established procedure, either make necessary entries in the land record or communicate, within a period***

7 AIR 2009 (NOC) 593.
8 2004 (1) ALD 99; 2003 (6) ALT 594.
9 S. 37 renumbered as sub-section (1) thereof by Act 27 of 2013, S. 25.
10 Inserted by Act 27 of 2013, S. 25.

of six months from the date of registration of waqf property under section 36, its objections to the Board.[11]

Reflections

Analogous section under Waqf Act 1954 is S.26, with the substitution of expression "Waqf Commissioner" for the expression "Board." Sub-section (2) inserted by the Amendment Act 69 of 1984 has been deleted.

This section discusses the particulars to be incorporated in the register of auqaf from clauses (a) to (f) under sub-section 1. These particulars are required to be incorporated even though they are exhaustive, but the register of waqf may also contain the details regarding the origin of waqf, the document number of the Waqf Deed, the name of the waqif, the purpose for which the waqf is dedicated, alternative purpose of the waqf if the existing purpose is extinguished, the intended or the prospective beneficiaries under the waqf, the line of succession of mutawalli, the scheme of administration or the instruction/intentions of the waqif, etc. Utmost care must be taken while registering the waqf institutions and their properties.

Sub-sections (2) and (3) are inserted by the Waqf Amendment Act 2013 (Act 27 of 2013), which require the Waqf Board to inform the government agencies and authorities about the registration of the properties as waqfs to enable them to make necessary entries in their records.

The Waqf Boards may also generate a master file containing the documents in original as far as possible in respect of the above-mentioned particulars and also the particulars mentioned under clauses (a) to (f) under sub-section 1 for its records.

Judicial response

Judicial response pertaining to this section is not found.

****

Section 38

Powers of Board to appoint Executive Officer:

(1) ***Notwithstanding anything contained in this Act, the Board may, if it is of the opinion that it is necessary so to do in the interest of the waqf,***

11 *Ibid.*

appoint on whole-time or part-time basis or in an honorary capacity, subject to such conditions as may be provided by regulations, an Executive Officer with such supporting staff as it considers necessary for any waqf having a gross annual income of not less than five lakh rupees:

Provided that the persons chosen for appointment should be a person professing Islam.

(2) *Every Executive Officer appointed under sub-section (1) shall exercise such powers and discharge such duties as pertain only to the administration of the property of the waqf for which he has been appointed and shall exercise those powers and discharge those duties under the directions, control and supervision of the Board.*

Provided that the Executive Officer who is appointed for a waqf having a gross annual income of not less than five lakh rupees shall ensure that the budget of the waqf is submitted, the accounts of the waqf are regularly maintained, and the yearly statement of accounts are submitted within such time as the Board may specify.

(3) *While exercising his powers and discharging his functions under sub-section (2), the Executive Officer shall not interfere with any religious duties or any usage or custom of the waqf sanctioned by the Muslim law.*

(4) *The salaries and allowances of the Executive Officer and his staff shall be fixed by the Board and in fixing the quantum of such salary the Board shall have due regard to the income of the waqf, the extent and nature of the duties of the Executive Officer and shall also ensure that the amounts of such salaries and allowances are not disproportionate to the income of the waqf and do not operate as an unnecessary financial burden on it.*

(5) *The salaries and allowances of the Executive Officer and his staff shall be paid by the Board from the Waqf Fund and, if the waqf generates any additional income as a result of appointment of the Executive Officer, the Board may claim reimbursement of amounts spend on the salaries and allowances from the fund of the waqf concerned.*

(6) *The Board may, for sufficient reasons, and after giving to the Executive Officer or a member of his staff, a reasonable opportunity of being heard, suspend, remove or dismiss the Executive Officer or a member of his staff from his post.*

(7) *Any Executive Officer or a member of his staff who is aggrieved by any order of removal or dismissal made under sub-section (6) may, within thirty days from the date of communication of the order, prefer an appeal against the order to the Tribunal and the Tribunal may,*

after considering such representation as the Board may make in the matter, and after giving a reasonable opportunity to the Executive Officer or a member of his staff of being heard, confirm, modify or reverse the order.

Reflections

Analogous section under Wakf Act 1954 is S.26 A inserted by the Amendment Act 69 of 1984.

Generally, a mutawalli or a Managing Committee is appointed for the administration of the waqf institution and its properties. This section confers power to the Waqf Board for the appointment of a Muslim Executive Officer and supporting staff for the waqf institutions whose gross annual income is not less than Rs. 5 lakh. Such an Executive Officer may be an employee of the Waqf Board or otherwise on salary/remuneration or on honorary basis, either full-time or part-time. He shall discharge his duties under the direction and supervision of the Board and submit the annual budget, annual accounts or any other report as required by the Board. But he shall not obstruct the religious, traditional and customary practices and affairs of the waqf institution.

Such Executive Officers, along with the supporting staff, may also be appointed for the major waqf institutions which are under the direct management of the Waqf Board.

The salary/remuneration of the Executive Officer and his supporting staff may be determined by the Waqf Board by taking into consideration the income of the waqf institution. The Executive Officer and his supporting staff may be suspended, removed or dismissed by the Board on sufficient grounds by giving reasonable opportunity to such official of being heard. The aggrieved employees are entitled to approach the Waqf Tribunal in such cases.

Judicial response

Judicial response pertaining to this section is not found

****

Section 39

Power of Board in relation to waqf which have ceased to exist:-

(1) ***The Board shall, if it is satisfied that the objects or any part thereof, of a waqf have ceased to exist, whether such cessation took place before***

or after the commencement of this Act, cause an inquiry to be held by the Chief Executive Officer, in the prescribed manner to ascertain the properties and funds pertaining to such waqf.

(2) *On the receipt of the report of inquiry of the Chief Executive Officer, the Board shall pass an order-*
   (a) *specifying the property and funds of such waqf;*
   (b) *directing that any property or funds pertaining to such waqf which have been recovered shall be applied or utilised for the renovation of any waqf property and where there is no need for making any such renovation or where utilisation of the funds for such renovation is not possible, be appropriated, to any of the purposes specific in sub-clause (iii) of clause (e) of sub-section (2) of section 32*

(3) *The Board may, if it has reason to believe that any building or other place which was being used for religious purpose or instruction or for charity has, whether before or after the commencement of this Act, ceased to be used for that purpose, make an application to the Tribunal for an order directing the recovery of possession of such building or other place.*

(4) *The Tribunal may, if it is satisfied, after making such inquiry as it may think fit, that such building or other place-*
   (a) *is waqf property;*
   (b) *has not been acquired under any law for the time being in force relating to acquisition of land or is not under any process of acquisition under any such law, or has not vested in the State Government under any law for the time being in force relating to land reforms; and*
   (c) *is not in the occupation of any person who has been authorised by or under any law for the time being in force to occupy such building or other place, make an order-*
      (i) *directing the recovery of such building or place from any person who may be in unauthorised possession thereof, and*
      (ii) *directing that such property, building or place be used for religious purpose or instruction as before, or if such use is not possible, be utilised for any purpose specified in sub-clause (iii) of clause (e) of sub-section (2) of section 32.*

<u>Reflections</u>

Analogous section under Wakf Act 1954 is S.26 B inserted by the Amendment Act 69 of 1984.

If the Waqf Board has satisfied that the objects of the waqf or any part thereof have ceased to exist, it should conduct an inquiry by the Chief Executive Officer in the prescribed manner. The Waqf Board shall formulate regulations for holding such inquiry. The principles of natural justice and fair play shall be the guiding principles in conducting such inquiry. All persons concerned with the waqf institution shall be given fair opportunity to be heard before concluding the inquiry.

Sub-section (2) stipulates that, on receipt of the inquiry report from the Chief Executive Officer, the boards shall pass orders specifying the property and funds of such waqf be utilised for the renovation of its waqf property or be appropriated to any of the purposes specified in sub-clause (iii) of clause (e) of sub-section (2) of section 32.

If the board is satisfied that any waqf property has ceased to be utilised for the purpose of waqf, it can make an application to the Waqf Tribunal for an order for the possession of the waqf property. Further, if the Tribunal is satisfied by an inquiry that the property in question is a waqf property and has not been vested in the State Government under any law for the time being in force and has not been under authorised possession of any person, it may pass an order directing the recovery and possession of such property or direct that such property be utilised for religious purposes or be utilised for any purpose specified in sub-clause (iii) of clause (e) of sub-section (2) of section 32.

Judicial response

Judicial response pertaining to this section is not found.

****

Section 40

Decision if a property is waqf property:-

(1) *The Board may itself collect information regarding any property which it has reason to believe to be waqf property and if any question arises whether a particular property is waqf property or not or whether a waqf is a Sunni waqf or a Shia waqf it may, after making such inquiry as it may deem fit, decide the question.*

(2) *The decision of the Board on a question under sub-section (1) shall, unless revoked or modified by the Tribunal, be final.*

(3) *Where the Board has any reason to believe that any property of any trust or society registered in pursuance of the Indian Trusts Act, 1882 (2 of 1882) or under the Societies Registration Act, 1860 (21 of 1860) or under any other Act, is waqf property, the Board may*

notwithstanding anything contained in such Act, hold an inquiry in regard to such property and if after such inquiry the Board is satisfied that such property is waqf property, call upon the trust or society, as the case may be, either to register such property under this Act as waqf property or show cause why such property should not be so registered;

Provided that in all such case, notice of the action proposed to be taken under this sub-section shall be given to the authority by whom the trust or society had been registered.

(4) ***The Board shall, after duly considering such cause as may be shown in pursuance of notice issued under sub-section (3), pass such orders as it may think fit and the order so made by the Board shall be final, unless it is revoked or modified by a Tribunal.***

Reflections

Analogous sections under Wakf Act 1954, is S.27 as amended under Amendment Act 69 of 1984.

Section (40) empowers the Waqf Board to decide the issue of whether a particular property is a waqf property or not, and, if it is a waqf property, whether it is a Shia Waqf or a Sunni Waqf after collecting necessary information and after conducting an inquiry in this matter. The decision of the Waqf Board shall be final unless modified or revoked by the Waqf Tribunal.

Sub-section (3) empowers the Waqf Board to call upon any trust or society if it has reason to believe that such a trust or society is managing the waqf property, to register such properties as waqf property or issue a show cause notice why such properties should not be registered as waqf. The orders passed by the board are final unless modified or revoked by the Waqf Tribunal.

Judicial response

The Division Bench of the Patna High Court in the case of Md. Yunus vs. Inspector General of Registration[12] has held that:

> It would be observed that the numerous objects which have been enumerated therein have no reference to any religious institutions of religion. They are all matters of general public benefit. It is well-established rule of construction that the expressions used in an enactment take their

12 AIR 1980 Pat 138.

> meaning and colour from the context in which they are used. We are, therefore, of the view that the expression charitable purpose as used in the Societies Registration Act does not embrace purposes which are religious or predominantly religious. If that be the correct view of law there cannot be any doubt that the Inspector General of Registration had no jurisdiction to register the Society in question under Section 3 of the Act.

Referring to the above judgement of the bench of the High Court of Jharkhand in Managing Committee of Ekra Mosque vs. State Of Bihar,[13] the court held that:

> Thus the Order of the minister (Annexure-1 of C.W.J.C. No. 4323 of 1998) authorizes the Society which was registered under the provisions of the Societies Registration Act, 1860 under the presidentship of the Respondent No. 8 to manage the Eqra Mosque and properties appertaining thereto, is wholly without jurisdiction.

A Division Bench of the Andhra Pradesh High Court in D. Venkata Krishna Rao and Others vs. Government of A.P., Rep. by Principal Secretary, Revenue Department and Others[14] observed that:

> Even if a wakf is not surveyed or mentioned in the report submitted by the Survey Commissioner under Section 4(3), even then there is an obligation for registration of every wakf, and as per Section 43, all the wakfs registered prior to the Wakf Act shall be deemed to have been registered there under. In this context, Section 40 assumes significance. Sub-section (3) thereof contains a non-abstante clause. This overrides other provisions in the Wakf Act. Notwithstanding anything contained in the other provisions of the Wakf Act, under Section 40(3) the Wakf Board may hold an enquiry and if it is satisfied that a property is a wakf property, can issue notice to the Trust or Society and then register under Section 36.

The High court of Andhra Pradesh further held that:

> For issuing the impugned errata notification, in our opinion, it may not be necessary for the Government to appoint a second Survey Commissioner nor for him to submit a report. Section 40 is wide enough to confer such powers on the Wakf Board.

13 AIR 2004 Jhar 3, 2003 (4) JCR 122 Jhar.
14 2012 (4) ALD 144; 2012 (6) ALT 379 (DB).

The Kerala High Court in Thayyil Kunhi Mohammed Haji and Ors vs. Darul Huda Islamic Academy,[15] has observed that enlistment of waqf property under section 5 and the decision of the Waqf Board under section 40 (1) of the Waqf Act 1995 or preconditions for invocation of the jurisdiction of Tribunal. Since the function of registration of property as waqf being that of the board, it is for the board to consider and decide the question at first instance before the Tribunal can be called upon to adjudicate the matter.

The Supreme Court in Madanuri Sri Rama Chandra Murthy vs. Syed Jalal[16] has held that the effect of section 40 of the Waqf Act 1995 is that, if any property has been omitted to be included in the list of auqaf by inadvertence or otherwise, then it was/is for the Waqf Board to take action as per the said provision. The decision of the Waqf Board shall be final unless it is revoked or modified by a civil court.

The Calcutta High Court in Masuda Begum and Ors vs. Roushan Ali[17] has held that:

> It is settled position of law that the record of rights does not create or extinguish title. The subject properties have been recorded in the C.S.R.O.R and R.S.R.O.R. as Pir Hazrat Pir Waqf Estate. The Board on the basis such entries in the said record of rights of the subject properties, has held that the properties are Waqf and enrolled the same as such. Section 40 of the said Act casts duty upon the Board to make objective inquiry to ascertain whether the subject properties are waqf or not. The requirement of such objectives inquiry assumes more importance when entries in C.S.R.O.R. and R.S.R.O.R. of the subject properties contradict the entries of L.R.R.O.R. of it.
>
> The Tribunal in the order impugned has discarded the L.O.R.R.O.R. of the subject properties on the ground that he petitioners have failed to establish the foundation of the entries in the said L.R.R.O.R. The Tribunal is not competent to decide the veracity of the entries in a record of rights in as much as the jurisdiction for the said purpose has been expressly conferred upon the authorities created under the provisions of the West Bengal Land Reforms Act. 1955.

****

15 AIR 2008 (NOC) 1178 (KER).
16 AIR 2017 SC 2653.
17 AIR 2019 Cal 275.

Section 41

Power to Cause Registration of Waqf and to Amend Register:-

> *The Board may direct a mutawalli to apply for the registration of a waqf, or to supply any information regarding a waqf or may itself cause the waqf to be registered or may at any time amend the register of auqaf.*

Reflections

Analogous section under Wakf Act 1954 is S.28.

This section empowers the State Waqf Board to direct the mutawalli or the Managing Committee to get the waqf institution registered. It can also call upon the Managing Committee or the mutawalli to furnish all the details about the functioning of the waqf institution. This section also empowers the board to amend the register of auqaf. But there must be sufficient reason and proper inquiry for amending the register of auqaf.

Judicial response:

Judicial response pertaining to this section is not found.

****

Section 42

Change in the management of Auqaf to be notified:-

(1) *In the case of any change in the management of a registered waqf due to the death or retirement or removal of the mutawalli, the incoming mutawalli shall forthwith, and any other person may notify the change to the Board.*

(2) *In the case of any other change in any of the particulars mentioned in section 36, the mutawalli shall, within three months from the occurrence of the change, notify such change to the Board.*

Reflections

Analogous section under Wakf Act 1954 is S.29.

The Management of the Waqf Institutions is bound under this section to keep the Waqf Boards informed about the changes in the management under the unforeseen circumstances such as death or the retirement of the mutawalli or naib mutawalli or change in the Managing Committee, etc. In case of any change in the matters relating to section (36), the mutawalli shall notify such a change to the Waqf Board within three months.

Judicial response

The High Court of Andhra Pradesh in A.P. State Wakf Board, Rep. by its Chief Executive Officer vs. Mir Qamar Hasan Razvi[18] held that:

> When the period of three years from the date of the appointment on 04.06.2008 had expired, the petitioner was justified in taking over the wakf by exercise of the powers u/s.65 of the Act ... In that view of the matter, the taking over of the management of the wakf by the Board is justified. The Tribunal, consequently, was not correct in allowing O.A.No.13 of 2011 in favour of the respondent herein.

****

Section 43

Auqaf registered before the commencement of this Act deemed to be registered:

> ***Notwithstanding anything contained in this Chapter, where any waqf has been registered before the commencement of this Act, under any law for the time being in force, it shall not be necessary to register the waqf under the provisions of this Act and any such registration made before such commencement shall be deemed to be a registration made under this Act.***

Reflections

Analogous section under Wakf Act 1954 is S.30.

If any waqf institution is registered under any law for the time being in force it need not be registered again under this Act and it is deemed to have been registered under this Act.

18 2012 (4) ALD 126; 2012 (3) ALT 791.

Judicial response

The High Court of Bombay, while disposing the Writ Petitions Nos. 2906 of 2004; No.899 of 2011; No.357 of 2011 by a common order, in Shaikh Yusuf Bhai Chawala vs. State of Maharashtra[19] WP NO. 2906 of 2004, dealt with the matter of registered trusts which were treated as waqf institutions by the Survey Commissioner of Waqf appointed by the Government of Maharashtra. The petitioners challenged the inclusion of their trusts in the list of auqaf as recommended by the Survey Commissioners. They also questioned the constitution of Waqf Board since sub-section (2) of section (13) requires the constitution of separate board for Shia Waqfs. The High Court of Bombay observed as under:

> Therefore, in our opinion, it would be appropriate to direct that till the Wakf Board is established, incorporated and constituted under the provisions of the Wakf Act and it becomes operative, the provisions of the Bombay Public Trust Act shall apply to the Muslims Public Trusts which are registered under the Bombay Public Trust Act.

This matter went in appeal before Honourable Supreme Court in Maharashtra State Board of Wakfs vs. Shaikh Yusuf Bhai Chawla and Ors[20] the Supreme Court in an interim order gave the following observation:

> In the present case, the difference between Trusts and Wakfs appear to have been overlooked and the High Court has passed orders without taking into consideration the fact that the Charity Commissioner would not ordinarily have any jurisdiction to manage the wakf properties.
>
> In these circumstances, in our view, it would be in the interest of all concerned to maintain the status quo and to restrain all those in management of the waqf properties from alienating and/or encumbering the waqf properties during the pendency of the proceedings before this Court. The order of the High Court staying the operation of its judgment has led to the revival of interim orders which have rendered such stay otiose. The said order of stay cannot also be continued during the pendency of these proceedings in its present form.

19 AIR 2012 (NOC) 112 (Bom).
20 2012 (5) SCR 1014.

VI MAINTENANCE OF ACCOUNTS OF AUQAF

Synopsis

Chapter VI under sections 44 to 71 of the Waqf Act 1995 discusses the finances, accounts and the administration of waqf institutions and their properties. The issues pertaining to waqf institutions such as presentation of budget, maintenance of accounts, audit of accounts, penalties in default, removal of mutawalli, assumption of waqf institutions under direct management of Waqf Board, supersession of managing committee, scheme of administration of waqf institution, lease of waqf property, recovery of alienated waqf property, etc., have been discussed in this chapter. Leasing of waqf property orally is not permitted. The maximum period of lease has been enhanced from 3 years to 30 years. Sale of waqf property, if any, shall be transacted through public auction only. The District Collectors/Magistrates, Additional District Collectors/Magistrates, Divisional Magistrates/Collectors shall implement the decisions of the State Waqf Boards. Any order under the Land Acquisition Act shall not be passed without consulting the State Waqf Board. A new provision under section 52 (A) has been made by the Amendment Act of 2013, which imposes two years rigorous imprisonment for any purchase or alienation of waqf property without prior sanction of the Waqf Board. The Chief Executive Officer of the State Waqf Board is empowered to make an application to the Waqf Tribunal for the eviction orders of the unauthorised occupants under the provisions of section 54.

Keywords: Accounts, Audit, Budget, Scheme, Supersession, Lease

****

Section 44

Budget:-

(1) ***Every <u>mutawalli</u>[1] shall, in every year prepare, in such form and at such time as may be prescribed, a budget in respect of the financial***

1 Substituted by Act 27 of 2013, S. 26 (a), for "wakf."

year next ensuing showing the estimated receipts and expenditure during that financial year.

(2) *Every such budget shall be submitted by the mutawalli at least thirty days*[2] *before the beginning of the financial year to the Board and shall make adequate provision for the following:-*

- (i) *for carrying out the objects of the waqf;*
- (ii) *for the maintenance and preservation of the waqf property;*
- (iii) *for the discharge of all liabilities and subsisting commitments binding on the waqf under this Act or any other law for the time being in force.*

(3) *In case the Board considers any item in the budget being contrary to the objects of the waqf and the provisions of this Act, it may give such direction for addition or deletion of such item as it may deem fit.*[3]

(4) *If in the course of the financial year the mutawalli finds it necessary to modify the provisions made in the budget in regard to the receipt or to the distribution of the amounts to be expended under the different heads, he may submit to the Board a supplementary or a revised budget and the provisions of sub-section (3) shall, as far as may be, apply to such supplementary or revised budget.*

Reflections

Analogous section under Wakf Act 1954 is S.31.

This section states that the mutawalli shall submit the budget for the next financial year to the Waqf Board at least one month before the commencement of the financial year in the prescribed format. Previously according to sub section (2) the annual budget had to be submitted by the mutawalli before three months of the commencement of the financial year. This period of three months has been reduced to one month by the Waqf Amendment Act 2013 (Act 27 of 2013). Sub-section (3) has been substituted by the Waqf Amendment Act 2013. Before substitution this sub-section read as under:

> "(3) the board may give such directions for making alterations, omission or addition in the budget as it may deem fit, consistent with the objects of the waqf and the provisions of the Act."

The budget shall contain receipts and payments expected in the ensuing financial year and the expenditure to be incurred for carrying out the object of the waqf. The mutawalli can submit a revised budget in case of any

2 Substituted by Act 27 of 2013, S. 26 (a), for "ninety days."

3 Substituted by Act 27 of 2013, S. 26 (b), for sub-section (3).

omissions and deletion in the budget. The Waqf Board shall provide the prescribed format in which it desires to obtain the budget estimates from the mutawallis or the managing committees of the waqf institutions.

This section also authorises the Waqf Board to direct the mutawalli for additions and deletions, if any, to be carried out in the budget and submit the revised budget. If the mutawalli feels that certain provisions in the budget are necessary to be modified, he may submit a supplementary or revised budget.

Judicial response

Judicial response pertaining to this section is not found.

****

Section 45

Preparation of budget of auqaf[4] *under direct management of the Board:-*

(1) *The Chief Executive Officer shall prepare, in such form and at such time as may be prescribed, a budget in respect of the financial year next ensuing showing the estimated receipts and expenditure for each of the auqaf under the direct management of the Board, showing therein the estimated receipts and expenditure and submit it to the Board for its approval.*

(2) *While submitting the budget under sub-section (1), the Chief Executive Officer shall also prepare statement giving details of the increase, if any, in the income of each waqf under the direct management of the Board and the steps which have been taken for its better management and the results accruing there from during the year.*

(3) *The Chief Executive Officer shall keep regular accounts and be responsible for the proper management of every waqf under the direct management of the Board.*

(4) *Every budget submitted by the Chief Executive Officer under sub-section (1) shall comply with the requirements of section 46 and, for this purpose; references therein to the mutawalli of the waqf shall be construed as pre-references to the Chief Executive Officer.*

(5) *The audit of accounts of every waqf under the direct management of the Board shall be undertaken by the State Examiner of Local Funds or any other officer appointed by the State Government for this purpose, irrespective of the income of the waqf.*

4 Substituted by Act 27 of 2013, S. 26 (a), for "wakfs."

(6) ***The provisions of sub-section (2) and (3) of section 47 and the provisions of section 48 and 49 shall, in so far as they are not inconsistent with the provisions of this section, apply to the audit of accounts referred to in this section.***

(7) ***Where any waqf is under the direct management of the Board, such administrative charges as may be specified by the Chief Executive Officer shall be payable by the waqf to the Board:***

Provided that the Chief Executive Officer shall not collect more than ten per cent, of the gross annual income of the waqf under the direct management of the Board as administrative charges.

Reflections

Analogous section under Wakf Act 1954 is S.31 A, inserted by the Amendment Act 69 of 1984.

This section provides that the Chief Executive Officer of the Waqf Board shall be responsible for the proper administration of the waqf institutions which are under the direct management of the Waqf Board. He shall keep proper accounts of such institutions and prepare the budget estimates of such waqf institutions and submit the same for the approval of the board. The Chief Executive Officer shall be construed as the mutawalli of waqf institutions, which are under the direct management of the Waqf Board. The audit of such waqf institutions shall be conducted by the Audit Officers/ Examiners of the Local Fund Audit of the State concerned. The relevant provisions of sections 47, 48 and 49 shall be relevant to the audit of such waqf institutions.

Judicial response

Judicial response pertaining to this section is not found.

****

Section 46

Submission of accounts of auqaf:-

(1) ***Every mutawalli shall keep regular accounts.***

(2) ***Before the 1st day of July[5] next, following the date on which the application referred to in section 36 has been made and thereafter before***

5 Substituted by Act 27 of 2013, S. 27, for "1st day of May."

the 1st day of July[6] in every year, every mutawalli of a waqf shall prepare and furnish to the Board a full and true statement of accounts, in such form and containing such particulars as may be provided by regulations by the Board, of all moneys received or expended by the mutawalli on behalf of the waqf during the period of twelve months ending on the 31st day of March, or, as the case may be, during that portion of the said period during which the provisions of this Act, have been applicable to the waqf.

Provided that the date on which the annual accounts are to be closed may be varied at the discretion of the Board.

Reflections

Analogous section under Wakf Act 1954 is S.32 with the addition of sub-sections 1 and 2 inserted by Waqf Amendment Act 34 of 1964.

The mutawalli shall maintain proper and regular accounts.

This sections pertain to preparation and submission of annual accounts by the mutawalli concerned to the Waqf Board on or before the first day of July every year. The Waqf Board can change the accounting year with its discretion. Before the Waqf Amendment Act 2013 this cut-off date was first day of May every year.

Judicial response

Judicial response pertaining to this section is not found.

****

Section 47

Audit of accounts of auqaf:-

(1) ***The accounts of auqaf submitted to the Board under section 46 shall be audited and examined in the following manner, namely:-***

(a) ***in the case of a waqf having no income or a net annual income not exceeding fifty thousand rupees,[7] the submission of a statement of accounts shall be a sufficient compliance with the provisions of***

6 Substituted by Act 27 of 2013, S. 27, for "1st day of May."

7 Substituted by Act 27 of 2013, S. 28 (I) (i), for "ten thousand rupees."

section 46 and the accounts of two per cent, of such auqaf shall be audited annually by an auditor appointed by the Board;

(b) *the accounts of the waqf having net annual income exceeding fifty thousand rupees*[8] *shall be audited annually, or at such other intervals as may be prescribed, by an auditor appointed by the Board from out of the panel of auditors prepared by the State Government and while drawing up such panel of auditors, the State Government shall specify the scale or remuneration of auditors;*

(c) *the State Government may, under intimation to the Board*[9] *at any time cause the account of any waqf audited by the State Examiner of Local Funds or by any other officer designated for that purpose by that State Government;*

(2) *The auditor shall submit his report to the Board and the report of the auditor shall among other things, specify all cases of irregular, illegal or improper expenditure or of failure to recover money or other property caused by neglect or misconduct and any other matter which the auditor considers it necessary to report; and the report shall also contain the name of any person who, in the opinion of the auditor, is responsible for such expenditure or failure and the auditor shall in every such case certify the amount of such expenditure or loss as due from such person.*

(3) *The cost of the audit of the accounts of a waqf shall be met from the funds of that waqf;*

Provided that the remuneration of the auditors appointed from out of the panel drawn by the State Government in relation to auqaf having a net annual income of more than fifty thousand rupees[10] *shall be paid in accordance with the scale of remuneration specified by the State Government under clause (c) sub-section (1):*

Provided further that where the audit of the accounts of any waqf is made by the State Examiner of Local Funds or any other officer designated by the State Government in this behalf, the cost of such audit shall not exceed one and a half per cent, of the net annual income of such waqf and such costs shall be met from the funds of the auqaf concerned.

----

8 Substituted by Act 27 of 2013, S. 28 (I) (i), for "ten thousand rupees."

9 Inserted by Act 27 of 2013, S. 28 (I) (iii).

10 Substituted by Act 27 of 2013, S. 28 (II), for "more than ten thousand rupees but less than fifteen thousand rupees."

Reflections

Analogous section under Wakf Act 1954 is S.33.

This section deals with the procedure of audit of the waqf institutions. Sub-section (1) stipulates that, for the waqf institutions having an annual income of less than Rs. 50,000, mere submission of statement of accounts shall be sufficient. But for the waqf institution having an annual income of more than Rs. 50,000, the Waqf Board shall appoint the auditors from the panel of auditors prepared by the State Government and their remuneration shall be determined.

The auditors are required to specify the improper and illegal expenditure and failure to recover the income or funds of the waqf, and the persons responsible for such failure or irregularity.

The expenditure towards audit shall be met from the funds of the waqf. This section also makes a proviso that, in case of audit by the examiners of the Local Fund Audit, the cost of the audit not exceeding one and a half per cent of the net annual income may be recovered from the waqf concerned.

The Waqf Act 1995 under this analogous section had provided for audit of accounts of the waqf institutions whose annual income is Rs. 10,000 or more previously. But this amount has been enhanced to Rs. 50,000 by the Amendment Act of 2013.

The audit of waqf institutions could have been made mandatory for the waqf institutions whose income is Rs. 1 lakh or more and whose mutawallis are eligible to elect a member of the Waqf Board under the electoral college of mutawallis.

Judicial response

Judicial response pertaining to this section is not found.

****

Section 48

Board to pass orders on auditor's report:-

(1) ***The Board shall examine the auditor's report, and may call for the explanation of any person in regard to any matter mentioned therein, and shall pass such orders as it thinks fit including orders for the recovery of the amount certified by the auditor under sub-section (2) of section 47.***
(2) ***The mutawalli or any other person aggrieved by any order made by the Board may, within thirty days of the receipt by him of the order, apply to the Tribunal to modify or set aside the order and the Tribunal***

may, after taking such evidence as it may think necessary, confirm or modify the order or remit the amount so certified, either in whole or in part, and may also make such order as to costs as it may think appropriate in the circumstances of the case.

(3) *No application made under sub-section (2) shall be entertained by the Tribunal unless the amount certified by the auditor under sub-section (2) of section 47 has first been deposited in the Tribunal and the Tribunal shall not have any power to stay the operation of the order made by the Board under sub-section (1).*

(4) *The order made by the Tribunal under sub-section (2) shall be final.*

(5) *Every amount for the recovery of which any order has been made under sub-section (1) or sub-section (2) shall, where such amount remains unpaid, be recoverable in the manner specified in section 34 or section 35 as if the said order were an order for the recovery of any amount determined under sub-section (3) of section 35.*

Reflections

Analogous section under Wakf Act 1954 is S.34.

This section empowers the Waqf Board to examine the auditor's report and pass orders for the recovery of inadmissible expenditure and the misappropriated amount as has been identified by the auditors. If any mutawalli or the managing committee is aggrieved by such an order, they may approach the Waqf Tribunal. But this section indicates that the Waqf Tribunal shall not pass any order unless the amount in question is deposited in the Tribunal. Though the Tribunal can decide the matter, it has no power to stay the operation of the orders passed by the board. The decision of the Tribunal shall be final. For the recovery of such an amount, the procedure specified in section 34 or 35 of the Act shall be followed.

Judicial response

Judicial response pertaining to this section is not found.

****

Section 49

Sums certified to be due recoverable as arrears of land revenue:-

(1) *Every sum certified to be due from any person by an auditor in his report under section 47 unless such certificate is modified or cancelled by an order of the Board or of the Tribunal made under section 48,*

and every sum due on a modified certificate shall be paid by such person within sixty days after the service of a demand for the same issued by the Board.

(2) ***If such payment is not made in accordance with the provisions of sub-section (1), the sum payable may, on a certificate issued by the Board after giving the person concerned an opportunity of being heard, be recovered in the same manner as an arrear of land revenue.***

Reflections

Analogous section under Wakf Act 1954 is S.35.

This section is the continuation of the preceding sections and provides for recovery of the amount certified to be due by the auditor under section 47, unless modified or cancelled by the board or the Tribunal, shall be payable within 60 days from the demand notice. Such an amount shall be recovered as arrears of land revenue; however, reasonable opportunity of being heard shall be provided to the person concerned.

Judicial response

Judicial response pertaining to this section is not found.

****

Section 50

Duties of Mutawalli:-

It shall be the duty of every mutawalli-

(a) ***to carry out the directions of the Board in accordance with the provisions of this Act or of any rule or order made there under;***

(b) ***to furnish such returns and supply such information or particulars as may from time to time be required by the Board in accordance with the provisions of this Act or of any rule or order made there under;***

(c) ***to allow inspection of waqf properties, accounts or records or deeds and documents relating thereto;***

(d) ***to discharge all public dues; and***

(e) ***to do any other act which he is lawfully required to do by or under this Act.***

Reflections

Analogous section under Wakf Act 1954 is S.36.

The mutawalli plays a pivotal role in the administration of waqf. The appointment, removal, duties and responsibilities of a mutawalli have been contentious issues before the courts of law. In the early 20th century, the status of a mutawalli was compared with that of a trustee in English Law. Though there are some similarities, there are also a lot of differences between the two. "The mutawalli has no ownership right on the waqf property; in that respect he is not a trustee in the technical sense; he holds the property as a manager for fulfilling the purpose, of the waqf," as described by Tyabji.[11] This provision under Muslim Law protects the waqf property from mismanagement, misappropriation and improper alienation of waqf property by the mutawalli.

Section 50 of the Act specifies the duties of mutawalli. The mutawalli is entrusted with the responsibility to follow the directions of the board and the waqif, furnish the required information to the board, co-operate with the inspection of the waqf properties and the accounts. Clauses (a) to (e) discuss the duties of the mutawalli which he is bound to comply with.

Judicial response

The duty of a mutawalli is to protect the waqf property and initiating legal action against the encroachers, trespassers and recovering possession of the waqf properties. The Bench of Patna High Court, in the case of Maulvi Reza Ansari vs. Shyamlal Shah,[12] has observed that:

> It is the Board alone which can institute and defend suits and proceedings in a court of law relating to wakfs after Wakf Act 1954 came into force and not the mutawalli. The execution proceedings instituted by the mutawalli have been rightly held to be not maintainable.

Contrary to this ruling of the Patna High Court, the High Court of Gujarat in Syed Khersha Sajanshah Mutvalli vs. Bhuj Municipality,[13] held that the mutawalli is entitled to file the suit for protection of waqf property, as it is a part of his duty. To arrive at this conclusion the High Court of Gujarat referred to the judgement of the Division Bench of High Court of Allahabad in Hashim Husain vs. Ahmad Raza,[14] which observed that

11 Badriddin Tyabji, *Muslim Law*, 3rd Edn. N.M. Tripathi, 1940.

12 AIR 1983 Pat 297.

13 AIR 1986 Guj 1; (1985) 1 GLR 437.

14 AIR 1974 All 305.

> Although it is true that a mutawalli is not a trustee within the meaning of the Act, or as understood either generally or under the Indian Trusts Act, but the nature of the duties which he is required to perform are more or less the same. A mutawalli stands in fiduciary relationship and it, is against the interest of society in general that such relationship should be allowed to be terminated unilaterally.

The Honourable Supreme Court of India, in Sayed Muhammed Mashur Kunhi Kaya Thangal vs. Badagara Jamayath Palli Dharas Committee,[15] has held that:

> The plaintiff could only succeed on the strength of its case and not on the weakness found in the case of the defendant, if any. The first appellate Court having elaborately considered the evidence placed on record in the light of the pleadings of the parties had come to the right conclusion in dismissing the suit of the plaintiff. The High Court in the second appeal, in our view, was not right in upsetting the findings of the fact recorded by the first appellate Court, that too without putting the parties on notice on the substantial question of law ... Under the circumstances and in the light of what is stated above, the impugned judgment cannot be sustained. In the result, the appeal is allowed, the impugned judgment is set aside except the direction given to the Wakf Board to act under section 63 of the Wakf Act 1995 and the suit filed by the plaintiff is dismissed. In other words, the direction given by the High Court to the Wakf Board to exercise power under section 63 of the Wakf Act 1995 is maintained.

A mutawalli cannot claim the benefit of being a tenant in the waqf property. The High Court of Karnataka in Karnataka Board of Wakf vs. Land Tribunal, Sira and Others,[16] has held that:

> It is no doubt true even in case of a wakf landed properties, if a person were to be found cultivating the land as tenant is entitled to claim occupancy rights by filling Form No. 7. But the person managing and administering the property of the wakf cannot be construed as a tenant in respect of the said property ... It is manifest that the person in possession of the land in capacity of the mutawalli cannot be construed as tenant and he is only a caretaker of the property and, therefore, not entitled for grant of occupancy right in respect of Wakf Properties.

****

15 AIR 2004 SC 4365.
16 AIR 2000 Kant. 141.

Section 51

Alienation of waqf property without sanction of Board to be void:-

(1) *Notwithstanding anything contained in the waqf deed, any lease of any immovable property which is waqf property, shall be void unless such lease is effected with the prior sanction of the Board:*[17]

Provided that no mosque, dargah, khanqah, graveyard, or imambara shall be leased except any unused graveyards in the States of Punjab, Haryana and Himachal Pradesh where such graveyard has been leased out before the date of commencement of the Waqf (Amendment) Act, 2013.

(1A) Any sale, gift, exchange, mortgage or transfer of waqf property shall be void ab initio:

Provided that in case the Board is satisfied that any waqf property may be developed for the purposes of the Act, it may, after recording reasons in writing, take up the development of such property through such agency and in such manner as the Board may determine and move a resolution containing recommendation of development of such waqf property, which shall be passed by a majority of two-thirds of the total membership of the Board:

Provided further that nothing contained in this sub-section shall affect any acquisition of waqf properties for a public purpose under the Land Acquisition Act, 1894 (1 of 1894) or any other law relating to acquisition of land if such acquisition is made in consultation with the Board:

Provided also that:-

(a) *the acquisition shall not be in contravention of the Places of Public Worship (Special Provisions) Act, 1991(42 of 1991);*
(b) *the purpose for which the land is being acquired shall be undisputedly for a public purpose;*
(c) *no alternative land is available which shall be considered as more or less suitable for that purpose; and*
(d) *to safeguard adequately the interest and objective of the waqf, the compensation shall be at the prevailing market value or a*

17 Substituted by Act 27 of 2013, S. 4, for sub-section 1 of section 51.

suitable land with reasonable solatium in lieu of the acquired property

[****] Sub-Section (2), (3), (4) and (5) omitted.[18]

Reflections

Analogous section under Wakf Act 1954 is S.36 A, inserted by Amendment Act 39 of 1964.

This section has been completely redrafted and Substituted by Act 27 of 2013. Prior to the Amendment this section read as under:

> Section 51 Alienation of waqf property without sanction of board is to be void.

(1) Notwithstanding anything contained in the Waqf Deed, any gift, sale exchange or mortgage of any immovable property which is waqf property, shall be void unless such gift, sale, exchange or mortgage is effected with the prior sanction of the board:

provided that no mosque, dargah or khangah shall be gifted, sold, exchanged or mortgaged except in accordance with any law for the time being in force.

(2) The board may, after publishing in the Official Gazette, the particulars relating to the transaction referred to in sub-section (1) invite any objections and suggestions with respect thereto, consider all objections and suggestions, if any, that may be received by it from the concerned mutawalli or any other person interested in the waqf, and accord sanction to such a transaction if it is of the opinion that such a transaction is:
- (i) Necessary or beneficial to the wakf;
- (ii) Consistent with the objects of the waqf;
- (iii) The consideration thereof is reasonable and adequate:
- (iv) Provided that the sale of the property sanctioned by the board shall be effected by public auction and shall be subject to confirmation by the board within such time as may be prescribed:

Provided further that the Tribunal may, on the application of the aggrieved mutawalli or other person, for reason to be recorded by it in

18 Sub-sections (2) (3) (4) and (5) omitted by Act 27 of 2013, S. 29 (ii).

writing, permit such sale to be made otherwise than by public auction, if it is of opinion that it is necessary so to do in the interest of the waqf.

(3) The utilisation or investment of the amount realised by the sale or exchange mortgage of any property shall be made by the mutawalli subject to the approval of the board, and where any amount has been raised by mortgage of any such property, the mutawalli or other person shall make repayment of the mortgage-debt and obtain a discharge of the mortgage-debt from the mortgagee within such reasonable time as the board may specify.
(4) Every approval given by the board under sub-section (3) shall be communicated to the mutawalli and shall also be published in the manner prescribed.
(5) The mutawalli, or any person having an interest in the waqf who is aggrieved by the decision given under sub-section (3), may, within 90 days from the date of communication to him of such a decision or the publication of the decision, as the case may be, prefer an appeal to the Tribunal against such a decision, and, thereupon, the Tribunal may, after giving the appellant and the board a reasonable opportunity of being heard, confirm, modify or set aside such a decision.

This section prohibits any transaction for sale, alienation or mortgage of waqf property without the prior sanction of the Waqf Board. It also provides that the necessary ingredients to be examined by the Waqf Board before according approval for sale or mortgage of such property. This section provides an exception to the unused graveyards in the States of Punjab, Haryana and Himachal Pradesh, which were already alienated. Such transactions shall be fair and transparent and shall be made through open auction. The section makes it mandatory for the acquisition of suitable property in lieu of the property disposed of.

Judicial response

Section 51 of the Waqf Act 1995 envisages that alienation of waqf property without the sanction of the Wakf Board shall be void. Further section 52 provides for recovery of the Wakf property transferred in contravention of section 51. In Mothukur and Velgodu Villages Mosques vs. Pandanna and Gokari (died) by L.Rs. and Others,[19] a division Bench of the High Court of Andhra Pradesh has observed that:

> At any rate, no prejudice is caused to the transferee, who is in occupation of the property, by non-issue of notice to the transferor. If a proper

19 2010 (1) ALD 76 (DB).

> notice is given to the person in occupation, that would constitute sufficient compliance of the fair procedure contemplated under the above mentioned statutory provision. Any other interpretation would render the provisions of section 36-A and 36-B nugatory.

While discussing the powers of the Waqf Board in alienation of waqf property the Andhra Pradesh High Court in Mohammedia Co-operative Building Society Ltd. vs. Lakshmi Srinivasa Co-operative Building Society Ltd. and Others,[20] observed that:

> It is only Wakf Board which has jurisdiction to accord necessary permission for purpose of alienation of wakf properties and Government cannot interfere with such transaction by issuing G.O. Further the sale transaction of wakf properties by defendant Dargah cannot be treated as policy, requiring prior permission of the State Government. Wakf Board did not apply its independent mind and simply followed Govt. Order while according permission; it amounts to violation of its statutory duty under section 36-A (Now section 51 of Wakf Act, 1995). The very sanction accorded by Govt., as otiose (i.e., unnecessarily becoming involved in a greater degree. Therefore, the sale transaction in favour of defendant society, have to be declared null and void.

The Wakf Board, even though it is the custodian of wakf properties, cannot directly lease out the wakf properties without the consent of the mutawalli. In the case of Markaz Constructions vs. Sugra Humayun Mirza Wakf,[21] the Bench of A.P. High Court observed that:

> Section 36A (section 51 of present Act) is only a supervisory control over the power granted to the mutawalli under the Wakf Deed ... The Board cannot supplant the mutawalli with reference to the powers granted under the Wakf Deed merely because the power of the mutawalli granted under the Wakf Deed is subject to the previous sanction of the Board.

The Bench of the Andhra Pradesh High Court further observed that the Wakf Board should have referred the matter to the mutawalli for consideration and the mutawalli should have advertised the proposal to attract better proposal for the development of the property. The matter went up to the Supreme Court. The Supreme Court confirmed the order of the Division Bench of A.P. High Court.

20 AIR 2007 (NOC) 1459.
21 (1996) 1 Andh WR 278 (DB).

The High Court of Patna in M/s. Namrita Construction Pvt. Ltd. & Anr. vs. State of Bihar & Others,[22] has taken the view that under the Waqf Act, 1995 the powers of the court in this regard have been vested in the Waqf Board and, therefore, even if the Deed of Waqf prohibits the mutawalli from making the sale, etc., of wakf property it would be open to the Wakf Board to grant approval for the sale or other forms of alienation. In fact, the overriding statutory powers of the Wakf Board in this regard have been made clear by the opening phrase "notwithstanding anything contained in the Wakf Deed" in section 51 of the Act. The Board, in granting such approval, will consider the wishes of the wakif(s) in this regard, but the same does not and cannot act as an absolute prohibition upon the powers of the board to accord such sanction if it finds such alienation of property to be necessary or beneficial to the wakf. It was accordingly held that a Deed of Wakf or a Scheme of Management cannot fetter statutory powers conferred upon Board by Parliament to grant sanction for alienation of wakf property under S.51 of the Act.

The Andhra Pradesh High Court in P. Radhakrishnaiah & Others vs. Andhra Pradesh Wakf Board, Hyderabad[23] has observed that service inams granted to the individuals for service to the mosques cannot be termed as grants to mosque. It is a grant to the named individual even though at the relevant time he happened to be office holder. And the Wakf Board is not entitled to that property treating it as wakf property. Since the defendants have purchased the property from the legal representatives of the service inamdars, they cannot be said to be in unauthorised possession. The suit by the Wakf Board filed after the expiry of 12 years is barred by limitations.

The Andhra Pradesh High Court in Mohd. Abdul Jabbar vs. Mohd. Ghulam Mustafa & Others,[24] has observed that if the Waqf Board ratified the action of the mutawalli for the alienation of waqf property, then the sale transaction cannot be said to have been illegal and there is no enforceability in the sale transaction.

In another case, the Andhra Pradesh High Court in Ramineni Sambasivarao and Others vs. Government of A.P. and Others,[25] has gone into the details of alienation of waqf property, and while referring to other citations observed that:

> An additional safeguard is provided under Rule 12(1) in that prior sanction of the Government is required for the sale of the wakf property. Rule 12(1) cannot be read in isolation and must be construed harmoniously with Section 51 of the Act, for it is a well settled principle or

22 AIR, 2009 (NOC) 3021 (Pat).
23 AIR 2008 (NOC) 569 (A.P.).
24 AIR 2008 (NOC) 1175 (A.P.).
25 2010 (4) ALD 710.

interpretation of statutes that the conferment of rule-making power by an Act does not enable the rule-making authority to make a rule which travels beyond the scope of the enabling Act or which is inconsistent therewith or repugnant thereto as held in State of Karnataka v H. Ganesh Kamat.[26]

Any power which the State Government may exercise under Section 97, to issue directions to the Board, can only be in furtherance of the mandatory, provisions of the act to ensure protection of Wakf property from encroachment, illegal alienation, transfers etc.

Section 97 of the Act does not empower the State Government either to relax or give a go-by to the provisions of Section 51 or to accord permission to the Chief Executive Officer of the A.P. State Wakf Board to sell wakf lands otherwise than by public auction. Section 97 does not, therefore, entitle the Government to direct alienation of wakf land except by way of public auction. The impugned order of the Government in so directing the Wakf Board is ultra vires Section 51 of the Wakf Act is without jurisdiction and must, accordingly, be quashed.

The Supreme Court considered the matter pertaining to alienation of wakf properties in D.M. Khasim Sab vs. Court Mohala Mosque Committee[27] and observed that the publication in the Official Gazette as mandated by sub-section (3) had not been done. The purpose for such a publication was to invite objections and suggestions with respect to the transaction referred to in sub-section (1). Hence it was held that, in the absence of compliance under sub-section (2), there was no valid sanction by the board.

Prior approval of the wakif or the court (qazi) (in the present Law the Waqf Board), is necessary for the sale, alienation or mortgage of wakf property. Ex-post facto sanction has never been contemplated by Islamic Jurists in Muhammadan Law. But in 1909 the High Court of Calcutta in Nimi Chand Adya vs. Gulam Hossain,[28] has referred to various texts of Islamic Jurisprudence to justify Ex-post facto sanction, which are as follows:

If a mutawalli wishes to mortgage or pledge the waqf property as security for loan, it is not valid, because such a course would render the waqf useless. Neither the mutawalli nor the people who frequent the mosque (that is the beneficiaries) can validly do so. If a mutawalli mortgages a house belonging to the waqf, and the mortgagee dwells in it, the

26 1983 AIR 550, 1983 SCR (2) 665.
27 (2004) 13 SCC 367.
28 (1909) 37 Cal 179; 3 IC 353.

jurists are of opinion that the latter is bound to pay customary rent (literally rent of a similar property) whether the house be in a condition to yield an income or not. This should be done as a measure to safeguard the waqf. (Fatawa Qadi Khan, AD 1196, Calcutta Edition 1835, Volume 4, page 218.) Text II.

If the waqf property has no money (literally income, profits, etc.) in the hands of the mutawalli the matter should be referred to the Cadi, (Quazi) so that the Cadi may order the mutawalli to borrow on (the security of) the waqf for the benefit of the waqf. The mutawalli may not borrow without the sanction of the Cadi. The circumstances which justify the borrowing arise when there is no income from the waqf property, thereby necessitating borrowing and contracting a loan. (Fatawa Qadi Khan, Volume 4, page 221.) Text III.

The saying of the Prophet addressed to Umar when he wanted to appropriate a piece of land belonging to him and called Thamgh "dedicate its corpus (asl), it shall not be sold nor inherited nor given away as a gift." (Hidayah by Burhan-al-din, AD 1197, Calcutta Edition, Volume II, page 888.) Text IV.

"When a valid waqf is made, its sale and transfer are not permitted. (Hidayah, Volume II, page 897. Text V)."

"It is reported from Imam Muhammad that it (waqf property) cannot be sold, inherited, not given away as a gift. (Hidayah, Volume II, page 907.) Text VI."

If the mutawalli is called upon to pay the land tax (khiraj) and tribute (jibayah) due from the waqf property, and he has not in his hands anything out of the income of the waqf, the jurisconsult Abu-l-Qasim says that it is lawful for him to borrow if the appropriate has authorised him to do so; otherwise he shall have to pay (that is, the debt incurred without the authority of the appropriator) out of his own property and not out of the income of the waqf. The jurisconsult Abu-l-Layth says that, when the mutawalli is confronted with an affair which makes it indispensable for him to borrow, he should do so with the sanction of the hakim, and then pay off the debt out of the income of the waqf, because the Cadi has the power of authorising the mutawalli to borrow on (the security of) the waqf. (Is'af by al-Tarabulusi, AD 1576, Cairo Edition, Text VII.

When the mutawalli wishes to borrow on the security of the waqf, in order to pay off the mortgage money (literally price of mortgage), he is empowered to do so with the sanction of the Cadi; otherwise not. Thus it is laid down in the Sirajiyyah. The circumstances which justify borrowing arise when there is no income of the waqf and thereby necessitates borrowing and contracting loan. But if there be any income of the waqf, and the mutawalli applies his own money for the benefit of the waqf, he may recover the amount from the income of the waqf. Thus it is laid down in the Fatawa Qadi Khan. (Fatawa 'Alamgiri, Calcutta Edition, Volume II, page 519.) Taxt. VIII.

It is not permitted to borrow on (the security of) waqf property, except when recourse to it becomes necessary for the benefit of the waqf, for example, for the purpose of repairs and purchase of seed grains. In such a case it is permitted, subject to the following two conditions: (1) the permission of the Cadi; but if the Cadi happens to be at a distance, he may borrow on his own authority; (2) when it was not possible to lease the property (literally corpus) and to spend the rents, etc., arising therefrom. (Durr al-Mukhtar by al-Hiskafi, AD 1677. Constantinople Edition, Volume III, page 649.) Text IX.

When it is indispensable to borrow, it is permitted with the sanction of the Cadi, if he does not happen to be at a distance from him (that is, the mutawalli), because the Cadi has general powers with respect to what is beneficial for the Muslims. And it is said it is permitted unrestrictedly (that is borrowing is permitted even without the sanction of the Cadi) for the purpose of repairs, but the first view is relied upon by the school. (Radd-al Muhtar by Ibn 'Abidin, AD 1836, Constantinople Edition, Volume III, page 649.) TEXT X.

It is laid down in the commentary of al-Tanwir: the mutawalli cannot borrow on (the security of) the waqf for the purpose of repairs, except with the permission of the Cadi. If the above-mentioned mutawalli (that is, the mutawalli mentioned in the question to which the Fatawa is the answer) borrows with his (Cadi's) permission for the purpose of repairing waqf property, the beneficiaries cannot demand their dues till the debt is satisfied. (Fataws Mahdiyah by Sheikh al-Islam Muhammad al-'Abbasi, Grand Mufti of Egypt, AD 1883, Volume II, page 469) Text XI.

12. It is not permitted to borrow on (the security of) waqf, except subject to the following three conditions: (1) for necessity, for example repairs; (2) permission of Cadi; (3) that it was not possible to lease the property and spend the income arising therefrom. (Fatawa Mahdiyah, Volume II, page 512.).

The High Court of Calcutta, after referring to the above texts, observed that:

These texts indicate that property which has been validly dedicated as wakf cannot, unless the Mutawalli is expressly empowered by the deed of endowment to do so, be ordinarily sold or mortgaged. If, however, necessity is established and the permission of the Kazi is obtained, such alienation is valid. Some of the texts, however, indicate that the Mutawalli may borrow on his own authority if the Cadi happens to be a distance.... This would seem to show that the previous permission of

> the Cadi is not a condition precedent, and Sir Roland Wilson appears to favour this view when he suggests that the transaction may be retrospectively confirmed by the Court … The texts, however, to which we have referred, indicate plainly that the consent of the Cadi is essential whenever he is available, and if so, there is no reason why approval subsequent to the transaction should not be treated as effective in the same manner as approval prior to the transaction. It is but rational to hold that the approval of the Cadi was deemed requisite, primarily with a view to make sure that the loan was necessary, and in this view, approval antecedent or subsequent, ought to be equally effectual.

This discordant ruling of the Calcutta High Court has been criticised by Amir Ali,[29] who opines that:

> Ex post facto sanction was never contemplated by the Mussalman jurists and the prior permission of the Judge was made an absolute condition to see not only that the loan was necessary, but also whether it was proper, that the terms were not onerous and there was no other mode of meeting the necessity.

However, Mulla[30] supports the notion of retrospective sanction when he says that

> a mutawalli has no power without the permission of the Court to mortgage, sell or exchange wakf property or any part thereof unless he is expressly empowered by the deed of wakf to do so. Mulla goes on to state that it has been held in Calcutta in Nimai Chand Addya v. Golam Hossein (1910) 37 Cal. 179, that a mortgage of wakf property though made without the previous sanction of the Court may be retrospectively confirmed by the Court and that the mortgage without the previous leave of the Court is not void ab initio.

However, the notion of retrospective sanction finds support by the High Court of Allahabad in Afzal Hussain vs. Chhedi Lal,[31] by the Calcutta High Court in Sailendranath vs. Hade Kaza,[32] by the Bombay High Court in Zafar Bai vs. Chhaganlal and by the Madras High Court in Abdul Kadir vs. Mahlar Rathul Kadiria Sabha Kayalpattinam,[33] and by the Orissa High

29 Mahommedan Law, Syed Ameer Ali, p. 490.
30 Mulla's Principles of Mahomedan Law, 10th Edn. 1933, p. 151.
31 AIR 1935 All 792; ILR (1935) 57 All 727; 155 IC 791.
32 AIR 1932 Cal 356; ILR (1932) 59 Cal 586; 137 IC 500.
33 AIR 1953 Mad 143.

Court in Saleb Khan vs. Madar Sahib.[34] Nimi Chand Adya vs. Gulam Hossain- (1909)37 Cal 179; 3 IC 353.

In Zafar Bai vs. Chhaganlal[35] the High Court of Bombay observed that:

> I see no distinction in principle between antecedent and subsequent sanction in the case of a long term lease if a mortgage by a Mutawalli can be validated by subsequent sanction as in – "Nemaichand v. Golam Hossein,"[36] and – "Afazal Hussain v. Chhedilal."[37] The test in both the cases is the same, viz., necessity or benefit to the institution.

Similarly the High Court of Madras in P.S. Abdul Kadir vs. Mahlar Rathul Kadiria Sabha Kayalpattinam,[38] held that:

> On the facts and in the circumstances above narrated it was clearly beneficial to the Mahlara that the Kayalpatnam property should be disposed of and the proceeds of the sale invested in a more remunerative property. Admittedly the Tuticorin property brought more income to the trust. The case was eminently fit for the exercise of the power of the court to grant retrospective sanction. We accordingly give the necessary sanction to the transaction.

In Abdul Hussain vs. Mohmmad Riza[39] it was observed:

> Considering the terms of the enactment and the scope and purpose of the Act is clear that the legislature intended of income of wakf properties for the purpose of providing some control on the management of properties which are admittedly wakf. It could not have intended to include in its scope the enquiry into the vital questions whether the disputed property is wakf property and the person in possession of it is a mutawalli, which are questions of fundamental character such as could be the subject-matter of a suit alone.

The High Court of Orissa while granting retrospective sanction for alienation of waqf property in Saleb Khan vs. Madar Sahib held that:

> But in view of the concurrent findings of fact about the legal necessity and the admitted position regarding the extent of the property that has been alienated and the total extent of the wakf property, we consider

34 AIR 1954 Ori 239.
35 AIR 1942 Bom 21; (1941) 43 Bom LR 854.
36 37 Cal 179.
37 57 All 727.
38 AIR 1953 Mad 143.
39 I.L.R. (1939) Nag. 564.

> that all necessary facts for the purpose of giving permission are available before us and we may therefore exercise discretion conferred by law and permit the two alienations. We may mention that in the Madras case cited above, permission was given at the first appellate stage. We would therefore permit the two alienations with retrospective effect and dismiss the plaintiff's suits.

However, sub-section (1) of section (51) has categorically made it clear that the sanction of the board is necessary for alienation, gift, sale or mortgage of the immovable waqf property, irrespective of the provisions of gift deed or any instrument. The newly inserted section 52A imposes up to two years' rigorous imprisonment for sale or alienation of waqf property without the sanction of the Waqf Board.

While dealing with the matter of mortgage of waqf property in Ganapathy Naicker vs. Special Officer for Wakfs, Madras,[40] the High Court of Madras,, while referring a decision of the Bench of the same Court in Adbul Kadir vs. Maharathul Kadiriya Sabba,[41] held that:

> In the circumstances, the proper order to make is to allow the petitions and direct the petitioners to apply to the Board for sanction. It is for the Board to consider the circumstances and grant sanction or refuse to grant it. In the event of the Board refusing to grant the sanction, the Board will be at liberty to take proceedings under section 36-B.

The validity of Acquisition of Certain Areas at Ayodhya by the Ayodhya Act (Act 33 of 1993) and the Presidential reference (No.1, of 1993) under Article 143 (1) of the Constitution of India to the Supreme Court came up for consideration before the Supreme Court in Dr. Ismail Faruqi vs. Union of India.[42] The Supreme Court held that:

> A temple, church or mosque, etc., Are essential immovable properties and subject to protection under Article 25 and 26. Every immovable property is liable to be acquired. Viewed in the proper perspective a mosque does not enjoy any additional protection which is not available to religious places of worship of other religions... There can be no reason to hold that a mosque has a unique or special status, higher than that of the places of worship of other religions in secular India to make it immune from acquisition by exercise of the sovereign or prerogative power of the State.

40 (1974)1 Mad LJ 239.
41 AIR 1953 Mad 143.
42 AIR 1995 SC 605.

A division bench of the High Court of Andhra Pradesh in Lanco Hills Technology Park … vs. Mahaboob Alam Khan and Others[43] held that:

> Even when the Wakf Board decides to alienate the wakf property, it can only be done after satisfying the conditionality's under Section 51(2), namely, such transaction is beneficial to the wakfs, in consistence with the objects of the wakf and consideration thereof is reasonable and adequate. Therefore, we are inclined to accept the submission of the Dargah and Wakf Board that the statement made by the CEO in the writ proceedings has no bearing on the question of "balance of convenience" at the time of considering the issue of permitting the petitioner to alienate the property.

In an interesting case of legal jugglery, a suit was filed in the Civil Court of Hamirpur District of U.P. (within the jurisdiction of Allahabad Bench of the High Court of Allahabad) for the allotment of wakf land situated in Bahraich District (within the jurisdiction of the Lucknow Bench of Allahabad High Court). The suit was dismissed as it was not cognisable at Hamirpur for the lack of territorial jurisdiction. The petitioner filed a writ petition in the Allahabad Bench of the High Court. The single judge, by interim order dated 11 June 2010 and 18 June 2010, directed allotment of the land to the petitioner in the "Mela area" and compliance of the orders. However, the Division Bench set aside the interim orders passed by the single judge. Aggrieved, the petitioner filed the petition for special leave. When the matter went to appeal before the Supreme Court in Raja Khan vs. U.P. Sunni Central Waqf Board & Anr[44] the court took a serious view of the matter and castigated strictures upon the single judge of the Allahabad Bench of the High Court who passed interim orders. The Supreme Court made the following observations:

> The above orders are shocking to say the least. We are of the opinion that the above two ex-parte interim orders of the single judge of the Allahabad High Court were clearly passed on extraneous considerations. This is for the following reasons:

(1) The property in question is in the district of Bahraich which is within the territorial jurisdiction of the Lucknow Bench of the Allahabad High Court. Hence, the writ petition could not have been validly filed or entertained in the Allahabad Bench of the High Court in view of the decision of this court in Nasiruddin vs. State Transport Appellate Tribunal AIR 1976 SC 331.

43 2012 (4) ALD 385; 2012 (4) ALT 136 (DB).
44 [2010] 13 (ADDL.) S.C.R. 1131 1132.

(2) The writ petition was not maintainable because ordinarily no writ petition lies against a private body.
(3) By the ex-parte order dated 11.6.2010 the writ petition has been practically allowed since by that ex-parte order the respondents 2, 3, & 4 (U.P. Sunni Central Waqf Board, District Magistrate, Bahraich and Committee of Management, Waqf No. 19, Dargah Sharif, Bahraich) have been directed to allot the land in the Mela of the aforesaid Waqf at plot Nos. 1760 to 1770 and 1826 to 1884 to the petitioner for the purpose of running circus, Jhoola, Merry-go-round etc., and possession of the allocated land was directed to be handed over within three days. Subsequently, on 18.6.2010, the same single Judge has passed an order directing the district Magistrate and SP, Bahraich to take appropriate action for compliance of the earlier order.

The faith of the common man in the country is shaken to the core by such shocking and outrageous orders such as the kind which have been passed by the single judge.

We are sorry to say but a lot of complaints are coming against certain judges of the Allahabad High Court relating to their integrity. Some judges have their kith and kin practicing in the same court, and within a few years of starting practice the sons or relations of the judge become multi-millionaires, have huge bank balances, luxurious cars, huge houses and are enjoying a luxurious life. This is a far cry from the days when the sons and other relatives of judges could derive no benefit from their relationship and had to struggle at the bar like any other lawyer.

We do not mean to say that all lawyers who have close relations with judges of the High Court are misusing those relationships. Some are scrupulously taking care that no one should lift a finger on this account. However, others are shamelessly taking advantage of these relationships.

There are also other serious complaints against some judges of the High Court.

The Allahabad High Court really needs some house cleaning (both Allahabad and Lucknow Bench), and we request Hon'ble the Chief Justice of the High Court to do the needful, even if he has to take some strong measures, including recommending transfers of the incorrigibles.

> We entirely agree with the view taken by the Learned Division Bench in the impugned judgment.

In M/S Namira Construction Pvt. Ltd. vs M/S Fazal Imam Public Charitable and Religious Trust,[45] the High Court of Patna, while dealing with the development of waqf property without permission of Waqf Board and

45 AIR 2019 (NOC) 473 PAT.

without the knowledge of the mutawalli, stated that the document dated 15 November 2002 sought to be relied on cannot be enforced in the absence of a valid and legal sanction, in as much as an alienation of the nature sought would be void ab initio in terms of section 51 of the Waqf Act 1995. It further observed that:

> once the agreement dated 15.11.2002 does not have a valid and legal existence, the proceedings undertaken under section 11(6) of the 1996 Act can go into this issue which is purely legal as the existence of a legally valid agreement is a sine qua non in order to apply the arbitration clause. In the instant case it is through this indirect method of the creation of an agreement dated 15.11.2002 that the arbitration clause is being invoked that exists in the agreement dated 09.09.2002 which is only valid development agreement. Thus in my opinion, the applicant cannot invoke the arbitration clause on the strength of a document which does not have a valid and legal existence. There is therefore, no arbitration clause available that can be invoked for the purpose of appointing an arbitrator.

****

Section 52

Recovery of waqf property transferred in contravention of section 51:-

(1) *If the Board is satisfied, after making any inquiry in such manner as may be prescribed, that any immovable property of a waqf entered as such in the register of waqf maintained under section 36, has been transferred without the previous sanction of the Board in contravention of the provisions of section 51 or section 56,*[46] *it may send a requisition to the Collector within whose jurisdiction the property is situate to obtain and deliver possession of the property to it.*

(2) *On receipt of a requisition under sub-section (1), the Collector shall pass an order directing the person in possession of the property to deliver the property to the Board within a period of thirty days from the date of the service of the order.*

(3) *Every order passed under sub-section (2) shall be served-*
   (a) *by giving or tendering the order, or by sending it by post to the person for whom it is intended; or*
   (b) *if such person cannot be found, by affixing the order on some conspicuous part of his last known place of abode or business, or*

46 Inserted by Act 27 of 2013, S. 30.

by giving or tendering the order to some adult male member or servant of his family or by causing it to be affixed on some conspicuous part of the property to which it relates:

Provided that where the person on whom the order is to be served, is a minor, service upon his guardian or upon any adult male member or servant of his family shall be deemed to be the service upon the minor.

(4) *Any person aggrieved by the order of the Collector under sub-section (2) may, within a period of thirty days from the date of the service of the order, prefer an appeal to the Tribunal within whose jurisdiction the property is situate and the decisions of the Tribunal on such appeal shall be final.*

(5) *Where an order passed under sub-section (2) has not been complied with and the time for appealing against such order has expired without an appeal having been preferred or the appeal, if any, preferred within that time has been dismissed, the Collector shall obtain possession of the property in respect of which the order has been made, using such force, if any, as may be necessary for the purpose and deliver it to the Board.*

(6) *In exercising his functions under this section the Collector shall be guided by such rules as may be provided by regulations.*

Reflections

Analogous section under Wakf Act 1954 is S.36 B, inserted by the amendment Act 34 of 1964.

This section provides for the recovery of waqf property alienated in contravention of section 51. The Waqf Board after considering and completing the procedure as mentioned in section 51 or 56 shall send a requisition to the District Collector/Magistrate concerned for recovery and possession thereof. The District Collector, upon receipt of the requisition, shall pass orders and serve the same to the person in possession of the waqf property to deliver the same to the waqf institution concerned within 30 days from the date of service of such orders. The aggrieved person may approach to the Waqf Tribunal and prefer an appeal within 30 days. The decision of the Tribunal shall be final.

The requisition to the District Magistrate/Collector is only an option available for recovery of the alienated waqf property. However, the option of filing a suit for recovery of the lost property or alienated waqf property in the Waqf Tribunal is always available to the mutawalli and to the Waqf Board.

Judicial response

The requisition to the District Magistrate/Collector is only an option available for recovery of the alienated waqf property. The Madras High Court in Tamil Nadu Wakf Board vs. S.A. Syed Masood and others,[47] observed that:

> If in a suit filed by a stranger, the Wakf Board can appear and plead as a party to the suit, there is no reason why the same right cannot be exercised by the Board itself in a civil suit filed by itself. The right to recover property is not for the first time created by the Statute. It is a common-law right. Section 36-B of the Wakf Act is only a summary procedure. Complicated questions of law and fact cannot be agitated before the Collector. The exhaustive remedy through a civil court is not taken away by virtue of Section 36-B of the Wakf Act.
>
> On the basis of the above said decisions, it can safely be held that the contention based on Section 36-B of the Wakf Act that the appellant's suit is barred under Section 9, C.P. Code has only to be rejected, and we do so.

A Bench of the High Court of Madras in Thangachi Nachial vs. Ahamed Hussain,[48] while referring to various judgements, has taken the view that a lawfully appointed trustee or mutawalli can institute a suit or legal proceeding to recover the alienated or encroached waqf property. But the mutawalli himself is party to the alienation and the person interested in waqf can institute legal proceedings by making the mutawalli or the Wakf Board a party to such suit. The court observed as under:

> The principles which regulate the right to institute suits in relation to trust properties are well settled as pointed out by Venkataramana Hao J. in Ahmed, Kutty v. Ayithraman Kutty, 1937–2 Mad LJ 301: (AIR 1937 Mad 819) (O). When there is a lawful trustee for an institution, he is the person competent to institute a suit in relation to the property of the institution, to take the necessary steps for safe-guarding and preserving it and to eject a trespasser and recover possession thereof for the trust, but the recovery of the property is only for and on behalf of the institution which he represents. But where a trustee has alienated the trust property and therefore would not proceed to recover possession of the same or has disabled himself otherwise from maintaining a suit in respect thereof or declines to institute a suit, it cannot be said that the institution is without a remedy.
>
> It is desirable and necessary to make the trustee a party to the suit, and where he is made a party it is open to the Court to mould the relief as

47 1995 AIHC 6317; (1995) 2 MLJ 514.
48 (1957) 1 MLJ 300; AIR 1957 Mad 194.

> the circumstances may require. If the suit is one brought for possession by the worshippers, the court can, after declaring the property to be trust property and setting aside the alienation, direct delivery of possession to the trustee. In cases where there is no trustee, it is open to the Court to direct delivery of possession to the worshippers on behalf of the trust.- Rangaswami Naidu vs. Krishna-swami Aiyar, 44 Mad LJ 116; (AIR 1923 Mad 276 (2)(P).
>
> This would not offend the principle that a trustee alone is competent to maintain a suit to eject a trespasser; See Kuvarbal v. Mir Alam Khan, ILR 7 Bom 170 (Q). Even a worshipper can recover possession of trust properties on behalf of the trust so that when proper proceedings are instituted for the management of the trust property and a trustee is appointed, he might hand over possession to the trustee. The general principle applicable to Muslim Wakf is the same as that applicable to the property of a Hindu idol. The rule of Hanafi Law that wakf property is taken to have ceased to be held in human ownership is applied to all such property even if the wakf be a wakf al-al-aulad Or wakf for the benefit of the descendants: Mahammad Jafar v. Taqi, AIR 1933 Oudh 517 (B). So when a waqf property is unlawfully alienated any person interested in the objects of the waqf may institute a suit to, set aside the altenations and for the enforcement of the provisions of the waqf; Kazi Hassan v. Balakrishna, ILR 24 Bom 170 (S).

It has been held, by the Karataka High Court in Rudramurthy vs. Karnataka Wakf Board[49] by the Karnataka High Court that section 36B of the Wakf Act 1954 (section 52 of the present Act) does not apply where the wakf property has been transferred long before the board came into existence. In such a case, the remedy is only by way of a suit. The High Court of Karnataka made the following observation:

> In view of the above it is clear that in pursuance of the impugned order, the Board could recover possession of the suit property only through the agency of the civil court and thus there is no immediate threat to the possession of the petitioner over the property in question.

Dealing with the scope sub-section (1) of section 52, the High Court of Allahabad in Afzal Houssain vs. First Additional District Judge[50] observed that:

> Action under Section 57 A can be taken only when the first condition is satisfied, namely that the property is entered as waqf property in the

49 AIR 1977 Kant 147.
50 AIR 1985 All 79.

register of waqfs maintained under Section 30. This is a jurisdictional fact and action under Section 57 A would be permissible only when the property is so entered. Under this provision it is not enough that the property is waqf property.

For recovery of waqf property under section 52 of the Act, the Andhra Pradesh High Court in Kadiyam Mullayya vs. District Judge, West Godavari[51] held that mere notice issued by the Collector to persons in possession of wakf property to hand over possession without prior notice of determination of their rights is not valid.

The High Court of Uttarakhand, in Smt. Salma Parveen vs. Uttarakhand Wakf Board & Others,[52] has held that to recover the wakf property transferred in contravention of section 51 of the Waqf Act, the board shall first raise objections before the District Collector under section 52 (2) and thereafter if aggrieved by the order of the Collector, file an appeal before the Waqf Tribunal.

Any person aggrieved by the orders of the District Collector/Magistrate in the recovery of the fraudulently alienated waqf property shall approach the Waqf Tribunal as has been mentioned earlier.

****

Section 52A

Penalty for alienation of waqf property without sanction of Board.[53]

(1) ***Whoever alienates or purchases or takes possession of, in any manner whatsoever, either permanently or temporarily, any movable or immovable property being a waqf property, without prior sanction of the Board, shall be punishable with rigorous imprisonment for a term which may extend to two years:***

Provided that the waqf property so alienated shall without prejudice to the provisions of any law for the time being in force, be vested in the Board without any compensation therefor.

(2) ***Notwithstanding anything contained in the Code of Criminal Procedure, 1973 (2 of 1974) any offence punishable under this section shall be cognizable and non-bailable.***

51 (1988) 1 Andh LT 160.
52 AIR, 2009 (NOC) 3023 (Utr).
53 Inserted by Act 27 of 2013, S. 31.

(3) ***No court shall take cognizance of any offence under this section except on a complaint made by the Board or any officer duly authorised by the State Government in this behalf.***
(4) ***No court inferior to that of a Metropolitan Magistrate or a Judicial Magistrate of the first class shall try any offence punishable under this section.***

Reflections

It is a newly inserted section under the Waqf Amendment Act 2013 hence no analogous section.

This section provides for punishment up to two years imprisonment if any person is in possession of the waqf property without the prior sanction of the board. This section declares that illegal possession of waqf property is a cognisable and non-bailable offence. The courts shall not take cognisance of such an offence unless there is a complaint by the board or an Officer authorised by the State Government in this regard.

Judicial response

A person should not be dispossessed arbitrarily from the property, even if it is a declared waqf property and even though fraudulent entries are made in any official records.

A division of Bench of Patna High Court in Shamimul Haque vs. The State Of Bihar[54] while upholding the order of the single judge observed that when it is found that the original writ petitioner was dispossessed illegally and arbitrarily on the oral orders passed by the S.D.O. Patna city, the same has been set aside and the original respondents are directed to restore the possession of the lands in question to the original writ petitioner, it cannot be said that the learned single judge has committed any error.

****

Section 53

Restriction on purchase of property on behalf of waqf:-

Notwithstanding anything contained in a waqf deed, no immovable property shall be purchased for or on behalf of any waqf from the

54 AIR 2019 PATNA 26 Paragraphs 6–7.

funds of any waqf except with the prior sanction of the Board, and the Board shall not accord such sanction unless it considers that the acquisitions of such property is necessary or beneficial to the waqf and that the price proposed to be paid there for is adequate and reasonable:

Provided that before such sanction is accorded, the particulars relating to the proposed transaction shall be published in the Official Gazette inviting objections and suggestions with respect thereto and, the Board shall, after considering the objections and suggestions that may be received by it from mutawalli or other persons interested in the waqf, make such order as it may think fit.

Reflections

Analogous section under Wakf Act 1954 is S.36 C, inserted by the Waqf Amendment Act (Act 69 of 1984).

Section 53 of the Waqf Act provides that no property shall be purchased on behalf of any Waqf without the prior sanction of the Waqf Board. The board, before according such a sanction, will publish the particulars of such transactions in the Official Gazette and local newspapers where such property is situated, calling for suggestions and objections, if any. The board should also consider that the transaction for the purchase of such property is transparent and the amount being paid for such property is adequate and reasonable.

Judicial response

Judicial response pertaining to this section is not found.

****

Section 54

Removal of encroachment from waqf property:-

(1) ***Whenever the Chief Executive Officer considers whether on receiving any complaint or on his own motion that there has been an encroachment on any land, building, space or other property which is waqf property and, which has been registered as such under this Act, he shall cause to be served upon the encroacher a notice specifying the particulars of the encroachment and calling upon him to show cause before a date to be specified in such notice, as to why an order requiring him to remove the encroachment before the date so specified should***

not be made and shall also send a copy of such notice to the concerned mutawalli.

(2) *The notice referred to in sub-section (1) shall be served in such manner as may be prescribed.*

(3) *If, after considering the objections, received during the period specified in the notice, and after conducting an inquiry in such manner as may be prescribed, the Chief Executive Officer is satisfied that the property in question is waqf property and that there has been an encroachment on any such waqf property, he may make an application to the Tribunal for grant of order of eviction for removing,*[55] *such encroachment and deliver possession of the land, building, space or other property encroached upon to the mutawalli of the waqf.*

(4) *The Tribunal, upon receipt of such application from the Chief Executive Officer, for reasons to be recorded therein, make an order of eviction directing that the waqf property shall be vacated by all persons who may be in occupation thereof or any part thereof, and cause a copy of the order to be affixed on the outer door or some other conspicuous part of the waqf property he may make an application to the Tribunal for grant of order of eviction for removing:*[56]

Provided that the Tribunal may before making an order of eviction, give an opportunity of being heard to the person against whom the application for eviction has been made by the Chief Executive Officer.

(5) *If any person refuses or fails to comply with the order of eviction within forty-five days from the date of affixture of the order under sub-section (2), the Chief Executive Officer or any other person duly authorised by him in this behalf may evict that person from, and take possession of, the waqf property.*

Reflections

Analogous section under Wakf Act 1954 is S.36 D, inserted by Waqf Amendment Act 1984 (Act 69 of 1984).

This section deals with the removal of encroachment from waqf property. The Chief Executive Officer, on receipt of any complaint about the encroachment, or acting suo motu, if he has reason to believe that there is

55 Substituted by Act 27 of 2013, S. 32(a), for "he may, by an order, require the encroacher to remove."

56 Substituted by Act 27 of 2013, S. 32(b), for sub-section (4).

an encroachment of waqf property, shall issue a notice to the encroacher calling upon him to remove the encroachment and deliver possession of the encroached property to the mutawalli, the managing committee or to an Officer authorised by him. On receipt of such notice, the encroacher may defend his case by submitting his own case before the Chief Executive Officer. Before Amendment Act 2013 (Act 27 of 2013), sub-section (3) had empowered the Chief Executive Officer to pass order of eviction, but now after proper enquiry he has to approach the Waqf Tribunal for an appropriate order. Sub-section (4) has been substituted and sub-section (5) is inserted by Waqf Amendment Act 2013 (Act 27 of 2013). Before substitution sub section was as follows:

> (4) Nothing contained in sub-section (3) shall prevent any person aggrieved by the order made by the chief executive officer under that sub-section from instituting a suit in a tribunal to establish that he has right, title or interest in the land, building, space or other property:
>
> Provided that no such suit shall be instituted by a person who has been let into possession of the land, building, space or other property as a lessee, licensee or mortgage by the mutawalli of the wakf or by any other person authorised by him in this behalf.

However, the Chief Executive Officer shall conduct an enquiry to find out the facts of the matter and approach the Tribunal for the eviction orders. The Tribunal, after giving reasonable opportunity of being heard to the encroacher, shall pass the necessary orders.

Judicial response

When the Chief Executive Officer initiates action against the encroachers for the removal of encroachment from the waqf property under this section, it is the Chief Executive Officer alone who has been delegated by such powers and not the Waqf Board. As observed by the High Court of Andhra Pradesh in Gajjala Venkateshwarlu and another vs. A.P. State Wakf Tribunal, Hyderabad,[57] tried to demarcate the two entities – the Waqf board and the Chief Executive Officer – and their powers.

The High Court of Andhra Pradesh in Muppu Raju Lakshmi vs. A.P. State Wakf board and Another,[58] while acknowledging the workload of a Chief Executive Officer has allowed the writ petition because of the absence of rules to be framed by the State Government under section 109 of Wakf Act 1995 and observed that:

57 2003 (3) ALD 269.
58 2010 (3) ALD 263.

> As the things stand now, in the State of Andhra Pradesh, an inquiry under section 54(3) of the Act can be conducted, only by the Chief Executive Officer. This may, no doubt, lead to heavy pressure on the functioning of the incumbent. However, that can be remedied, only by framing the relevant Rules.

In the case of Agrapu Venkatamma vs. Revenue Divisional Officer, Srikakulam and Others,[59] the High Court of Andhra Pradesh held that the Chief Executive Officer has quasi-judicial powers under section 54 of this Act. Justice L. Narasimha Reddy observed that:

> Thus, there is a distinction and also separation of powers of the Wakf board and the Chief Executive Officer. The powers of the Chief Executive Officer and the functions of the Wakf board are distinct and separate. Section 32 deals with the functions of the board. Independent and separate powers are also vested on the Chief Executive Officer and the Chief Executive Officer is not merely an officer who executes the resolutions of the Wakf board alone.
>
> Under Section 54 of the Act, the Chief Executive Officer is empowered to receive any complaint with regard to any encroachment of any land; building or other property which is wakf property registered under the Wakf Act and issue a show-cause notice on the encroacher calling upon the encroacher to show-cause why he should not be removed from the encroachment. After submitting the explanation under Section 54 (2), the Chief Executive Officer alone is empowered to pass an order under Section 54 (3). Under Section 54(4), any person aggrieved by the order passed by the Chief Executive Officer under Section 54(3), is entitled to institute a suit in a Tribunal to establish his right, title and interest in the land, building, space or property. But under proviso to Section 54 (4), the lessee, licensee or mortgagee is not entitled to institute a suit. Under Section 55, if the order passed by the Chief Executive Officer under Section 54(3) becomes final, then the Chief Executive Officer may apply to the Divisional Magistrate within the local limits for eviction of the encroacher and such Magistrate is empowered to remove the encroacher.

The Andhra Pradesh High Court has ruled in the case of Building Mosque Wakf, Vijayawada vs. Sheik Meera and Sons,[60] that:

> Therefore, Mutawalli has also power to issue quit notice and recover possession from the tenants which is part of his powers of management and

59 2007 (2) ALT 595.
60 2011 (1) ALD 611.

> administration of wakf or wakf properties. Both the courts below therefore are not right in concluding that the Mutawalli in the present case had no authority to issue notice of eviction and file the suit for eviction.

In another case, Hameed Ali vs. A.P. State Wakf board,[61] the Andhra Pradesh High Court observed that:

> Further, it is a well settled principle that if the order of the authorities is in contravention of fundamental right or the violation of principles of natural justice or if the order is wholly without jurisdiction. It is always open for the aggrieved party to challenge the same in a writ proceeding under Article 226 of the Constitution of India. A catena of decisions on this point would reveal that even the order is wholly without jurisdiction; even this Court is entitled to interdict the proceedings at the stage of show-cause notice also.

The Honourable High Court appears to give the impression that, whenever the fundamental rights or the principles of natural justice are violated, then the remedy under Article 226 of the Constitution of India is always available.

The High Court Madras, in the case of Mutawalli Larabsha Dharga vs. the Panruti Municipality,[62] held that:

> Further, as per Section 54 (3) of the Wakf Act, when any order has been passed by the Chief Executive Officer of the Wakf board, that the property is a wakf property and the person in possession of the property is an encroacher and directed the encroacher to deliver possession of the property to the Mutawalli of the Wakf, any person aggrieved by such order, may institute a suit in a Tribunal to establish that he has right/title/interest in the land, building, space or other property.

In the year 2019, a division Bench of the Kerala High Court while dealing with a case of the removal of encroachments from the waqf property in the P.K. Hamza Hajee vs. Kerala State Waqf board,[63] rendered the ruling as follows:

> The Chief Executive Officer himself has to initiate the proceedings under Section 54. He is bound to conduct an enquiry based on the objection if any received from the alleged "encroacher." On satisfaction about the encroachment, he is bound to approach the Wakf Tribunal for getting an order of removal of the encroachment. There is

61 2001 (4) ALD 594.
62 C.R.P. (NPD) Nos. 1607, 2916 and 2320 of 2010.
63 AIR 2019 Kerala 182.

no provision in the Wakf Act or under the Lease Rules authorising the Chief Executive Officer to delegate such powers to any other officer of the Wakf board.

****

Section 55

Enforcement of orders made under section 54:-

Where the person, ordered under sub-section (4)[64] of section 54 to remove any encroachment, omits or fails to remove such encroachment, within the time specified in the order or, as the case may be, fails to vacate the land, building, space or other property to which the orders relates, within the time aforesaid, the Chief Executive Officer may refer the order of the Tribunal to the Executive Magistrate[65] within the local limits of whose jurisdiction the land, building, space or other property is situated for evicting the encroacher, and thereupon, such Magistrate shall make an order directing the encroacher to remove the encroachment, or, as the case may be, vacate the land, building, space or other property and to deliver possession thereof to the concerned mutawalli and in default of compliance with the order, remove the encroachment or, as the case may be, evict the encroacher from the land, building, space or other property and may, for this purpose, take such police assistance as may be necessary.

Reflections

Analogous section under Wakf Act 1954 is S.36 E inserted by Waqf Amendment Act 1984 (Act 69 of 1984).

This section deals with the procedure of enforcement and execution of the orders passed under the provisions of section 54 of the Act. The Chief Executive Officer shall send the orders of the Tribunal to the District Collector/Magistrate, under whose jurisdiction the encroached property is situated for eviction of the encroachers and delivering possession to the mutawalli, the managing committee or the Officer authorised/designated in this behalf. The District Collector/Magistrate shall take the help of the police force as may be necessary for the execution of the orders.

64 Substituted by Act 27 of 2013, S. 33 (a), for sub-section (3)."

65 Substituted by Act 27 of 2013, S. 33 (b), for apply to the sub-divisional magistrate.

Judicial response

The High Court of Andhra Pradesh in Nanda Seshikala and Others vs. A.P. State Wakf Board and Others[66] has observed that:

> As already pointed out, the powers of the Chief Executive Officer under Section 54(1) are totally distinct and recognized by the statute. Therefore, since the Chief Executive Officer issued notices invoking his jurisdiction under Section 54(1) of the Act and the consequential proceedings were issued under Section 55 of the Act, the only course open to the petitioners is to approach the Tribunal constituted under Section 83 of the Act.

The Madhya Pradesh High Court in Sufi Tafseer Mohammad vs. State of Madhya Pradesh[67] held that there was no need of a second inquiry for taking action under section 55 of the Act. The court, while disposing of the case, held as under:

> A bare perusal of the aforesaid provision revels that no second enquiry is warranted under section 55 whether once an order of eviction is passed under section 54. The provision as contained under section 55 is in the nature of power to execute the order of eviction.

****

Section 55A

Disposal of property left on waqf property by unauthorised occupants.[68]

(1) ***Where any person has been evicted from any waqf property under sub-section (4) of section 54, the Chief Executive Officer may, after giving fourteen days' notice to the person from whom possession of the waqf property has been taken and after publishing the notice in at least one newspaper having circulation in the locality and after proclaiming the contents of the notice by placing it on conspicuous part of the waqf property, remove or cause to be removed or dispose of by public auction any property remaining on such premises.***

(2) ***Where any property is sold under sub-section (1), the sale proceeds shall, after deducting the expenses relating to removal, sale and such***

66 2003 (5) ALD 796, 2003 (5) ALT 466.

67 W.P. No. 9935/2011.

68 Inserted by Act 27 of 2013, S. 34.

other expenses, the amount, if any, due to the State Government or a local authority or a corporate authority on account of arrears of rent, damages or costs, be paid to such person, as may appear to the Chief Executive Officer to be entitled to the same:

Provided that where the Chief Executive Officer is unable to decide as to the person to whom the balance of the amount is payable or as to the appointment of the same, he may refer such dispute to the Tribunal and the decision of the Tribunal thereon shall be final.

Reflections

This is a new section inserted by Waqf Amendment Act 2013 (Act 27 of 2013), hence no analogous section under Wakf Act 1954.

This section provides for the serving of 14 days' notice to the encroacher to remove or cause to remove by public auction the remains on the premises. Alternatively, such notice may be affixed at a conspicuous place on the premises of the waqf property and the same may be published in the local newspaper.

Judicial response

The Bihar Wakf Act 1947 as amended by Bihar Wakf (Amendment and Validating Act) 1950, wherein there was provision of a Majlis whose decision stands good and effectual. A Division Bench of the Patna High Court in Amar Nath Alias Bunti vs. State of Bihar and Others held that the occupant of the wakf property having given possession by the Majlis is not an encroacher. The bench has set aside the order of the Waqf Tribunal as well as the order of single judge of the same Court.

****

Section 56

Restriction on power to grant lease of waqf property:-

(1) ***A lease for any period exceeding thirty years[69] of any immovable property which is waqf property shall, notwithstanding anything contained in the deed or instrument of waqf or in any other law for the time being in force, be void and of no effect:***

69 Substituted by Act 27 of 2013, S. 35 (a) (i), for "A lease or sub-lease for any period exceeding three years."

Provided that a lease for any period up to thirty years may be made for commercial activities, education or health purposes, with the approval of the State Government, for such period and purposes as may be specified in the rules made by the Central Government:[70]

Provided further that lease of any immovable waqf property, which is an agricultural land, for a period exceeding three years shall, notwithstanding anything contained in the deed or instrument of waqf or in any other taw for the time being in force, be void and of no effect:

Provided also that before making lease of any waqf property, the board shall publish the details of lease and invite bids in at least one leading national and regional news papers.

(2) *A lease for a period of one year but not exceeding thirty years*[71] *of immovable property which is waqf property shall, not withstanding anything contained in the deed or instrument or waqf or in any other law for the time being in force, be void and of no effect unless it is made with the previous sanction of the board.*

(3) *The board shall, in granting sanction for lease [******]*[72] *or renewal thereof under this section review the terms and conditions on which the lease is [****] proposed to be granted or renewed and make its approval subject to the revision of such terms and conditions in such manner as it may direct:*

Provided that the Board shall immediately intimate the State Government regarding a lease for any period exceeding three years of any waqf property and thereafter it may become effective after the expiry of forty-five days from the date on which the Board intimates the State Government[73]

(4) *Every rule made by the Central Government under this section shall be laid, as soon as may be after it is made, before each House of Parliament, while it is in session for a total period of thirty days, which may be comprised in one session or in two or more successive sessions, and if, before the expiry of the session immediately following the session or the successive sessions aforesaid, both Houses agree in making any modification in the rule or both Houses agree that the rule*

70 Inserted by Act 27 of 2013, S. 35 (a) (ii).

71 Substituted by Act 27 of 2013, S. 35 (b), for "A lease or sub-lease for any period exceeding one year and not exceeding three years."

72 The word "or sub-lease" omitted by Act 27 of 2013, S. 35 (c) (i).

73 Inserted by Act 27 of 2013, S.35 (c) (ii).

should not be made, the rule shall thereafter have effect only in such modified form or be of no effect, as the case may be; so, however, that any such modification or annulment shall be without prejudice to the validity of anything previously done under that rule[74]

Reflections

Analogous section under Wakf Act 1954 is S.36 F inserted by Waqf Amendment Act 1984 (Act 69 of 1984).

This section imposes certain restrictions upon leasing up of properties. It restricts leasing of agricultural land for more than three years. However, it gives an exception to leasing of immovable property for the commercial development or for educational and health purposes for a period up to 30 years. Sub-section (2) specifies that any lease of waqf property for a period of one year and not exceeding 30 years without the sanction of the board shall be void. The board is authorised to review the terms and conditions of the lease. Any lease of immovable property for a period more than 3 years and less than 30 years shall have the approval of the State Government. However, such grant of lease can have effect after the expiry of 45 days from the date of such communication to the State Government. This implies that if the State Government does not respond to such communication within 45 days it is deemed to have the approval of the State Government.

Sub-section (4) of this section, is inserted by Waqf Amendment Act 2013 (Act 27 of 2013). It deals with the regulations to be framed by the Central Government under this section. Such regulations shall be tabled before both the Houses of Parliament when both the Houses of Parliament are in session for at least 30 days in a single spell or in different spells. These regulations shall be effective as have been modified or amended by the Parliament.

Judicial response

The Waqf Act under section 56 imposes certain restrictions on grant of lease of waqf properties. The provision as mentioned in the above section that any lease of immovable property exceeding three years without the sanction of the board/Government is void, has been held by a Bench of the Madras High Court in H. Idayathulla vs. Larab Sha Dharba, Panruti.[75] The Bench observed that:

74 Inserted by Act 27 of 2013, S. 35 (d).
75 (2007)2 MLJ 1034.

> Therefore the contention of the respondents 2 to 6 that one of the Mutawalli had given on lease initially for a period of 11 months with an intention to continue it as a permanent lease, is unsustainable in view of the statutory bar contained in Section 36-F of the Wakf Act, 1954, corresponding to Section 56 of the Wakf Act, 1995.

However, the High Court of Allahabad in Ramdhani vs. Jankirai,[76] has held that:

> A lease deed of any agricultural land which is under a waqf cannot be created for more than three years and for other properties, such a lease cannot be created for more than a period of one year unless the permission of the District Judge, now the Waqf board, is obtained. Thus by no stretch of imagination, it can be said that the lease is void ab initio.
>
> My view on the above point is further strengthened by the observation made in a Madras case in Sundaramurthi Nair vs. Chotti Bibi (AIR 1942 Mad 641) where it was held that a lease granted by a Mutawalli in respect of waqf land for more than three years without the sanction of the court was not void ab initio under the Mohammedan Law and was only voidable. It was also held that such leases are operative or binding on the mutawalli who granted it unless they are declared to be invalid.

The High Court of Uttarakhand, in the case of Management Committee vs. State of Uttarakhand & Others,[77] observed that a grant of permission for raising construction above a tenanted shop by Chief Executive Officer of Waqf board without approval from waqf and thereby creating lease and continuation of possession of new construction, is without jurisdiction.

****

Section 57

Mutawalli entitled to pay certain costs from income of waqf property:-

> ***Notwithstanding anything contained in the waqf deed, every mutawalli may pay from the income of the waqf property any expenses properly incurred by him for the purpose of enabling him to furnish any particulars, documents or copies under section 36 or any accounts under section 46 or any information or documents required by the***

76 AIR 1971 All 533.
77 AIR 2017 UTTARAKHAND 87.

Board or for the purpose of enabling him to carry out the directions of the Board.

Reflections

Analogous section under Wakf Act 1954 is S.34.

Section 57 of the Act authorises the mutawalli to pay from the income of the waqf any proper expenditure incurred to furnish any particulars or documents under section 36 and 46 of this Act or to provide any information or documents required by the board to comply with the directions of the board.

Judicial response

Judicial response pertaining to this section is not found.

****

Section 58

Power of Board to pay dues in case of default by mutawalli:-

(1) ***Where a mutawalli refuses to pay or fails to pay any revenue, cess, rates or taxes due to the Government or any local authority, the Board may discharge dues from the Waqf Fund and may recover the amount so paid from the waqf property and may also recover damages not exceeding twelve and a half per cent of the amount so paid.***

(2) ***Any sum of money due under sub-section (1) may, on a certificate issued by the Board after giving the mutawalli concerned an opportunity of being heard, be recovered in the same manner as an arrears of land revenue.***

Reflections

Analogous section under Wakf Act 1954 is S.38.

This section provides that in case of any default by the mutawalli to pay any revenue, cess, taxes, etc., due to the Government or to the local authority, the Waqf Board can remit the same from the Waqf Fund and recover the same from the mutawalli along with damages not exceeding 12½ per cent of the amount so paid. The explanation of the mutawalli may be called for and he may be given a reasonable opportunity to submit his explanation. Such an amount can be recovered from the mutawalli in the same manner as arrears of land revenue.

Judicial response

Judicial response pertaining to this section is not found.

****

Section 59

Creation of reserve fund:-

> ***For the purpose of making provisions for the payment of rent and of revenue, cess, rates and taxes due to the Government or any local authority, for the discharge of the expenses of the repair of the waqf property and for the preservation of the waqf property, the Board may direct the creation and maintenance, in such manner as it may think fit, of a reserve fund from the income of a waqf.***

Reflections

Analogous section under Wakf Act 1954 is S.39.

This section authorises the Waqf Board for the creation of a reserve fund from the Waqf Fund to meet the unforeseen expenses and discharge of the liabilities towards land revenue, cess, taxes, etc., and for the preservation of waqfs. The Waqf Board may formulate regulation for the operation of such fund.

Judicial response

Judicial response pertaining to this section is not found.

****

Section 60

Extension of time:-

> ***The Board may, if it is satisfied that it is necessary so to do, extend the time within which any act is required to be done by the mutawalli under this Act.***

Reflections

Analogous section under Wakf Act 1954 is S.40.

This section authorises the Waqf board to extend the time limit if any mutawalli failed to comply with its directions or any mutawalli is at default in fulfilling the requirements under this Act within the prescribed time limit.

Judicial response

Judicial response pertaining to this section is not found.

****

Section 61

Penalties:-

(1) *If a mutawalli fails to-*
- (a) *apply for the registration of a waqf;*
- (b) *furnish statement of particulars of accounts or returns as required under this Act;*
- (c) *supply information or particulars as required by the Board;*
- (d) *allow inspection of waqf properties, accounts, records or deeds and documents relating thereto;*
- (e) *deliver possession of any waqf property, if ordered by the Board or Tribunal;*
- (f) *carry out the directions of the Board;*
- (g) *discharge any public dues; or*
- (h) *do any other act which he is lawfully required to do by or under this Act,*

he shall, unless he satisfies the court or the Tribunal that there was reasonable cause for his failure, be punishable with fine which may extend to <u>*ten thousand rupees for non-compliance of clauses (a) to (d) and in case of non-compliance of clauses (e) to (h), he shall be punishable with imprisonment for a term which may extend to six months and also with fine which may extend to ten thousand rupees.*</u>[78]

(2) *Notwithstanding anything contained in sub-section (1), if-*
- (a) *a mutawalli omits or fails, with a view to concealing the existence of a waqf, to apply for its registration under this Act,-*

78 Substituted by Act 27 of 2013, S. 36, for "eight thousand rupees."

(i) *in the case of a waqf created before the commencement of this Act, within the period specified there for in sub-section (8) of section 36;*

(ii) *in the case of any waqf created after such commencement, within three months from the date of the creation of the waqf; or*

(b) *a mutawalli furnishes any statement, return or information to the Board, which he knows or has reason to believe to be false, misleading, untrue or incorrect in any material particular.*

he shall be punishable with imprisonment for a term which may extend to six months and also with fine which may extend to fifteen thousand rupees.

(3) *No court, shall take cognizance of an offence punishable under this Act save upon compliant made by the Board or an officer duly authorised by the Board in this behalf.*

(4) *No court inferior to that of a Metropolitan Magistrate or a Judicial Magistrate of the first class shall try any offence punishable under this Act.*

(5) *Notwithstanding anything contained in the Code of Criminal Procedure, 1973, (2 of 1974) the fine imposed under sub-section (1), when realised, shall be credited to the Waqf Fund.*

(6) *In every case where offender is convicted after the commencement of this Act, of an offence punishable under sub-section (1) and sentenced to a fine, the court shall also impose such term of imprisonment in default of payment of fine as is authorised by law for such default.*

Reflections

Analogous section under Wakf Act 1954 is S.41.

This section enumerates the duties of mutawalli under clause (a) to (h). Any deviation under (a) to (d) may attract a fine up to Rs. 10,000 and deviations under (e) to (h) will be punishable with imprisonment for a term which may extend to 6 months and also with fine which may extend to 10,000 rupees. This section contemplates that the concealing of the existing waqf or a failure to register the existing waqf will attract fine and imprisonment. But no court shall take cognisance of such an offence unless an application is made by the Waqf Board or an Officer authorised by the board in this behalf. No court inferior to the Metropolitan Magistrate or the Judicial First Class Magistrate shall try such offence. The fine imposed under this section shall be credited to the Waqf Fund.

Judicial response

Judicial response pertaining to this section is not found.

****

Section 62

Mutawalli not to spend any money belonging to waqf for self defence:-

> ***No mutawalli shall spend any money out of the funds of the waqf, of which he is the mutawalli, for meeting any costs, charges, or expenses which are or may be, incurred by him, in relation to any suit, appeal or any other proceeding for, or incidental to, his removal from office or for taking any disciplinary action against himself.***

Reflections

Analogous section under Wakf Act 1954 is S.41 A, inserted by Waqf Amendment Act 1984 (Act 69 of 1984).

This section prohibits the mutawalli from spending any amount from the income of the waqf to meet any expenditure towards the legal expenses to defend himself in case of his removal or to meet the expenses to defend himself from the disciplinary actions.

Judicial response

Judicial response pertaining to this section is not found.

****

Section 63

Power to appoint mutawalli in certain cases:-

> ***When there is a vacancy in the office of the mutawalli of a waqf and there is no one to be appointed under the terms of deed of the waqf, or where the right of any person to act as mutawalli, is disputed, the Board may appoint any person to act as mutawalli for such period and on such condition as it may think fit.***

Reflections

Analogous section under Wakf Act 1954 is S.42.

Whenever a vacancy in the office of the mutawalli is created and there is no claim for the same, section 63 authorises the Waqf Board to appoint any person as mutawalli for such a period and on such terms and conditions as it thinks fit.

Judicial response

The Supreme Court, in a recent case of appointment of mutawalli in Syeda Nazira Khatoon vs. Syed Zahiruddin[79] Ahmed Baghdadi, while quoting from its judgement in Ahmad GH Arif vs. Commissioner of Wealth Tax,[80] observed that:

> In the instant case, the wakf deed does not give the mutawalli any such power to select another person as the future mutawalli on his demise, by creating a trust deed or any other instrument to that effect. In the absence of such an authorization, the transfer of the office of 5 mutawalli by Syed Badruddin Ahmed by way of a trust deed in favour of his wife clearly went beyond the purview of his powers and the settled principles of Mohammedan law.

The full bench of Allahabad High Court, in the matter of Moattar Raza vs. Joint Director of Consolidation U.P.,[81] has ruled that:

> "The legal status and position of a Mutawalli under a Wakf under the Mussalman law is that of a manager or superintendent."

A Bench of the High Court of Andhra Pradesh, in Andhra Pradesh Wakf board vs. Mohamed Hidayatullah[82] has taken interpretation of this section when it observed that under section 42 (now section 63) the board can appoint a mutawalli and made the following observations:

> As long as the mutawalli is effectively working in office and as long as there are no other proceedings pending against him, we do not think the board has any power to direct the mutawalli to hand over the record to the committee or to the board. No proceedings of whatever kind are pending against the mutawalli. The impugned order therefore directing

79 AIR 2019 SC 4676.
80 AIR 1971 SC 1691.
81 AIR 1933 All 407.
82 AIR 1974 AP 287.

> the mutawalli to hand over the record is not in accordance with law and cannot be sustained.
>
> The wakf board, without assuming direct management of the wakf or removing the mutawalli, cannot keep back in its custody or possession the records relating to the wakf. It has to hand over the entire property belonging to the wakf to the mutawalli. It is true that the board has special powers of supervision directly or indirectly through the committee constituted under Section 16 of the Act. But that does not mean that the board can direct the mutawalli to hand over the entire property to the managing committee or to the board without having any recourse to Section 43 or S, 43-A.

In Syed Akbar Shah vs. Tamil Nadu Wakf board,[83] a Bench of the High Court of Madras described the scope of section 42 of the Wakf Act 1954 (now section 63) as under:

> Section 42 of the Act is divisible into two compartments. The first one is that the Board has jurisdiction to appoint a person to act as mutawalli for such period and on such condition as it may think fit, if there is a vacancy in the office of mutawalli of a wakf and no one has been appointed as per the terms of the instrument of wakf. The second compartment relates to a contingency where the right of the person in occupation of the office is disputed by others. These two divisions contemplated in section 42 enable independently and separately the Wakf Boards to act and exercise their jurisdiction statutorily conferred on them, to appoint mutawallis in the two above specified cases. We are therefore, of opinion that one is not telescoped with the other.

In the year 1892, in Piran vs. Abdul Karim,[84] a case came up for hearing before the Bench of Calcutta High Court consisting of Justice MacPherson Justice Ameer Ali. Speaking for the Bench, Justice Ameer Ali, while referring to the classic books of Mohammedan Jurisprudence and the practices of the appointment of sajjada and mutawalli, elaborately observed as under:

> According to the two disciples (of Abu Hanifa), “wakf” signifies the appropriation of a particular article in such a manner as subjects it to the rules of divine property, whence the appropriator’s right in it is extinguished, and it becomes a property of God, by the advantage of it resulting to His creatures. The two disciples therefore hold appropriation to be absolute, though differing in this, that Aboo Yoosaf holds the

83 1978 TNLJ 410.
84 1892 ILR 19 Cal 203.

appropriation to be absolute from the moment of its execution, whereas Mahomed holds it to be absolute only on the delivery of it to a mutwali (or procurator), and, consequently, that it cannot be disposed of by gift or sale.

"It is stated from Shaik-ul-Islam Abdul Hassan that all the mashaikhs (jurists) declare that if they (the congregation) do appoint a mutawalli, it would be as valid as if the appointment was made with the permission of the Kazi."

> And in the Radd-ul-Muhtar it is stated that the modern Mahomedan lawyers recognize the validity of an appointment by the congregation. So also in the Wajiz-ul-Muhtar. it is clear, therefore, that the election of the plaintiff is not invalid under the Mohammadan Law. Besides, it seems to me that the appointment of a sajjadanashin of a durgah must, to a large extent, be regulated by the practice followed in the particular durgah or neighbouring dargahs.
>
> Herklot describes the custom in vogue in the durgahs existing in Southern India. And, so far as I am aware, that is consistent with the practice prevailing in other parts of India, viz., that upon the death of the last incumbent, generally on the day of what is called the sium or teja ceremony (performed on the third day after his decease), the fakirs and murids of the durgah, assisted by the heads of neighbouring durgahs, install a competent person on the guddi; generally the person chosen is the son of the deceased or somebody nominated by him, for his nomination is supposed to carry the guarantee that the nominee knows the precepts which he is to communicate to the disciples. In some instances the nomination takes the shape of a formal installation by the electoral body, so to speak, during the life-time of the incumbent. But in every case the person installed is supposed to be competent to initiate the murids into the mysteries of the tarikat (the holy path).

In the case of Vidya Varuthi Thirtha Swamigal vs. Balusamy Iyer,[85] speaking for the judicial committee of the Privy Council, Justice Ameer Ali observed that:

> The manager of the wakf is mutawalli, the governor superintendent or curator. In Jeevandas Shah's case the Judicial Committee called him "procurator" which related to a Khankha, a Mohammadan institution analogous in many respects to a Mutt where Hindu religious instruction

85 AIR 1922 PC 123; 48 IA 302; ILR 44 Mad 831; 65 IC 161.

> is dispensed. The head of these Khankhas which exist in large numbers in India is called Sajjadanashin. He is the teacher of religious doctrines and rules of life and the manager of the institution and the administrator of its charities and has in most cases a larger interest in the usufruct than an ordinary mutawalli. But neither the sajjadanashin nor the mutawalli has any right in the property belonging to the Wakf; the properties are not vested in him and he is not a trustee in the technical sense.

The above observation of Justice Ameer Ali differentiates between a mutawalli and a sajjadahnashin. The Wakf Act 1995 includes sajjadahnashin in the definition of a mutawalli. In Syed Shah Mohammad Kazim vs. Syed Abi Saghir,[86] Justice Muhammad Noor observed that:

> Khanqahs cannot exist and continue without a sajjadanashin. In other systems the personal expenditure of the head of such an institution has been curtailed to almost nothing by enjoining celibacy, as for instance in the case of Christian monasteries or Hindu Mutts. But Islam prohibits celibacy and a saint with a family is the rule rather than an exception. In these circumstances devotees and adherence of khanqas have always made provision for maintenance of the sajjadanashin and his family so that he may devote all his time to imparting religious and spiritual instructions to his disciples and be free from secular cares. A sajjadanashin is an integral part of the institution and the central figure so as to speak therein. Its existence depends on his personality. In him is supposed to continue the spiritual line. Therefore provision for his maintenance and that of his descendants is a provision for him as the head of the institution. It is a trust and not a personal grant.

Section 61 of the Act imposes penalties to the mutawalli if he deviates from the established procedure and the provisions of the Act. Further section 63 authorises the Waqf board to appoint a mutawalli when there is no mutawalli to look into the affairs of the waqf, when there is a vacancy in the office of mutawalli, when there is no one to be appointed as a mutawalli as per terms of the deed of waqf or when there are rival claimants. In addition to this, section 64 of the Act authorises the Waqf Board to remove a mutawalli. It gives detailed grounds and circumstances under which a mutawalli can be removed.

The High Court of Allahabad, in Syed Muhammad Ahmad Hasan vs. Shia Central board of Wakf,[87] while dealing with the appointment of mutawalli, has quoted the Privy Council (AIR 1936, P.C., 253 (2)) "Where a power is given to do a certain thing in a certain way the thing must be done

86 AIR 1932 Pat 33; (1932) 11 Pat 288; 136 IC 417.
87 AIR 2009 All, 38.

in that way or not at all. Other methods of performance are necessarily forbidden," and observed that:

> When under Section 64(3) a specific mode of exercise of power i.e., by a special majority is provided, the said power cannot be delegated to one member of the board. In view of exercise of such powers by a special mode the power is not capable of delegation. Any other interpretation shall make the requirement provided in Section 64(3) redundant and meaningless. Special majority has been provided for specific object i.e., to make the removal only when 2/3rd of members of board agree, permitting one member to do it is to permit a thing to be done in a manner which is not permissible under the Act.

In Kerala, the Wakf Board vs. Alam Aboobaker Sait,[88] the Bench of the Kerala High Court in a similar case observed as follows:

> On a plain reading of section 42 of the Act, it appears that the power to appointment can be exercised only when there is a vacancy. It is an enabling provision which entitles the Wakf board to step in when there is vacuum, there being none to look after the affairs of the wakf as a mutawalli. It is also necessary to note that the power conferred by section 42 is not to appoint a person as the mutawalli. The stipulation that such appointment shall be made for such period and on such conditions as it may think fit also suggests that it is not the regular appointment of a mutawalli that is contemplated by section 42 of the Act.

The Allahabad High Court, in Maulvi Abdul Rahman Siyai vs. Sardar Maqbool Hasan & Others,[89]while interpreting the relevant sections of the Act, has given the following observations in respect of appointment and removal of mutawalli.

> Hence the provision in Sub-section (5) of Section 43 cannot be made use of for the purpose of removing the person already in office as a mutawalli for the purpose of giving effect to the order of appointment made under Section 42 of the Act. The Legislature would not have conferred power of removal without giving adequate power or making adequate provision for enforcing such an order as has been done in Sub-section (5) of Section 43. This is another reason for us to come to the conclusion that the power conferred by Section 42 of the Act does not empower the Wakf Board to remove a person who is already functioning as a mutawalli.

88 AIR 1987 Ker 176 (DB).
89 AIR 2009 All 62.

The High Court of Andhra Pradesh, in Mulla Rahim Saheb and Others vs. A.P. State Wakf Board and Another,[90] held that:

> The Board is bound to make an enquiry and for the said purpose has to issue notice and provide reasonable opportunity to the Mutawalli concerned before he is removed from his office as Mutawalli. In the instant case, no such procedure is followed by the Board and they were bound to follow the said procedure in so far as it relates to the 1st petitioner who is admittedly a hereditary Mutawalli and about which there is no dispute.

In another case, Shaik Ghouse Mohiuddin vs. Andhra Pradesh State Wakf board,[91] the Andhra Pradesh High Court held that:

> A reading of the provisions of Section 63 of the Act would amply demonstrate that a person can be appointed as Mutawalli in the above circumstances, but while making such appointment by the Wakf Board in favour of any person to act as Mutawalli, the period for which the said person is appointed should be specified in the order.

In Khajeh Salimulah vs. Abdul Khair,[92] the High Court of Calcutta in its judgement dated 30 August 1901 held that:

> It is indisputable that a claim to office and to property appurtenant thereto may be barred by limitation. If the office (of mutawalli) is not hereditary, Article 120 is applicable. If, on the other hand, the office is hereditary, Article 124 governs the matter ... It is clear, therefore, that the claim of the plaintiff to the office of mutawalli became barred by limitation upon the expiry of six years from the date of the towliatnamah of Faizunnessa, dated the 29th January 1877. Even if Article 124 or Article 144 were held applicable, the title must be taken to have been extinguished by limitation in 1889.

A Bench of the High Court of Calcutta consisting of A. Mookerjee and E. Fletcher, in the case of Kassim Hussan vs. Hazra Begam,[93] has observed that:

> In our opinion, it is fully established by satisfactory evidence that Hazra Bibi has held the office of mutawalli from 1880 and has been

90 1997 (2) ALD 79; 1997 (2) ALT 136.
91 AIR 2002 AP 344; 2002 (1) ALD 751.
92 37 Cal 263.
93 AIR 1920 Cal 800; 60 Ind Cas 165.

> in possession thereof by performance of the duties attached thereto, either herself or through her deputies for a period of not less than thirty-six years. What then is the legal effect of such possession of the office, even if we assume for a moment that her nomination to the office of mutawalli was not validly made or was not confirmed by a Kazi or by a judicial officer of equivalent status? The obvious answer is that the plaintiff has acquired a good title to the office of mutawalli by reason of her possession thereof for the statutory period.

In Gulam Samdani vs. Andhra Pradesh Wakf Board,[94] the Andhra Pradesh High Court held that sections 44 and 45 of the Waqf Act 1954 (now sections 70 and 71) do not empower the Waqf Board to remove a mutawalli and appoint another mutawalli pending enquiry. The court observed thus:

> But the section does not contemplate the appointment of a receiver pending enquiry. The enquiry contemplated under Section 45 is with reference to the matters mentioned in Section 44 of the said Act. Under Section 44 of the Act an enquiry should be instituted, on the application of any person interested in a wakf, relating to the administration of the wakf. Therefore, either under Section 44 or under Section 45 of the Act the question of appointment of a receiver pending such an enquiry does not arise.

In Gulam Ali vs. Secretary, Karnataka Board of Wakfs,[95] the High Court of Karnataka while quashing the orders of the Waqf Board and for the constitution of the Managing Committee for the Waqf as an interim arrangement, held that the board had no power to remove the mutawalli for modification of the scheme already framed by it. The court observed as under:

> The scheme is framed with a view to properly administer the wakf in conformity with the direction, purposes and any usage or custom of the wakf sanctioned by the Muslim Law. Therefore, there is no option left to the Wakf Board to over-come the provisions of the scheme and appoint an adhoc committee. Such an act cannot at all be sustained as it is directly in conflict with the provisions of the scheme. As long as there is no obstacle for implementing the scheme or appointing the committee as per the scheme, it is not permissible for the Wakf Board to appoint an adhoc committee under S. 42 of the Act.

In the case of Mst. Aziza Kabathin vs. State of West Bengal,[96] a High Bench of Calcutta, while quashing the orders of the West Bengal Commissioner of waqf, observed that:

94 AIR 1975 AP 104.
95 AIR 1985 Kant 242.
96 AIR 1984 Cal 326.

> It is now an established principle of law that the Commissioner of Wakfs in making an appointment Under Section 40 of the Act shall try to give effect to the wishes of the wakif and appoint Mutawalli from amongst the members of the family of the wakif. It is true that the Commissioner of Wakfs had repeatedly asked the appellants Nos. 2 and 3 to get themselves substituted as Mutawallis of the wakf estate (EC 690). But after their refusal, it was the duty of the Commissioner to enquire whether there was any other member of the family of the wakif who could be appointed a Mutawalli of the wakf estate. If none was available from the family of the wakif or the last holder of the office of the Mutawalli, the Commissioner might appoint independent and disinterested persons to the office of Mutawalli. In the instant case we find that the applicants Nos. 1 and 2 are the sons of the late Abdul Ali who was the last Mutawalli. The Commissioner should have considered their case for appointment as Mutawalli. A stranger is not at all desirable to be introduced into a wakf estate consisting of the family dwelling house, tanks, orchard etc., although it is disputed whether the family dwelling house is comprised within the wakf-al-al-Aulad.

The High Court of Andhra Pradesh, in Syed Jamil Ahmed (Died) Per Lrs. vs. Meer Ahmed Ali Khan (Died) Per Lrs,[97] ruled that the post of mutawalli is not hereditary and held as under:

If the Mutawalli is appointed by the Wakf Board, Mutawalliship is not hereditary and the legal heir of the Mutawalli cannot be termed Mutawalli as the appointment comes to an end immediately after the death of the person who has been appointed as Mutawalli.

The High Court of Andhra Pradesh, in Syed Shah Mohammed Raju Hussaini ... vs. Andhra Pradesh State Wakf Board,[98] held that:

> It is evident that to exercise power under the provision, any of the two circumstances must exist, namely, (a) there is a clear vacancy of the Mutawalliship and (b) there is a dispute as to the competence or eligibility of the existing mutawalli of a wakf. Admittedly, the petitioner is functioning as mutawalli of the wakf and the impugned order does not refer to any dispute as to the eligibility or competence of the petitioner. Therefore, there was no basis for the first respondent to exercise the power under Section 63 of the Act.

****

97 2002 (6) ALD 318, 2002 (5) ALT 174.
98 2007 (3) ALD 345, 2007 (2) ALT 511.

Section 64

Removal of Mutawalli:-

(1) *Notwithstanding anything contained in any other law or the deed of waqf, the Board may remove a mutawalli from his office if such mutawalli-*
   (a) *has been convicted more than once of an offence punishable under section 61; or*
   (b) *has been convicted of any offence of criminal breach of trust or any other offence involving moral turpitude, and such conviction has not been reversed and he has not been granted full pardon with respect to such offence; or*
   (c) *is of unsound mind or is suffering from other mental or physical defect or infirmity which would render him unfit to perform the functions and discharge the duties of a mutawalli; or*
   (d) *is an undischarged insolvent; or*
   (e) *is proved to be addicted to drinking liquor or other spirituous preparations, or is addicted to the taking of any narcotic drugs; or*
   (f) *is employed as a paid legal practitioner on behalf of, or against, the waqf; or*
   (g) *has failed without reasonable excuse, to maintain regular accounts for two consecutive years or has failed to submit, in two consecutive years, the yearly statement of accounts, as required by sub-section (2) of section 46; or*
   (h) *is interested, directly or indirectly, in a subsisting lease in respect of any waqf property, or in any contract made with, or any work being done for, the waqf or is in arrears in respect of any sum due by him to such waqf; or*
   (i) *continuously neglects his duties or commits any misfeasance, malfeasance, misapplication of funds or breach of trust in relation to the waqf or in respect of any money or other waqf property; or*
   (j) *wilfully and persistently disobeys the lawful orders made by the Central Government, State Government, Board under any provision of this Act or rule or order made thereunder;*
   (k) *misappropriates or fraudulently deals with the property of the waqf.*

(2) *The removal of a person from the office of the mutawalli shall not affect his personal rights, if any, in respect of the waqf property either as a beneficiary or in any other capacity or his right, if any, as a sajjadanashin.*

(3) *No action shall be taken by the Board under sub-section (1) unless it has held an inquiry into the matter in a prescribed manner and the decision has been taken by a majority of not less than two-thirds of the members of the Board.*

(4) *A mutawalli who is aggrieved by an order passed under any of the clauses (c) to (j) of sub-section (1), may, within one month from the date of the receipt by him of the order, appeal against the order to the Tribunal and the decision of the Tribunal on such appeal shall be final.*

(5) *Where any inquiry under sub-section (3) is proposed, or commenced, against any mutawalli, the Board may, if it is of opinion that it is necessary so to do in the interest of the waqf, by an order suspend such mutawalli until the conclusion of the inquiry.*

Provided that no suspension for a period exceeding ten days shall be made except after giving the mutawalli a reasonable opportunity of being heard against the proposed action,

(6) *Where any appeal is filed by the mutawalli to the Tribunal under sub-section (4), the Board may make an application to the Tribunal for the appointment of a receiver to manage the waqf pending the decision of the appeal, and where such an application is made, the Tribunal shall, notwithstanding anything contained in the Code of Civil Procedure, 1908, (5 of 1908) appoint a suitable person as receiver to manage the waqf and direct the receiver so appointed to ensure that the customary or religious rights of the mutawalli and of the waqf are safeguarded.*

(7) *Where a mutawalli has been removed from his office under sub-section (1), the Board may, by order, direct the mutawalli to deliver possession of the waqf property to the Board or any officer duly authorised in this behalf or to any person or committee appointed to act as the mutawalli of the waqf property.*

(8) *A mutawalli of a waqf removed from his office under this section shall not be eligible for re-appointment as a mutawalli of that waqf for a period of five years from the date of such removal.*

Reflections

Analogous section under Wakf Act 1954 is S.43.

This section specifies the circumstances under which a Wakf Board is authorised to remove a mutawalli. It has listed clauses (a) to (k) above under which a mutawalli can be removed from his office. Sub-section (2) under this section provides that the removed mutawalli is entitled to his personal rights such as his designation as sajjadanashin, his right as a beneficiary, his right to perform any religious rites or his rights in respect of the waqf property.

The mutawalli shall not be removed unless an inquiry is held and the decision has been taken by the board by a majority of not less than two-thirds of the members present. A mutawalli who is aggrieved by the decision of the board may appeal against the order of the Waqf Board before the Tribunal, and the decision of the Tribunal shall be final. The Wakf Board can suspend a mutawalli until the conclusion of the inquiry and the mutawalli shall deliver the possession of the waqf properties as directed by the

Waqf Board. Further, sub-section 8 specifies that a removed mutawalli shall not be eligible for re-appointment for a period of five years from the date of such removal. Honesty and integrity shall be indispensable qualities of a mutawalli, without which the purpose for which the wakf is dedicated would be jeopardised.

Judicial response

A Bench of the High Court of Andhra Pradesh, in Andhra Pradesh Wakf Board vs. Mohamed Hidayatullah,[99] has taken interpretation of this section when it observed that, under section 42 (now section 63), the board can appoint a mutawalli and made the following observations:

> The wakf Board, without assuming direct management of the wakf or removing the Mutawallis, cannot keep back in its custody or possession the records relating to the wakf. It has to hand over the entire property belonging to the wakf to the mutawalli. It is true that the Board has special powers of supervision directly or indirectly through the committee constituted under Section 16 of the Act. But that does not mean that the Board can direct the mutawalli to hand over the entire property to the managing committee or to the Board without having any recourse to Section 43 or S, 43-A.

This judgement has been discussed in the preceding section as well. However this judgement is relevant in respect of removal of mutawalli as well. A division Bench of the High Court of Madras in Kadhar Sheriff vs. Tamil Nadu State Wakf Board,[100]while referring to this decision of the Andhra Pradesh High Court has held that:

> If the Board finds that the mutawalli is not fit to continue in management, it can take appropriate proceedings against him. When the Board finds that there is no case for the removal of the mutawalli, then it cannot resort to a procedure by which he becomes non est. Such a procedure cannot be brought in even with the aid of the doctrine of implied powers. We hold that the order of the Wakf Board appointing Executive Officers and appointing managing committee in these cases are ultra vires the powers of the Board and null and void as they cannot be supported by any of the provisions of the Act.

The Waqf Board is authorised to appoint a mutawalli, constitute a committee, appoint a receiver as and when necessary. But it cannot suspend a legally appointed mutawalli for the sake of appointing another mutawalli or

99 AIR 1974 AP 287.
100 AIR 1987 Mad 40; (1987)1 MLJ 159.

constituting a managing committee. The Madras High Court, in the case of T.E. Mohamed Sheriff vs. Superintendent of Waqfs, Central Zone,[101] took the view that the Waqf Board cannot initiate the appointment of a mutawalli, a committee or a receiver pending any inquiry for the removal of mutawalli. Justice Ismail observed that:

> In my view, the Board has no jurisdiction to interfere with the administration of the properties by the petitioner on the ground that he has failed to submit proper accounts and also failed to pay the contributions; nor is the Board justified in interfering with the said administration on the ground that action is being taken to remove him from Mutawalliship.

The High Court of Madhya Pradesh in Intezamia Committee Idgah, Morar vs. M.P. Wakf Board[102], held that:

> Thus, in this light, if we peruse the aforesaid principle laid down by the Hon'ble Supreme Court, there does not remain any doubt that there is an express exclusion of the jurisdiction of the Civil Court under the Wakf Act. The claim of the defendant under these circumstances that the Civil Court had no jurisdiction is correct. The Civil Court has got no jurisdiction with respect to any matter, which is required by or under the Act has to be determined by a Tribunal and if under Section 43(4A) an appeal lies against the order of removal to the Tribunal, the Civil Court had no jurisdiction.

In K.P. Zainulabdeen vs. Tamil Nadu Wakf Board,[103] the learned single judge, while rejecting the contention of the petitioner, held that:

> Whenever the Board is obliged to conduct an inquiry, it is open to the Board having regard to the provisions contained in S. 45 of the Act to hold such inquiry into either itself or by authorising somebody to hold such an inquiry ... This is not a case where the Board had abdicated its powers in favour of the Enquiry Committee. The Enquiry Committee has been constituted to gather the materials and submit the same with its recommendations to the Board for deciding the further course of action in exercise of its powers under Ss. 43, 43(A) and 44. I see no merit in this objection on behalf of the petitioners and the procedure adopted by the Board is quite in accordance with law and well within its competence and authority.

101 AIR 1971 Mad 243.
102 AIR 1996 MP 47;1996 (0) MPLJ 37.
103 AIR 1992 Mad 298.

The learned single judge of the High Court of Karnataka Justice D.V. Shylendra Kumar, in Syed Enayathullah vs. State of Karnataka,[104] while dealing with the removal of the mutawalli took the view that, even after the report of Lokyukta, the Waqf Board shall initiate action against the mutawalli by conducting an inquiry under section 64 of the Act. The judge observed that:

> The immediate effect of the report of the Lok Ayukta would have been to place the petitioner under suspension and order of suspension deemed to have been issued by the appointing authority, the Wakf Board. In fact the Government also had called upon the Board to take further action as per law under the provisions of the Wakf Act. If any action is contemplated against the Mutawalli particularly for his removal, procedure as contemplated in Section 64 of the Wakf Act, will have to be followed. The compliance of requirement of Sub-section (3) of Section 64 of the Wakf Act is mandatory.

In O.M.S. Sheik Udman Aalim Sahib vs. Tamil Nadu Wakf Board[105] the learned single judge held that even the availability of the alternative remedy for the petitioner under section 83 of the Waqf Act 1995 to move the Tribunal against the order of the Waqf Board, the remedy of writ jurisdiction under Article 226 of the Constitution cannot be denied and the court cannot be expected to close its eyes even in respect of cases of this type. The court observed as under:

> It is settled proposition that the existence of an alternative remedy is not a bar for the jurisdiction of this Court under Article 226 of the Constitution of India but only a self restraint which is not warranted in this case. In appropriate cases, this Court exercises its power wherever the necessity to avail the alternative remedy is found to be unnecessary in the circumstances of the case, and the Court is not expected to close its eyes even in a case of this type.

The High Court of Andhra Pradesh, in K.M. Safiullah vs. A.P. State Wakf Board and Others,[106] while dealing with the matter of the issue of how to show cause notice to the mutawalli under section 64 of the Waqf Act 1995, observed that:

> The enumeration of the allegations in the show cause notice would in no way work to the disadvantage of the petitioner, and on the other

104 AIR 2004 Kant 295.
105 (2004) 4 LW 274.
106 2003 (2) ALD 440, 2003 (2) ALT 253.

> hand, enables him to deal with them properly and effectively, in the representation or explanation, which he may submit to the impugned show cause notice.

The High Court of Uttarakhand in Mohd. Idris alias Idris Baba vs. Uttaranchal Wakf Board through its Chief Executive Officer[107] made the following observation in respect of the Powers of the Survey Commissioner of Waqfs vis-à-vis appointment of a mutawalli:

> It is to be seen whether the revisionist was appointed by a competent person. In the case at hand, revisionist was appointed by Assistant Survey Commissioner. Work of Assistant Survey Commissioner has been defined in sub-section (2) of section 4 of the Act, wherein there is no mention that he has a power even to appoint adhoc Administrator to perform the act of mutawalli under the Act.

A case pertaining to the removal of a mutawalli under section 64 of Waqf Act 1995 for not residing in the station and for not maintaining the waqf institution properly came up before The High Court of Karnataka in Syed Shah Tayyab Khadri vs. State of Karnataka.[108] The High Court ruled that any order passed without following the provisions and procedures is illegal and liable to be quashed.

****

Section 65

Assumption of direct management of certain auqaf by the Board:-

(1) ***Where no suitable person is available for appointment as a mutawalli of a waqf, or where the Board is satisfied, for reasons to be recorded by it in writing, that the filling up of the vacancy, in the office of a mutawalli is prejudicial to the interests of the waqf, the Board may by notification in the Official Gazette, assume direct management of the waqf for such period or periods, not exceeding five years in the aggregate, as may be specified in the notification.***

(2) ***The State Government, may, on its own motion or on the application of any person interested in the waqf, call for the records of any case for the purpose of satisfying itself as to the correctness, legality or propriety of the notification issued by the Board under sub-section (1) and pass such orders as it may think fit and the orders so made by the***

107 AIR 2013 Uttarakhand 72.
108 AIR 2019 Karnataka 201.

State Government shall be final and shall be published in the manner specified in sub-section (1).

(3) *As soon as possible after the close of every financial year, the Board shall send to the State Government a detailed report in regard to every waqf under its direct management, giving therein-*
   (a) *the details of the income of the waqf for the year immediately preceding the year under report;*
   (b) *the steps taken to improve the management and income of the waqf;*
   (c) *the period during which the waqf has been under the direct management of the Board and explaining the reasons as to why it has not been possible to entrust the management of the waqf to the mutawalli or any committee of management during the year; and*
   (d) *such other matters as may be prescribed.*

(4) *The State Government shall examine the report submitted to it under sub-section (3), and after such examination issue directions or instructions to the Board as it may think fit and the Board shall comply with such directions or instructions on receipt thereof.*

(5) *Notwithstanding anything contained in sub-section (1), the Board shall take over the administration of a waqf, if the waqf Board has evidence before it to prove that management of the waqf has contravened the provisions of this Act.*[109]

Reflections

Analogous section under Wakf Act 1954 is S.43A, inserted by the Amendment Act (Act 69 of 1984) and again amended by the Wakf Amendment Act 1984 (Act 69 of 1984).

This section provides that the Waqf Board can take the waqf institution under its management and control when no suitable person is available for the appointment of mutawalli or where it appears that appointment of mutawalli would be prejudicial to the interest of the waqf. The assumption of the waqf under the direct management of the board shall be notified in the Official Gazette and specify the period not exceeding five years in the notification. Sub-section (2) authorises the State Government to examine the legality correctness of propriety of the notification and pass such orders as it may think fit under the circumstances of the case. The Waqf Board shall provide the details of the waqf institution under its direct management to the State Government in the manner prescribed in sub-section (3). The State Government, after examining such a report, may issue direction for compliance by the board.

109 Inserted by Act 27 of 2013, S. 37.

Judicial response

Section 65 of the Waqf Act 1995 empowers the State Waqf Board to take a waqf institution under its direct management if the circumstances so warrant. But no institution shall be under the direct management of the Waqf Board for more than five years. The High Court of Karnataka, in P. Mohammed Dastagir vs. Karnataka Board of Wakf and Others,[110] observed that the requirement of recording reasons in writing for such appointment of an administrator is necessary only at the first stage when the board assumes management of wakf. The High Court observed as under:

> The appointment was therefore only in the nature of nominating the petitioner as an Agent of the Board, to look after the affairs of the Masjid. If the petitioner was doing so it was not for the sake of any monetary gain or other advantage, but only in the spirit of service to the Masjid. Now that the Board has in its wisdom, considered it proper to terminate the said appointment and appoint another person in his place, the petitioner can make no grievance.

****

Section 66

Powers of appointment and removal of mutawalli when to be exercised by the State Government:-

Whenever a deed of waqf or any decree or order of a court of any scheme of management of any waqf provides that a court or any authority other than a Board may appoint or remove a mutawalli or settle or modify such scheme of management or otherwise exercise superintendence over the waqf, then notwithstanding anything contained in such deed of waqf, decree, order or scheme, such powers aforesaid shall be exercisable by the State Government.

Provided that where a Board has been established, the State Government shall consult the Board before exercising such powers.

Reflections

Analogous section under Wakf Act 1954 is S.43 B, inserted by the Amendment Act (Act 69 of 1984).

Section (66) empowers the State Government to exercise the power to appoint or remove a mutawalli or settle or modify any scheme of

110 AIR 1998 Kant. 297.

management enunciated by a deed, decree or order of a court. However, the State Government shall consult the Wakf Board before exercising the powers under this section.

Judicial response

Judicial response pertaining to this section is not found.

****

Section 67

Supervision and supersession of committee of management:-

(1) *Whenever the supervision or management of a waqf is vested in any committee appointed by the waqf, then, notwithstanding anything contained in this Act, such committee shall continue to function until it is superseded by the Board or until the expiry of its term as may be specified by the waqf, whichever is earlier:*

Provided that such committee shall function under the direct control and supervision of the Board and abide by such directions as the Board may issue from time to time;

Provided further that if the Board is satisfied that any scheme for the management of a waqf by a committee is inconsistent with any provision of this Act or of any rule made there under or with the directions of the waqf, it may, at any time, modify the scheme in such manner as may be necessary to bring it in conformity with the directions of the waqf or of the provisions of this Act and the rules made there under.

(2) *Notwithstanding anything contained in this Act and in the deed of the waqf, the Board may, if it is satisfied, for reasons to be recorded in writing, that a committee, referred to in sub-section (1) is not functioning properly and satisfactorily, or that the waqf is being mismanaged and that in the interest of its proper management, it is necessary so to do, by an order, supersede such committee, and, on such supersession, any direction of the waqf, in so far as it relates to the constitution of the committee, shall cease to have any force:*

Provided that the Board shall, before making any order superseding any committee, issue a notice setting forth therein the reasons for the proposed action and calling upon the Committee to show cause within such time, not being less one month, as may be specified in the notice, as to why such action shall not be taken.

(3) *Every order made by the Board under sub-section (2) shall be published in the prescribed manner and on such publication shall be binding on the mutawalli and all persons having any interest in the waqf.*

(4) *Any order made by the Board under sub-section (2)shall be final:*

Provided that any person aggrieved by the order made under sub-section (2) may, within sixty days from the date of the order, appeal to the Tribunal:

Provided further that the Tribunal shall have no power to suspend the operation of the order made by the Board pending such appeal.

(5) *The Board shall, whenever it supersedes any committee under sub-section (2), constitute a new committee of management simultaneously with the order made by it under sub-section (2).*

(6) *Notwithstanding anything contained in the foregoing sub-sections, the Board may, instead of superseding any committee under sub-section (2), remove any member thereof if it is satisfied that such member has abused his position as such member or had knowingly acted in a manner prejudicial to the interests of the waqf, and every such order for the removal of any member shall be served upon him by registered post:*

Provided that no order for the removal of the member shall be made unless he has been given a reasonable opportunity of showing cause against the proposed action:

Provided further that any member aggrieved by any order for his removal from the membership of the committee may, within a period of thirty days from the date of service of the order on him, prefer an appeal against such order to the Tribunal and the Tribunal may, after giving a reasonable opportunity to the appellant and the Board of being heard, confirm, modify or reverse the order made by the Board and the order made by the Tribunal in such appeal shall be final.

Reflections

Analogous section under Wakf Act 1954 is S.43C, inserted by the Amendment Act (Act 69 of 1984).

Section (67) states that whenever the management of a waqf is vested in a committee appointed by the waqf shall continue to work until the expiry of its term or until it is superseded by the board whichever is earlier. Such committees are required to function under the direct control of the waqf and comply with the directions issued by the Waqf Board. If the Waqf Board finds that the Committee of a waqf is not functioning or indulging in mismanagement or misappropriation of the funds of the waqf, the Waqf Board can supersede such a committee, but, before such action, a notice shall be served to the committee calling upon its explanation. The committee shall be given a fair opportunity to present its case and justification to the board. The order passed by the board shall be published in the prescribed manner. Such order of the board shall be binding on the mutawalli and all persons having any interest in the waqf. Such order of the board shall be final. Any person aggrieved by such order may appeal to the Tribunal within 60 days from the date of the order. However, the Tribunal shall not have the powers to suspend the operation of the order made by the board pending such appeal.

The board is authorised to constitute a new committee in place of the superseded committee. It can also remove a particular person from the committee. However, before passing such an order, the person removed from the committee shall be given a reasonable opportunity of being heard. The order removing such a person shall be served to him by the registered post.

Any person aggrieved by such orders of the board may prefer an appeal within 30 days of the service of the order to him, before the Waqf Tribunal. The Tribunal may confirm, modify or reverse the order made by the board. The order of the Tribunal in such an appeal shall be final.

Judicial response

The High Court of Madhya Pradesh, in Abdul Karim vs. M.P. State Waqf Board,[111] upheld the delegation of powers to the Chairman for the constitution of Managing Committee. The constitution of such Management Committee is considered as valid.

Amjad Ali Mirza, being deceased, his heirs Nagma Begum & Others vs. Board of Wakfs & Others:[112]

As such, the deed of 1926 makes it categorically clear that the transfer was not in favour of the committee members in their personal capacity or for their individual interest but solely for the worship of the Mohammedan community.

> The purpose of a waqf ought to be considered in the context of Islam. Since Allah, the God Almighty is formless from the Islamic perspective, the expression of devotion to Allah could not be deified through

111 AIR 2019 (NOC) 502 (M.P).
112 AIR 2019 (NOC) 188 (CAL).

> a particular symbol alone or a single structure but had to be expressed through various religious activities and rituals. Hence, a dedication for the Mohammedan community to perform the worship of Allah as well as to hold religious functions, tantamount to a dedication to Allah, though there may not be any formal dedication in the name of Allah.

In Managing Committee Masjid, Idgah, Mysore vs. State of Karnataka and Others,[113] the Karnataka High Court observed that sub-section (2) of section 67 of the Act provides that a Committee like the petitioner, in which the management of a waqf is vested, can be superseded only if, (a) it is not functioning properly and satisfactorily, or (b) that the waqf is being mismanaged and that, in the interest of its proper management, it is necessary so to do. Sub-section (5) of section 67 of the Act specifically and in unambiguous terms provides that a new Committee of management has to be constituted simultaneously with the supersession of the existing Committee. Therefore, a new Committee cannot be constituted unless the old Committee is superseded under and in accordance with the statutory provisions contained therein. The court, while quashing the order of the Karnataka Wakf Board, observed that:

> Admittedly the Act does not concede any doctrine of pleasure or subjective or secretive act in favour of the Board. It has been advisedly so done, since, or else it would have been ultra vires the transparency and reasonableness clause, namely, Art 14 of the Constitution of India. Therefore, the pleasure clause and Condition No. 9 of Annexure-A are clearly ultra vires the powers of the Board. Those are accordingly declared as null and void and non-est and they cannot be relied upon by the Board for any purpose whatsoever.

In another case,, Karnataka High Court in Janab Shastry Khaja Hussain vs. Karnataka Wakf Board,[114] wherein the issue of "doctrine of pleasure" of the Wakf Board was discussed in connection with section 16 of the Wakf Act, 1954 (section 18 of new Act) empowers the board to constitute Committees for supervision of waqfs. The court observed that:

> The scheme in question is said to have been framed six years later in the year 1990 when the said provision did not exist. It is therefore difficult to see how such a scheme can still be recognised to be one which has a valid statutory sanction behind it. Secondly, because all that the scheme provides is that the term of office of the Members, shall not exceed 5 years. The scheme does not make the Committee, immune from dissolution or removal within the outer limit of 5 years. In other words

113 1998 AIHC 2723.
114 1997 AIHC 4146.

> the doctrine of pleasure is not watered-down by the scheme nor any security of tenure provided. Thirdly because the scheme does not indicate whether the same was retrospective in the sense that it would apply even to Committees that had been appointed earlier to the year 1990. Suffice it to say that since the terms subject to which the Committee was appointed themselves authorised the Board to wind up the Committee at its pleasure, it is difficult to see how any such order of dissolution could be said to be bad particularly when the Members of the Committee so appointed had accepted the said appointment on those terms without any reservation.

The Andhra Pradesh High Court, in Sk. Abdul Saleem vs. A.P. State Wakf Board,[115] recorded the following observation:

> It is also relevant to note that Sub-section (2) specifically provides that the order of supersession shall be 'for the reasons to be recorded in writing'. The said words employed in Sub-section (2) make it clear that the Board while passing an order of supersession is bound to record reasons. In other words, the satisfaction of the Board shall be reflected from the reasons assigned in the order of supersession.

The High Court of Andhra Pradesh held that the Waqf Board cannot reconstitute the committee without any valid reason and following the proper procedure. While delivering the Judgement in Janab Gori Sultan and Others vs. A.P. State Wakf Board and Others,[116] it observed:

> The 1st respondent does have the power to supersede, or replace a committee constituted by it, before the term, for which it appointed, had expired. Such an exercise, however, must precede an enquiry into the allegation of misconduct. The necessary procedure is prescribed under Section 67 of the Act. It clearly mandates that before a Committee is superseded, notice setting forth the reasons must be issued to the effected parties. A show-cause notice of not less than one month is mandatory. By calling it as reconstitution, the 1st respondent cannot supersede the committee appointed by it, in contravention of Section 67 of the Act. On this ground alone, the impugned order dated 22-11-2005 is liable to be set aside.

****

115 2006 (2) ALD 501, 2006 (2) ALT 76.
116 2007 (4) ALD 31.

Section 68

Duty of mutawalli or committee to deliver possession of records, etc:-

(1) ***Where any mutawalli or committee of management has been removed by the Board in accordance with the provisions of this Act, or of any scheme made by the Board, the mutawalli or the committee so removed from the office (hereinafter in this section referred to as the removed mutawalli or committee) shall hand over charge and deliver possession of the records, accounts and all properties of the waqf, (including cash) to the successor mutawalli or the successor committee, within one month from the date specified in the order.***

(2) ***Where any removed mutawalli or committee fails to deliver charge or deliver possession of the records, accounts and properties (including cash) to the successor mutawalli or committee within the time specified in sub-section (1), or prevents or obstructs such mutawalli or committee, from obtaining possessing thereof after the expiry of the period aforesaid, the successor mutawalli or any member of the successor committee may make an application, accompanied by a certified copy of the order appointing such successor mutawalli or committee, to any District Magistrate, Additional District Magistrate, Sub-Divisional Magistrate or their equivalent***[117] ***within the local limits of whose jurisdiction any part of the waqf property is situated and, thereupon, such District Magistrate, Additional District Magistrate, Sub-Divisional Magistrate or their equivalent***[118] ***may, after giving notice to the removed mutawalli or members of the removed committee, make an order directing the delivery of charge and possession of such records, accounts and properties (including cash) of the waqf to the successor mutawalli or the committee, as the case may be, within such time as may be specified in the order.***

(3) ***Where the removed mutawalli or any member of the removed committee, omits or fails to deliver charge and possession of the records, accounts and properties (including cash) within the time specified by any Magistrate***[119] ***under sub-section (2), the removed mutawalli or every member of the removed committee, as the case may be, shall be punishable with imprisonment for a term which may extend to six months or with fine which may extend to eight thousand rupees, or with both.***

(4) ***Whenever any removed mutawalli or any member of the removed committee omits or fails to comply with the orders made by any***

117 Substituted by Act 27 of 2013, S. 38 (i), for "Magistrate of the first class" and "Magistrate," respectively.

118 *Ibid.*

119 Substituted by Act 27 of 2013, S. 38 (ii), for "the magistrate."

Magistrate[120] *under sub-section (2), the Magistrate may authorise the successor mutawalli or committee to take charge and possession of such records, accounts, properties (including cash) and may authorise such person to take such police assistance as may be necessary for the purpose.*

(5) *No order of appointment of the successor mutawalli or committee shall be called in question in the proceedings before any Magistrate*[121] *under this section.*

(6) *Nothing contained in this section shall bar the institution of any suit in a competent civil court by any person aggrieved by any order made under this section, to establish that he has right, title and interest in the properties specified in the order made by any Magistrate*[122] *under sub-section (2).*

Reflections

Analogous section under Wakf Act 1954 is S.43 E, inserted by the Wakf Amendment Act 1984 (Act 69 of 1984).

Section 68 is a continuation of the preceding sections. This section provides that the mutawalli or the committee of management removed from the office shall hand over records, documents, accounts and all properties of the wakf to the successor mutawalli or committee within one month. In case of failure of the superseded committee, the successor may approach the District Collector/Magistrate who may direct the superseded committee or any member for compliance of orders. But no order of appointment of a mutawalli or a committee shall be called in question. Failure to comply with the orders of the district Collector/Magistrate will attract a fine of Rs. 8,000 or imprisonment of up to 6 months or both. However, any person aggrieved may approach a competent civil court to establish that he has right, title and interest in the properties specified in the order made by any Magistrate under sub-section (2).

Judicial response

The Honourable Supreme Court of India, in Sayed Muhammed Mashur Kunhi Kaya Thangal vs. Badagara Jamayath Palli Dharas Committee,[123] has held that:

120 *Ibid.*
121 *Ibid.*
122 *Ibid.*
123 AIR 2004 SC 4365.

The first appellate Court having elaborately considered the evidence placed on record in the light of the pleadings of the parties had come to the right conclusion in dismissing the suit of the plaintiff. The High Court in the second appeal, in our view, was not right in upsetting the findings of the fact recorded by the first appellate Court, that too without putting the parties on notice on the substantial question of law. In the result, the appeal is allowed, the impugned judgment is set aside except the direction given to the Wakf Board to act under section 63 of the Wakf Act 1995 and the suit filed by the plaintiff is dismissed. In other words, the direction given by the High Court to the Wakf Board to exercise power under section 63 of the Wakf Act 1995 is maintained.

****

Section 69

Power of Board to frame scheme for administration of waqf:-

(1) *Where the Board is satisfied after an enquiry, whether on its own motion or on the application of not less than five persons interested in any waqf, to frame a scheme for the proper administration of the waqf, it may, by an order, frame such scheme for the administration of the waqf, after giving reasonable opportunity and after consultation with the mutawalli or others in the prescribed manner.*[124]

(2) *A scheme framed under sub-section (1) may provide for the removal of the mutawalli of the waqf holding office as such immediately before the date on which the scheme comes into force:*

Provided that where any such scheme provides for the removal of any hereditary mutawalli, the scheme shall also provide for the appointment of the person next in hereditary succession to the mutawalli so removed, as one of the members of the committee appointed for the proper administration of the waqf.

(3) *Every order made under sub-section (2) shall be published in the prescribed manner, and, on such publication, shall be final and binding on the mutawalli and all persons interested in the waqf:*

Provided that any person aggrieved by an order made under this section may, within sixty days from the date of the order, prefer an

124 Substituted by Act 27 of 2013, S. 39, for sub-section (1).

appeal to the Tribunal and after hearing such appeal, the Tribunal may confirm, reverse or modify the order:

Provided further that the Tribunal shall have no power to stay the operation of the order made under this section.

(4) ***The Board may, at any time by an order, whether made before or after the scheme has come into force, cancel or modify the scheme.***
(5) ***Pending the framing of the scheme for the proper administration of the waqf, the Board may appoint a suitable person to perform all or any of the functions of the mutawalli thereof and to exercise the powers, and perform the duties, of such mutawalli.***

Reflections

Analogous section under Wakf Act 1954 is S.43 F, inserted by the Wakf Amendment Act 1984 (Act 69 of 1984).

Section (69) authorises the Waqf Board to frame a scheme for the proper administration of the waqf after consultation with the mutawalli. There shall be a representation of at least five persons interested in the waqf. Sub-section (1) has been substituted by the Waqf Amendment Act 2013 (act 27 of 2013). Prior to substitution, this section read as under:

> (1) whenever the board is satisfied, whether on its own motion or on the application of not less than five persons interested in any wakf, that it is necessary or desirable to frame a scheme for the proper administration of the wakf, it may by an order frame such scheme for the administration of the wakf, after consultation with the mutawalli or the applicant in the prescribed manner.

Such a scheme may provide for the removal of the mutawalli before the date on which the scheme comes into force. If the Waqf Deed provides for the appointment of hereditary mutawalli, the scheme so framed shall have the provision for the nomination or appointment of a person next in hereditary succession, as one of the members of the committee constituted under the scheme for the proper administration of the waqf. The order of such a scheme shall be published in the prescribed manner and shall be final and binding on the mutawalli and all the persons interested in the waqf.

Any person aggrieved by such scheme may prefer an Appeal to the Tribunal, and, after hearing the parties concerned, the Tribunal may confirm, modify or reverse such an order of the Waqf Board. This section also provides that the Tribunal shall have no power to stay the operation of the order made under this section.

The Waqf Board is also authorised to cancel or modify such a scheme. The Waqf board can also appoint an administrator or a person to perform all or any of the functions and duties of the mutawalli.

Judicial response

Judicial response pertaining to this section is not found.

****

Section 70

Inquiry relating to administration of waqf:-

> ***Any person interested in a waqf may make an application to the Board supported by an affidavit to institute an inquiry relating to the administration of the waqf and if the Board is satisfied that there are reasonable grounds for believing that the affairs of the waqf are being mismanaged, it shall take such action thereon as it thinks fit.***

Reflections

Analogous section under Wakf Act 1954 is S.44.

Section 70 provides for an inquiry relating to the administration of waqf. Any person interested in waqf may make an application along with an affidavit to the Waqf Board to initiate an inquiry relating to the administration of waqf. If the Waqf Board is satisfied that there are reasonable grounds to believe that the affairs of waqf are being mismanaged, it shall take action as it thinks fit and necessary.

Judicial response

In a recent case in Mir Qamar Hasan Razvi vs. A.P. State Wakf Board Hyderabad,[125] the High Court of Andhra Pradesh, while dismissing the petition, ruled that since the Waqf Act 1995 provides an efficacious alternative remedy to the petitioner to challenge the order of the Chief Executive Officer A.P. State Waqf Board before the State Waqf Tribunal, the petitioner has to avail the said remedy.

****

125 2011 (5) ALD 407.

Section 71

Manner of holding inquiry:-

(1) ***The Board may, either on an application received under section 70[126] or on its own motion-***
  (a) ***hold an inquiry in such manner as may be prescribed; or***
  (b) ***authorise any person in this behalf to hold an inquiry into any matter relating to a waqf and take such action as it thinks fit.***

(2) ***For the purposes of an inquiry under this section, the Board or any person authorised by it in this behalf, shall have the same powers as are vested in a civil court under the Code of Civil Procedure, 1908 (5 of 1908) for enforcing the attendance of witnesses and production of documents.***

Reflections

Analogous section under Wakf Act 1954 is S.45, inserted by the Amendment Act (Act 69 of 1984).

Section 71 prescribes the manner in which an inquiry has to be conducted when an application is received under section 70 or on its own motion. The board may authorise or appoint a person to hold an inquiry into the matters of administration of waqf and the take necessary action based on the findings of the inquiry. This section simply specifies a person to be an Inquiry Officer. It does not specify whether that person should be Judicial Officer, an Executive Magistrate or an Officer of the Waqf Board.

The Inquiry Officer shall have the same powers as are vested is a Civil Court under the Code of Civil Procedure 1908 (5 of 1908) for enforcing the attendance of witnesses and production of documents. However, before initiating any action based on the finding of the inquiry, the explanation of the mutawalli or the person affected shall be obtained and considered by the board.

Judicial response

The Andhra Pradesh High Court is of the view that, when the Act contemplates that an inquiry has to be conducted by the Chief Executive Officer, it should invariably be conducted by him or there shall be regulations to prescribe the manner of appointment of Inquiry Officer in such cases. In the

126 Substituted by Act 27 of 2013, S. 40, for "73."

case of Muppu Raju Lakshmi vs. Andhra Pradesh, the State Wakf Board Rep. by its Chief Executive Officer and Another[127] held that:

> As the things stand now, in the State of Andhra Pradesh, an inquiry under section 54(3) of the Act can be conducted, only by the Chief Executive Officer. This may, no doubt, lead to heavy pressure on the functioning of the incumbent. However, that can be remedied, only by framing the relevant Rules.

127 2010 (3) ALD 263; 2010 (3) ALT 244.

VII FINANCE OF THE BOARD

Synopsis

This chapter, from section 72 to 82, deals with the finances of the State Waqf Boards. Payment of Waqf Fund Contribution by the waqf institutions from their income to the Waqf Board or from the annuity; powers of the Waqf Board to borrow funds with the approval of the State Government; budget, finances, accounts and audit of the State Waqf Boards; recovery of dues to the Waqf Boards as arrears of revenue, etc., are discussed in this chapter. The Waqf Amendment Act 2013 has attempted to strengthen the role of Waqf Boards by making a provision that Orders under the Land Acquisition Act in respect of waqf lands shall not be passed without consulting the State Waqf Board concerned. The Chief Executive Officer of the State Waqf Board has been authorised to file an application before the Waqf Tribunal to evict the unauthorised occupants.

Keywords: Income, Annuity, Arrears, Corpus

****

Section 72

Annual contribution payable to Board:-

(1) ***The mutawalli of every waqf, the net annual income of which is not less than five thousand rupees, shall pay annually, out of the net annual income derived by the waqf, such contributions, not exceeding seven percent of such annual income as may be prescribed, to the Board for the services rendered by such Board to the waqf.***

Explanation I.- For the purposes of this Act, "net annual income" shall mean the gross income of the waqf from all sources, including nazars and offerings which do not amount to contributions to the corpus of the waqf, in a year after deducting there from the following, namely:-

(i) *the land revenue paid by it to the Government;*

(ii) *the rates, cesses, taxes and licence fees, paid by it to the Government or any local authority;*

(iii) *expenditure incurred for all or any of the following purposes in respect of lands directly under cultivation by the mutawalli for the benefit of the waqf, namely:-*[1]

(a) *maintenance of, or repairs to, irrigation works, which shall not include the capital cost of irrigation;*

(b) *seeds or seedlings;*

(c) *manure;*

(d) *purchase and maintenance of agricultural implements;*

(e) *purchase and maintenance of cattle for cultivation;*

(f) *wages for ploughing, watering, sowing, transplanting, harvesting, threshing and other agricultural operation:*

Provided that the total deduction in respect of an expenditure incurred under this clause shall not exceed twenty per cent [2] *of the income derived from lands belonging to the waqf:*

Provided further that no such deduction shall be permitted in respect of waqf land given on lease, by whatever name called, whether batai or share cropping or any other name.[3]

(iv) *expenditure on sundry repairs to rented buildings, not exceeding five per cent, of the annual rent derived there from, or the actual expenditure, whichever is less;*

(v) *sale proceeds of immovable properties or rights relating to, or arising out of immovable properties, if such proceeds are reinvested to earn income for the waqf:*

Provided that the following items of receipts shall not be deemed to be income for the purposes of this section, namely:-

(a) *advances and deposits recovered and loans taken or recovered;*

(b) *deposits made as security by employees, lessees or contractors and other deposits, if any;*

(c) *withdrawals from banks or of investments;*

(d) *amounts recovered towards costs awarded by courts;*

1 Inserted by Act 27 of 2013, S. 41(i).

2 Substituted by Act 27 of 2013, S. 41(ii), for "ten per cent."

3 Inserted by Act 27 of 2013, S. 41(iii).

(e) *sale proceeds of religious books and publications where such sales are undertaken as an un-remunerative enterprise with a view to propagating religion;*
(f) *donations in cash or kind or offerings made by the donors as contributions to the corpus of the waqf:*

Provided that the interest on income, if any, accruing from such donations or offerings shall be taken into account in calculating the gross annual income;

(g) *voluntary contributions received in cash or kind for a specific service to be performed by the waqf and expended on such service;*
(h) *audit recoveries.*

Explanation II.-In determining, the net annual income for the purposes of this section, only the net profit derived by any waqf from its remunerative undertakings, if any, shall be taken as income, and in respect of its non-remunerative undertakings, such as, schools, colleges, hospitals, poor homes, orphanages or any other similar institutions, the grants given by the Government or any local authority or donations received from the public or fees collected from the pupils of educational institutions shall not be taken as income.

(2) *The Board may in the case of any mosque or orphanage or any particular waqf reduce or remit such contribution for such time as it thinks fit.*

(3) *The mutawalli of a waqf may realise the contributions payable by him under sub-section (1) from the various persons entitled to receive any pecuniary or other material benefit from the waqf, but the sum realisable from any one of such persons shall not exceed such amount as shall bear to the total contribution payable, the same proportion, as the value of the benefits receivable by such person bears to the entire net annual income of the waqf:*

Provided that if there is any income of the waqf available in excess of the amount payable as dues under this Act, other than as the contribution under sub-section (1), and in excess of the amount payable under the waqf deed, the contribution shall be paid out of such income.

(4) *The contribution payable under sub-section (1) in respect of a waqf shall, subject to the prior payment of any dues to the Government or any local authority or of any other statutory first charge on the waqf property or the income thereof, be a first charge on the income of the waqf and shall be recoverable, on a certificate issued by the Board*

after giving the mutawalli concerned an opportunity of being heard, as an arrear of land revenue.

(5) *If a mutawalli realises the income of the waqf and refuses to pay or does not pay such contribution, he shall also be personally liable for such contribution which may be realised from his person or property in the manner aforesaid.*

(6) *Where, after the commencement of this Act, the mutawalli of a waqf fails to submit a return of the net annual income of the waqf within the time specified there for or submits a return which, in the opinion of the Chief Executive Officer is incorrect or false in any material particular, or which does not comply with the provisions of this Act or any rule or order made there under, the chief Executive Officer may assess the net annual income of the waqf to the best of his judgment or revise the net annual income as shown in the return submitted by the mutawalli and the net annual income as so assessed or revised shall be deemed to be the net annual income of the waqf for the purposes of this section:*

> *Provided that no assessment of net annual income or revision of return submitted by mutawalli shall be made except after giving a notice to the mutawalli calling upon him to show cause, within the time specified in the notice, as to why such assessment or revision of the return shall not be made and every such assessment or revision shall be made after considering the reply if any, given by the mutawalli.*

(7) *Any mutawalli, who is aggrieved by the assessment or revision made by the Chief Executive Officer, under sub-section (6), may prefer an appeal to the Board within thirty days from the date of receipt of the assessment or revision of return and the Board may, after giving the appellant a reasonable opportunity of being heard, confirm, reverse or modify the assessment or revision or the return and the decision of the Board thereon shall be final.*

(8) *If, for any reason, the contribution or any portion thereof leviable under this section has escaped assessment in any year, whether before or after the commencement of this Act, the Chief Executive Officer may, within five years from the last date of the year to which such escaped assessment relates serve upon the mutawalli a notice assessing him with the contribution or portion thereof which has escaped assessment, and demanding payment thereof within thirty days from the date of service of such notice, and the provisions of this Act and the rules made there under, shall, as far as may be, apply as if the assessments were made under this Act, in the first instance.*

Reflections

Analogous section under Wakf Act 1954 is S.46.

Section 72 of the Wakf Act provides for the payment of annual contribution at the rate of seven per cent by the Mutawalli of the waqf whose annual income is five thousand or more to the Waqf Board. The method of calculation of the annual income and the admissible deductions have been discussed under this section. But these deductions shall not exceed 20 per cent of the gross annual income of the waqf. The Waqf Amendment Act 2013 (Act 27 of 2013) has enhanced these admissible expenditures from 10 per cent to 20 per cent. In case of lease of agricultural lands these deductions are not admissible. In respect of Waqf-alal-Aulad the annual contribution shall be calculated over the amount allocated for the pious, religious or charitable purposes.

The Chief Executive Officer of the Waqf Board is authorised to review the net annual income for the determination of annual contribution payable by the mutawalli. If any mutawalli is aggrieved by the decision of the Chief Executive Officer, he may appeal to the Waqf Board and the decision of the Board shall be final.

The Waqf Board is authorised to recover the arrears of the annual contribution from the mutawalli or from his personal property as arrears of land revenue. The Waqf Board is also authorised to reduce or waive the annual contribution for such time as it thinks fit in case of any mosque or orphanage or any particular waqf. Any deviation on the part of the mutawalli in the payment of the contribution will attract penal action under section 61 of this Act.

The payment of annual contribution could have been limited to the waqf institutions whose annual income is Rs. 1 lakh or more and whose mutawallis are entitled to vote and elect the members of the Waqf Board under the electoral college of mutawallis.

Judicial response

A batch of writ petitions were filed before the Kerala High Court challenging the levy of annual contribution of Waqf Fund as violative of Article 14 of the Constitution. It was contended that the levy fell unevenly and inequitably on different waqfs. A learned Single Judge of the High Court of Kerala held that so long as what is taxed is not what ultimately comes into the hands of the owner as net income, and the levy is not a percentage of such net income, the incidence of the levy varies from person to person and violates Article 14 of the Constitution.

The Kerala Waqf Board, which was the first respondent in the writ petition, went in appeal. The Bench of the Kerala High Court, in this case

Kerala Wakf Board vs. Union of India,[4] while upholding the levy of annual contribution held that:

> Alleged inequalities arising from the nature of enjoyment of properties or even the nature of the properties owned by a wakf cannot be made a ground for supporting the contention that an impost such as a fee at a uniform rate on the gross income of wakfs taking into account the services rendered to each wakf is violative of Article 14 of the Constitution as we are not able to discern any clear hostile discrimination or the singling out of any wakf or any class of wakfs for special or peculiar treatment. The discrimination if any, as stated already, seems to arise out of fortuitous circumstances.

However, the provisions and the explanations under this section provide for the exclusion of certain expenditures to arrive at the net annual income for the calculation of waqf contribution.

The High Court of Kerala in Thorayil Juma Masjid Mannalu Committee, Madakkallur vs. Kerala Wakf Board, Ernakulam,[5] held that the order passed by the Wakf Board in exercise of its appellate jurisdiction under section 72 (7) of the Waqf Act 1995 was final, and that such an order cannot be challenged before the Waqf Tribunal.

****

Section 73

Power of Chief executive Officer to direct banks or other person to make payments:-

(1) ***Notwithstanding anything contained in any other law for the time being in force, the Chief Executive Officer, if he is satisfied that it is necessary and expedient so to do, make an order directing any bank in which, or any person with whom any money belonging to a waqf is deposited, to pay the contribution, leviable under section 72, out of such money, as may be standing to the credit of the waqf in such bank or may be deposited with such person, or out of the moneys which, may, from time to time, be received by bank or other person for or on behalf of the waqf by way of deposit, and on receipt of such orders, the bank or the person, as the case may be, shall when no appeal has been preferred under sub-section (3), comply with such orders, or were an appeal has been preferred under sub-section (3), shall comply with the orders made by the Tribunal on such appeal.***

4 AIR 1975 Ker 123 (DB); ILR 1974 (2) Kerala P. 316
5 AIR 2007 (NOC) 1341 Ker. 2007 Ker, L.T. 231.

(2) *Every payment made by a bank or other person in pursuance of any order made under sub-section (1), shall operate as a full discharge of the liability of such bank or other person in relation to the sum so paid.*

(3) *Any bank or other person who is ordered under sub-section(1) to make any payment may, within thirty days from the date of the order, prefer an appeal against such order to the Tribunal and the decision of the Tribunal on such appeal shall be final.*

(4) *Every Officer of the bank or other person who fails, without any reasonable excuse, to comply with the order made under sub-section (1) or, as the case may be, under sub-section (3), shall be punishable with imprisonment for a term which may extend to six months or with fine which may extend to eight thousand rupees, or with both.*

Reflections

Analogous section under Wakf Act 1954 is S.46 A, inserted by the amendment Act 69 of 1984.

In case the annual contribution is due to the Waqf Board under section (72), this section empowers the Chief Executive Officer of the Waqf Board to recover the annual contributions or arrears from any bank or person with whom the money belonging to the waqf institution is kept or deposited. The Chief Executive Officer of the Waqf Board may pass order calling upon such a bank or individual to remit the contribution. Such payment to the Waqf Board shall be treated as full discharge of liability of such bank or person.

The bank or person aggrieved by such an order can prefer an appeal before the Waqf Tribunal within 30 days from the date of the receipt of such an order. The decision of the Tribunal shall be final. The Section also provides that failure to make the payment will attract a penalty of Rs. 8,000 or imprisonment for 6 months or both.

Judicial response

Judicial response relating to this section is not found.

****

Section 74

Deduction of contribution from perpetual annuity payable to the waqf:-

(1) *Every authority empowered to disburse any perpetual annuity payable to a waqf under any law relating to the abolition of zamindaries*

or jagirs, or laying down land ceilings, shall, on receipt of a certificate from the Chief Executive Officer, specifying the amount of contribution payable by the waqf under section 72 which remains unpaid, deduct before making payment of the perpetual annuity to the waqf, the amount specified in such certificate and remit the amount so deducted to the Chief Executive Officer.

(2) *Every amount remitted under sub-section (1) to the Chief Executive Officer shall be deemed to be a payment made by the waqf and shall to the extent of the amount so remitted, operate as a full discharge of the liability of such authority with regard to the payment of the perpetual annuity.*

Reflections

Analogous section under Wakf Act 1954 is S.46 B, introduced by the Wakf Amendment Act 1984 (Act 69 of 1984).

The Waqf Fund contribution shall be deducted from the perpetual annuity payable to any waqf institution by any authority and be remitted to the Chief Executive Officer of the Waqf Board. Such deduction and remittance shall be treated as full discharge of liability of such authority.

Judicial response

Judicial response relating to this section is not found.

****

Section 75

Power of Board to borrow:-

(1) *For the purpose of giving effect to the provisions of this Act, the Board may, with the previous sanction of the State Government, borrow such sum of money and on such terms and conditions as the State Government may determine.*

(2) *The Board shall repay the money borrowed, together with any interest or costs due in respect thereof, according to the terms and conditions of the loan.*

Reflections

Analogous section under Wakf Act 1954 is S.47.

With the prior sanction of the State Government the Waqf Board can borrow money for giving full effect to the provisions of this Act. The Board, after borrowing the loan on such terms and conditions, shall repay the same on the terms and conditions as may be specified.

Judicial response

Judicial response relating to this section is not found.

****

Section 76

Mutawalli not to lend or borrow moneys without sanction:-

(1) *No mutawalli, Executive Officer or other person in charge of the administration of a waqf shall lend any money belonging to the waqf or any waqf property or borrow any money for the purposes of the waqf except with the previous sanction of the Board:*

Provided that no such sanction is necessary if there is an express provision in the deed of waqf for such borrowing or lending, as the case may be.

(2) *The Board may, while according sanction, specify any terms and conditions subject to which the person referred to in sub-section (1) is authorised by him to lend or borrow any money or lend any other waqf property.*

(3) *Where any money is lent or borrowed, or other waqf property is lent in contravention of provisions of this section, it shall be lawful for the Chief Executive Officer:*

   (a) *to recover an amount equal to the amount which has been so lent or borrowed, together with interest due thereon, from the personal funds of the person by whom such amount was lent or borrowed;*

   (b) *to recover the possession of the waqf property lent in contravention of the provisions of this Act, from the person to whom it was lent, or from persons who claim title to such property through the person to whom such property was lent.*

Reflections

Analogous section under Wakf Act 1954 is S.47 A, inserted by the Wakf Amendment Act 34 of 1964.

This section prohibits the mutawalli, Executive Officer or any person in charge of administration of waqf from lending or borrowing any money on behalf of the waqf without the prior approval of the Board. However, if there is a provision under the Waqf Deed it can be followed accordingly. The Waqf Board, while according permission, may prescribe terms and conditions specific to a particular transaction and for a waqf institution.

The Chief Executive Officer may recover the possession of the waqf property lent in contravention of the provisions of this Act, from the person to whom it was lent, or from persons who claim title to such property through the person to whom such property was lent. The Chief Executive Officer may also recover the amount which has been so lent or borrowed, from the personal funds of the person by whom such an amount was lent or borrowed.

Judicial response

Judicial response relating to this section is not found.

****

Section 77

Waqf Fund:-

(1) *All moneys received or realised by the Board under this Act and all other moneys received as donations, benefactions or grants by the Board shall form a fund to be called the Waqf Fund.*
(2) *All moneys received by the Board, as donations, benefactions and grants shall be deposited and accounted for under a separate sub-head.*
(3) *Subject to any rules that may be made by the State Government in this behalf, the Waqf Fund shall be under the control of Board, so, however, that the Waqf Fund under the control of common Waqf Board shall be subject to rules, if any, made in this behalf by the Central Government.*
(4) *The Waqf Fund shall be applied to*
   (a) *repayment of any loan incurred under section 75 and payment of interest thereon;*
   (b) *payment of the cost of audit of the Waqf Fund and the accounts of auqaf;*
   (c) *payment of the salary and allowances to the officers and staff of the Board;*

(d) *payment of travelling allowances to the Chairperson, members, of the Board;*
(e) *payment of all expenses incurred by the Board in the performance of the duties imposed, and all exercise of the powers conferred, by or under this Act;*
(f) *payment of all expenses incurred by the Board for the discharge of any obligation imposed on it by or under any law for the time being in force.*
(g) *payment of maintenance to Muslim women as ordered by a court of competent jurisdiction under the provisions of the Muslim Women (Protection of Rights on Divorce) Act, 1986 (25 of 1986).*[6]

(5) ***If any balance remains after meeting the expenditure referred to in sub-section (4), the Board may use any portion of such balance for the preservation and protection of waqf properties or for such other purposes as it may deem fit.***

Reflections

Analogous section under Wakf Act 1954 is S.48, as Amended by the Wakf Amendment Act 34 of 1964.

This section provides for the constitution of Waqf Fund to meet the expenditure incurred on audit of auqaf, salaries of the employees, allowances to the Chair-Person, repayment of loans or for the discharge of any duty by the Waqf Board under this Act. In case of common Waqf Boards, the application of the Waqf Fund shall be subject to the rules formulated by the Central Government.

Sub-Section (4) lists the heads of expenditure on which the Waqf Fund can be spent. A new clause (g) has been inserted under sub-section 4 by the Waqf Amendment Act 2013 (Act 27 of 2013) which specifically provides for payment of maintenance to Muslim women on orders of a court of competent jurisdiction under the provisions of the Muslim Women (Protection of Rights on Divorce) Act, 1986 (25 of 1986).

Judicial response

Judicial response relating to this section is not found.

****

6 Inserted by Act 27 of 2013, S. 42.

Section 78

Budget of Board:-

(1) *The Board shall in every year prepare, in such form and at such time as may be prescribed, a budget for the next financial year showing the estimated receipts and expenditure during that financial year and forward a copy of the same to the State Government.*
(2) *On receipt of the budget forwarded to it under sub-section (1), the State Government shall examine the same and suggest such alterations, corrections, or modifications to be made therein as it may think fit and forward such suggestions to the Board for its consideration.*
(3) *On receipt of the suggestions from the State Government the Board may make written representations to that Government with regard to the alterations, corrections or modifications suggested by that Government and the State Government shall, after considering such representations, communicate, within a period of three weeks from the date of receipt thereof, to the Board its final decision in relation to the matter and the decision of the State Government shall be final.*
(4) *On receipt of the decision of the State Government under sub-section (3), the Board shall incorporate in its budget all the alterations, corrections, modifications finally suggested by the State Government and the budget as so altered, corrected or modified, shall be the budget which shall be passed by the Board.*

Reflections

Analogous section under Wakf Act 1954 is S.49, as Amended by Wakf Amendment Act (Act 69 of 1984).

This section speaks about the procedure for preparation of annual budget and submission of the same to the State Government by the Waqf Board. The State Government on examination of the budget may suggest alterations, additions or deletions which have to be incorporated by the Board before passing it. On receipt of such suggestions from the State Government, the Waqf Board may address a representation to the State Government under sub-section (3). However, the decision of the State Government shall be final.

Sub-section (1) envisages preparation of budget by the Waqf Board. Sub-section (2) authorises the State Government to carry out modification and alterations in the budget. Sub-section (3) stipulates that the decision of the State Government is final. Again, sub-section (4) contemplates that the Board shall pass the budget as modified by the State Government. Whereas under sub-section (4) the Board has no option except to ratify the budget as modified and altered by the State Government.

Judicial response

Judicial response relating to this section is not found.

****

Section 79

Accounts of Board:-

> ***The Board shall cause to be maintained such books of account and other books in relation to its accounts in such form and in such manner as may be provided by regulations.***

Reflections

Analogous section under Wakf Act 1954 is S.50.

The Waqf Board shall maintain proper books of accounts as may be prescribed by the regulations. This section does not mention the types of accounts that are required to be maintained. It could have discussed the types of accounts that a Waqf Board shall maintain. It is advisable if the Board maintains separate accounts for each waqf institution.

Judicial response

Judicial response relating to this section is not found.

****

Section 80

Audit of accounts of Board:-

(1) ***The accounts of the Board shall be audited and examined annually by such auditor as may be appointed by the State Government.***
(2) ***The auditor shall submit his report to the State Government and the report of the auditor shall, among other things, specify whether the accounts of every waqf under the direct management of the Board have been kept separately and whether such accounts have been audited annually by the State Examiner of Local Funds and shall***

also specify all cases of irregular, illegal or improper expenditure or of failure to recover money or other property caused by neglect or misconduct and any other matter which the auditor considers it necessary to report; and the report shall also contain the name of any person who, in the opinion of the auditor is responsible for such expenditure or failure and the auditor shall in every such case certify the amount of such expenditure or loss as due from such person.

(3) *The cost of the audit shall be paid from the Waqf Fund.*

Reflections

Analogous section under Wakf Act 1954 is S.51.

This section provides for the audit of the accounts of the Waqf Board by the auditors appointed by the State Government. The auditors shall submit the audit report to the State Government specifying the illegal or improper expenditure, if any, the failures in the recovery of the amount due to the Board, the misuse of funds and the persons responsible for such misuse, the comments on the accounts of the waqf institution under the direct management of the Board and any other matter which in the opinion of the auditors is worth reporting to the State Government. The auditor shall also discuss in his/their report whether the accounts of the waqf under the direct management are kept separately, and whether the accounts were examined by the officials of Local Fund Audit of the State concerned.

Judicial response

Judicial response relating to this section is not found.

****

Section 81

State Government to pass orders on auditor's report:-

The State Government shall examine the auditor's report and may call for the explanation of any person in regard to any matter mentioned therein, and shall pass such orders on the report as it thinks fit and a copy of the said auditor's report, along with orders shall be forwarded by the State Government to the Council within a period of thirty days of laying of such report before each House of the State Legislature

where it consists of two Houses or where such Legislatures consist of one House, before that House.[7]

Reflections

Analogous section under Wakf Act 1954 is S.52.

This section authorises the State Government to examine the auditor's report and pass orders as it thinks fit in the circumstances of the case to call for the explanation of the delinquent persons, if any, as mentioned in the auditor's report. A copy of the auditor's report shall be forwarded by the state Government to the Central Waqf Council within a period of 30 days of placing such a report before State Legislature.

Judicial response

Judicial response relating to this section is not found.

****

Section 82

Dues of Board to be recovered as arrears of land revenue:-

(1) ***Every sum certified to be due from any person by auditor in his report under section 80, be paid by such person within sixty days after the service of a demand notice by the Board.***
(2) ***If such payment is not made in accordance with the provisions of sub-section (1), the sum payable may, on a certificate issued by the Board, after giving the person concerned an opportunity of being heard, be recovered as an arrear of land revenue.***

Reflections

Analogous section under Wakf Act 1954 is S.53.

This section provides for the recovery of the amount due as certified by the auditors, which shall be paid by such person within 60 days from the

7 Inserted by Act 27 of 2013, S. 43.

date of service of demand notice. However, a reasonable opportunity shall be given to such a person of being heard. The amount due may be recovered as an arrears of land revenue.

Judicial response

Judicial response relating to this section is not found.

VIII JUDICIAL PROCEEDINGS

Synopsis

This chapter, under Sections 83 to 95 of the Act, deals with the establishment of Waqf Tribunals by the State Government, judicial proceedings, expeditious decision of the cases bar on the jurisdiction of the Civil Courts, appointment of receiver, mandatory notice of cases to the Waqf Board, etc., section 83 empowers the State Government to constitute a Waqf Tribunal. Section 85 of the Act bars the jurisdiction of civil courts. The Waqf Tribunal shall have jurisdiction to try all matters pertaining to the waqf. Section 7 of the Act says that whether a particular property is a waqf property or not, and whether a waqf specified in the list of waqf is a Shia Waqf or a Sunni Waqf shall be referred to the Waqf Tribunal. With the Waqf Amendment Act 2013, the Waqf Tribunal no longer remains a single-member body.

The Waqf Amendment Act 2013 has also made a provision that the Waqf Tribunal can assess the damages due to unauthorised possession of waqf property and pass orders for the recovery through District Magistrates. The Waqf Tribunal shall entertain the application submitted by the Chief Executive Officer for the eviction of unauthorised occupants of the waqf property. With the Waqf Amendment Act 2013 the Waqf Tribunal no longer remains a single member body.

Keywords: Tribunal, Jurisdiction, Receiver, Notice of suits, Civil Procedure Code 1908, Land Acquisition Act 1894

****

Section 83

Constitution of Tribunals, etc.:-

(1) ***The State Government shall, by notification in the Official Gazette, constitute as many Tribunals as it may think fit, for the determination of any dispute, question or other matter relating to a waqf or waqf***

property, eviction of a tenant or determination of rights and obligations of the lessor and the lessee of such property, under this Act and define the local limits and jurisdiction of such Tribunals;[1]

(2) *Any mutawalli, person interested in a waqf or any other person aggrieved by an order made under this Act, or rules made there under, may make an application within the time specified in this Act or where no such time has been specified, within such time as may be prescribed, to the Tribunal for the determination of any dispute, question or other matter relating to the waqf.*

(3) *Where any application made under sub-section (1) relates to any waqf property which falls within the territorial limits of the jurisdiction of two or more Tribunals, such application may be made to the Tribunal within the local limits of whose jurisdiction the mutawalli or any one of the mutawallis of the waqf actually and voluntarily resides, carries on business or personally works for gain, and, where any such application is made to the Tribunal aforesaid, the other Tribunal or Tribunals having jurisdiction shall not entertain any application for the determination of such dispute, question or other matter:*

Provided that the State Government may, if it is of opinion that it is expedient in the interest of the waqf or any other person interested in the waqf or the waqf property to transfer such application to any other Tribunal having jurisdiction for the determination of the dispute, question or other matter relating to such waqf or waqf property, transfer such application to any other Tribunal having jurisdiction, and, on such transfer, the Tribunal to which the application is so transferred shall deal with the application from the stage which was reached before the Tribunal from which the application has been so transferred, except where the Tribunal is of opinion that it is necessary in the interests of justice to deal with the application afresh.

(4) *Every Tribunal shall consist of-*[2]

- (a) *one person, who shall be a member of the State Judicial Service holding a rank, not below that of a District, Sessions or Civil Judge, Class I, who shall be the Chairman;*
- (b) *one person, who shall be an officer from the State Civil Services equivalent in rank to that of the Additional District Magistrate, Member;*
- (c) *one person having knowledge of Muslim law and jurisprudence, Member,*

1 Substituted by Act 27 of 2013, S. 44 (a), for sub-section (1).
2 Substituted by Act 27 of 2013, S. 44 (b), for sub-section (4).

and the appointment of every such person shall be made either by name or by designation.

(4A) The terms and conditions of appointment including the salaries and allowances payable to the Chairman and other members other than persons appointed as ex officio members shall be such as may be prescribed."

(5) *The Tribunal shall be deemed to be a civil court and shall have the same powers as may be exercised by a civil court under the Code of Civil Procedure, 1908, (5 of 1908) while trying a suit, or executing a decree or order.*
(6) *Notwithstanding anything contained in the Code of Civil Procedure, 1908, (5 of 1908) the Tribunal shall follow such procedure as may be prescribed.*
(7) *The decision of the Tribunal shall be final and binding upon the parties to the application and it shall have the force of a decree made by a civil court.*
(8) *The Execution of any decision of the Tribunal shall be made by the civil court to which such decision is sent for execution in accordance with the provisions of the Code of Civil Procedure, 1908 (5 of 1908).*
(9) *No appeal shall lie against any decision or order whether interim or otherwise, given or made by the Tribunal:*

Provided that a High Court may, on its own motion or on the application of the Board or any person aggrieved, call for and examine the records relating to any dispute, question or other matter which has been determined by the Tribunal for the purpose of satisfying itself as to the correctness, legality or propriety of such determination and may confirm, reverse or modify such determination or pass such other order as it may think fit.

Reflections

Analogous section under Wakf Act 1954 is S.55 and sub-section 4 and 4 A were substituted by Waqf Amendment Act 2013 (Act 27 of 2013).

Section 83 of the Act provides for the constitution of Waqf Tribunal or Tribunals by the State Government for the determination of any dispute or other matter relating to a waqf or waqf property. The State Government shall define the jurisdiction of such a Tribunal. This section provides for the determination of all the disputes by the Tribunal, including rent control and tenancy cases. Sub-section (1) has been substituted by the Waqf Amendment Act 2013 (Act 27 of 2013). The substitution of this section nullifies the recent Supreme Court Judgement which held that the Tribunal does not have the jurisdiction to try the cases pertaining to rent control and tenancy. Prior to substitution, sub-section (1) read as under:

> (1) The state government shall, by notification in the official gazette, constitute as many tribunal as it may think fit, for the determination of any dispute, question or other matter relating to a wakf or wakf property under this Act and define the local limits and jurisdiction under this Act of each of such tribunal.

The Waqf Amendment Act 2013 has changed the composition of Tribunal. Now it shall consist of a Chair-Person who is not below the rank of District Judge or Class 1 Civil Judge; one state civil service officer not below the rank of Additional District Magistrate and a person having knowledge of Muslim Law and jurisprudence. This composition of the Waqf Tribunal with two members in addition to the presiding officer has been provided by the Waqf Amendment Act 2013 (Act 27 of 2013). Prior this amendment, the sub-section (4) read as under:

> (4) Every tribunal shall consist of one person, who shall be a member of the state judicial service holding a rank, not below that of a District, Session or Civil Judge, class I, and the appointment of every such person may be made either by name or by designation.

Any person interested in waqf or a mutawalli of a waqf may institute a suit or file an application before the Tribunal within such time as provided under this Act. The Tribunal shall have the same powers as may be exercised by a Civil Court under the Civil Procedure Court 1908 (5 of 1908). The execution of the orders of the Tribunal shall be made by the Civil Courts.

Judicial response

The Supreme Court, in Syed Mohideen & Another vs. Ramanathapura Peria Mogallam jamath & Others (Civil Appeal No. 492 of 2003),[3] reiterated the powers of the Waqf Tribunal by saying:

> We, however, may make it clear that in terms of Section 83(5) of the Wakf Act, 1995 the Wakf Tribunal is deemed to be a civil court and has the same powers as are exercised by civil court under the Code of Civil Procedure, 1908 while trying a suit or executing a decree or order. The civil courts are in turn competent to issue injunctions in terms of Order XXXIX Rules 1 and 2 and Section 151 C.P.C. Similar orders can,

3 [2010] 8 S.C.R. 777

> therefore, be passed by the Wakf Tribunal also in suits that are legally triable by it if a case for grant of such injunction or direction is made out by the party concerned.

The High Court of Allahabad, in Zaheer Ahmad vs. Wakf No. 13 Hauz Wali Masjid, Sarwat Gate, Muzaffar Nagar & Others,[4] held that:

> The language used under Section 83(2) of the Act also reveals that by using the expression "or" between the phrase "any mutawalli or person interested in a Wakf" and "any other person aggrieved by an order made under this Act or Rules made there under", the legislature has intended to make distinction between aforesaid persons.

The Indore Bench of Madhya Pradesh High Court, in Subhan Shah vs. M.P. Wakf Board,[5] held that:

> The order passed by the Tribunal appears to be just and proper and has been passed within its jurisdiction by the Tribunal, under Sub-section (3) of Section 32 the Tribunal can settle schemes of management for a wakf, give a direction for the utilisation of income of wakf consistent with the object of the wakf and as per its object and have rightly held that the plaintiffs are also entitled for Wajifa and have rightly and legally framed a scheme for the distributions of the offerings and Wajifa amongst them.

The Wakf Board filed an appeal in the matter before the Supreme Court Appeal (civil) 6975 of 2004. The Supreme Court after considering the facts of the case referred the case back to the Wakf Tribunal.

The Himachal Pradesh High Court in Jeet Mohammaed vs. Jatinder Kaur & Another,[6] has held that any Muslim is a person interested in wakf and can approach the Waqf Tribunal to file a petition in respect of a waqf matter. It observed that:

> When these aspects are kept in mind, it is obvious that any person who professes Islam is a person interested in the management of the Wakf Board. He can raise dispute(s) before the Wakf Tribunal that such property is being frittered away or are being sold against the intention of the creator of the Wakf. The State in its wisdom has barred the jurisdiction of the civil Courts and vested the same in a tribunal. The intention behind this is that the property of the Wakf is not wasted and caught

4 AIR 2009 (NOC) 1080, (All).
5 AIR 2004 MP, 22.
6 AIR 2009 HP, 44.

> up in delays caused by legal niceties but the same are dealt with expeditiously by a Tribunal.

The High Court of Andhra Pradesh in T. Shivalingam vs. A.P. Wakf Tribunal,[7] while dealing with the jurisdiction of the Wakf Tribunal observed that:

> This is a highly misconceived Writ Petition. A suit has been filed by the respondents before A.P. State Wakf Tribunal seeking eviction of the petitioner from the property belonging to Wakf. A Writ of Prohibition has been filed on the ground that the Tribunal has no jurisdiction to entertain suits of the present nature i.e., suit for eviction. Section 7 of the Act is not a bar for entertaining of such suits but it only lays down that disputes regarding nature of property as to whether it is Wakf property or not can be decided only by the Tribunal.

On the other hand, the same High Court of Andhra Pradesh in Chowk Mosque, Nandiyal, vs. P.V.H. Maqbul Basha,[8] has taken a different view and observed that:

> Suit for permanent injunction restraining defendants from interfering with construction of shops in mosques premises does not fall within the ambit of Section 6, 70, 83 of the Wakf Act, 1995 and therefore the question of instituting a suit in the Tribunal does not arise.

However, a Division Bench of High Court of Andhra Pradesh, while referring to the above cases when its attention was drawn in Syed Muneer vs. Chief Executive Officer, A.P. State Wakf Board, Hyd,[9] upheld the view expressed in the T. Shivilingam case that the Waqf Act bars the jurisdiction of the civil court to decide any dispute relating to waqf property. The Division Bench observed:

> Assuming that in the writ petition a jurisdictional fact is required to be gone into, the same can also be directed to be gone into by the Tribunal at the first instance.

A Division Bench of the High Court of Andhra Pradesh, in M. Bikshapathi vs. Government of Andhra Pradesh,[10] held that the jurisdiction of the Waqf Tribunal cannot be limited by reading section 6 alone providing for the

7 1999 (3) ALD 646.
8 1999 AIHC 1758.
9 2001 (4) ALD 430 (DB).
10 1999 (6) ALD 270 (DB).

decision to determine the nature of the waqf property, i.e., to the effect of whether it is a waqf property or not; whether it is a Shia Waqf or Sunni Waqf and who is the interested person who can institute a suit. Section 6 further specifies that the person interested shall, in relation to the property, include every person who, though not interested in the waqf concerned, is interested in such property.

In the case of Allauddin Charities and Zakath Wakf vs. Hameed Ali,[11] the High Court of Andhra Pradesh referred to this judgement and held that, under sub-section (5) of section 83, the Tribunal constituted under sub-section (1) of section 83 shall be deemed to be a Civil Court and shall have the same powers as may be exercised by a Civil Court under the Code of Civil Procedure while trying a suit or executing a decree or order. Therefore, when the Tribunal has been conferred with the power to determine any dispute, question or other matter relating to a waqf or waqf property under the Act and acts as a Civil Court for all purposes, this Court, in exercise of the jurisdiction under Article 226 of the Constitution, cannot permit a party to bypass such statutory remedy and assign itself the role of statutory authority or Tribunal by dealing with the disputed questions of fact or title.

The confusion regarding the jurisdiction of the Waqf Tribunal and the Civil Courts continued with the incoherent judgements rendered by various High Courts. The High Court of Andhra Pradesh, in Adoni Syed Khader Macci-Ul Bhokari Darga Katta and Macci Mhader Saheb Darga Katta Committee, Adoni vs. Shaikan Bee and others[12] held that, when a dispute is relating to eviction of a tenant in occupation of waqf property, a petition can be filed before the civil Court only and not before the Waqf Tribunal.

The High Court of Madhya Pradesh has taken a firm view in Intizamia Committee Idgah, Morar vs. M.P. Wakf Board[13] and held that, when decision of the Tribunal is made final, the jurisdiction of Civil Court stands ousted.

In Thorayil Juma Masjid Mannalu Committee, Madakkallur vs. Kerala Wakf Board, Ernakulam,[14] the High Court of Kerala held that the order passed by Wakf Board in exercise of its appellate jurisdiction under section 72(7) is final and such an order cannot be challenged before the Waqf Tribunal under section 83 of the Waqf Act, 1995.

Division Bench of the Madras High Court, consisting of Honourable Mr. Justice Markandey Katju, Chief Justice (as His Lordship then was) and D. Murugesan, J., in Salam Khan vs. Tamil Nadu Wakf Board,[15] took a broad view of the jurisdiction of Waqf Tribunal and observed:

11 2002 (1) ALD 67 (DB).
12 2011 (4) ALT 812 (DB).
13 AIR 1996 MP, 47.
14 AIR 2007 (NOC) 1341 Ker. 2007 Ker, L.T. 231.
15 (2005) 1 LW 676.

> In our opinion, all matters pertaining to Wakfs should be filed in the first instance before the Wakf Tribunal constituted under Section 83 of the Wakf Act, 1995 and should not be entertained by this Court straight away under Article 226 of the Constitution of India. Thus Wakf Tribunal can decide all disputes, questions or other matters relating to a Wakf or Wakf property. The words 'any dispute, question or other matters relating to a Wakf or Wakf property', are in our opinion, words of very wide connotation. Any dispute, question or other matters whatsoever and in whatever manner arises relating to a Wakf for or Wakf property can be decided by the Wakf Tribunal.
>
> We may further clarify that the party can approach a Wakf Tribunal even if no order has been passed under the Act against which he is aggrieved. It may be mentioned that sections 83 (1) and 84 of the Act do not confine the jurisdiction of the Wakf Tribunal to the determination of the correctness or otherwise of an order passed under the Act. No doubt, section 83(2) refers to orders passed under the Act, but in our opinion, section 83(1) and 84 of the Act, are independent provisions and they do not require an order to be passed under the Act before invoking the jurisdiction of the Wakf Tribunal.

This matter went out to the Supreme Court in SLP (C) No. 4156/2005, but the Supreme Court dismissed the Special Leave Petition in *limine* with the words "we see no reason to interfere."

The Andhra Pradesh High Court, in Shaik Ameer and Another vs. A.P. State Wakf Board and Another,[16] while discussing the locus standi parties to the case before the Waqf Tribunal, held that:

> If the petitioners are of the view that the respondents cannot maintain the suit, they can, certainly, raise this ground in their written statement and being a pure question of law, the Tribunal can decide it as a preliminary issue.

The High Court of Andhra Pradesh, while dealing with the writ petition in Yousuf Begum vs. Wakf Board, Hyderabad,[17] observed that:

> When the land is claimed by the Wakf Board, such dispute has to be resolved by the Wakf Tribunal constituted under the Wakf Act ... Further, if the relief as claimed is granted it would amount to compelling the Wakf Board to relinquish their right to manage the Wakf property and also to compel them to abdicate their duty under various

16 2007(5) ALT221
17 2010 (6) ALD 273.

> provisions of the Wakf Act. Such a writ cannot be issued by this Court. The petitioner is, therefore, given liberty to avail the remedy before the Wakf Tribunal.

But the Bench of the Honourable Supreme Court of India comprising Justice Markandey Katju and Justice T.S. Thakur, J.J. has taken the following view while dealing with a civil appeal No. 1182 of 2006 in the case of Ramesh Gobindram (deceased by L.Rs.) vs. Sugra Humayun Mirza Wakf.[18] The Bench observed that:

> What is noteworthy is that under Section 6 read with Section 7 (supra) the institution of the Civil Court is barred only in regard to questions that are specifically enumerated therein. The bar is not complete so as to extend to other questions that may arise in relation to the wakf property.
>
> The bar of jurisdiction contained in Section 85 is in that sense much wider than that contained in Section 6(5) read with Section 7 of the Wakf Act. While the latter bars the jurisdiction of the Civil Court only in relation of questions specified in Sections 6(1) and 7(1), the bar of jurisdiction contained in Section 85 would exclude the jurisdiction of the Civil Courts, not only in relation to matters that specifically fall in Sections 6 and 7 but also other matters required to be determined by a Tribunal under the Act.
>
> There is, in our view, nothing in Section 83 to suggest that it pushes the exclusion of the jurisdiction of the Civil Courts extends beyond what has been provided for in Section 6(5), Section 7 and Section 85 of the Act.
>
> A suit seeking eviction of the tenants from what is admittedly wakf property could, therefore, be filed only before the Civil Court and not before the Tribunal. The contrary view expressed by the Tribunal and the High Court of Andhra Pradesh is not, therefore, legally sound. So also the view taken by the High Courts of Rajasthan, Madhya Pradesh, Kerala and Punjab & Haryana in the decisions referred to earlier do not declare the law correctly and shall to the extent they run counter to what we have said here in above stand overruled. The view taken by the High Courts of Allahabad, Karnataka, Madras and Bombay is, however, affirmed. In the result these appeals succeed and are hereby allowed.

A Division Bench of the High Court of Andhra Pradesh in Lanco Hills Technology Park vs. Mahaboob Alam Khan and Others[19] discussed the

18 AIR 2010 Supreme Court, 2897, AP.

19 2012 (4) ALD 385; 2012 (4) ALT 136 (DB).

principles of interlocutory injunction and held that the Waqf Tribunal has the same powers of Civil Court under the Civil Procedure Court and that the same principles of adjudication will apply to the Waqf Tribunal as well. The Court observed that:

> The Court granting interlocutory injunction is required to apply three tests, namely, prima facie test, balance of convenience test and irreparable injury test.
>
> What emerges from the above conspectus is that the grant of interlocutory injunction is a discretionary remedy and in the exercise of judicial discretion, in granting or refusing to grant, the court will take into reckoning the following as guidelines: (1) Whether the persons seeking temporary injunction has made out a prima facie case. This is sine qua non. (2) Whether the balance of convenience is in his favour that is whether it could cause greater inconvenience to him if the injunction is not granted than the inconvenience which the other side would be put to if the injunction is granted. As to that the governing principle is whether the party seeking injunction could be adequately compensated by awarding damages and the defendant would be in a financial position to pay them. (3) Whether the person seeking temporary injunction would suffer irreparable injury. It is, however, not necessary that all the three conditions must obtain. "With the first condition as sine qua non, at least two conditions should be satisfied by the petitioner conjunctively and a mere proof of one of the three conditions does not entitle a person to obtain temporary injunction.
>
> The Wakf Tribunal has the same powers of the civil Court under CPC while trying a suit or executing a decree or order (sub-section (5) of Section 83). In the absence of any rules referable to Section 86(6) prescribing the procedure to be followed by the Wakf Tribunal, all the principles for grant of interlocutory injunctions are equally applicable even in an application or suit filed before the Wakf Tribunal.

The High Court of Uttaranchal in Sardar Abdul Wahid Khan vs. District Judge Dehradun and Others[20] has taken the view that an aggrieved person can approach the Waqf Tribunal in case any orders or proceedings are not issued due to the inaction of the authorities on the matters traversing the Waqf Act. The Court thus observed as under:

> Under Section 83 (5) of the Waqf Act, 1995 the Tribunal has all powers of the Civil Court under the Code of Civil Procedure, and hence it has also powers under Order 39 Rules 1,2 and 2A of the Code

20 Writ Petition No. 499 of 2010 (M/S).

> of Civil Procedure to grant temporary injunctions and enforce such injunctions.
>
> Hence, it cannot be said that a party can approach the Wakf Tribunal only against an order passed under the Act. In our opinion, even if no order has been passed under the Act, the party can approach the Wakf Tribunal for the determination of any dispute, question, or other matters relating to a wakf or wakf property, as the plain language of Sections 83 (1) and 84 indicates.

The High Court of Madras, in the case of Muthavalli Larabsha Dharga vs. the Panruti Municipality,[21] held that:

> Therefore, a reading of Section 83 of the Wakf Act, makes it clear that the Wakf Tribunal, constituted under the Act is not a Civil Court and is a persona designata and it is only deemed to be a Civil Court and the Tribunal can also follow such procedures, as may be prescribed, notwithstanding, anything contained in C.P.C.

An interesting case came up for hearing before the Honourable Supreme Court of India in Raja Khan vs. U.P. Sunni Central Waqf Board & Another[22] in the year 2010. The crux of the matter was that a suit was filed in the Civil Court of Hamirpur District of U.P. (within the jurisdiction of Allahabad Bench of the High Court of Allahabad) for the allotment of waqf land situated in Bahraich District (within the jurisdiction of the Lucknow Bench of Allahabad High Court). The suit was dismissed as it was not cognisable at Hamirpur for the lack of territorial jurisdiction. The petitioner filed a writ petition in the Allahabad Bench of the High Court. The single judge, by an interim order dated 11 June 2010 and 18 June 2010 directed allotment of the land to the petitioner in the "Mela area" and compliance of the orders. However, the Division Bench set aside the interim orders passed by the single judge. Aggrieved, the petitioner filed an appeal before the Supreme Court. The Bench of the Supreme Court consisting of Justice Markandey Katju and Justice Gyan Sudha Mishra took a serious view of the matter and castigated strictures upon the single judge of the Allahabad Bench of the High Court who passed interim orders with following observations:

> The above orders are shocking to say the least. We are of the opinion that the above two ex-parte interim orders of the Single Judge of the Allahabad High Court were clearly passed on extraneous considerations. This is for the following reasons:

21 C.R.P. (NPD) Nos.1607, 2916 and 2320 of 2010.
22 [2010] 13 (ADDL.) S.C.R. 1131 1132.

(1) The property in question is in the district of Bahraich which is within the territorial jurisdiction of the Lucknow Bench of the Allahabad High Court. Hence, the writ petition could not have been validly filed or entertained in the Allahabad Bench of the High Court in view of the decision of this court in Nasiruddin vs. State Transport Appellate Tribunal AIR 1976 SC 331.
(2) The writ petition was not maintainable because ordinarily no writ petition lies against a private body.
(3) By the ex-parte order dated 11.6.2010 the writ petition has been practically allowed since by that ex-parte order the respondents 2, 3, & 4 (U.P. Sunni Central Waqf Board, District Magistrate, Bahraich and Committee of Management, Waqf No. 19, Dargah Sharif, Bahraich) have been directed to allot the land in the Mela of the aforesaid Waqf at plot Nos. 1760 to 1770 and 1826 to 1884 to the petitioner for the purpose of running circus, Jhoola, Merry-go-round etc., and possession of the allocated land was directed to be handed over within three days. Subsequently, on 18.6.2010, the same single Judge has passed an order directing the district Magistrate and SP, Bahraich to take appropriate action for compliance of the earlier order.

The faith of the common man in the country is shaken to the core by such shocking and outrageous orders such as the kind which have been passed by the Single Judge.

The Allahabad High Court really needs some house cleaning (both Allahabad and Lucknow Bench), and we request Hon'ble the Chief Justice of the High Court to do the needful, even if he has to take some strong measures, including recommending transfers of the incorrigibles.

We entirely agree with the view taken by the Learned Division Bench in the impugned judgment.

The division Bench, chaired by the Chief Justice of High Court of Patna while hearing a Letters Patent Appeal No. 1026 of 2018, in Dr. Mahrukh Khan vs. The State Of Bihar[23] observed that, in the case of a dispute of waqf property, the appropriate forum would be the Waqf Tribunal. The appeal was dismissed with a liberty to the appellants to approach the Waqf Tribunal.

****

23 Air 2019 (NOC) 737 PAT.

Section 84

Tribunal to hold proceedings expeditiously and to furnish to the parties copies of its decision:-

> ***Whenever an application is made to a Tribunal for the determination of any dispute, question or other matter relating to a waqf or waqf property it shall hold its proceedings as expeditiously as possible and shall as soon as practicable, on the conclusion of the hearing of such matter give its decision in writing and furnish a copy of such decision to each of the parties to the dispute.***

Reflections

Analogous section under Wakf Act 1954 is S.55 A, inserted by Waqf Amendment Act 1984 (Act 69 of 1984).

Section 84 contemplates that the Tribunal should hold the proceedings as expeditiously as possible. The copies of its orders shall be provided to the parties concerned.

Judicial response

Judicial response pertaining to this section is not found.

****

Section 85

Bar of jurisdiction of civil courts:-

> ***No suit or other legal proceeding shall lie in any civil court, revenue court and any other authority[24] in respect of any dispute, question or other matter relating to any waqf, waqf property or other matter which is required by or under this Act to be determined by a Tribunal.***

Reflections

Analogous section under Wakf Act 1954 is S.55 C, inserted by Waqf Amendment Act 1984 (Act 69 of 1984).

24 Substituted by Act 27 of 2013, S. 45, for "civil court."

This section bars the jurisdiction of Civil Courts, Revenue Courts or any other authority under any Law. The words "Civil Courts, Revenue Court or any other authority" have been inserted by Waqf Amendment Act (Act 27 of 2013).

Judicial response

The Supreme Court in Board of Wakf, West Bengal vs. Anis Fatima Begum[25] in (Civil Appeal No. 5297 of 2004) has held that:

> The Wakf Tribunal can decide all disputes, questions or other matters relating to a Wakf or Wakf property. The words "any dispute, question or other matters relating to a Wakf or Wakf property" appearing in Sections 83 and 84 of Act are words of very wide connotation. ...Under Section 83 (5) of the Wakf Act, 1995, the Tribunal has all powers of the civil court under the Code of Civil Procedure, and hence it has also powers under Order 39 Rules 1, 2 and 2A, CPC to grant temporary injunctions and enforce such injunctions. Hence, a full fledged remedy is available to any party if there is any dispute, question or other matter relating to a Wakf or Wakf property.
>
> Even if no order has been passed under the Act, the party can approach the Wakf Tribunal for the determination of any dispute, question or other matters relating to a Wakf or Wakf property, as the plain language of Sections 83 (1) and 84 indicates.
>
> It is well-settled that when there is a special law providing for a special forum, then recourse cannot be taken to the general law. Since the matter fell under the purview of the Wakf Act, only the Wakf Tribunal has jurisdiction in the matter, and not the civil court.

The High Court of Kerala in Musaliar vs. T.K. Muhammad Sahib[26] held that since the management of the Wakf does not fall within the powers of the Tribunal, the dispute is not liable to be resolved by the Tribunal. Consequently, the learned Judge held that the civil court has jurisdiction. But a bench of the same court has overruled this decision in Aliyathammada vs. Pattakkal Chriyakoya[27] and held that:

> the words "any dispute, question or other matters relating to a Wakf or Wakf property" under section 85 are wide enough to take within its sweep not only matters which are specially conferred on the Tribunal by the various provisions of the Act but also any dispute, question or other

25 [2010] 13 (ADDL.) S.C.R. 1063 1064.
26 AIR 2003 Ker. 84.
27 AIR 2003 Ker. 366.

matters relating to a Wakf or Wakf property since those powers have also been conferred on the Tribunal by the Wakf Act 1995.

A Bench of Kerala High Court, in Badagara Jumayath Palli Dharas Committee vs. Peedikayalakath Ummar Kutty Haji and Others,[28] held that:

> we find that Section 7 (5) of the Act merely says that the tribunal shall not have jurisdiction to determine any matter which is the subject-matter of any suit or proceedings instituted or commenced in a civil court under sub-section (1) of Section 6, before the commencement of this Act or which is the subject-matter of any appeal from the decree passed before such commencement. Section 7(5) of the Act clearly exempts appeal from the bar of jurisdiction. Hence, we are of the view that this court is perfectly competent to decide the question regarding wakf in this appeal.

A Bench of High Court of Madras consisting of Markanday Katju and F.M. Ibrahim Khalifulla in Mukram Sherif vs. Moideen Sherif,[29] dealing with the jurisdiction of Tribunal under section 85 of Waqf Act 1995 relied upon the above judgement in Salam Khan vs. Tamil Nadu Wakf Board,[30] and the dismissal of the Special Leave Petition in S.L.P. (C) 4156/2005 by the Supreme Court and ruled that all the disputes relating to a waqf have to be filed before the Waqf Tribunal constituted under section 83 of the Waqf Act. In another case V.S.D. Sikkandar vs. K.M. Khader Gani,[31]a Bench of High Court of Madras ruled that:

> A harmonious construction of the various provisions of the Wakf Act 1995 which came into force on 1.1.1996, particularly section 85 of the Act, the civil court ceases to have jurisdiction to try any suit relating to a Wakf or Wakf property.

A Bench of the High Court of Rajasthan in the case of Sayed Abdul Vasit & Others vs. Addl. Civil Judge & Others,[32] while dealing with the jurisdiction of Tribunal has held that:

> An extremely limited jurisdiction has been bestowed on the Tribunal. The Tribunal does not have the same jurisdiction as a civil Court. Therefore, any issue unrelated to nature of property or status of wakf

28 AIR 2002 Ker. 56.
29 (2005) 2 LW 615 (DB).
30 (2005) 1 LW 676.
31 (2006) 4 MLJ 1800.
32 AIR 2009 (NOC) 1394, (Raj).

> would be outside jurisdiction of Tribunal and within the jurisdiction of civil Court ... Since the instant case relates to recovery or rental money and grant of permanent injunction, obviously the case does not relate to the nature of the property or the status of the wakf. Hence, clearly the Tribunal does not have the jurisdiction to try the present suits. Thus, the jurisdiction vests wholly in civil Court. Merely, because the property is a wakf property, it would not oust the jurisdiction of civil Court.

The High Court of Bombay, while dealing with a similar case in Abdul Kadar & Others, vs. Masjid Juma Darwaja,[33] held that:

> A dispute between landlord and tenants is not arising under Wakf Act and, therefore, is not cognizable either u/S. 7(1) or then u/S. 83 (1) thereof. Wakf Act has been enacted for better administration and regulation of Wakfs and to have effective control over them. The Tribunals created there under are for the purpose of determining questions which arise under the Wakf Act. The dispute between landlord and tenants does not arise under Wakf Act at least in present facts.

The High Court of Karnataka, in Dattaray Hanamantrao Bidikar & Another vs. Smt. Dilshad Begum & Others,[34] held that:

> The jurisdiction of the Civil Court is barred and that is made clear u/S. 85 of the Act by use of the words "other matter which is required by or under this Act to be determined by a Tribunal". So, it is only in the circumstances, stated in Sec. 85 that the jurisdiction of the Civil Court is barred and the said provision does not apply to all sorts of suits instituted by the parties before the Civil Court.

The High Court of Andhra Pradesh, in P. Rama Rao & Others vs. High Court of A.P., represented by its Registrar,[35] observed that:

> Therefore, it is now made very clear that the bar of jurisdiction of Civil Courts contemplated under Section 85 of the Wakf Act, 1995 would be effective only w.e.f., the constitution of Wakf Tribunal and till such time the jurisdiction of the Civil Court should continue as a rightful forum for the adjudication of the Wakf disputes.

33 AIR 2009 (NOC) 1704 (Bom).
34 AIR 2009 (NOC) 1705 (Kar).
35 2000 (1) ALD 298 (DB) = 2000 (1) ALT 210 (DB).

The High Court of Kerala, in T.M. Muhammed Sahib and another vs. Arakkal Mohammed Ibrahim,[36] held that:

> Wordings used in Section 85 of the Wakf Act that "no suit shall lie" means no fresh suit can be filed and it will not affect pending suits particularly when there is no provision in the Act for transferring existing pending suits to the Wakf Tribunal.

In the case of Anjuman A. Burhani vs. Daudi Bohra Jamaet, Registered Society & Another,[37] the Honourable High Court of Rajasthan, while upholding the jurisdiction of the Wakf Tribunal in all matters pertaining to the waqf, ruled that:

> The language of Sections 83 and 85 of the Act confers such wider jurisdiction upon the Tribunal and, therefore, in the opinion of this Court, the Court below erred in rejecting the application under Order 7, Rule 11. C.P.C. filled by the defendant-petitioner. The present controversy falls within the domain and jurisdiction of the Wakf Tribunal and therefore, the Civil Court had no jurisdiction in the matter in view of Section 85 of the Act.

Similarly, the Division Bench of the High Court of Madhya Pradesh, in Wakf Imambara Imlipura, Khandwa vs. Smt. Khursheeda Bi & Others,[38] while referring to a number of judgements of various High Courts and the Supreme Court in the matter of the jurisdiction of Waqf Tribunal, held that:

> In M. Satyaranayana vs. State of Karnataka, AIR 1986 SC 1162 it has been laid down that a Statute cannot be construed merely with reference to grammar. Statute whenever the language permits must be construed reasonably and rationally to give effect to the intention and purpose of the legislature. For giving effect to the intention and purpose of the Legislature the interpretation of ouster of Civil Court jurisdiction is a reasonable consideration as that is expressly provided by the statute.
>
> In the circumstances, we hold that Section 85 of the Waqf Act ousts the jurisdiction of Civil Court to try such cases of ejectment of tenant; the Waqf Tribunal shall try such cases. The orders passed by the Civil Court and Waqf Tribunal to the contrary are set aside. The cases be made over / presented to the "Waqf Tribunal to be tried in accordance with law.

36 AIR 2007 (NOC) 1104 Ker.
37 AIR 2009 Rajasthan, 150.
38 AIR 2009 MP, 238.

The Supreme Court in Sardar Khan vs. Syed Najmul Hasan[39] observed that:

> On a conjoint reading of sub-section (5) of section 7 and section 85, the result would be that the Act will not be applicable to the pending suits or proceedings or appeals or revisions which have commenced prior to 1.1.1996 i.e., coming into force of the Wakf Act, 1995.

The High Court of Madras, in Samuthra Vijaya Nainar vs. Sirukadambur Masjid rep. by its Mutawallis,[40] held that the suit O.S 230/1990 cannot be transferred to the Tribunal as the suit had been instituted prior to the commencement of the Waqf Act 1995. It further observed:

> By virtue of sub-section (5) of section 7 the bar of jurisdiction of civil courts under section 85 of the Wakf Act 1995 is not applicable to pending suits or appeals or revisions instituted or commenced under sub-section (1) of section 6 prior to 1.1.1996 when the Wakf Act 1995 came into force, as held by the Supreme Court in Sardar Khan vs. Syed Najmul Hasan.[41]

The Bench of Honourable Supreme Court of India consisting of Justice Markandey Katju and Gyan Sudha Mishra, in another case Board of Wakf, West Bengal vs. Anees Fatima Begum and Another,[42] rendered the judgement that:

> In our opinion all matters pertaining to Wakfs should be filed in the first instance before the Wakf Tribunal constituted under Section 83 of the Wakf Act 1995 and should not be entertained by the Civil Court or by the High Court straightaway under Article 226 of the Constitution of India.

It has been held by a Division Bench of this Court, (High Court of Madras) to which one of us (Markandey Katju, Chief Justice) was a party, in W.A. No.2344 of 2000 and W.P. Nos. 12710 and 15945 of 2000 (Salam Khan v. The Tamil Nadu Wakf Board), decided on 31.1.2005, reported in 2005-1-LW 676, that all disputes relating to wakf should be filed in the first instance before the Wakf Tribunal, constituted under Sec.83 of the WakfAct, 1995 and the writ petitions should not be entertained directly by this Court under Art.226 of the Constitution as there is alternative remedy. Against the aforesaid judgment of the Division Bench of this Court, a Special Leave

39 AIR 2007 SC 1447.
40 (2007) 4 MLJ 580.
41 AIR 2007 SC 1447.
42 2011 (1) ALD 61 (SC).

Petition, viz., SLP (C) No.4156 of 2005, was filed in the Supreme Court and the said Special Leave Petition was dismissed.

The Allahabad High Court in Smt. Kubra Khatoon and others vs. Allahtala Malik Waqf Masoom Hasan, Amroha[43] held that eviction notice and eviction suit in respect of waqf property filed prior to the enforcement of Amendment Act 2013, is lawful and within jurisdiction. The decree of eviction and the tenant is also lawful. The tenant is not entitled to permanent tenancy.

****

Section 86

Appointment of a receiver in certain cases:-

> ***Notwithstanding anything contained in the Code of Civil Procedure, 1908, (5 of 1908) or in any other law for the time being in force, where any suit or other legal proceeding is instituted or commenced-***

(a) ***by or on behalf of a Board-***
   - (i) ***to set aside the sale of any immovable property, which is waqf property, in execution of a decree or order of a civil court;***
   - (ii) ***to set aside the transfer of any immovable property, which is waqf property, made by the mutawalli thereof, whether for valuable consideration or not, without or otherwise than in accordance with, the sanction of the Board;***
   - (iii) ***to recover possession of the property referred to in clause (a) or clause (b) or to restore possession of such property to the mutawalli of the concerned waqf; or***

(b) ***by a mutawalli to recover possession of immovable property, which is waqf property, which has been transferred by a previous mutawalli or by any other person,[44] whether for valuable consideration or not, without otherwise than in accordance with the sanction of the Board, and which is in the possession of the defendant, the court may, on the application of the plaintiff, appoint a receiver of such property and direct such receiver to pay from time to time to the plaintiff, out of the income of the property, such amount as the court may consider to be necessary for further prosecution of the suit.***

----

43 AIR 2018 (NOC) 212 (ALL).

44 Inserted by Act 27 of 2013, S. 46.

Reflections

Analogous section under Wakf Act 1954 is S.55 D, inserted by Waqf Amendment Act 1984 (Act 69 of 1984).

Section 86 of the Act provides for appointment of a receiver by the court if the waqf property is transferred, alienated in contravention of the provisions of this Act. The receiver may be directed by the courts to pay out of the income of the property such amount as the court may consider necessary.

Judicial response

Judicial response pertaining to this section is not found.

****

Section 87

Bar to the enforcement of right on behalf of unregistered wakfs: Omitted[45]

Reflections

Analogous section under Wakf Act 1954 is S.55E, inserted by Wakf Amendment Act 1984 (Act 69 of 1984).

This section imposed a bar on the enforcement of rights on behalf of unregistered waqf. But this section has been omitted by Waqf Amendment Act 2013 (Act 27 of 2013). Before omission, this section read as under:

> Bar to the enforcement of right on behalf of unregistered wakfs:
>
> (1) Notwithstanding anything contained in any other law for the time being in force, no suit, appeal or other legal proceeding for the enforcement of any right on behalf of any wakf which has not been registered in accordance with the provisions of this Act, shall be instituted or commenced or heard, tried or decided by any court after the commencement of this Act, or where any such suit, appeal or other legal proceeding had been instituted or commenced before such commencement, no such suit appeal or other legal proceeding shall be continued, heard, tried or decided by any court after such commencement unless such wakf has been registered, in accordance with the provisions of this Act.

45 Waqf Amendment Act, 2013 (Act 27 of 2013).

(2) The provisions of sub-section (1) shall apply as far as may be, to the claim for set-off or any other claim made on behalf of any wakf which has not been registered in accordance with the provisions of this Act.

But the Amendment Act of 2013 has omitted this section.

Judicial response

Section 87 of the Wakf Act 1995 bars the enforcement of right on behalf of unregistered wakfs. The High Court of Madras in Shanmugham and another Appellants vs. Tamil Nadu State Wakf Board, Madras, Respondent,[46] held that:

> The fact remains that the suit was filed by the Wakf. It is settled proposition of law that an appeal is a continuation of the original proceeding and until final decision is rendered in proceeding, the suit is presumed to be pending. Acceptance of such interpretation by the learned counsel for the appellant on Section 87 of the Act, will only lead to a glaring discrimination namely that Section 87 would apply in case where the Wakf Board had lost the suit and not in case where the Wakf Board had succeeded in the suit. Such a construction is neither rational nor warranted and hence not acceptable.

The Supreme Court in Tamil Nadu state Wakf Board vs. Hatija Ammal[47] observed that:

> The High Court is justified in holding that the Wakf Board had no right to institute suit for declaration that any property is a wakf property as the scheme of the Act clearly indicates. The High Court further found that as far as the appellant is concerned with regard to title of any property, it must comply with the requirements of Sections 4,5 and 6 or 27 of the Act, which means that if any property is not published as wakf property as required under Section 5(2) of the Act or the Board has not invoked the special power under Section 27, the Wakf Board cannot file a suit for declaration and possession and on that basis upheld the order made by the Trial Court as affirmed by the First Appellate Court.

****

46 AIR 1999 Mad. 96.
47 AIR 2002 SC 402.

Section 88

Bar to challenge the validity of any notification, etc.:-

> ***Save as otherwise expressly provided in this Act, no notification or order or decision made, proceeding or action taken, by the Central Government or the State Government under this Act or any rule made there under shall be questioned in any civil court.***

Reflections

Analogous section under Wakf Act 1954 is S.55 F, inserted by Waqf Amendment Act 1984 (Act 69 of 1984).

Section 88 imposes restrictions on the Civil Courts for trying or entertaining any notification, order or decision made or action taken by the Central or State Government under the provisions of this Act.

Judicial response

Judicial response pertaining to this section is not found.

****

Section 89

Notice of suits by parties against Board:-

> ***No suit shall be instituted against the Board in respect of any act purporting to be done by it in pursuance of this Act or of any rules made there under, until the expiration of two months next after notice in writing has been delivered to, or left at, the office of the Board, stating the cause of action, the name, description and place of residence of the plaintiff and the relief which he claims; and the plaint shall contain a statement that such notice has been so delivered or left.***

Reflections

Analogous section under Wakf Act 1954 is S.56.

This section makes a provision for serving two months' notice to the Waqf Board for instituting any case against the Waqf Board. The notice shall mention name description place of residence of the plaintiff, the claim of relief, etc. The plaint shall also contain a statement that such notice has been served to the Waqf Board.

Judicial response

The Waqf Act under section 89 says that two months' notice shall be given to the Waqf Board before filing a suit or initiating any legal proceedings in matters of waqf. The High Court of Andhra Pradesh, in A.P. State Wakf Board, Hyderabad vs. Sabita Joshi and Others,[48] while dealing with the matter pertaining to issue of notice under section 89, observed that:

> Once the suit has been adjudicated on merits, without the defendant in it, raising any objection, as to the failure to issue notice, the acceptance of the plea at a later stage would render the entire exercise futile. Even if a plea was not raised, the petitioner could have insisted on framing of an issue touching it. No such effort was made.
>
> The second reason is that, instant case, a writ petition filed by the respondents was opposed by the petitioner, on several grounds. Accepting that plea, this, court disposed of the writ petition, leaving it open to the respondents to file a suit within a time stipulated therein.
>
> In case the petitioner wanted that a suit must be preceded by the service of notice, under Section 89 of the new Act, such a contention ought to have been raised before this Court itself. For all practical purposes, the petitioner waived the objection, even if it is otherwise tenable. Hence, the plea cannot be accepted.

The serving of notice to the Waqf Board is mandatory in the initiation of any suit or case against the Wakf Board or the wakf property. The Madras High Court in Madras State Wakf Board ... vs. B.A. Jamal Muhammed And Others[49] held that:

> These provisions are almost analogous to the provisions of Section 80, Civil Procedure Code ... In view of the fact that it has been found that the subject-matter of dispute in this case was wakf property it was necessary for the plaintiffs to serve the statutory notice provided under Section 53, Muslim Wakf Act, before the institution of the suit.

****

48 2010 (6) ALD 651.
49 (1966) 2 MLJ 104.

Section 90

Notice of suits, etc., by courts:-

(1) ***In every suit or proceeding relating to a title to or possession of a waqf property or the right of a mutawalli or beneficiary, the Court or Tribunal shall issue notice to the Board at the cost of the party instituting such suit or proceeding.***
(2) ***Whenever any waqf property is notified for sale in execution of a decree of a civil court or for the recovery of any revenue, cess, rates of taxes due to the Government or any local authority, notice shall be given to the Board by the Court, Collector or other person under whose order the sale is notified.***
(3) ***In the absence of a notice under sub-section (1), any decree or order passed in the suit or proceeding shall be declared void, if the Board, within six months[50] of its coming to know of such suit or proceeding, applies to the court in this behalf.***
(4) ***In the absence of a notice under sub-section (2), the sale shall be declared void, if the Board, within one month of its coming to know of the sale, applies in this behalf to the court or other authority under whose order the sale was held.***

Reflections

Analogous section under Wakf Act 1954 is S.57, as amended by Waqf Act 1984 (Act 69 of 1984).

This section makes it obligatory on the part of courts or Tribunal to issue notice to the Waqf Board in every case relating to a title or possession of waqf property or right of a mutawalli or a beneficiary. Such notice shall be issued by the Tribunal or the courts at the cost of the party instituting such case. Notice shall also be issued to the Waqf Board in case of execution of a decree by the Civil Court or for recovery of revenue, cess or taxes due to the Government. In the absence of such notice, under sub section (1), the proceedings shall be declared void if the Waqf Board applies to the concerned court or authority within six months of its coming to know of such proceedings. In the absence of such notice, under sub section (2), the sale shall be declared void if the Waqf Board applies to the concerned court or authority within one month of its coming to know of such a sale.

50 Substituted by Act 27 of 2013, S. 48, for "one month."

Judicial response

The Supreme Court (bench of Chief Justice Hidayatulla), in Mst. Ayesha Bibi vs. Commissioner of Wakf, West Bengal,[51] held that:

> The language of the fourth sub- section of s. 70 is quite clear that the Commissioner must not have knowledge previously of the suit. Where the Commissioner has knowledge of the suit he, cannot claim a second knowledge as the start of the limitation. In other words, his presence as a party in the suit after summons to him must be treated as a notice to him under the first sub- section of S.70.
>
> We regret this result and only hope that some way will be found out of the difficulty created by the-foolish action of the Commissioner in leaving the field clear for the compromise of the suit.

When a party's name is struck out from the suit comes to an end as far as that party is concerned as held by the Judicial Committee of the Privy Council in Haveli Shah vs. Khan Sahib Shaikh Painda Khan.[52]

A five-judge Bench of the Supreme Court in Garikapatti Veeraya vs. Subbiah Choudhury[53] referred to the reasoning of the Judicial Committee in the Colonial Sugar Refining Company's case {(1) (1878) I.L.R. 3 Cal. 662 (3) [1905] A.C. 369 at page 665} that it was quite true that the suitor cannot enter Court C without going through Court B, but neither can he enter Court B till Court A has given its decision, and observed that:

> That the legal pursuit of a remedy, suit, appeal and second appeal are really but steps in a series of proceedings all connected by an intrinsic unity and are to be regarded as one legal proceeding. The right of appeal is not a mere matter of procedure but is a substantive right. "The right to go from court to court in appeal is the right which vests at the date of the institution of the proceedings in the court of the first instance. It is true, as pointed out by Rankin C.J. that the litigant cannot go from Court A to Court B or from Court B to Court C unless and until an adverse order actually is made but the right to go up to Court C vests, not at the date of the adverse judgment or the date of the filing of the appeal but, at the date of the institution of the original proceedings.

The judgement of a Bench of the High Court of Calcutta comprising Justice D. Mitter and Justice Pattersonin Commissioner of Wakfs vs. Mahmuda

51 1970 AIR 287; 1970 SCR (1) 583; 1969 SCC (2) 305.
52 AIR 1926 PC 88.
53 1957 AIR 540; 1957 SCR 388.

Bibi and Others[54] is also relevant to quote here. The bench, while dealing a case under the Bengal Waqf Act 1934, held that:

> Section 70, Clause (4) enacts that in the absence of a notice under Sub-section (1) any decree or order passed in the suit or proceedings would be void if the Commissioner applies to the Court within one month of his knowledge. It is contended that the words "suit or proceedings" would include an "appeal" and as the proceedings for the appointment of the receiver were initiated in the appeal, it must be regarded as a suit or proceedings within the meaning of Section 69 or Section 70. We are unable to accede to this contention. The words "suit or proceeding" must be regarded in its ordinary sense and cannot be held to include "appeal." A reference to Sub-section 11 and 15, Civil P. C., 1908, would show that a suit does not include an appeal. With reference to res judicata (S.13 of 1882) it has been held that a suit does not include an appeal; see Bharaselal Choudhury v. Sartchandra (1896) 23 Cal 415. See also Amarsangji Dungerji v. Dipsingji Jhala 1925 Bom 241, at p. 449. Our attention has been drawn by Mr. Suhrawardy to a decision of this Court to which I was a party, and the language used there is to the effect that an appeal is really a continuation of the suit. Something of that kind is also said in the decision of the case in Samed Sheikh v. Naba Gopal Ghose 1914 Cal 614. The decision to which I was a party is reported in Faizunnessa Bibi v. Gholam Rabbani (1935) 62 Cal 1132.
>
> The suit was instituted long before the promulgation of the Act of 1936, and any right or rights, which were acquired at the time of the institution of the suit or even after the passing of the decree which was long before the promulgation of the Act in 1936, cannot be affected by the provisions of the latter Act. It was open to the parties before the promulgation of the Act to settle their dispute in a suit by or against a Mutawalli without reference to the officer who had not come into existence then.

****

Section 91

Proceedings under (Land Acquisition Act) Act 1 of 1894:-

(1) ***If, in the course of proceedings under the Land Acquisition Act, 1894 or under any law for the time being in force relating to the acquisition of land or other property, <u>and before an award is made, in case the</u>***

54 AIR 1936 Cal 480, 166 Ind Cas 212.

property*[55] *under acquisition is waqf property, a notice of such acquisition shall be served by Collector on the Board and further proceedings shall be stayed to enable the Board to appear and plead as a party to the proceeding at any time within three months from the date of the receipt of such notice.

> ***Explanation: - The reference to the Collector in the foregoing provisions of this sub-section shall, in relation to any other law referred to therein, be construed, if the Collector is not the competent authority under such other law to make an award of the compensation or other amount payable for the acquisition of land or other property there under, as a reference to the authority under such other law competent to make such award.***

(2) ***Where the Board has reason to believe that any property under acquisition is waqf property, it may at any time before the award is made appear and plead as a party to the proceeding.***
(3) ***When the Board has appeared under the provisions of sub-section (1) or sub-section (2), no order shall be passed under section 31 or section 32 of the Land Acquisition Act, 1894 or under the corresponding provisions of the other law referred to in sub-section (1) without giving an opportunity to the Board to be heard.***
(4) ***Any order passed under section 31 or section 32 of the Land Acquisition Act, 1894 or under the corresponding provisions of the other law referred to in sub-section (1) without giving an opportunity to the Board to be heard, shall be declared void if the Board, within one month of its coming to know of the order, applies in this behalf to the authority which made the order.***

Reflections

Analogous section under Wakf Act 1954 is S.58, as amended by Waqf Amendment Act 1984 (Act 69 of 1984).

In the matters of land acquisition under any law, if it is found before the award is made that the property in question is a waqf property, the Land Acquisition Officer shall give notice to the Waqf Board and no orders shall be passed without hearing the case of the Waqf Board. The order/award passed shall be void if the Waqf Board within one month of coming to know of such an order applies in this behalf to such an authority. This

55 Substituted by Act 27 of 2013, S. 49, for "it appears to the collector before an award is made that any property."

provision will enable the Waqf Board in the proper safeguarding of the waqf property.

Judicial response

Judicial response pertaining to this section is not found.

****

Section 92

Board to be party to suit or proceeding:-

> ***In any suit or proceeding in respect of a waqf or any waqf property the Board may appear and plead as a party to the suit or proceeding.***

Reflections

Analogous section under Wakf Act 1954 is S.59.

Section 92 entitles the Wakf Boards to be a party in any suit where the wakf institution or wakf properties are involved.

Judicial response

Judicial response pertaining to this section is not found.

****

Section 93

Bar to compromise of suits by or against mutawallis:-

> ***No suit or proceeding in any court by or against the mutawalli of a waqf relating to title to waqf property or the rights of the mutawalli shall be compromised without the sanction of the Board.***

Reflections

Analogous section under Wakf Act 1954 is S.60.

This section prohibits compromise of any kind in respect of the waqf property or the rights of the mutawalli without the sanction of the Waqf Board.

Judicial response

Judicial response pertaining to this section is not found.

****

Section 94

Power to make application to the Tribunal in case of failure of mutawalli to discharge, his duties:-

(1) ***Where a mutawalli is under an obligation to perform any act which is recognised by Muslim law as pious, religious or charitable and the mutawalli fails to perform such act, the Board may apply to the Tribunal for an order directing the mutawalli to pay to the Board or to any person authorised by the Board in this behalf the amount necessary for the performance of such act.***

(2) ***Where a mutawalli is under an obligation to discharge any other duties imposed on him under the waqf and the mutawalli wilfully fails to discharge such duties, the Board or any person interested in the waqf may make an application to the Tribunal and the Tribunal may pass such order thereon as it thinks fit.***

Reflections

Analogous section under Wakf Act 1954 is S.61, as amended by Waqf Amendment Act 1984 (Act 69 of 1984).

If the Mutawalli fails to perform any duty as per the object of the waqf, which is religious or pious, the Waqf Board or any person interested in the waqf may approach the Tribunal for an appropriate direction or orders. The Waqf Board may apply to the Tribunal for the appropriate orders for the payment of such an amount for the performance of such an act/ceremony.

Judicial response

Judicial response pertaining to this section is not found.

****

Section 95

Power of appellate authority to entertain appeal after expiry of specified period:-

> ***Where, under this Act any period has been specified for the filing of any appeal, the appellate authority may, if it is satisfied that the appellant was prevented by sufficient cause from preferring the appeal within the period so specified, entertain the appeal after the expiry of the said period.***

Reflections

Analogous section under Wakf Act 1954 is S.61 A, as inserted by Waqf Amendment Act 1984 (Act 69 of 1984).

This section authorises the appellate authority to pardon the delay in filing the appeal if it is satisfied that there are sufficient reasons which caused the delay in filing the appeal. The expression "appellate authority" has not been defined in the Act. However, it refers to the authority which is entitled to hear an appeal under this act.

Judicial response

Judicial response pertaining to this section is not found.

IX MISCELLANEOUS

Synopsis

This chapter deals with the miscellaneous issues governing Waqf Administration. The Act provides certain powers to the government to check the misuse of powers by the Waqf Boards and also for the protection of waqf properties. The final chapter of the Act from sections 96 to 113 largely deals with the governance of waqfs and provides for the powers of the State and Central Governments. The Central Government is empowered to regulate the secular activities of the waqf institutions, whereas the State Government is authorised to give directions to the State Waqf Boards from time to time. The State Government shall submit an annual report to the state legislature. If the Waqf Board fails to discharge its duties and responsibilities the State Government can supersede it. The Survey Commissioner of Waqf and the Officers and Members of the Waqf Board are deemed to be public servants. The Waqf Amendment Act 2013 has added new provisions as section 104 A and 104 B. Section 104 A prohibits sale, gift, mortgage, or transfer of waqf property. Section 104 B provides for the restoration of waqf properties under the occupation of the Government agencies to the Waqf Board. The Provisions of Limitation Act 1963 shall not apply for the recovery of waqf properties. The provisions of this Act shall apply to Evacuee Properties as well. The State Government is empowered to make rules and the State Waqf Board is authorised to frame regulations in consonance with this Act for the better administration of the waqf institutions.

Keywords: Deed, Custom, Alienation, Limitations, Evacuee, Supersession

****

Section 96

Power of Central Government to regulate secular activities of auqaf:-

(1) *For the purpose of regulating the secular activities of auqaf, the Central Government shall have the following powers and functions, namely:-*
   (a) *to lay down general principles, and policies of waqf administration in so far as they relate to the secular activities of the auqaf;*
   (b) *to co-ordinate the functions of the Central Waqf Council and the Board, in so far as they relate to their secular functions;*
   (c) *to review administration of the secular activities of auqaf generally and to suggest improvements if any.*

(2) *In exercising its powers and functions under sub-section (1), the Central Government may call for any periodic or other reports from any Board and may issue to the Board such directions as it may think fit and the Board shall comply with such directions.*

Explanation: - For the purposes of this section "secular activities" shall include social, economic, educational and other welfare activities.

Reflections

Analogous section under Wakf Act 1954 is S.62, as amended by Wakf Amendment Act (Act 69 of 1984).

This section empowers the Central Government to lay down principles and policies for the administration of the secular activities of the waqf institution, to establish a co-ordination between the Central Waqf Council and the Waqf Boards and to suggest improvement in the waqf administration. The explanation to this section describes "secular activities" as including social, economic, educational and welfare activities. Sub-section (2) authorises the Central Government to call for periodic reports from the Waqf Boards and the boards shall comply with such directions.

Judicial response

Judicial response relating to this section is not found.

****

Section 97

Directions by State Government:-

Subject to any directions issued by the Central Government under section 96, the State Government may, from time to time, give to the Board such general or special directions as the State Government

thinks fit and in the performance of its functions, the Board shall comply with such directions:

> *Provided that the State Government shall not issue any direction being contrary to any waqf deed or any usage; practice or custom of the waqf.*[1]

Reflections

Analogous section under Wakf Act 1954 is S.63.

Apart from the powers of the Central Government to issue directions to the Waqf Boards under section 96, this Act empowers the State Government to issue directions to the State Waqf Boards from time to time. The directions issued by the State Government shall not be in contravention to the directions issued by the Central Government. A proviso has been added to this section by Waqf Amendment Act 2013 (Act 27 of 2013), which states that the State Government shall abstain from issuing any direction to the State Waqf Board in contravention of the waqf deed, usage, customs and practices of the waqf.

Judicial response

In the case of Managing Committee, Wakf vs. State Of Andhra Pradesh And Others[2] the High Court of Andhra Pradesh set aside the orders of the Andhra Pradesh Government appointing the third respondent as mutawalli of the waqf on the grounds that the government cannot exercise the powers under section 97 of the Act and cannot interfere with an order passed by the Waqf Board in exercise of its statutory powers under section 32 of the Act.

A Division Bench of the High Court of Andhra Pradesh in Markaz Constructions vs. S.H. Mirza Wakf,[3] has given directions to the mutawalli, asking him, inter alia, to invite fresh offers. The petitioners have filed these petitions for special leave from the judgement and order of the Division Bench. When the matter went up to the Supreme Court in an appeal, the Bench of the Supreme Court headed by the Chief Justice (as he then was) A.M. Ahmedi in this case of Markaz Constructions vs. Sugra Humayun Mirza Wakf & Others[4] observed that looking to all the

1 Inserted by Act 27 of 2013, S. 50.
2 2000 (5) ALT 626.
3 1996 (1) ALD 952 (DB).
4 1996 SCALE (6) 84.

circumstances, we do not consider this a matter where intervention under Article 136 is required.

The powers of the State Government to issue directions to the Waqf Boards for better performance of the Waqf Board have been questioned in the Courts of Law time and again. In Syed Muzaffar Hussain vs. State of U.P.,[5] the High Court of Uttar Pradesh held that:

> The order of the State Government under section 63 of the old Wakf Act 1954, (Under Sec 97 of the Wakf Act, 1995) is not confined to render of policy only and the State Government is empowered to issue directions restraining the Board's acts during the period between expiry of its normal term and reconstitution of new Wakf Board.

A Bench of the High Court of Andhra Pradesh in Majlis-e-shura Dasti Parcha Bafi Hermain Sharifain Wakf Committee vs. A.P. Wakf Board, Hyderabad and Others[6] interpreted section 97 of the Act and held that:

> In any event, the words "subject to any directions issued by the Central Government" cannot but mean that in the event of there being any direction by the State Government and in the event of there are similar directions by the Central Government, the directions of the State Government shall be subject to the directions of the Central Government and not independently of it.

In the case of Masjid-e-Islamabad vs. Karnataka Wakf Board,[7] the Karnataka Government issued a direction to the Waqf Board to appoint Abdullah Khazi as administrator of the waqf, displacing the legally elected governing body of the managing society which is registered as a society under the Societies Registration Act. The single Judge of Karnataka High Court Justice K.S. Puttaswamy has observed that:

> The Government cannot act as a manager, director, controller or supervisor of every waqf in the state.
>
> On the above analysis of section 15 and 63 of the Act it follows the order or directions issued by the Minister for wakfs and the consequent order made thereto by the Board are wholly without jurisdiction and are manifestly illegal and they are therefore liable to be quashed.

5 1984 LLJ 31.

6 1998 (5) ALD 236; 1998 (5) ALT 761.

7 AIR 1981 Kant 154.

The Andhra Pradesh High Court in Managing Committee, Wakf, Jamia Masjid, Jaggayyapet[8] observed:

> The statutory power and authority conferred upon the Wakf Board under the provisions of the Act cannot be allowed to be guided or structured by the State Government in an individual case or issue as the same would amount to controlling or guiding the statutory power of the Wakf Board by the State Government.

The High Court of Andhra Pradesh, in Ramineni Sambasivarao and others vs. Government of A.P. and others,[9] ruled that the power conferred to the state government under section 97 of Waqf Act 1995 is in furtherance of the provisions of Waqf Act and not a discretionary one. It observed that:

> Section 97 does not, therefore, entitle the Government to direct alienation of wakf land except by way of public auction. The impugned order of the Government in so directing the Wakf Board is ultra vires Section 51 of the Wakf Act is without jurisdiction and must, accordingly, be quashed.

When a statute vests discretionary power in a particular authority, that discretion has to be exercised by that very authority without interference by some other person or authority even though superior to it. Therefore, the government cannot overstep its authority and exercise the powers which should necessarily be exercised by the Waqf Board as per the Act.

The High Court of Andhra Pradesh, while giving a description of the powers of the Government in Association of A.P. Sajjada Nasheens, Mutawallis and Khidmat Guzaran of Wakfs rep. by its President, Soofi Shah Mohd. Sabir Ali and Another vs. Secretary representing the Union of India (UOI), (Law) Department and Others,[10] observed that:

> It cannot be gain said that it is the duty of the State to preserve, protect, maintain, administer and improve the wakf properties.... It is of utmost importance, therefore, that wakfs should be maintained properly and their resources should be utilized for the objects and the purposes of dedications. But unfortunately, many of the existing wakfs are allowed to fall into decadence by the impact of twin factors of neglect and misuse.

8 2000 (5) ALT 626.
9 2010 (4) ALD 710.
10 2010 (1) ALT 112.

The Andhra Pradesh High Court, in M. Govinda Rao and Others vs. A.P. State Wakf Board and Others,[11] gave the following observation as far as the powers of the Government were concerned:

> The most effective manner of ensuring compliance of this condition is sale of wakf lands by public auction. Not only would such a mode be transparent it would, by its being held in open public view and gaze, and its being subjected to public scrutiny, also ensure that the best possible price is received on the sale of such lands. The first proviso to Section 51(2) of the Act, which seeks to achieve this salutary public purpose of securing the best price possible on the sale of wakf lands, is mandatory and cannot be dispensed with.

****

Section 98

Annual report by State Government:-

> ***As soon as may be after the close of a financial year, the State Government shall cause a general annual report on the working and administration of the State Waqf Board and the administration of auqaf in the State during the year to be prepared and laid before each House of the State Legislature where it consists of two Houses, or where such Legislature consists of one House, before that House, and every such report shall be in such form and shall contain such matters as may be provided by regulations.***

Reflections

Analogous section under Wakf Act 1954 is S.63 A, as inserted by Wakf Amendment Act (Act 69 of 1984).

The State Government shall prepare an annual report on close of the financial year. The annual report shall contain the information as may be provided in the regulation, including the functioning of the Waqf Board and the administration of auqaf. The annual report shall be placed before the State Legislature. This section does not describe the last date before which the annual report shall be placed before the legislature.

11 2008 (2) ALT 429.

<u>Judicial response</u>

Judicial response pertaining to this section is not found.

****

Section 99

Power to supersede Board:-

(1) *If the State Government is of opinion that the Board is unable to perform or has persistently made default in the performance of, the duty imposed on it by or under this Act or has exceeded or abused its powers, or has wilfully and without sufficient cause failed to comply with any direction issued by the Central Government under section 96 or the State Government under section 97, or if the State Government is satisfied on consideration of any report submitted after annual inspection, that the Board's continuance is likely to be injurious to the interests of the auqaf in the State, the State Government may, by notification in the Official Gazette, supersede the Board for a period not exceeding six months:*

Provided that before issuing a notification under this sub-section, the State Government shall give a reasonable time to the Board to show cause why it should not be superseded and shall consider the explanations and objections, if any, of the Board:

<u>*Provided further that the power of the State Government under this section shall not be exercised unless there is a prima facie evidence of financial irregularity, misconduct or violation of the provisions of this Act.*</u>[12]

(2) *Upon the publication of a notification under sub-section (1) superseding the Board,-*
   (a) *all the members of the Board shall, as from the date of supersession, vacate their offices as such members;*
   (b) *all the powers and duties which may, by or under the provisions of this Act, be exercised or performed by or on behalf of the Board shall, during the period of supersession, be exercised and performed by such person or persons as the State Government may direct; and*
   (c) *all property vested in the Board shall, during the period of supersession vest in the State Government.*

12 Inserted by Act 27 of 2013, S. 51 (a).

(3) ***On the expiration of the period of supersession specified in the notification issued under sub-section (1), the State Government may-***
(a) ***extend the period of supersession by another six months with reasons to be recorded in writing and, the period of continuous supersession shall not exceed more than a year; or;***[13]
(b) ***reconstitute the Board in the manner provided in section 14.***

Reflections

Analogous section under Wakf Act 1954 is S.64, as amended by Wakf Amendment Act (Act 69 of 1984).

This section empowers the State Government to supersede the State Waqf Board by notification in the Official Gazette, for a period not exceeding six months, when it is found that the board is in persistent default of performance of its duties or has abused its powers or failed to comply with the directions of Central/State Government. The board shall be given sufficient opportunity to submit its explanation before such supersession.

A second proviso has been added under this section by Waqf Amendment Act 2013, which specifies that the State Government shall exercise such powers only when there is a prima facie evidence of financial irregularity, misconduct or violation of the provisions of this Act.

After issue of notification in the Official Gazette regarding supersession of the board, the board shall seize to exist; the members, including the Chair-Person, shall relinquish their office; and the functions of the board shall be performed by a person designated by the State Government and the assets of the board shall be deemed to be the assets of the State Government.

Clause (a) to sub-section (3) has been substituted by Amendment Act 2013 which states that on expiry of the supersession the State Government may extend the period of supersession for a period not more than six months. It implies that in any case the period of supersession shall not exceed one year. It shall reconstitute the board during such period.

Judicial response

The law empowers the State Government to supersede the Waqf Board in case of persistent default of discharge of its duties and responsibilities. The Government of Kerala superseded the Waqf Board vide its orders dated

13 Substituted by Act 27 of 2013, S. 51 (d0, for Cl. (a). Prior to its substitution, Cl. (a) read as under:- "(a) extend the period of supersession for such further period as it may consider necessary; or ..."

29 August 1983. The Kerala Waqf Board and its Chair-Person approached the High Court of Kerala in Kerala Wakf Board vs. State of Kerala[14] the High Court of Kerala had observed that:

> The impugned order has been made on the mistaken assumption that the Board persistently violated its duties and persistently abused its power. This misconceived assumption has eroded the very basis of the order. I have no doubt that the officer who made the order on behalf of the Government acted in good faith. But the order is unsustainable. It is wrong in law and unsupported by evidence. It is grossly unreasonable, unjust and oppressive. It is therefore ultra vires the power of the Government.

Dealing with a similar case, a Bench of the Patna High Court in Bihar State Sunni Wakf Board vs. State of Bihar[15] had observed that:

> The persistent default in the performance of the duty imposed on it cannot be gathered by a solitary instance of any irregularity or illegality.
>
> Supersession of a statutory body is a serious matter. It is governed by the statute and the provisions contained therein must be strictly followed. Section 64 of the Wakf Act does not give a blanket power to supersede the Board as and when the respondents and its authorities desire to do so or for any reason whatsoever.

There is another case between Bihar State Sunni Wakf Board vs. State of Bihar,[16] wherein the Supreme Court observed that:

> On plain reading of the said provision, it would be obvious that the opinion of the State Government to supersede the Board is not a subjective opinion. It has to be based on objective findings and for the reasons to be recorded in writing. The persistent default in the performance of the duty imposed on it cannot be gathered by a solitary instance of irregularity or illegality.

While discussing the powers of the Waqf Board vis-à-vis the powers of the State and Central Governments in regulating the activities of waqf institutions, the High Court of Madras in Raichand J. Shah vs. State of Tamil Nadu & Secretary, Tamil Nadu Wakf Board[17] the High Court of Madras analysed the powers of the Waqf Board in relation to the powers of the Central and State Governments and observed that:

14 AIR 1984 Ker 57.
15 AIR 1993 Pat 89.
16 AIR 1993 Pat 89.
17 (2002) 4 LW 213.

> Resolutions made by the Board, which in the opinion of the State Government are detrimental to the interest of the Wakfs, are certainly capable of being interfered with and in respect of which directions are capable of being given by the State Government for which express provision is made in section 63 of the Wakf Act 1954.

The Andhra Pradesh High Court, in M. Govinda Rao and Others vs. A.P. State Wakf Board and Others,[18] described the powers of the State Government in superseding the Waqf Board in the following words:

> The contention that, since wakf lands are not shown under Section 18, the respondents as cultivating tenants are entitled for the statutory protection under Section 15 of the Act, and to have the preferential right to purchase the lands under their cultivation, are submissions required merely to be noted to be rejected.

****

Section 100

Protection of action taken in good faith:-

> ***No suit or other legal proceeding shall lie against the Board or Chief Executive Officer or Survey Commissioner or any other person duly appointed under this Act in respect of anything which is in good faith done or intended to be done under this Act.***

Reflections

Analogous section under Wakf Act 1954 is S.65.

The Waqf Act under this section provides immunity to the Board, the Chief Executive Officer, the Survey Commissioner of the Waqf and any other person duly appointed under this Act in respect of anything having done or intended to have done in good faith under this Act. The words "good faith" imply anything done honestly, whether negligently or diligently.

Judicial response

The Andhra High Court, in Syed Munavvaruddin Quadri vs. Chief Executive Officer, A.P.,[19] while discussing the regulations framed by A.P. State Waqf

18 2008 (2) ALT 429.
19 2007 (3) ALD 711, 2007 (4) ALT 192.

Board regarding conduct of Elections to the Managing Committees of the Waqf Institutions, observed as under:

> The "conduct of election of members of Managing Committee" is very conspicuous by its absence in Section 110(2) of the Act. This would also lend support that the Parliament did not contemplate the election of a Managing Committee of a wakf. Therefore, the decision of the first respondent to order election of Managing Committee of Jamia Mosque was itself without any authority or power. If this writ petition is allowed, it would amount to resurrecting an illegality. Writ of Mandamus cannot be issued to validate an illegal thing. (See Maharaja Chintamani Saran Nath Shahdeo vs. State of Bihar, Supreme Court Judgement in Civil Appeal No. 5451 of 1995 decided on 7 October 1999.)

****

Section 101

Survey Commissioner, members and officers of the Board deemed to be public servants:-

(1) ***The Survey Commissioner, members of the Board, every officer, every auditor of the Board and every other person duly appointed to discharge any duties imposed on him by this Act or any rule or order made thereunder, shall be deemed to be public servants within the meaning of section 21 of the Indian Penal Code (45 of 1860).***

(2) ***Every mutawalli of a waqf, every member of managing committee, whether constituted by the Board or under any deed of waqf, every Executive Officer and every person holding any office in a waqf shall also be deemed to be a public servant within the meaning of section 21 of the Indian Penal Code (45 of 1860).***

Reflections

Analogous section under Wakf Act 1954 is S.66, as substituted by Wakf Amendment Act (Act 69 of 1984).

This section stipulates that the members of the board, Survey Commissioner of the Waqf, Chief Executive Officer, auditors, mutawallis, members of the Managing Committees or any other persons appointed to discharge the duties under this Act to be public servants within the meaning of section 21 of the Indian Penal Code (45 of 1860). This stipulation of public servants takes such officers/persons under the purview of Anti-Corruption Laws.

Judicial response

Judicial response pertaining to this section is not found.

****

Section 102

Special provision for reorganisation of certain Boards:-

(1) *Where on account of the reorganisation of States under any law providing reorganisation of States, the whole or any part of a State in respect of which a Board was, immediately before the day of such reorganisation, functioning has been transferred on that day to another State and by reason of such transfer, it appears to the Government of a State in any part of which the Board is functioning that the Board should be dissolved or that it should be reconstituted as an Intra-State Board for the whole or any part of that State, the State Government may frame a scheme or such dissolution or such reconstitution, including proposals regarding the transfer of the assets, rights and liabilities of the Board to any other Board or State Government and the transfer or re-employment of employees of the Board and forward the scheme to the Central Government.*

(2) *On receipt of a scheme forwarded to it under sub-section (1), the Central Government may, after consulting the Council and the State Governments*[20] *concerned, approve the scheme with or without modifications and give effect to the scheme so approved by making such order as it thinks fit.*

(3) *An order under sub-section (2) may provide for all or any of the following matters, namely:-*

   (a) *the dissolution of the Board;*

   (b) *the reconstitution in any manner whatsoever of the Board including the establishment, where necessary, of a new Board.*

   (c) *the area in respect of which the reconstituted Board or new Board shall function and operate;*

   (d) *the transfer, in whole or in part, of the assets, rights and liabilities of the Board (including the rights and liabilities under any contract made by it) to any other Board or State Government and the terms and conditions of such transfer;*

   (e) *the substitution of any such transferee for the Board, or the addition of any such transferee, as party to any legal proceeding to*

20 Substituted by Act 27 of 2013, S. 52, for "after consulting the state governments."

which the Board is a party; and the transfer of any proceeding pending before the Board to any such transferee;

(f) *the transfer or re-employment of any employee of the Board to or by, any such transferee and subject to the provisions of law providing for the reorganisation of the concerned State, the terms and conditions of service applicable to such employees after such transfer or re-employment; and*

(g) *such incidental, consequential and supplemental matters as may be necessary to give effect to the approved scheme.*

(4) *Where an order is made under this section transferring the assets, rights and liabilities of any Board, then, by virtue of that order, such assets, rights and liabilities of the Board shall vest in, and be the assets, rights and liabilities of, the transferee.*

(5) *Every order made under this section shall be published in the Official Gazette.*

(6) *Every order made under this section shall be laid before each House of Parliament, as soon as may be, after it is made.*

Reflections

Analogous section under Wakf Act 1954 is S.66, as inserted by Wakf Amendment Act (Act 30 of 1959), and amended by Waqf Amendment Act 1984 (Act 69 of 1984).

This section provides for the dissolution of the Waqf Board and the reconstitution of the board as an Intra-State Board for the whole or any part of the state in case of reorganisation of states under any law. The State Government shall frame a scheme for such dissolution and reconstitution of the Waqf Board providing for transfer of assets, liabilities, transfer of employees, etc., and forward such a scheme to the Central Government. The Central Government, after consulting State Governments concerned, may approve the scheme with or without modifications and due affect to the scheme as it thinks fit. Sub-section (3) lists the matter which shall be included, among other things, in the scheme. Every order in this regard shall be published in the Official Gazette and tabled before both the houses of parliament.

Judicial response

Judicial response pertaining to this section is not found.

****

Section 103

Special provision for establishment of Board for part of a State:-

(1) *Where on account of the territorial changes brought about by any law providing for the reorganisation of any state, this Act is as from the date on which that law comes into force applicable only to any part or parts of a State but has not been brought into force in the remaining part thereof, then notwithstanding anything contained in this Act, it shall be lawful for the Government of the State to establish one or more Boards for such part or parts in which this Act is in force and in such a case any reference in this Act to the word "State" in relation of a Board shall be construed as a reference to that part of the State for which the Board is established.*

(2) *Where any such Board has been established and it appears to the Government of the State that a Board should be established for the whole of the State, the State Government may, by order notified in the Official Gazette dissolve the Board established for the part of the State or reconstitute and reorganise such Board or establish a new Board for the whole of the State and thereupon, the assets, rights and liabilities of the Board for the part of the State shall vest in and be the assets, rights and liabilities of the reconstitution Board or the new Board, as the case may be.*

Reflections

Analogous section under Wakf Act 1954 is S.66 B, as inserted by Wakf Amendment Act (Act 30 of 1959) and amended by Wakf Amendment Act 1984 (Act 69 of 1984).

Section 103 envisages provision of the establishment of Waqf Board for part of a state in case of territorial changes brought about by any law for the reorganisation of any state. This section authorises the State Government to constitute more than one Waqf Boards for administrative and geographical convenience. Similarly, this section provides for constitution of a single Waqf Board where more than one Waqf Boards are functioning in such a state.

Judicial response

Judicial response relating to this section is not found.

****

Section 104

Application of Act to properties given or donated by persons not professing Islam for support of certain waqf:-

Notwithstanding anything contained in this Act where any movable or immovable property has been given or donated by any person not professing Islam for the support of a waqf being:

(a) ***a mosque, idgah, imambara, dargah, khanqah or a maqbara;***
(b) ***a Muslim graveyard;***
(c) ***a choultry or a musafirkhana,***

then such property shall be deemed to be compromised in that waqf and be dealt in the same manner as the waqf in which it is so comprised.

Reflections

Analogous section under Wakf Act 1954 is S.66 C, as inserted by Wakf Amendment Act (Act 34 of 1964).

This section provides for donations/contributions of movable or immovable properties by Non-Muslims to the waqf institutions such as a mosque, idgah, imambara, dargah, khangah; maqbara; a Muslim graveyard; a choultry or a musafarkhana. This section makes such donations/contribution acceptable. It may not be out of place to mention here that the waqf jurisprudence allows a Non-Muslim to donate for a waqf and accepts a Non-Muslim to function as a mutawalli.

Judicial response

Judicial response pertaining to this section is not found.

****

Section 104A

Prohibition of sale, gift, exchange, mortgage or transfer of waqf property.— [21]

(1) ***Notwithstanding anything contained in this Act or any other law for the time being in force or any waqf deed, no person shall sell, gift,***

21 Inserted by Act 27 of 2013, S. 53.

exchange, mortgage or transfer any movable or immovable property which is a waqf property to any other person.

(2) *Any sale, gift, exchange, mortgage or transfer of property referred to in sub-section (1) shall be void ab initio.*

Reflections

It is a new section inserted by Wakf Amendment Act 2013 (Act 27 of 2013) hence there is no analogous section in Wakf Act 1954.

This is a new section inserted by Waqf Amendment Act 2013 (Act 27 of 2013). This section prohibits sale, gift, mortgage or transfer of waqf property to any person. Such transfer or alienation shall be void ab initio. This section declares such a transaction to be void even if there is such provision in the Waqf Deed.

Judicial response

Judicial response pertaining to this section is not found.

****

Section 104B

Restoration of waqf properties in occupation of Government agencies to Waqf Board.— [22]

(1) *If any waqf property has been occupied by the Government agencies it shall be returned to the Board or the mutawalli within a period of six months from the date of the order of the Tribunal.*

(2) *The Government agency may, if the property is required for a public purpose, make an application for determination of the rent, or as the case may be, the compensation, by the Tribunal at the prevailing market value.*

Reflections

It is a new section inserted by Wakf Amendment Act 2013 (Act 27 pf 2013), hence no analogous section in Wakf Act 1954.

22 Inserted by Act 27 of 2013, S. 54.

This is again a new section inserted by Waqf Amendment Act 2013 (Act 27 of 2013). This section provides that any government agency in occupation of waqf property shall vacate and hand over the same to the Waqf Board or a mutawalli; however, if such an agency requires the property in its occupation it shall apply to the Waqf Board/Tribunal for the determination of rent/compensation as the case may be.

Judicial response

The Supreme Court, in Sayyed Ali vs. Andhra Pradesh Wakf Board, Hyderabad,[23] having discussed the law under Andhra Pradesh (A.A.) Inams (Abolition and Conversion into Ryotwari) Act, 1956 and the Waqf Act 1995, and also citing relevant judgements observed as under:

> "The plea of res judicata presupposes that there is inexistence a decree or judgment which is legal, but when the judgment is non est in law, no plea of res judicata can be founded on such a judgment."

In Mathura Prasad vs. Dossibai, AIR [1971] SC 2355, the court observed as follows:

> A question of jurisdiction of the Court, or of procedure, or a pure question of law unrelated to the right of the parties to a previous Suit, is not res judicata in the subsequent suit ... Similarly, by an erroneous decision if the Court assumes jurisdiction which it does not possess under the statute the question cannot operate, as res judicata between the same parties, whether the cause of action in the subsequent litigation is the same or otherwise:

****

Section 105

Power of Board and Chief Executive officer to require copies of documents, etc., to be furnished:-

> ***Notwithstanding anything contained in any law for the time being in force, it shall be lawful for the Board or the Chief Executive Officer to require any person having the custody of any record, register, report or other document relating to a waqf or any immovable property, which is waqf property, to furnish subject to the payment of necessary costs, copies of, or extracts from, any such record, register, report or***

23 AIR 1998 SC, 972.

document and every person to whom such a requisition is made, shall furnish, as soon as may be practicable, to the Board or Chief Executive Officer copies or extracts from the required record, register, report or other document.

Reflections

Analogous section under Wakf Act 1954 is S.66 D, as inserted by Wakf Amendment Act 1984 (Act 69 of 1984).

Under this section the Waqf Board and its Chief Executive Officer are conferred with the right to obtain any document or record relating to waqf or waqf property on payment of any fee from any office or agency.

Judicial response

Judicial response pertaining to this section is not found.

****

Section 106

Powers of Central Government to constitute common Boards:-

(1) *Where the Central Government is satisfied that by reasons of-*
   (i) *the smallness of the Muslim population in two or more States,*
   (ii) *the slender resources of the auqaf in such States, and*
   (iii) *the disproportion between the number and income of the auqaf and the Muslim population in such States,*

   it is expedient in the interests of the auqaf in the States and the Muslim population of such States, to have, instead of separate Boards for each of such States, a common Board, it may, after consultation with the Council and the Government[24] *of each of the concerned States, establish, by notification in the Official Gazette, a common Board for such States as it may deem fit, and may, by the same or any subsequent notification specify the place at which the principal office of such common Board shall be located.*

(2) *Every common Board established under sub-section (1) shall, as far as practicable, consist of the persons specified in sub-section (1) or, as the case may be, sub-section (7) of section 14.*

24 Substituted by Act 27 of 2013, S. 55, for "after consultation with the government."

(3) ***Whenever any common Board is established under sub-section (1):***

(a) ***all powers vested in the State Government under any deed of waqf or any provision of law for the time being in force relating to auqaf, shall stand transferred to, and vested in, the Central Government and, thereupon, references in such deed of waqf or law to the State Governments shall be construed as references to the Central Government:***

Provided that while establishing a common Board for two or more States, the Central Government shall ensure that at least one representative of each of the concerned States is included as a member of the Board;

(b) ***references in this Act to a State shall be construed as references to each of the States for which the common Board has been established;***

(c) ***the Central Government may, without prejudice to any rule applicable to a Board in a State, make, by notification in the Official Gazette, rules regulating the conduct of business by and affairs of, the common Board.***

(4) ***The common Board shall be a body corporate, with objects not confined to one State, having perpetual succession and a common seal with power to acquire and hold property and to transfer any such property, subject to such conditions and restrictions as may be specified by the Central Government, and shall by the said name sue or be sued.***

Reflections

Analogous section under Wakf Act 1954 is S.66 F, as inserted by Wakf Amendment Act 1984 (Act 69 of 1984).

This section authorises the Central Government to constitute a Waqf Board for more than two states if it has reason to believe that constitution of a separate board is not viable due to a negligible number of waqf institutions or meagre income from the waqf institutions, etc. If a single Waqf Board is constituted for two or more than two states, all the powers bestowed on the State Government shall stand transferred to the Central Government. However, a representative of each of such state governments shall be included in the board.

Judicial response

Judicial response relating to this section is not found.

****

Section 107

Act 36 of 1963 not to apply for recovery of waqf properties:-

> ***Nothing contained in the Limitation Act, 1963 shall apply to any suit for possession of immovable property comprised in any waqf or for possession of any interest in such property.***

Reflections

Analogous section under Wakf Act 1954 is S.66 G, as inserted by Wakf Amendment Act 1984 (Act 69 of 1984).

This section exempts application of Limitation Act 1963 (Act 36 of 1963) in case of any suit for possession of immovable Waqf property or for any interest in such property.

Judicial response

In Vaidya Varthi Thirtha Swamigal vs. Balusamy Iyer,[25] delivering the judgement Mr. Ameer Ali observed:

> Neither under the Hindu Law nor in the Mohammadan system is any property conveyed to a shebait or a mutawalli in the case of a dedication. Nor is any property vested in him; whatever property he holds for the idol or the institution, he holds as manager with certain beneficial interest regulated by custom or usage. Under the Mohammadan Law, the moment a wakf is created all rights of property pass out of the wakif and vest in God Almighty. The curator whether called mutawalli or sajjadanashin or by any other name, is merely a manager. He is certainly not a "trustee" as understood in the English system.

A Bench of the High Court of Madras, in Khaji Mohamed Hossain vs. Majiday Mahmood jamait Managing Committee,[26] has held that as the society had been for a period of 14 years in undisputed management of the mosque in derogation of the right of the previous mutawalli, it must be deemed to have acquired the right of mutawalli by prescription.

25 AIR 1922 PC 123; 48 IA 302; ILR 44 Mad 831; 65 IC 161.
26 AIR 1940 Mad, 167.

The Supreme Court in T Kaliamurthi & Another vs. Five Gori Thaikal Wakf & Others,[27] has discussed at length the matter pertaining to limitations for filing suit and observed that:

> In view of the above authorities, we are of the view that in the present case, once it is held that the suit for possession of the suit properties filed at the instance of the wakf were barred under the Limitation Act, 1908, the necessary corollary would be to hold that the right of the wakf to the suit properties stood extinguished in view of Section 27 of the Limitation Act, 1963 and therefore, when Section 107 came into force, it could not revive the extinguished rights.

The High Court of Andhra Pradesh, in A.P. State Wakf Board, vs. Smt. Sabita Joshi and Others,[28] held that:

> More than all, the petitioner did not raise any plea as to limitation in the suit, much less any issue was framed on it. After a full-fledged trial has taken place and the Tribunal rendered its judgment, the plea is raised for the first time before this Court. Therefore, it cannot be accepted.

The Andhra Pradesh High Court, in Managing Committee, Masjid-e-Ibrahimia Rep. by Secretary, A.M. Yousuf Hussain vs. Hyderabad Allwyn Metal Works Ltd., Now Called as Voltas Ltd.,[29] observed that:

> No provision similar or analogous to Section 107 of the Wakf Act, 1995 is found in the Wakf Act, 1954. Section 6(1) of the Wakf Act, 1954 provides limitation of one year from the date of publication of notification in the official gazette as required under Sub-section (2) of Section 5, for filing civil suit. This provision has no relevance, for in the instant case, the suit was already filed and it ended in a decree. As per Article 136 of the Limitation Act, 1963, the decree shall have to be executed within a period of 12 years. In the instant case, though the petitioner-plaintiff obtained decree, they did not execute it within a period of 12 years, and filed the E.P. after lapse of 25 years.
>
> If there was stay granted by this Court in second appeal of the judgment and decree of the first appellate Court, then the period of limitation of 12 years for executing the decree, would start to run from 30-07-1980, on which date, the Supreme Court, dismissed the S.L.P. And if from 30-07-1980, the period of limitation of 12 years was to be

27 AIR 2009 SC, 840.

28 Civil Revision Petition No.1324 of 2010.

29 AIR 2006 AP 330; 2006 (4) ALD 769; 2006 (4) ALT 736.

reckoned, then the judgment and decree, should have been executed on or before 29-06-1992 (sic. 29-7-1992), which the petitioner did not do. Inasmuch as the petitioner-plaintiff filed the E.P. for executing the decree in 2005, i.e. after lapse of more than two decades from the date the decree attained finality and became executable, it is clearly barred by limitation, and no exception can be taken to the order of the Court below rejecting the E.P. on the ground that it is barred by limitation.

For the foregoing reasons, there is no merit in the C.R.P., and the same is accordingly dismissed. However, having regard to the provisions of the Wakf Act, it is left open to the petitioner to take recourse to the remedies available to them there under and in accordance with law.

****

Section 108

Special provision as to evacuee waqf properties:-

The provisions of this Act shall apply, and shall be deemed always to have applied, in relation to any evacuee property within the meaning of clause (f) of section 2 of the Administration of Evacuee Property Act, 1950 which immediately before it became such evacuee property within the said meaning was property comprised in any waqf and, in particular any entrustment (whether by transfer of any documents or in any other manner and whether generally or for specified purpose) of any such property to a Board made before the commencement of this Act in pursuance of the instructions of the Custodian under the Administration of Evacuee Property Act, 1950 shall have, and shall be deemed always to have had, notwithstanding anything contained in any other provision of this Act, effect as if such entrustment had operated to-

(a) *vest such property in such Board in the same manner and with the same effect as in a trustee of such property for the purposes of sub-section (1) of section 11 of the Administration of Evacuee Property Act, 1950 (31 of 1950) with effect from the date of such entrustment, and*

(b) *authorise such Board to assume direct management of the waqf concerned for so long as it might deem necessary.*

Reflections

Analogous section under Wakf Act 1954 is S.66 H, as inserted by Wakf Amendment Act 1984 (Act 69 of 1984).

This section makes a provision for the application of this Act to the evacuee property as defined under section (2) clause (f) of the Administration of Evacuee Property Act, 1950 (Act 31 of 1950).

Judicial response

Judicial response relating to this section is not found.

****

Section 108A

Act to have overriding effect.— [30]

> ***The provisions of this Act shall have overriding effect notwithstanding anything inconsistent therewith contained in any other law for the time being in force or in any instrument having effect by virtue of any law other than this Act.***

Reflections

New Section inserted by Act 27 of 2013, hence there is no analogous section in Wakf Act 1954.

This section makes a provision of an overriding effect of the Waqf Act 1995 in case of any inconsistency in any other law for the time being in force. This is a very important provision enacted by the Parliament for the protection of waqf properties and for the removal and clarification of ambiguities, uncertainty and inconsistency caused due to any provision under any other law for the time being in force.

Judicial response

Judicial response pertaining to this section is not found.

****

30 Inserted by Act 27 of 2013, S. 56.

Section 109

Power to make Rules:-

(1) *The State Government may, by notification in the Official Gazette, make rules to carry out the purposes of this Act, other than those of Chapter III.*

(2) *In particular, and without prejudice to the generality of the foregoing powers, such rules may provide for all or any of the following matters, namely:*

i. *the qualifications required to be fulfilled by a person to be appointed as a mutawalli under clause (i) of section 3;*
(ia) other particulars which the report of the Survey Commissioner may contain under clause (f) of sub-section (3) of section 4.[31]

ii. *any other matter under clause (f) of sub-section (4) of section 4;*

iii. *the particulars which a list of Auqaf published under sub-section (2) of section 5, may contain;*

iv. *the manner of election of members of the Board by means of a single transferable vote, under sub-section (2) of section 14;*

v. *the terms and conditions of service of the Chief Executive Officer under sub-section (2) of section 23;*

vi. *the conditions and restrictions subject to which the Chief Executive Officer or any other officer may inspect any public office, records or registers under sub section (1) of*[32] *section 29;*
(vi a) the period within which the mutawalli or any other person may produce documents related to waqf properties under sub-section (2) of section 31;[33]
(vi b) the conditions under which an agency of the Government or any other organisation may supply copies of records, registers and other documents under sub-section (3) of section 31.

vii. *The conditions subject to which an Executive Officer and supporting staff may be appointed under sub-section (1) of section 38;*

viii. *the manner in which an inquiry may be held by the Chief Executive Officer under sub-section (1) of section 39;*

31 Substituted by Act 27 of 2013, S. 57 (a), for Cl. (i). Prior to its substitution, Cl. (i) read as under:- "(i) other particulars which the report of the survey commissioner may contain, under clause (f) of sub-section (3) of section (4); ..."

32 Substituted by Act 27 of 2013, S. 57(b), for "under."

33 Inserted by Act 27 of 2013, S. 57(c).

ix. *the form in which, and the time within which, a separate budget for Auqaf under the direct management of the Board shall be prepared under sub-section (1) of section 45;*

x. *the interval at which accounts of Auqaf may be audited in pursuance of the provisions of sub-section (1) of section 47;*

xi. *[*****] omitted.*[34]

xii. *the guidance subject to which the Collector shall recover the property transferred in contravention of the provisions of this Act. under section 52;*

xiii. *the manner of service of notice issued under sub-section (1) of section 54 and the manner in which any inquiry is to be made under sub-section (3) of that section;*

xiv. *the manner in which any inquiry may be held under section 64 or section 71;*

xv. *the other matters which may be specified in the report submitted under sub-section (3) of section 65;*

xvi. *the manner of publication of order made under sub-section (2) of section 67;*

xvii. *the manner in which consultation may be made with mutawalli under sub-section (1) of section 69;*

xviii. *the manner of publication of order made under sub-section (3) of section 69;*

xix. *the rate at which contribution is to be made by a mutawalli under section 72;*

xx. *the payment of moneys into the Waqf Fund, the investment, the custody and disbursement of such moneys under section 77;*

xxi. *the form in which, and the time within which, the budget of the Board may be prepared and submitted under section 78;*

xxii. *the time within which application is to be made to the Tribunal under sub-section (2) of section 83;*

(xxii a) The term and condition of appointment including the salaries and allowances payable to the chairman and other members other than persons appointed as ex officio members under sub-section (4-A) of section 83;[35]

xxiii. *the procedure which the tribunal shall follow under sub-section (6) of section 83;*

34 Cl. (xi) omitted by Act 27 of 2013, S. 57 (d). Prior to its omission, Ci. (xi) read as under:- "(xi) the time within which, the sale of any property is to be informed under the first proviso to sub-section (2) of section 51 and the manner in which the approval given under sub-section shall be published; ..."

35 Inserted by Act 27 of 2013, S. 57 (e).

xxiv. *the form in which the annual report is to be submitted and the matters which such report shall contain under section 98; and*

xxv. *any other matter which is required to be, or may be, prescribed.*

Reflections

Analogous section under Wakf Act 1954 is S.67.

This section authorises the state government to frame rules for the functioning of the Waqf Board and the administration of waqf institutions, except on those matters provided under Chapter III of the Act. The subject matter on which the rules and regulations shall be prepared has been provided under sub-section (2). These rules shall be notified in the Official Gazette.

Judicial response

The decision of the Andhra Pradesh High Court, in Syed Munavvaruddin Quadri vs. Chief Executive Officer, A.P. State Wakf Board & Others,[36] discusses the powers of the State Government and the Waqf Board under section 109 and 110. The judgement in this case has been quoted under the following section.

****

Section 110

Powers to make regulations by the Board:-

(1) *The Board may, with the previous sanction of the State Government, make regulations not inconsistent with this Act or the rules made there under, for carrying out its functions under this Act.*
(2) *In particular, and without prejudice to the generality of the foregoing powers, such regulations may provide for all or any of the following matters, namely:*
    (a) *the time and places of the meetings of the Board under sub-section (1) of section 17;*
    (b) *the procedure and conduct of business at the meetings of the Board;*
    (c) *the constitution and functions of the committees and the Board and the procedure for transaction of business at the meetings of such committees;*

36 2007 (3) ALD 711.

(d) *the allowances or fees to be paid to the Chairperson or members of the Board or members of committees;*

(e) *the terms and conditions of service of the officers and other employees of the Board under sub-section (2) of section 24;*

(f) *the forms of application for registration of Auqaf further particulars to be contained therein and the manner and place of registration of Auqaf under sub-section (3) of section 36;*

(g) *further particulars to be contained in the register of Auqaf under section 37;*

(h) *the form in which, and the time within which, the budgets of Auqaf may be prepared and submitted by the Mutawalli and approved by the Board under sub-section (1) of section 44;*

(i) *the books of accounts and other books to be maintained by the Board under section 79;*

(j) *fees payable for inspection of proceedings and records of the Board or for issue of copies of the same;*

(k) *persons by whom any order or decision of the Board may be authenticated; and*

(l) *any other matter which has to be, or may be, provided by regulations.*

(3) *All regulations made under this section shall be published in the Official Gazette and shall have effect from the date of such publication.*

Reflections

Analogous section under Wakf Act 1954 is S.68.

This section confers powers to the state Waqf Boards to frame regulations in consonance with the Act and rules framed by Central and State Governments. The matters on which the board can frame regulations have been listed in sub-section (2). These regulations shall be notified in the Official Gazette.

Judicial response

The issue of formulation of Rules and Regulations by the State Government and the State Waqf Board under section 109 and 110 respectively came up for consideration before the Andhra Pradesh High Court in Syed Munavvaruddin Quadri vs. Chief Executive Officer, A.P. State Wakf Board & others.[37] The High Court rendered the following observation:

37 2007 (3) ALD 711.

This would also lend support that the Parliament did not contemplate the election of a Managing Committee of a Wakf. Learned Standing Counsel for Wakf Board does not dispute the legal position. Therefore, the decision of the first respondent to order election of Managing Committee of Jamia Mosque was itself without any authority or power. If this writ petition is allowed, it would amount to resurrecting an illegality. Writ of Mandamus cannot be issued to validate an illegal thing.

****

Section 111

Laying of Rules and Regulations before State Legislature:-

> ***Every rule made under section 109 and every regulation made under section 110 shall be laid, as soon as may be after it is made, before the State Legislature.***

Reflections

Analogous section under Wakf Act 1954 is S.68A.

This section provides for placing the rules framed under section 109 and regulations formulated under section 110, before the state legislature.

Judicial response

Judicial response pertaining to this section is not found.

****

Section 112

Repeal and savings:-

(1) ***The Waqf Act, 1954 (29 of 1954) and the Waqf (Amendment) Act, 1984 (69 of 1984) are hereby repealed.***

(2) ***Notwithstanding such repeal, anything done or any action taken under the said Acts shall be deemed to have been done or taken under the corresponding provisions of this Act.***

(3) ***If, immediately before the commencement of this Act, in any State, there is in force in that State, any law which corresponds to this Act that corresponding law shall stand repealed:***

Provided that such repeal shall not affect the previous operation of that corresponding law, and subject thereto, anything done or any action taken in the exercise of any power conferred by or under the corresponding law shall be deemed to have been done or taken in the exercise of the powers conferred by or under this Act as if this Act was in force on the day on which such things were done or action was taken.

Reflections

Analogous section under Wakf Act 1954 is S.69.

This section provides for the repealing of Wakf Act 1954 (Act 29 of 1954), and the Waqf Amendment Act 1954 (Act 69 of 1984). However, sub-section (2) of this section saves the action taken under these repealed Acts to have done and taken under the corresponding provisions of this Act.

Judicial response

The High Court of Andhra Pradesh, in Chintala Uday Shankar and Others vs. Subedar Saheb Choultry, Trust,[38] while discussing the revision petition observed as under:

> As already stated the Subedar Saheb Choultry Committee has not filed any revision against the said orders of the Rent Appellate Court wherein its claim has been rejected.
>
> In view of the concurrent findings recorded by both the authorities below and more so when the appeal filed by purchasers has been allowed holding that the plaintiff has failed to establish its title and that the plaintiff never exercised its right to manage the schedule property as wakf property from 1920 till the date of filing of the suit in 1994 and as the schedule property ceased to be a wakf property as per the judgments under Exs. B3, B4 and B6 as observed above, I do not see any illegality, irregularity or impropriety in the orders under revision.

A Judgement of the Bench of the Supreme Court of India consisting of Dalveer Bhandari, Ruma Pal, Dr. Ar. Lakshmanan, Dalveer Bhandari would be more appropriate to discuss under section 112 of the Waqf Act 1995. In M/S Gammon India Ltd vs. Spl. Chief Secretary & Others,[39] dealing with the question of the jurisdiction of the repealed Act of A.P.G.S. Tax Act

38 2007 (2) ALD 213.
39 (2006) 3 SCC 354.

1957, after the enactment of A.P.V.A. Tax Act 2005, the Supreme Court held that:

> On the touchstone of the principles of law culled out from the judgments of various courts applied to the facts of these cases lead to a definite conclusion that the Assistant Commissioner (Commercial Taxes), Warangal Division was fully justified in initiating and completing the proceedings under the A.P.G.S. Tax Act even after it is repealed.

The validity and continuity of the Waqf Board constituted under the provisions of previous Act, i.e., Wakf Act 1954 was questioned in Muslim Minority Front vs. Andhra Pradesh,[40] before the High Court of Andhra Pradesh, which held that:

> The new Board shall assume office on the appointment of the members thereof and the members appointed under Section 11 of the Wakf Act, 1954 shall have no claim whatsoever for any office in the Board. Since a declaration to the above effect may not be sufficient, let a direction issue to the State Government to complete the formalities as contemplated Under Section 14 of the new Act by 30-6-1996. Let a further direction issue accordingly that consequent upon the notification Under Section 14(9) of the Wakf Act, 1995 respondents 4 to 13 shall vacate their office.

****

Section 113

Power to remove difficulties:-

(1) ***If any difficulty arises in giving effect to the provisions of this Act, the Central Government may, by order, not inconsistent with the provisions of this Act, remove the difficulty:***

> ***Provided that no such order shall be made after the expiry of the period of two years from the commencement of this Act.***

(2) ***However, order made under this section shall be laid, as soon as may be after it is made, before each House of Parliament.***

----

40 (1996) 2 ALT 30.

Reflections

Analogous section under Wakf Act 1954 is S.70.

This section confers the powers to the Central Government to remove any difficulty by an order for the proper implementation of this Act. Such removal of the difficulty shall not be inconsistent with the provisions of this Act. However, such orders passed by the government shall be placed before the Houses of Parliament as soon as possible.

Judicial response

Judicial response pertaining to this section is not found.

Table of cases

S.No.	Names of the parties	Citation	Page No.
1.	Abdul Fata *v* Russomoy Chowdhuri	ILR (1894) 22 Cal 619 PC: 22 IA,76	27, 28
2.	Abdul Gaffar *v* Rahmat Ali	AIR, 1930, Oudh, 245	
3.	Abdul Hussain vs. Mohmmad Riza	ILR (1939) Nag 564	177
4.	Abdul Jalil *v* Uttar Pradesh	AIR, 1984, SC, 882	
5.	Abdul Kadar *v* Masjid Juma Daewaja	AIR, 2009 (NOC) 1704 (Bom).	262
6.	Abdul Karim v. M.P. State Waqf Board	AIR 2019 (NOC) 502 (M.P)	221
7.	Abdul Karim *v* Rahimabai	AIR, 1946, Bom, 342: 1946, 48, Bom, LR, 67	63
8.	Abdul Khadeer Beig vs. Government of Andhra Pradesh	2008 (2) ALD 33	108
9.	Abdul Khaleel *v* Karnataka Wakf Board	1988, (1), CLJ, 251	112
10.	Abdul Qavi *v* Asaf Ali	AIR, 1962, All, 364	
11.	Abdul Rafey *v* Banni Begam	15, IC, 36	8
12.	Abdul Rafi *v* Shamsul Haq	AIR, 1969, All, 35	
13.	Abdul Rahim *v* Narain Das,	1922 (50), IA, 84	
14.	Abdul Rahiman Musaliar *v* Muhammad	AIR,2003,Ker,84	
15.	Abdul Rahman *v* Murugappa	AIR, 1924, Mad, 577	
16.	Abdul Rais *v* Madhya Pradesh Wakf Board	(2005)3, LW, 241; (2005)1, SCC, 741	85
17.	Abdul Razack *v* Jimbabai	(1911), 14 Bom, LR, 295: 14, IC, 988	
18.	Abdul Sah *v* Mahoboob	AIR, 1972, Mys, 60	
19.	Abdul Sattar *v* Abdul Hameed	AIR, 1944, Mad, 504	
20.	Abdul Sukur *v* Abubakker	54, Bom, 358	

(*Continued*)

(*Continued*)

S.No.	*Names of the parties*	*Citation*	*Page No.*
21.	Abdul Wahab *v* Sughra Begum	AIR, 1932, All, 248: ILR (1932), 54, All 455: 136, IC, 619	9
22.	Abdulla *v* Ali Kunhi	1957, Ker, LJ, 849	
23.	Abdullah *v* Zain	1888, (13), Bom, 555	
24.	Abu Sayed *v* Bakar	ILR, (1901), 24, All, 190	
25.	Advocate General *v* Fathima	9, Bom, HCR, 19	
26.	Advocate General *v* Yusuf Ali,	AIR 1921, Bom, 338: 84 IC, 759: (1922) 24,	7, 9
27.	Afzal Houssain *v* Addl. District Judge	AIR, 1985, All, 79	184
28.	Afzal Hussain *v* Chhedilal	AIR, 1935, All, 792: ILR (1935) 57, All, 727: 155, IC 791	176
29.	Agha Ali *v* Altaf Hasan	ILR, 14, All, 429 (FB)	
30.	Agrapu Venkatamma v. Revenue Divisional Officer, Srikakulam	2007 (2) ALT 595	190
31.	Ahamed Kutty *v* Ayithraman Kutty	(1987)2, MLJ, 301	
32.	Ahmed Arif *v* Commissioner Wealth Tax,	AIR, 1971, SC,1691	
33.	Ahmed Ashraf *v* Murtaza	AIR, 1935, Oudh 299: ILR (1935) 11 Lah 93: 154,IC, 1023	
34.	Ahsanullah *v* Ziauddin	1937, All, LJ, 585 (PC)	
35.	Akbar *v* Mohamed Ansar	(1990)1, MLJ,342	
36.	Akhtar Ahmaed *v* Andhra Pradesh	AIR, 1964, AP, 244	114
37.	Akkode Jumayath vs P.V. Ibrahim	[2013] 7 S.C.R. 1033 1034; AIR 2013 SC 3530	
38.	Alam Aboobacker *v* Kerala Wakf Board	AIR, 1982, Ker , 322	
39.	Ali Bakhtiyar *v* Altaf Hossain	AIR, 1933, Cal 581: ILR (1933)60 Cal 790: 145, IC, 638	62
40.	Ali Hussain *v* Fazal	ILR (1914), 36 All, 431: 23, IC, 291	
41.	Ali Makin Naqvi etc. *v* U.P. Shia Wakf Board	AIR, 2009 (NOC) 593 (All).	135, 145
42.	Ali Mohamed *v* Ali Akbar	AIR, 1928, Lah, 58	

(*Continued*)

(*Continued*)

S.No.	Names of the parties	Citation	Page No.
43.	Aliyathammada *v* Pattakkal Cheriyakoya	AIR, 2003, Ker, 366	260
44.	Ali Zaman *v* Akbar Ali	AIR, 1937, PC, 127	
45.	Allah Baksh *v* Mohamed Umar	AIR, 1929, Lah, 444	
46.	Allah Rakhi *v* Mohd. Rahim,	1993, 61 (IA), 50, All.	
47.	All India Lawyers Union *v* Union of India	(1992)2, LW, 577	
48.	A.M. Ali Akbar *v* Keelakkarni Masjid Committee	AIR 2001, Mad 431; (2001)2 LW 753	
49.	Alma Latifi Masima Latifi, *in re*	AIR, 1962, Bom, 227	
50.	Allauddin Charities and Zakath Wakf vs. Hameed Ali	2002 (1) ALD 67 (DB)	253
51.	Amir Alam *v* State of Uttar Pradesh	AIR, 2002, All, 215	49, 71
52.	Amjad Ali Mirza, v Board of Wakfs	AIR 2019 (NOC) 188(CAL)	
53.	Amir Khan *v* Sheik Sulaiman	(1968)2, MLJ, 559	
54.	Amir Singh *v* Badardin	AIR, 1940, Lah, 119	
55.	Amjadullah Siddiqui *v* Mirza Nizamuddin	AIR, 1982, AP, 342	
56.	A.M. Mohideen Packker *v* Tamil Nadu Wakf Board	1983, TNLJ, 418	
57.	A.P. Moidu *v* P.V. Narayanan	AIR 2017 (NOC) 287 KER	64
58.	A.P.M.S.Mohamed Ali Marikayar *v* Special Officer Wakfs, Madras	(1969)2, MLJ, 556	
59.	A.M.S.Mohamed Yousuf *v* Tamil Nadu Wakf Board	1998, 1LW, 470	
60.	Andhra Pradesh Wakf Board *v* Dowlat Bibi	AIR, 1983, AP, 57	60
61.	Andhra Pradesh State Wakf Board v Mavuru Sundaramma	2007 (5) ALD 267, 2007 (6) ALT 365	80, 85
62.	Andhra Pradesh Wakf Board *v* Mohamed Hidayatullah	AIR, 1974, AP, 287	112, 203, 213
63.	Anis Fatima *v* Board of Wakf, Bengal	AIR, 2004, Cal, 91, (DB)	
64.	Anjuman Burhani *v* Daudi Bohra Jamaet,	AIR 2009, Rajasthan, 150.	263
65.	Anjuman Islamia *v* Muhammed Hussain	1981, All, LJ, 1120	

(*Continued*)

(*Continued*)

S.No.	*Names of the parties*	*Citation*	*Page No.*
66.	Anjuman Islamia *v* Najim	AIR, 1982, MP, 17	
67.	Appasamy Odayar *v* Subramaniya	(1889), ILR, 12, Mad, 26 (PC); 15 IA, 167	
68.	A.P. State Wakf Board, Hyd. v All India Shia Conference	AIR 2000 SC 1751, 2000 (2) SCR 78	83
69.	A.P.State Wakf Board, *v* Sabita Joshi	2010 (6) ALD 651	269, 297
70.	A.P.State Wakf Board v. Mir Qamar	2012 (4) ALD 126, 2012 (3) ALT 791	155
71.	A.R.A. Basith Charitable Trust *v* Karnataka State Board of Wakf	AIR, 2009 (NOC) 2697 (Kar).	
72.	Arif Hussain *v* Additional District Judge Etawah	AIR 2008 (NOC) 1417	
73.	Arur Singh vs. Badar Din and others	AIR 1940 Lahore, 119	60
74.	Asha Bibi *v* Nabissa	AIR, 1957, Mad, 583	
75.	Ashwin Kumar Ghosh *v* Ananda	AIR, 1952, SC, 363	
76.	Asma Jafar Imam *v* State of Bihar	AIR, 1965, Pat, 48	64
77.	A.S.Narayana Deekshitulu *v* Andhra Pradesh	AIR, 1996, SC, 1765	
78.	Association of A.P. Sajjada Nasheens, Mutawallis, *v* Union of India	2010 (4) ALD 136 (DB)	102
79.	Ayesha *v* Commissioner of Wakfs, West Bengal	AIR, 1970, SC, 287	
80.	Azizunnissa *v* Sirdar Ali	AIR, 1927, Bom, 387: (1927) 29, Bom. LR, 343: 102 IC, 129	7
81.	Backer Ali *v* Anjuman Ara	ILR, 25, All, 236, (PC); (1902)30, IA, 94	58
82.	Badagara Jumayadh Committee *v* Peedikayalakath Ummer kutty	AIR, 2002, Ker, 56	89, 261
83.	Badarla Suryakumari *v* Badaria Vamana	AIR 2010 A.P, 209; 2010 (5) ALD, 373(FB).	
84.	Badrul Islam Ali *v* Ali Begum	(1935)16, Lah, 782	
85.	Ballaabh *v* Noor Mohamed	AIR, 1936, PC, 83; (1936)40, CWN, 499; 70, Mad, LJ,55; 160, IC, 576	

(*Continued*)

(*Continued*)

S.No.	*Names of the parties*	*Citation*	*Page No.*
86.	Bank of Augusta *v* Earle Peter's Court	Rep (US), 588	
87.	Banubi *v* Narasingrao	ILR, 31, Bom, 250	
88.	Bank of Augusta *v* Earlen Peter	Court Rep (US), 588	
89.	Banubi *v* Narsingrao	ILR, 31, Bom, 250	
90.	Baqulla Khan *v* Gulam	AIR, 1935, All, 616	
91.	Barkatulla *v* Committee of Management,	1966, ATLJ, 454	
92.	Basheer Ahamed v State of West Bengal	AIR, 1976, Cal, 142	42, 50
93.	Beli Ram *v* Mohamed Afzal	AIR, 1948, PC, 168: ILR (1949), Lah 1:50, Bom, LR, 674	
94.	Benoikumar Acahrjee *v* Ahmaed Ali	AIR, 1942, Cal, 467 (1)	
95.	B. Gowra Reddy vs. Government of Andhra Pradesh	AIR 2002 AP 313	86
96.	Biba Jan *v* Kalb Hussain	ILR, (1909)31, All, 136: 1 IC, 763	7, 8
97.	Bihar Sunni Wakf Board *v* State of Bihar,	6642 of 1990 dated 21-09-1991	
98.	Bihar Sunni Wakf Board *v* State of Bihar	AIR, 1993, Pat, 89	285
99.	Bikanimia *v* Shukhlal	ILR (1893)20, Cal, 116, (FB)	61, 62
100.	Birjad Mohal *v* Humayum	AIR, 1944, Pat, 234: ILR (1944)23, Pat, 203	
101.	Blair *v* Duncan	1902, AC, 37	
102.	Board of Muslim Wakfs vs. Smt. Hadi Begum	AIR 1992 SC 1083	86
103.	Board of Wakfs, Rajasthan *v* Radhakrishnan	AIR, 1979, SC, 289	67, 85
104.	Board of Wakf, West Bengal *v* Anis Fatima Begum	2011 (1) ALD 61 (SC) (2010) 13 (ADDl) SCR 1063	260, 264
105.	Building Mosque Wakf, Vijayawada *v* Sheik Meera	2011 (1) ALD 611	190
106.	Chhedilal Misra v. Civil Judge Lucknow	2007 (4) SCC 632	55
107.	Chintala Uday Shankar v. Subedar Saheb Choultry, Trust	2007 (2) ALD 213	305

(*Continued*)

(*Continued*)

S.No.	*Names of the parties*	*Citation*	*Page No.*
108.	Chintaman *v* Ramgopal	AIR, 1948, Nag, 385	
109.	Chowk Mosque, Nandiyal, *v* P.V.H. Maqbul	1999, AIHC, 1758	252
110.	C. K. Mohammed *v* Karnataka Board of Wakfs.	AIR, 2009 (NOC) 1706 (Kar).	69
111.	C.S. Peeran *v* Tamil Nadu State Wakf Board	AIR, 1969, Mad, 350: (1968)2, MLJ, 365	134
112.	Commissioner, Hindu Endowments *v* Sri Lakshmindra Shirur Mutt	AIR, 1954, SC, 282	42, 47, 48
113.	Commissioner of Wakfs *v* Ayesha Bibi	AIR, 1966, Cal, 68	
114.	Commissioner of Wakfs *v* Mehamuda Bibi	AIR, 1936, Cal, 480	272
115.	Commissioner of Wakfs *v* Mohammed Mohsin,	(1875)15, DLR, 167	
116.	Commissioner of Wakfs, West Bengal *v* Kazi Rashid Ali	AIR, 1958, Cal, 413	58
117.C	Court of Appeal in Picture Houses v Wednesbury Corp	(1947) 2 KB 680	114
118.	Dial Chand *v* Syed Karamut	16, WR, 116	
119.	Datatray Hanamantrao *v* Dilshad Begum	AIR, 2009 (NOC) 1705 (Kar).	262
120.	Digyadarshan Rajindra *v* Andhra Pradesh	AIR, 1970, SC, 181	
121.	Dilworth *v* Commissioner for Land	LR, 1899, AC, 99	
122.	D.M. Khasim *v* Court Mosque Committee	(2004)13, SCC, 367	173
123.	Dr. Mahrukh Khan vs The State Of Bihar	AIR 2019 (NOC) 737 PAT	258
124.	D. Venkata Krishna Rao and Others vs. Government of A.P.	2012 (4) ALD 144; 2012 (6) ALT 379 (DB).	75, 85, 152
125.	Eshan Beg *v* Rahmat Ali	ILR (1934), 10 Luck, 547	
126.	Eng Hock *v* Emperor	AIR, 1934, Rangoon, 178	
127.	Farid Abdul Latif Noorani *v* Sayed Sadiq	AIR, 2009 (NOC) 1935 (Bom).	122
128.	Fatima Bai *v* Gulam Hussain	9, Bom, LR, 1337	
129.	Fatima Bibi *v* Advocate General, Bombay	ILR, (1881)6, Bom, 42	8, 9
130.	G.M.A. Bhaimia *v* Madras State Wakf Board	(1968)1, MLJ, 410	

(*Continued*)

(*Continued*)

S.No.	*Names of the parties*	*Citation*	*Page No.*
131.	Gajjala Venkateshwarlu and Another v A.P. State Wakf Tribunal, Hyderabad	2003 (3) ALD 269	121, 189
132.	Gananasambandha Sannadhi *v* Velu Pandaram	23, Mad, 271, (PC)	
133.	Ganapathy Naicker *v* Special Officer for Wakfs, Madras	(1974)1, Mad, LJ, 239	178
134.	Ganee *v* Husen	10, BHCR, 7	
135.	Gangabai *v* Thavar	1, Bom, HCROC, 71	
136.	Garikapatti Veeraya *v* Subbiah	1957, SCR, 388, AIR 1957 540	271
137.	Gaselfar *v* Ahmedi Bibi	AIR, 1930, All, 169	
138.	Gora *v* Rajasthan Board of Wakf.	AIR, 2009 (NOC) 1393 (Raj).	61, 65
139.	Grimond *v* Drimond	1905, AC, 124	
140.	Gulam Abbas *v* Uttar Pradesh	AIR, 1981, SC, 2198	83
141.	Gulam Ahamed *v* Abdul Rasheed	AIR, 1933, Lah, 905	
142.	Gulam Ali *v* Sultan Khan	AIR, 1967, Ori, 55	7
143.	Gulam Ali *v* Secretary, Karnataka Wakf Board	AIR, 1985, Kant, 242	209
144.	Gulam *v* Abdul Majeed	AIR, 1957, AP, 941:	
145.	Gulam Samdani *v* Andhra Pradesh Wakf Board	AIR, 1975, AP, 104	209
146.	Gulisthan Shadi Mahal Trust, Bangalore, vs. Karnataka Board of Wakfs	2002 AIHC 999 Karn HC	78
147.	Gunga Gobind Mundul *v* The Collector of 24 Pargunnahs	(1866-67)11, MIA, 345, (PC)	
148.	Guruvaboyan *v* Director of Survey Chenai	(2004)1, MLJ, 245, (DB)	
149.9	Habib Ashraf v Syed Wajihuddin	AIR, 1933, Oudh, 222:	
150.	Hafiz Mohamed Zafar *v* Uttar Pradesh Sunni Board of Wakfs	AIR, 1965, All, 33	42, 48
151.	Haji Ali Akbar vs Wakf Alal Allah/ Alal Khair Wakf	AIR 2019 (NOC) 344 ALL	
152.	H. Idayathulla *v* Larab Sha Dharga, Panruti	(2007)2, MLJ, 1034	196
153.	Haji Ibrahim Trust *v* Madras State Wakf Board	AIR, 1965, Mad, 121	
154.	Haji Abdul Razak *v* Ali Baksh	AIR, 1946, Lah, 200	

(*Continued*)

(*Continued*)

S.No.	*Names of the parties*	*Citation*	*Page No.*
155.	Haji Anwar *v* Punjab Wakf Board	AIR, 1980, P&H, 306	109, 117
156.	Hameed Ali vs. A.P. State Wakf Board	2001 (4) ALD 594	191
157.	Hanooman Prasad *v* Babooee	6, MIA, 393	
158.	Hari Prasad *v* Usman	AIR, 1943, All 2:	
159.	Hashim Haroon *v* Gonnsali	AIR, 1942, Sind, 137:	8
160.	Hashim Hussain *v* Ahamed Raza	AIR, 1974, All, 305, (DB)	166
161.	Haveli Shah *v* Khan Shahib Shaikh	AIR, 1926, PC, 88	271
162.	Himachal Wakf Board *v* Maulana Mumtaz	AIR, 2008, H.P, 94.	
163.	Hindurao Balwant *v* Krishnarao	AIR, 1982, Bom, 216	
164.	Hindu Public vs. Rajdhani Puja Samithee	1999 (2) SCC 853	70
165.	Hussain *v* Salah	AIR, 1953, Hyd, 195	
166.	Hussain *v* Subhan Khan	AIR, 1931, Oudh, 375	
167.	Ibrahim Khan *v* Ahamed Sait	32, All, 503	8
168.	Ibrahimsab & Ors. *v* Kashimsha & Ors	AIR 2008 (NOC) 2448	
169.	Imdad Ali *v* Ashiq	AIR, 1929, Oudh, 25	
170.	India Cement *v* Union of India,	(2007) 2 SCC 181.	
171.	Intazamiya Committee *v* M.P. Wakf Board	AIR, 1996, MP, 47	214, 253,
172.	Irfan *v* Official Receiver	AIR, 1934, All, 837	
173.	Irshad Hussain *v* Makut Mandhar	AIR, 1927, All, 377	
174.	Ismail Faruqi (Dr.) *v* Union of India	AIR, 1995, SC, 605	178
175.	Ismail Haji *v* Umar Abdulla	AIR, 1929, Bom, 155	
176.	Ismail *v* Umar	AIR, 1942, Bom, 155:	
177.	Ismail *v* Wahadani	26, Bom, 308 (14), Bom, LR 120: (1918), NWN, 270	
178.	Ismail Sait *v* Hamidi Begum	AIR, 1921, Pat, 125	8
179.	Ismail Khan *v* The secretary, Tamil Nadu Wakf	(2004)4, LW, 642	
180.	J.K. Cotton Mills *v* State of Uttar Pradesh	AIR, 1961, SC, 1170	

(*Continued*)

(*Continued*)

S.No.	*Names of the parties*	*Citation*	*Page No.*
181.	Jado Singh *v* Nathur Singh	ILR, 48, All, 592	
182.	Jagan Nath Das *v* Birbhadra	19, CAL; 776	
183.	Jagir Singh *v* Ranbir Singh	AIR, 1979, SC, 381	
184.	Jahesan *v* Aybar Hussain	ILR, 7, All, 178	
185.	Jainulabudeen *v* Jainulabudeen	(1981)1, MLJ, 332 (DB)	68
186.	Jaipur Jung *v* Director of Endowment	AIR, 1963, SC, 985	
187.	Janab Khaja Hussain *v* Karnataka Board of Wakf	1997, AIHC, 4146	112, 222
188.	Janab Gori Sultan v A.P. State Wakf Board	2007 (4) ALD 31	223
189.	Janab Hisamuddin *v* Niyamathulla	(2007)2, MLJ, 1069	
190.	Jan Mohamad *v* Mohomood Ali	AIR, 1974, All, 124	
191.	Jawahara *v* Akbar	ILR, 7, All, 178, (FB)	56
192.	Jeet Mohammed *v* Jatinder	AIR 2009 HP, 44.	68, 69, 251
193.	Jeevandas *v* Kubeer-oo-deen	(1840)2, MIA,390	
194.	Jinjira *v* Fakrulla	AIR, 1922, Cal, 429:	
195.	Jugotmony *v* Ramjanee	1884 (10), Cal, 533	
196.	Kachch Wakf Board, *v* Kachch Memon Jamat,	1998, AIHC, 4943	
197.	Kadhar Sheriff *v* Tamil Nadu Wakf Board	AIR, 1987, Mad, 40:	213
198.	Kadir Ibrahim *v* Rahmatullah	33, Mad, 118: 4 IC, 136	
199.	Kadir Murthuza *v* Mohamed	AIR, 1943, Mad, 234:	62
200.	Kadiyam Mullayya *v* District Judge, Godavari	(1988)1, Andh, LT, 160	185
201.	Kagitala Venkata v. Smt. Sabarunnisa	AIR 2018 (NOC) 137, HYD	89
202.	Kaku Chanchuramana *v* Palapu Arunachalam	AIR, 1935, Mad, 857	
203.	K.M. Safiullah vs. A.P. Wakf Board	2003 (2) ALD 440, 2003 (2) ALT 253	215
204.	K.M. Shaida *v* Delhi Iron Company	1971, All, LJ, 510	
205.	K.P. Zinulabdeen *v* Tamil Nadu Wakf Board	(1991)2, LW, 678	214
206.	K.T.M. Syed Ibrahim *v* Tamil Nadu Wakf Board	(1992)2, LW, 108	

(*Continued*)

(*Continued*)

S.No.	*Names of the parties*	*Citation*	*Page No.*
207.	Karnataka Wakf Board *v* Govt. of India	1995, AIHC, 6666	74
208.	Karnataka Wakf Board *v* Govt. of India	(2004)10, SCC, 779	144
209.	Karnataka Wakf Board v Land Tribunal	AIR 2000 Kant. 141	167
210.	Karnataka State Board of Wakfs *v* Mohammed	AIR, 1982, Kant, 309	
211.	Karnataka Wakf Board *v* State of Karnataka	AIR, 1996, Kant, 55	
212.	Karnataka Wakf Board *v* State of Karnataka	AIR, 2003, SC, 2467	82
213.	Kassim *v* Hazra	AIR, 1920, Cal, 800	208
214.	Kassimiah Charitites *v* Madras State Wakf Board	AIR, 1964, Mad, 18	
215.	Kazi *v* Baalkrishna	24, Bom, 170	
216.	Kerala Wakf Board *v* Abdul Sattar	AIR, 1975, Kerala, 123	
217.	Kerala Wakf Board *v* Alam Aboobacker	AIR, 1987, Ker, 176, (DB)	
218.	Kerala Wakf Board *v* State of Kerala	AIR, 1984, Ker, 57	285
219.	Kerala Wakf Board *v* Union of India	AIR, 1975, Ker, 123, (DB)	236
220.	Kerala Wakf Board *v* Valia Maliyekkal	AIR, 1985, Ker, 228	
221.	Khader Sheriff *v* Tamil Nadu Wakf Board	AIR, 1987, Mad4 0:	
222.	Khajah Soleman *v* Nawab Salimullah	AIR, 1922, PC, 107:	29
223.	Khajeh Salimulla *v* Abdul Khair	37, Cal, 263	208
224.	Khaji Mohamed *v* Majiday Jamait Committee	AIR, 1940, Mad, 167	296
225.	Khalil Ahamad *v* Sheik Mohammed	AIR, 1965, All, 320	57
226.	Khaliluddin *v* Sriram	AIR, 1934, All, 176:	
227.	Khan Bahadur *v* The Assistant Controller,	(1961)2, MLJ, 372	
228.	Khatoon v.Allahtala Malik Waqf	AIR 2018 (NOC) 212 (ALL)	
229.	Kidambi Raghavachariyar *v* Thiramalai Ansari	26, Mad, 113	

(*Continued*)

(*Continued*)

S.No.	*Names of the parties*	*Citation*	*Page No.*
230.	Kulsam Bi *v* Mohamed Sattar	AIR, 1948, Nag, 183	7
231.	Kulsom Bibee *v* Gulam	(1905)10, Cal, WN, 449	
232.	Kuttavan *v* Mamona	ILR, 35, Mad, 681;	
233.	Kuvarbai *v* Miralam	7, Bom, 170	
234.	Lala Hem Chand *v* Lalapearey	AIR, 1942, PC, 64	
235.	Lala Jhaolal *v* Ahamdulla	AIR, 1934, All, 335	
236.	Lanco Hills Technology Park vs. Mahaboob Alam Khan	2012 (4) ALD 385, 2012 (4) ALT 136 (DB)	179, 255
237.	Latifunnisa *v* Shaharbanu	AIR, 1932, Oudh, 108	
238.	Luchimipal *v* Amiralam	ILR, (1882)9, Cal, 176	8, 9
239.	M.A. Azeem Baig *v* A.P. State Wakf Board,	AIR 2010 (NOC) A.P. 922.	123
240.	M.A. Aziz *v* A.P. State Wakf Board	AIR, 1998, AP, 61	124
241.	Macci Mhader Saheb Darga Committee, Adoni v Shaikan Bee	2011 (4) ALT 812 (DB)	253
242.	Macduff, *in re*	(1896)2 CH, 463	
243.	Madanuri Srirama v. Syed Jalal	AIR 2017 SC 2653	153
244.	Madras Wakf Board *v* Jamal	1966(2), MLJ, 103	
245.	Madras Wakf Board *v* Kazi Mohiuddin	1974 (1), MLJ, 258	
246.	Madras State Wakf Board *v* Jamal Mohammad	(1966) 2, MLJ, 104	269
247.	Madras Wakf Board *v* Kazi Moideen	AIR, 1974, Mad, 225	
248.	Madras State Wakf Board *v* Mohamed	(1971)84, LW, 261	
249.	Madras State Wakf Board *v* Revenue Divisional Officer	(1966)1, MLJ, 212	
250.	Mahabab Hussain *v* Nasirudeen	AIR, 1928, Nag, 44	
251.	Mahabir Prasad *v* Syed Mustafa	AIR, 1937, PC, 174:	8
252.	Mahachalar Rahman *v* Faizur Rahman	35, IC, 880, Cal	7,8
253.	Mahant Beseshwar *v* Sashinath	AIR, 1943, Pat, 289	
254.	Mahanth Singh *v* U Ba Yi	AIR, 1939, PC, 110	
255.	Maharashtra State Board of Wakfs vs. Shaikh Yusuf Bhai Chawla	2012 (5) SCR 1014	156

(*Continued*)

(*Continued*)

S.No.	*Names of the parties*	*Citation*	*Page No.*
256.	Mahazar Hussain *v* Abdul Hadi	ILR, (1911)33, All, 400: 9 IC, 753	7, 8
257.	Mahendra Nath *v* Delraddi	AIR, 1966, Cal, 285 (FB)	
258.	Majlis-e-shura Dasti Parcha vs. A.P. Wakf Board, Hyderabad	1998 (5) ALD 236, 1998 (5) ALT 261	280
259.	Majlis *v* State of Karnataka	AIR, 2003, Kant, 81	
260.	M.L. Azeez *v* Secretary Wakf Board	1204 of 1965	
261.	Ma Mi *v* Kalandrammal	AIR, 1927, PC, 22:	
262.	Management Committee V. State of Uttarakhand	AIR 2017 UTTARAKHAND 87	
263.	Management Committee v. State of Uttarakhand	AIR 2017 UTTARAKH 87	197
264.	Managing Committee Mysore *v* State of Karnataka	1998, AIHC, 2723	222
265.	Managing Committee Ekra Mosque *v* State of Bihar	AIR, 2004, Jhar, 3	144, 152
266.	Managing Committee, Masjid-e-Ibrahimia v. Hyderabad Allwyn Metal Works Ltd	AIR 2006 AP 330 2006 (4) ALD 769	297
267.	Managing Committee, Wakf v. State Of Andhra Pradesh	2000 (5) ALT 626	279, 281
268.	Manickchand *v* Saleh Mohamed	AIR, 1969, SC, 571	
269.	Manjula Varsheney vs. A.P. State Wakf Board	2000 (1) ALD 452, 1999(6) ALT 725	135
270.	Mansoor Kasim Mulla *v* Guddu	AIR 2010 (NOC) Bom 835, AIR 2010 (NOC) BOM 835	121
271.	Manzoor Ahmad *v* State	AIR 2008 (NOC) 1177	
272.			
273.	Mariambai *v* Md. Jaffar Rahim	AIR, 1973, Mad, 191	8
274.	Mariambi *v* Fatmabi	31, Bom, LR, 135	
275.	Markaz Constructions *v* Sugra Humayun Wakf	AIR, 1996, SC, 2763:	171, 279
276.	Mashuddin *v* Bullabah	ILR, (1912)35, All 68: 17 IC, 471	
277.	Masjid-e-Islamabad *v* Karnataka Wakf Board	AIR, 1981, Kant, 154	280

(*Continued*)

(*Continued*)

S.No.	*Names of the parties*	*Citation*	*Page No.*
278.	Masjid Shahid Ganj *v* Gurdwara Committee	AIR, 1940, PC, 116	64
279.	Masood Ali *v* Zabid Ali	AIR, 1954, All, 355	
280.	Masuda Begum & Ors v Roushan Ali	AIR 2019 Cal 275	153
281.	Maula Bu *v* Hafizuddin	AIR, 1926, Lah, 372	
282.	Maulana Mustafa *v* Union of India	AIR, 2002, Guj, 252	
283.	Maule Shah *v* Ghane Shah	AIR, 1938, PC, 202	
284.	Maulvi Mohamed Fahimul Haq *v* Jegat Bullay	ILR, (1923)2, Pat, 391	
285.	Maulvi Rahman *v* Sardar Maqbool	AIR 2009 All, 62	207
286.	Maulvi Reza Ansari *v* Shyamlal Shah	AIR, 1983, Pat, 297	166
287.	Mayadhar Subudhi Tana *v* Orissa Board of Wakfs	AIR, 1966, Ori, 208	
288.	Mazbar Ali *v* Mardaj	AIR, 1958, AP, 8	
289.	Mazfar Hussain *v* Adiya Saran	AIR, 1948, PC, 42:	
290.	M. Bikshapathi vs. Government of A. P	1999 (6) ALD 270 (BD)	79, 252
291.	Md. Ali *v* Dinesh Chandra	AIR, 1940, Cal, 417	
292.	Md. Admad Ali v Arastu Talimi Trust Hyd	2994 (1) ALD 99, 2003 (6) ALT 594	145
293.	Mohd. Idris Baba vs. Uttarkhand Wakf Board	AIR 2013 Uttarakhand 72	77, 136, 216
294.	Md. Immam *v* B. B. Mariam	ILR, 8, Pat, 484	
295.	Md. Moinuddin *v* Md. Mustafa	AIR 2010 Pat 24	
296.	Meeran Sahib *v* Madras Wakf Board	1967, MLJ, 425	
297.	Meran Bakh *v* Gulam Nabi	14, Lah, 624	
298.	Minorities Welfare Association, Hyd vs. Syed Shah Akbar Nizamuddin	2011 (6) ALD 722	77
299.	Miru *v* Ramgopal	AIR, 1935, All, 891:	60
300.	Mirza Fida *v* Yakub	1925, PC, 101	
301.	M. Govinda Rao *v* Andhra Pradesh Wakf Board	AIR 2008 (NOC) 1901	282, 286
302.	Mir Qamar *v* A.P.State Wakf Board,	2011 (5) ALD, 407.	228
303.	Mohamed Afzal *v* Din Mohamed	AIR, 1947, Lah, 117	

(*Continued*)

(*Continued*)

S.No.	*Names of the parties*	*Citation*	*Page No.*
304.	Mohamed Ali *v* Kader	(1999)2, LW, 36	
305.	Mohamed Bibi *v* Sulaiman	AIR, 1926, Mad, 1110	
306.	Mohamed Hasan *v* Umardaras	ILR, 29, All, 633	
307.	Mohamed *v* Tamil Nadu Wakf Board	(1980)1, MLJ, 235	
308.	Mohd. Imadullah *v* Mst. Bismilla	AIR, 1922, PC 384	
309.	Mohamed Ismail Ariff *v* Ahmed	ILR, 43, Cal, 1085: 35 IC 30: (1916)43, IA, 127	
310.	Mohamed Jafar *v* Taqi Khan	AIR, 1933, Oudh, 517: ILR (1934)9, Luck 170:	
311.	Mohamed Karim *v* Abdul Gaffor	AIR, 1964, MP, 227	
312.	Mohamed Mahin *v* Madras State Wakf Board	(1967)1, MLJ, 65	62
313.	Mohd. Mohideen *v* State Wakf Board	AIR, 1963, Mad, 132	
314.	Mohamed Rustom Ali *v* Mustaq Hussain	AIR, 1921, PC, 105:	
315.	Mohamed Sabir Ali *v* Tahir Ali	AIR, 1957, All, 94	
316.	Md. Saleem ur Rahman vs. A.P. State Wakf Board	2007 (4) ALT 834	113
317.	Mohamed Shafindeen *v* Catur Bhaj	1958, Raj, LW, 461	
318.	Mohamed Shah *v* Fasihudeen Ansari	AIR, 1956, SC, 713	
319.	Mohamed Wasi *v* Bachchan Sahib	AIR, 1955, All, 68	
320.	Mohammed Yusuf v Inspector General of Registration Patna	AIR 1980 PAT 138	151
321.	Mohamed Yasin *v* Rahmath	AIR, 1947, All, 201 (FB):	
322.	Mohamed Yusuf *v* Mohamed Sadiq	AIR, 1933, Lah, 501:	9
323.	Mohammed Ali *v* Dinesh	AIR, 1940, Cal, 417	
324.	Mohammed Badrul *v* Shah Hasan	AIR, 1935, All, 278:	
325.	Mohammed Raza *v* Yadgar Hussain	AIR, 1924, PC, 109	
326.	Mohammed Sabeer Ali *v* Thahir Ali	AIR, 1957, All, 94	
327.	Mohammed Sait *v* Mst. Sakina Begum	AIR, 1935, Lah, 626,	

(*Continued*)

(*Continued*)

S.No.	*Names of the parties*	*Citation*	*Page No.*
328.	Mohammed *v* Mohammed	(1996)10, SCC, 705	56
329.	Mohammad Zafar *v* State of U.P.	AIR 2008 (NOC) 1174	
330.	Mohammedia Co-operative *v* Lakshmi Srinivasa Co-operative Building Society	AIR 2007 (NOC) 1459.	171
331.	Mohd. Abdul Jabbar *v* Mohd. Ghulam	AIR 2008 (NOC) 1175 (A.P)	172
332.	Mohd. Harun & Anr. *v* Nissar Ahmed	AIR 2008 (NOC) 2767	
333.	Mohd. Idris *v*. Uttaranchal Wakf Board	AIR 2013 Uttarakhand 72	136
334.	Mohesh Narain Munshi *v* Tarucknath Moitra	20, IA, 30, (PC)	
335.	Moideen Bibi Ammai *v* Ratnavelu Mudali	AIR, 1927, Mad, 69	
336.	Mokshamdanlal *v* Hariprasad Vishnuprasad	AIR, 1959, Bom, 650	
337.	Moqattar Raza *v* Joint Director Uttar Pradesh	AIR, 1970, All, 509	203
338.	Motishah *v* Abdul Gaffar	AIR, 1956, Nag, 38, 42	
339.	Morice *v* Bishop of Durham	(1804)10, Ves, 522	
340.	Moulvee Abdoolah *v* Rajeswari Dossea	(1946)7, Sch. Rep, 268	
341.	M.P. Wakf Board vs. Subhan Shah	(2006) 10 SCC 696	79
342.	M/S Gammon India Ltd vs. Spl. Chief Secretary	(2006) 3 SCC 354	305
343.	Mothukur *v* Pandanna	2010 (1) ALD 76 (DB)	169
344.	M.S. Hameed *v* Mohamed	AIR, 2003, Mad, 179	
345.	M.S.S. Wakf Board College *v* Mohamed	(2006)1, LW, 386	
346.	M/s. Mahalakshmi Oil Mills *v* Andhra Pradesh	AIR, 1989, SC, 335	
347.	Mst. Ayesha Bibi *v* Commissioner of Wakfs, Bengal	AIR, 1970, SC, 287	271
348.	Mst. Aziza Kabathin *v* State of West Bengal	AIR, 1984, Cal, 326	209
349.	Mst. Bibi Kubra *v* Jainandan	AIR, 1955, Pat, 270	
350.	Mst. Bismillah *v* Muhammed Ali	AIR, 1927, Oudh, 85	

(*Continued*)

(*Continued*)

S.No.	*Names of the parties*	*Citation*	*Page No.*
351.	Mst. Mubarak Jan *v* Mst. Taj Begam	AIR, 1938, Lah, 453	
352.	Mst. Musharaf Begam *v* Mt. Sikarndar	AIR, 1928, All, 516:	
353.	M/s. Namrita Construction *v* State of Bihar	AIR, 2009 (NOC) 3021 (Pat).	172
354.	Mst. Peeran *v* Hafiz Md.	AIR, 1966, All, 201	
355.	Mst. Zohra Khaton *v* Janab Mohammed	AIR, 1978, Cal, 133	
356.	Mst. Rukia Begam *v* Surajmal	AIR, 1936, All, 404	
357.	Mt. Abadi Begum *v* Khaniz Zanib	AIR, 1927, PC, 2	
358.	Mt. Ali Begam *v* Badr-ul-Islam Ali	AIR, 1938, PC, 184:	58
359.	Mubarak Ali *v* Ahmed Ali	AIR, 1935, Lah, 414:	
360.	Muhamed Bibi *v* Sulaiman	AIR, 1926, Mad, 1110	
361.	Muhammad Rustom *v* Mustaq	AIR, 1921, PC, 105:	
362.	Muhammad *v* Razia	32, IA, 86	
363.	Muhammed Ayub *v* Amir	AIR, 1939, Cal, 268: 43,	
364.	Mukarram *v* Anjuman-un-Nissa	AIR, 1924, All, 223:	9
365.	Mukram Sherif *v* Moideen Sherif	(2005)2, LW, 615, (DB)	261
366.	Mulla Rahim Saheb and Ors. *v* A.P. State Wakf	1997, (2), ALD, 79	208
367.	Mundaria *v* Shyam Sunder	AIR, 1963, Patna, 98	
368.	Muneerul Islamic Sangam *v* Valiya Peedikakal	AIR, 2004, Ker, 311	
369.	Murdan Sardar *v* Secretary of State	AIR, 1939, Cal, 313	
370.	Muppu Raju *v* A.P. State Wakf Board	2010 (3) ALD 263.	189
371.	Musaliar vs. T.K. Muhammad Sahib	AIR 2003 KER 84	260
372.	Musahib Khan *v* Rajkumar	AIR, 1938, Oudh, 238:	
373.	Musharaj *v* Siccander	AIR, 1928, All, 518	
374.	Muslim Minority Front *v* Govt. A.P.,	1996(2) ALT, 30;	107, 306
375.	Muslim Orphanage *v* Khatoon Bi	AIR, 1958, Mys, 28	7
376.	Muslim Wakfs, Rajasthan vs. Radhakrishnan	AIR1979 SC 289	

(*Continued*)

(*Continued*)

S.No.	*Names of the parties*	*Citation*	*Page No.*
377.	Mutawalli Larabsha Dharga v Panruti Municipality	CRP (NPD) 1607, 2916, 2320/2010	191, 257
378.	Muzafar Ahamed *v* Indrakumar Das	AIR, 1944, Cal, 40	
379.	Mysore Board of Wakfs *v* Lakshmiah Setty	AIR, 1974, Kant, 28	
380.	N.A. Azeezullah *v* T.N. Wakf Board	WA 109 of 1980	
381.	Namira Construction v Fazal Imam Charitable Trust	AIR 2019 (NOC) 473 PAT	180
382.	Nagindas *v* Mohamed	ILR, 46, Bom, 312	
383.	Nagma Begum v Board of Wakfs	AIR 2019 (NOC) 188 CAL	221
384.	Nanak Chandra *v* Chandra Kishore	AIR, 1970, SC, 446	
385.	Nanda Seshikala v. A.P.State Wakf Board	2003 (5) ALD 796, 2003 (5) ALT 466	193
386.	Nanhoon Beg *v* Gulam	AIR, 1951, Nag, 314	
387.	Naraini Devi (Smt.) *v* Smt. Ramo Devi	AIR, 1976, SC, 2198	
388.	Narayanamoorthy *v* Achayya Sastrulu	AIR, 1925, Mad, 411	133
389.	Narayan Pershad *v* State of Hyderabad	AIR, 1955, Hyd, 82	
390.	Nashoda Khatoon *v* Md. Ibrahim	AIR, 1932, Cal, 93	
391.	Nawab Sayed Ali *v* Iffat Hameedi Begum	AIR, 1942, Cal, 180	
392.	Nawab Shahrukh *v* Sayed Inayat	AIR, 1975, All, 452	
393.	Nawab Usman Ali *v* Choudry Faezullah	AIR, 1959, MP, 377	48
394.	Nawab Zain *v* Director of Endowments	AIR, 1963, SC, 985	59
395.	Nazira *v* Sukhdarshan	1936, All, LJ, 651	
396.	Nimi Chand Adya *v* Gulam Hossain	(1909)37 Cal, 179: 3 IC, 353	173, 177
397.	Noor Mohamed *v* U.P. Sunni Wakf Board	(2003)11, SCC, 782	
398.	O.M.S. Udman *v* Tamil Nadu Wakf Board	(2004)4, LW, 274	215

(*Continued*)

(*Continued*)

S.No.	*Names of the parties*	*Citation*	*Page No.*
399.	Palani Muslim Dharmaparipalana Sangam *v* Tamil Nadu Wakf Board	(1975)1, MLJ, 201	
400.	Palaniappa Chetty *v* Devasikamany	44, IA, 147: 40, Mad 709 (PC)	
401.	Pannalal Patil *v* State of Andhra Pradesh	AIR, 1996, SC, 1023	
402.	P. A. Sulaiman *v* Hanafi Jumanath	1996, AIHC, 2760	
403.	Pathukutti *v* Avathalakutti	ILR, (1988)13, Mad, 66 (FB)	
404.	Pathukutti Umma *v* Nedungudi Bank	AIR, 1937, Mad, 731:	
405.	Peeran Sahib *v* Madras State Wakf Board	1967, MLJ, 425	
406.	Phul Chand *v* Akbar	ILR (1896)19, All, 211	8
407.	Piran *v* Abdul Karim	ILR, (1891)19, Cal, 203	204
408.	P.K. Kutty Haji *v* State of Kerala	AIR, 2009 (NOC) 596 (Ker).	110
409.	P.K.Hamza v Kerala State Wakf Board	AIR 2019 KER 182	191
410.	P.K.M. Kutty Haji *v* State of Kerala	AIR 2009 (NOC) 596 Ker	110, 115
411.	P. Mohammed Dastagir *v* Karnataka Board of Wakf	AIR, 1998, Kant, 297	218
412.	P.M. Venkatachalapathy *v* Syed Anwar	(2006)1, LW, 803	
413.	P.S. Abdul Kadir vs. Mahlar Rathul Kadiria Sabha Kayalpattinam	AIR 1953 Mad 143	177, 178
414.	P. Radhakrishnaiah. *v* A.P.Wakf Board	AIR 2008 (NOC) 569 A.P	172
415.	Praful Goradia v Union of India	(2011) 1 SCR 579	95
416.	Pragdasji Bhagwandasji *v* Ishwarlalbhai	AIR, 1952, SC, 143	
417.	P. Rama Rao *v* High Court of A.P.,	2000 (1), ALD, 298 (DB)	262
418.	Privy Council *v* Vave Lebbai Marakkayar	41, IA, 21, (PC)	
419.	Pullin Behari *v* Davar	AIR, 1946, Cal, 83:	
420.	Punjab Wakf Board *v* Shakur Masih	AIR, 1997, SC, 104	

(*Continued*)

(*Continued*)

S.No.	Names of the parties	Citation	Page No.
421.	Punjab Wakf Board *v* Gram Panchayat	AIR, 2000 SC 3488	83, 85
422.	Punjab Wakf Board *v* Vijay Kumar	AIR, 2009 (NOC) 2465 (P&H).	
423.	Puratabur Co. *v* Cane Commissioner, Bihar	AIR, 1970, SC, 1986	
424.	Quadir Baksh *v* Sadullah	AIR, 1938, Oudh 77:	
425.	Quebeca Light Heating Power *v* Bandary	AIR, 1920, PC, 181	
426.	Radhakanta *v* Commissioner Endowments,	AIR, 1981, SC, 798	
427.	Radhakrishnan *v* State of Rajasthan	AIR, 1967, Raj,1	67, 69, 75
428.	Rahiman *v* Bagridan	AIR, 1936, Oudh, 213:	
429.	Rahmath Bi *v* State Wakf Board	AIR, 1982, Mad, 202	
430.	Rahmatullah Khaleem *v* A.P. Wakf Board	AIR, 1983, AP, 116	
431.	Raichand J. Shah *v* State of Tamil Nadu	(2002) 4, LW, 213	134, 285
432.	Raja Khan vs. U.P. Sunni Central Waqf Board	(2010) 13 (ADDL) SCR 1131	179, 257
433.	Raja of Palghat *v* Raman Unni	41, Mad, 4	
434.	Ramanathan Chettiar *v* Vava Labbai	ILR (1911)34, Mad, 12	8, 9
435.	Ram Charan *v* Fatima	ILR(1915)42, Cal, 933:	7, 8
436.	Ramdhani *v* Jankirai	AIR, 1971, All, 553	197
437.	Ramesh Gobindram *v* Sugra Humayun Wakf	AIR, 2010 SC, 2897, AP.	255
438.	Ramineni *v* Government of A.P.	2010 (4) ALD 710	172, 281
439.	Ram Murthi *v* Puran Singh	AIR, 1963, Punj, 393	
440.	Rana Parween Siddiqui v. Union of India	AIR 2018 Delhi 90	108
441.	Ranjan *v* Mst. Rahmani	AIR, 1932, Oudh, 71	
442.	Rao Sir Bahadur Singh *v* State of Uttar Pradesh	AIR, 1953, SC, 394	
443.	Rasamaya Chowduri *v* Abul Fata	ILR (1891)18, Cal, 399	61
444.	Rashid Unnisha *v* Ata Rasool	AIR, 1958, All, 67	63
445.	Rashiduddin *v* Nasiruddin	AIR, 1929, Lah, 721	
446.	Rashuddin *v* Atarh	AIR, 1958, All, 67	

(*Continued*)

(*Continued*)

S.No.	*Names of the parties*	*Citation*	*Page No.*
447.	Ratilal Gandhi *v* State of Bombay	AIR, 1954, SC, 388	42, 48, 49, 100
448.	Raushar Ali *v* Mohamed Sherif	AIR, 1936, Lah, 87	
449.	Rengasamy Goundan *v* Alagayammal	AIR, 1915, Mad, 1133	
450.	Rengasamy Naidu *v* Krishnasamy Iyer	44, MLJ, 116	
451.	Riland, *in re*	1881, WN, 173	
452.	Rudramurthy *v* Karnataka Wakf Board	AIR, 1977, Kant, 147	184
453.	Runchordas *v* Parvathi	23, Bom, 725	
454.	Ruqia Begum *v* Surajmal	AIR, 1936, All, 404	
455.	Saalmi Haji v Muhammedkutty	AIR 2019 (NOC) 778(KER)	
456.	Sachindranath Rai *v* Mahraj Bahadur Singh	AIR, 1922, PC, 187	
457.	Sackville-West *v* Holmesdale Viscount	(1870)4, HL, 543	
458.	Sahruvan Nachiar *v* G.S. Mohamed Hussain	AIR, 2001, Mad, 36	
459.	Sailendranath *v* Hade Kaza	AIR, 1932, Cal, 456:	176
460.	Saith Kapor *v* Jagmohan	AIR, 1981, SC, 136	
461.	Sajjadanashin Mia Baksh *v* Allah Bi	(1921) 8, (Lah. 111)	
462.	Sajjad Ali Khan *v* Jagmohandas	4 CWN, 320	
463.	Sakina *v* Laddan	2, Cal, LJ, 218	
464.	Salam Khan *v* Tamil Nadu Wakf Board	(2005) 1 LW, 676	253, 261
465.	Saleb Khan *v* Madar Sahib	AIR, 1954, Ori, 239	177
466.	Salebhai *v* Safiabee	(1912)36, Bom, LR, III	
467.	S. Moosa *v* Tamil Nadu Wakf Board	(2003)2, LW, 44	
468.	Samuthra Vijaya *v* Sirukadambur Masjid	(2007)4 MLJ, 580	264
469.	Sardar Khan *v* Syed Najmul Hassan	(2007) 3, MLJ, 366, (SC)	88, 264
470.	Sarkum vs. Rehman Baksh	1896-1824 Cal. 83 p.91	18
471.	Satdas *v* Rambai	21, IC, 275	8
472.	Sattar Ismail *v* Hameed	AIR, 1944, Mad, 504:	8
473.	Sattar Khan v High School Boarding Committee	(2018) 4 SCC 613	71

(*Continued*)

(*Continued*)

S.No.	*Names of the parties*	*Citation*	*Page No.*
474.	Sayed Abdul Vasit *v* Addl. Civil Judge	Air, 2009 (NOC) 1394 (Raj).	261
475.	Sayed Md. *v* Sayed Gobar	ILR, 6, Bom, 88	
476.	Sayed Muhammed *v* Badagara Jamath Committee	AIR, 2004, SC, 4365	167, 225
477.	Sayyed Ali *v* Andhra Pradesh Wakf Board	(1998)2, SCC, 642;	
478.	Secretary Mahakuma *v* U.P. Sunni Wakf Board	1984, LLJ, 37	
479.	Shah Wajihuddin *v* Shah Murtaza	AIR, 1930, Oudh, 32	
480.	Shahar Banoo *v* Aga Mohamed	34, IA, 46	
481.	Shahzadee *v* Khaja Hussain	(1869)12, WR, 498	
482.	Shaik Ameer and Another vs. A.P. State Wakf Board	2007 (5) ALT 221	254
483.	Shaikh Bashir Ahamed *v* Shaik Jabbar	AIR, 1968, Pat, 29	
484.	Shaik Ghouse *v* State Wakf Board	AIR, 2002, AP, 344	208
485.	Shaik Mastan Sahib *v* Palayani Balarami	AIR, 1953, Mad, 958	
486.	Shaikh Yusuf Bhai Chawala vs. State of Maharashtra	AIR 2012 (NOC) 112 Bom. 2012 (5) SCR 1014	102, 103, 156,
487.	Shama Churan Roy *v* Abdul Kabeer	3, CWN, 158	
488.	Shameem Sulthana *v* Syed Ibrahim	2011 (4) ALD 379.	
489.	Shamimul Haque vs. State Of Bihar	AIR (2019) Pat 26	186
490.	Shamsuddin *v* Tuticorin Jamia Masjid	AIR, 1984, Mad, 276	
491.	Shanmugham *v* T.N.State Wakf Board,	AIR, 1999, Mad, 96	267
492.	Sk. Abdul Saleem vs. A.P. State Wakf Board	2006 (2) ALD 501, 2006 (2) ALT 76	223
493.	S.K. Habibuddin *v* Orissa Board of Wakf	1998, AIHC, 4833	
494.	Sheikh Mohamed *v* Shah Trust	(2004),1, LW, 425	
495.	Shoukat Ali Ansari *v* State of Rajasthan	AIR, 1999, Raj, 175	108

(*Continued*)

(*Continued*)

S.No.	Names of the parties	Citation	Page No.
496.	Shia Youngmen *v* Syed Fatah Ali Shah	AIR, 1941, Lah, 145 (FB):	
497.	Siraj ul Haq *v* Board of Wakfs	1959, SCJ, 367	
498.	Siraj ul-Khan's case	AIR, 1959, SC, 198	
499.	Soofi Shah Sabir Ali v Union of India (UOI),	2010 (1) ALT 112	281
500.	Smt. Faiqa Khatoon *v* Riyazur Rahman	AIR, 2009 (NOC) 1703All	
501.	Smt. Kamla Mohini v. H.P. Waqf Board Shimla	AIR 2019 HP1	80
502.	Smt. Kubra Khatoon v. Allahtala Malik Waqf	AIR 2018 (NOC) 212 (ALL)	265
503.	Smt. Salma *v* Uttarakhand Waqf Board	AIR, 2009 (NOC) 3023 (Utr).	185
504.	Sri Radhakrishna Rice Mill Co. *v* Jumma Majeed	AIR, 2003, AP, 70	
505.	Sri Silambani Devasthanam, *v* Chidambaram	AIR, 1943, Mad, 691	
506.	State of Bombay *v* R.M.D. Chamarbaugwala	AIR, 1957, SC, 679	
507.	State of West Bengal *v* Union of India	AIR, 1963, SC, 1241	
508.	State Wakf Board, Madras *v* Abdul Azeez	(1967)1, MLJ, 190	
509.	Subhan Shah *v* M.P. Wakf Board	AIR, 1997, MP, 8	251
510.	Subramania Aiyar *v* Prayag Dossjee Varu	AIR, 1917, Mad, 355	
511.	Sufi Tafseer Mohammad vs. State of M P	WP. NO. 9935/2011	193
512.	Sultana Begum *v* Prem Chand	AIR, 1997, SC, 1006	
513.	Sunnath Mosque Committee Puliampatti *v* Land Administration Commissioner	(1998)1, LW, 69, (SN)	
514.	Sunni Central Board of Wakfs *v* Sirajul	AIR, 1954, All, 88	7
515.	Syed Ahamed *v* Julaiha Bibi	AIR, 1947, Mad, 176:	8
516.	Syed Ahmed *v* Hafiz Zahid	AIR, 1934, (A11), 732	
517.	Syed Akbar Shah *v* T.N. Wakf Board	1978, TNLJ, 410	204
518.	Syed Ali Jasser *v* Shafi	1981, All, LJ, 669	
519.	Syed Ali *v* Syed Mohamed	AIR, 1928, Pat, 441:	9

(*Continued*)

(*Continued*)

S.No.	*Names of the parties*	*Citation*	*Page No.*
520.	Sayyed Ali and Others *v* A.P. Wakf Board,	AIR, 1998, SC, 972 (1998) 2 SCC 642	84, 85, 293
521.	Syed Akbar Nizamuddin *v* Mohd. Hashim	2011 (6) ALD, 86.	
522.	Syed Ansaruddin *v* T.N Wakf Board	(1992)2, LW, 685	
523.	Syed Anwar Basha *v* Jamia Masjid, Karur	(1966)1, MLJ, 379	
524.	Syed Edullah Shah *v* State Wakf Board	AIR, 1966, Mad, 439:	
525.	Syed Fazal Pookoya *v* Union of India	AIR, 1993, Ker, 398	101
526.	Syed Enayathullah *v* State of Karnataka	AIR, 2004, Kant, 295	215
527.	Syed Hameed *v* Tamil Nadu Wakf Board	(2000)1, LW, 623	
528.	Syed Hasan *v* Muzaffarpur Properties Pvt. Ltd.	AIR 2008 (NOC) 2675	55
529.	Syed Jamil Ahmed v Meer Ahmed Khan	2002 (6) ALD 318, 2002 (5) ALT 174	210
530.	Syed Khersha *v* Bhuj Municipality	AIR, 1986, Guj,1	166
531.	Syed Ahmad *v* Shia Board of Waqf, U. P.	AIR 2009, All, 38.	
532.	Syed Shah Tayyab Khadri v. State of Karnataka	AIR 2019 KAR 201	
533.	Syed Mohamed Labie *v* Md. Hanifa	AIR, 1976, SC, 1569	7, 57, 60
534.	Syed Mohideen *v* Sofia Khatun	AIR, 1940, Cal, 167	
535.	Syed v Ramanathapura Peria Mogallam Jamath	(2010) 8 SCR 777	250
536.	Syed Mohammad Khan *v* Waqf Board	AIR, 2009 (NOC) 198 (All).	
537.	Syed Moinuddin *v* T.N.Wakf Board	(1998)1, LW, 134	
538.	Syed Moinuddin *v* Tamil Nadu Wakf Board,	AIR, 1998, Mad, 129	
539.	Syed Muhammad *v* Shia Central Board of Waqf	AIR 2009 All, 38	206
540.	Syed Munavvaruddin *v* Chief Executive Officer, A.P. Wakf Board	2007 (3) ALD 711	286, 302, 303

(*Continued*)

(*Continued*)

S.No.	*Names of the parties*	*Citation*	*Page No.*
541.	Syed Muneer vs. Chief Executive Officer, A.P. State Wakf Board, Hyd	2001 (4) ALD 430 (DB)	252
542.	Syed Muzaffer Hussain *v* State of U.P.	1984, LLJ, 31	280
543.	Syeda Nazira Khatoon vs Syed Zahiruddin Ahmed Baghdadi	AIR 2019 SC 4676	203
544.	Syed Pershah *v* Tamil Nadu Wakf Board	(1976)89, LW, 708	
545.	Syed Shah Kadiri *v* Mohamed Lebbai	(1958)2, MLJ, 199	
546.	Syed Shah Hussaini *v* Union of India	AIR, 1999, Kant, 112	135
547.	Syed Shah Kazim *v* Syed Abi Saghir	AIR, 1932, Pat, 33:	65, 206
548.	Syed Shah Raju Hussaini v A.P. State Wakf Board	2007 (3) ALD 345, 2007 (2) ALT 511	210
549.	Syed Shah Tayyab Khadri vs. State of Karnataka	AIR 2019 Kar 201	216
550.	Syed Sibte Rasul *v* Sibte Nabi	AIR, 1943, All, 74:	9
551.	Syed Waqarul Ahad *v* State of Rajasthan	AIR 2009 (NOC) 3022 Raj	
552.	T.A. Ahammed Kabeer V. State of Kerala	AIR 2017 (NOC) 72 KER	109
553.	Tamil Nadu State Wakf Board *v* Hatija	AIR, 2002, SC, 402	79, 267
554.	Tamil Nadu Wakf Board *v* Hadhija (dead) by LRs	AIR, (2002)1, LW, 384, (SC)	
555.	T.Nadu Wakf Board *v* M. Ebrahim Musuee	AIR, 1979, Mad, 231	64
556.	T.N. Board *v* S.A. Syed Masood	(1995) 2, LW, 308	183
557.	T.Nadu. Wakf Board *v* S.J. Syed Basha	(2000)2, LW, 510	67
558.	T.N. Wakf Board *v* Syed Imam Sahib	AIR, 1983, Mad, 297	
559.	T.E. Mohamed Sheriff *v* Superintendent of Wakfs, Central Zone	AIR, 1971, Mad, 243	214
560.	T.Kaliamurthi *v* Five Gori Thaikal Wakf	AIR, 2009, SC 840 Mad	297
561.	T.M. Muhammed Sahib v Arakkal Mohammed Ibrahim	AIR 2007 (NOC) 104 KER	263

(*Continued*)

(*Continued*)

S.No.	*Names of the parties*	*Citation*	*Page No.*
562.	T. Shivalingam *v* A.P. Wakf Tribunal	1999 (3), ALD, 646	89, 252
563.	T.S. Yusuf *v* Tamil Nadu Wakf Board	AIR, 1982, Mad, 115	
564.	Thakur Md. Ismail *v* Thakur Shabir Ali	AIR, 1962, SC, 1722	
565.	Thangachi Nachial *v* Ahamed Hussain	(1957)1, MLJ, 300	183
566.	Thanka Mayil *v* Pappa Fathima Bibi	(1960)1, Mad, LJ, 150	
567.	Thayyil Kunhi Mohammed *v* Darul Academy	AIR 2008 (NOC) 1178	153
568.	The Cantonment Board, Ambala *v* Piyarilal	AIR, 1966, SC, 108	
569.	The Commissioner, Hindu Religious Endowments, Madras *v* Swamiar Shriur Mutt,	AIR, 1962, SC, 1733	
570.	The Commissioner, Hindu Endowments v. Sri Lakshmindra Thirtha Swamiar	AIR 1954 SC 282	47, 100, 101
571.	The Executive Committee *v* P.A.G. Hussain	(1996)2, LW, 788	
572.	Thorayil Juma Masjid *v* Kerala Wakf Board,	AIR 2007 (NOC) 1341 Ker.	236, 253
573.	Tilkayat Shri Govindlalji *v* State of Rajashtan	AIR, 1963, SC, 1638	42, 50
574.	T.S.A. Guptha vs. Joint Collector-II	2008 (2) ALD 184	79
575.	Tulsamma's case	AIR, 1977, SC, 1944;	
576.	U. Mohamed Khalilullah *v* Tamil Nadu Wakf	(2006)3, MLJ, 856	
577.	Union of India *v* T.R. Verma	AIR, 1957, SC, 882	
578.	U.P. Sunni Board Wakfs *v* Mazhar Hassan	AIR, 2001, SC, 3359	55
579.	Usman Ali Khan *v* Faezullah	AIR, 1959, MP, 377	100
580.	Usman Sahib *v* Karnataka Board of Wakf	AIR, 1996, MP, 47	
581.	Usman *v* Karnataka Board of Wakf	AIR, 1932, Pat, 33	
582.	Uttar Pradesh Sunni Central Wakf *v* Sirajul Haq	AIR, 1963, All 537	
583.	Vembu *v* Srinivasa	23, MLJ, 638	

(*Continued*)

(*Continued*)

S.No.	*Names of the parties*	*Citation*	*Page No.*
584.	Vidya Swamigal *v* Balusamy Iyer	AIR, 1922, PC, 123:	56, 66, 205, 296
585.	VSD Sikkandar *v* K.M. Khader Gani	(2006)4, MLJ, 1800	261
586.	V.T. Doraisamy *v* Thaikal Wakf	(2000)2, LW, 66	
587.	Vuppuluri Atchayya *v* Sri Kanchumarti Rao	ILR, 39, Mad, 195 (FB)	
588.	Wakf Board vs. Alam Aboobaker Sait	AIR 1987 KER 196 (DB)	207
589.	Wakf Board, Ambala *v* Nar Singh & Ors	AIR 2008 (NOC) 2372	
590.	Wakf Board, A *v* B. Ramana Reddy	AIR, 1999, SC, 3374	
591.	Wakf Imambara *v* Smt. Khursheeda Bi	AIR 2009, MP. 238.	263
592.	Wahid Ali *v* Ashraf Hussain	37, Cal, 262	
593.	Wali Mohamed *v* Smt. Rahmabee	(1999)3, LW, 267	
594.	Waqf Masjid, Railway, *v* Ashok Sethi	AIR 2011 Uttarakhand 68	
595.	Yashpal Lala *v* Allatala Malik Waqf	AIR, 2006, All, 115	
596.	Yousuf Begum *v* Wakf Board, Hyderabad	2010 (6) ALD 273	134, 254
597.	Yusuf Khan *v* Misal Khan	73, IC, 99	9
598.	Zafar Bai *v* Chhaganlal	AIR, 1942, Bom, 21:	
599.	Zafar Hussain *v* Mian Muhammed	AIR, 1937, Lah, 552:	
600.	Zafar Hussain *v* Ghiasuddin	AIR, 1937, Lah 552;	
601.	Zaheer Ahmad *v* Masjid Muzaffar Nagar	AIR 2009 (NOC) 1080 (All)	251
602.	Zainab *v* Jamal Khan	AIR, 1951, Nag, 428	
603.	Zain Yar Jung *v* Director of Endowment	AIR, 1963, SC, 955	

Bibliography

Abu al-Hasan Burhan-Aldin al-Fargani al-Marghinani, *Hedaya*, 2nd Edn., Tr. by Charles Hamilton, Kitab Bhavan, New Delhi, 1870, Rp. 1994.

Alauddin Haskafi Durrul-Mukhtar, *Commentary of Tanvirul Absar of Md. Bin Abdullah*, Tr. by B.M. Dayal, Kitab Bhavan, New Delhi, 1913, Rp. 2008.

Ameer Ali Syed, *Mohammedan Law*, 4th Edn., Vol. I, Himalayan Books, New Delhi, 1912, Rp. 1985.

Athar Hussain, *Waqf Law and Administration in India*, 2nd Edn., Eastern Book Co., Lucknow, 1973.

Baillie Neil, *Digest of Mohammedan Law*, 4th Edn., Premier Book House, Lahore, 1965.

Coulson, N.J., *A History of Islamic Law*, Universal Law Publishing Company, Delhi, 1997.

Derret, J.D.M., *Religion Law and the State in India*, Faber & Faber, London, 1968.

Fakhruddin Hasan, *Fatawa-I-Qazi Khan*, English Tr. by Muhammad Yusuf Khan Bahadur and Wilayat Husain, Kitab Bhavan, New Delhi, Rp. 1994.

Henri Cattan, *Law of Wakf (Law in the Middle East)*, Middle East Institute, Washington, 1955.

Hunter, W.W. *Indian Mussalman*, Trubner and Company, London, 1876.

Imam Malik Muwatta *(Compiled during the reign of Mansur, Abbasid Caliph)*, 9th Edn., Eng. Tr. by Rahimuddin Muhammad, Kitab Bhavan, New Delhi, 2010.

Joseph Schacht, *The Origin of Mohammedan Jurisprudence*, Clarendon Press, Oxford, 1950.

Kozlouski Gregory, *Muslim Endowments & Society in British India*, Cambridge University Press, Cambridge, 1985.

Mulla D. Fardunji, *Principles of Mohammedan Law*, Revised by Hidayatullah, 19th Edn., 15th reprint, Laxis Nexis, Butterworth, New Delhi, 2007.

Oxford, *Encyclopedia of Modern Islamic World, Vol. IV – Article: Wakf.* Oxford University Press, London, 1991.

Philip K. Hitti, *The History of Arabs*, 2nd Edn., Macmillan, London, 1940.

Pickthal Md. Marmaduke, *The Meaning of Holy Quran*, English Tr., Universal Book Stall, New Delhi, Rp. 1994.

Rahim Abdul, *Muhammadan Jurisprudence*, 2nd Edn., Allahabad Law Agency, Faridabad, 2004.

Ramanatha Aiyar. *The Law Lexicon*, 4th Edn., Rev. by Shakil Ahmad Khan, Lexis Nexis, New Delhi, 2017.

Tyabji Badruddin, *Personal Law of Muslims in India and Pakistan*, 4th Edn., N.M. Tripathi, Bombay, 1968.

Verma, B.R., *Islamic Law-Personal Being Commentaries on Mohammedan Law*, 6th Edn., Allahabad Law Publishers, Allahabad, 1986.

Yousuf Ali Abdullah, *Translation and Commentary on the Holy Quran*, Kitab Bhavan, New Delhi, 1934, 2nd Rp. 1991.

Index

For Product Safety Concerns and Information please contact our EU
representative GPSR@taylorandfrancis.com
Taylor & Francis Verlag GmbH, Kaufingerstraße 24, 80331 München, Germany

www.ingramcontent.com/pod-product-compliance
Ingram Content Group UK Ltd.
Pitfield, Milton Keynes, MK11 3LW, UK
UKHW020155200926
475702UK00016B/2712
9780367696504